An intellectual titan of
the Renaissance,

ERASMUS OF ROTTERDAM,

one of the most learned men of his or any
other age, still possesses the power to shock
us from our lethargy and to focus the
mind's eye on truth.

In *The Praise of Folly*, as readers of Professor Dolan's witty translation will discover, Erasmus dissolves in the acid of his
wit and scorn the wickedness and the pretensions of his age—and ours. No folly or
evil is spared—whether it be arid intellec-
tualism or the bestiality of war.

But we meet in these pages another Erasmus
as well, a man whose humanism is, above
all, Christian and whose vision of the
dynamic Christ was—and is—a call to
charity and peace in an age of intolerance,
strife, and hatred.

This Mentor volume, selected and translated with an introduction and commentary
by a noted historian and scholar, is especially pertinent today, when Christians seek
unity and men of goodwill search, with hope
as their guide, for peace on earth.

*The text includes a short biography of
Erasmus and a list of selected readings.*

SIGNET and MENTOR Books of Interest

THE
ESSENTIAL
ERASMUS

SELECTED AND NEWLY TRANSLATED
WITH INTRODUCTION AND COMMENTARY BY

JOHN P. DOLAN

A MENTOR BOOK from.
NEW AMERICAN LIBRARY
TIMES MIRROR
New York and Scarborough, Ontario
The New English Library Limited, London

MENTOR TRADEMARK REG. U.S. PAT. OFF. AND FOREIGN COUNTRIES
REGISTERED TRADEMARK——MARCA REGISTRADA
HECHO EN CHICAGO, U.S.A.

SIGNET, SIGNET CLASSICS, MENTOR, PLUME AND MERIDIAN BOOKS
are published *in the United States* by
The New American Library, Inc.,
1301 Avenue of the Americas, New York, New York 10019,
in Canada by The New American Library of Canada Limited,
81 Mack Avenue, Scarborough, Ontario M1L 1M8,
in the United Kingdom by The New English Library Limited,
Barnard's Inn, Holborn, London, E.C. 1, England

FIRST MENTOR PRINTING, JUNE, 1964

6 7 8 9 10 11 12 13 14

PRINTED IN THE UNITED STATES OF AMERICA

Contents

Introduction

Two years after the terrible destruction of World War II, when Europe stood at the crossroads between renewal or self-destruction, the late Cardinal Archbishop of Paris, Emmanuel Suhard, penned a now-famous pastoral letter in which he outlined a plan for a new sacral culture, a Christian transformation of life. He wrote:

> It will perhaps be the great honor of our time to have started what others will carry through, a humanism in proportion to the world and God's plan. . . . Need we add that the task is incumbent upon the intellectuals, as it was in the time of the great Doctors of the Church. They must bend every possible effort to the creation of a Christian society in which the kingdom of God will be sought above all else. The first apostolate of this present crossroads is in the realm of thought.[1]

We can think of no better words to introduce the works of a man who over four centuries before stood on the frontier of a new era, an era that presaged an intellectual awakening that looked to a rejuvenation of a religion addressed to all of mankind and that aimed at the fulfillment of the Mystical Body of Christ. For the world of the early sixteenth century embraced the hope that society and institutions, not merely individuals, could be changed for the better. The rediscovery of the world of antiquity had given Church leaders a new dimension, a rich and variable source upon which to draw in rebuilding the Christian world. There was a shared belief that a free unfolding of the human spirit in the framework of a Christo-centric philosophy would usher in a new and marvelous age.

[1] E. Suhard, *Growth or Decline* (Chicago: Editions Fides, 1948), pp. 56–57.

The coincidence of rapid social change with the classical revival at the end of the Middle Ages had produced an aura of
optimism among the educated of Europe that saw the possibility of making Christianity a more dynamic force in society.
Few men shared this optimism more deeply and none contributed more earnestly to its implementation than Erasmus
of Rotterdam. If none was more disillusioned at its tragic failure, few have been more frequently accused by posterity for
sharing responsibility in that same failure.

The unfolding of history points to nothing more clearly than
to the constant prematurity of reforming idealism. Any message, be it theological or philosophical, must be evaluated in
terms of history as the uninterrupted welling of life in a multitude of currents and countercurrents formed by changing
influences and varied impulses. The dissemination of ideas is
a process that must often be nurtured by the passage of time.
Few, if any, great minds have enjoyed fame in their lifetime,
and even fewer have been understood. Yet it is the unique
distinction of Erasmus that his genius radiated a brilliance
even during his lifetime that has seldom been equaled. That
he survived the onslaught of the Counter-Reformation and the
Counter-Renaissance is sufficient testimony to his greatness.
His rediscovery, century after century, by a Shakespeare, a
Grotius, a Montaigne, a Voltaire points to the timeless uni-
versality of his attraction. Yet the web of Clio has so deftly
entangled him in the snarls of misjudgment that even to this
day, in spite of the post-war *renascentia erasmiana,* he remains
more celebrated than actually known.[2]

His belief that society might be renovated through the principles of self-sacrifice and his conviction that the reform of
the Church depended upon a better self-knowledge of its
members, thus entailing a slow and prolonged process, never
found acceptance in the radical and immediate programs of
would-be reformers. He was admittedly no saint.[3] He was not
even a reformer in the accepted sense of the word. For, as
Gilson points out, "the real reformer is not the man who sees
that a reform is needed; nor is he the man who, in season and
out of season, preaches the necessity of reform; the true reformer is the man who achieves it." [4] Yet no one can deny his
constant insistence that for mankind nothing is more important

[2] "Erasme, malgré le nombre croissant de ceux que étudient son temps
et son oeuvre est plus célèbre que connu." E. L. Halkin, *Les Colloques
d'Erasme* (Brussels: 1946), p. 3.

[3] *Desiderii Erasmi Roterdami Opera Omnia,* ed. J. Clericus (Leiden:
1703–1706), IX, 197; "Ego mihi non arrogo sanctimoniam."

[4] E. Gilson, *Reason and Revelation in the Middle Ages* (New York:
Charles Scribner's Sons, 1938), p. 70.

than a daily striving for perfection in personal piety.[5] To those
who berate him for neglecting the mystical foundations of religion it must be pointed out that his very skepticism reveals a
blending of belief in things unseen that could proceed only
from a deep sense of the interior element in all spirituality.
His constant refusal to be ensnared by the visionary attraction
of the unreal is ever counterbalanced by a studied determination to maintain his belief in the invisible. It is this that gives
his realism, in the face of the perplexities of everyday life, an
unexpected glow even today. The very superficiality ascribed
to Erasmus by his critics is often evidenced in their own failure
to penetrate the depths of his Neo-Platonic spiritualism—a
spiritualism that had enabled Christianity to transform the ancient paganism of the Greco-Roman world.

A sampling of a few contemporary critics of Erasmus might
perhaps throw some light on the enigmatic shadow that continues, after almost four centuries, to darken his name and
orthodoxy. The prominent English historian Philip Hughes
singles him out for what he terms his "unreasoned vindictive-
ness" and his failure to perceive the great issues of the time.
He is representative of so many of his coreligionists who see in
Erasmus a sort of sixteenth-century Benedict Arnold.

> Erasmus, filled with contempt for the barbarous latinity
> of too many of his scholastic contemporaries, and for
> their barbarous indifference to the vast opportunities for
> new knowledge opened to them by the revival of Greek
> studies, and rending with interest, hate for hate, had dis-
> missed, unstudied, the whole vast achievement. He pre-
> ferred not to know the great technique that had been
> built up, and when, for example, in the controversy with
> Luther, he comes to defend the freedom of the will, his
> ignorance of the very nature of the problem led him into
> the most extraordinary of blunders.[6]

A second variation of a common judgment of Erasmus is
that he is basically an ethical humanitarian, a sincere and
dedicated scholar but one whose ethical concerns are somehow
divorced from a thoroughly Christian foundation. Roland
Bainton acknowledges the sincerity of Erasmus' Christianity
and pays high tribute to him as a scholar.

[5] *Opus Epistolarum Desiderii Erasmi Roterdami*, ed. P. S. Allen
(London and New York: Oxford University Press, 1906–1958), IX, p.
401, hereafter cited *E. E.*

[6] P. Hughes, *The Reformation in England* (London: Hollis & Carter,
1948), I, p. 344.

Yet the same author relegates Erasmus' defense of the freedom of investigation to a form of Renaissance confidence in the power of reason rather than a concern for a more positive theology and Christian peace.[7] Speaking of the young Erasmus, Harbison also remarks: "The dominant note is a naïve secularism, combined with a soul-hearted acceptance of Christian ethics. . . . He moralized antiquity and strips Christianity to a great extent of its miraculous and mystical elements."[8] Describing Erasmus as the hero of liberal Christianity, Preserved Smith reiterates the same theme:

> That he saw through the accretions of superstition, dogma and ritual to the "philosophy of Christ"; that he let his mind play freely on the sacred arcana of the traditional faith; that he recognized reason as the final arbiter in these matters as well as in social and political affairs—all this is the whole genius of Erasmus.[9]

Albert Hyma, one of his best known American critics, also describes Erasmus as a forerunner of modern liberal Christianity:

> Erasmus spoke in 1515 as hundreds of well known churchmen have spoken in the twentieth century. In his opinion, it mattered little whether the miracles recorded in the Bible actually happened or not. As for the doctrine of transubstantiation, of purgatory, and of justification by faith and words, he believed that they might be interpreted in various ways. . . . He said on many occasions that to imitate the life of Jesus was far more important than to argue about dogma. . . . Science meant almost nothing to him. Dogma on the other hand meant little more. . . . It was easy for Erasmus to criticize existing conditions, but he disliked the work of constructing different conditions.[10]

Of the members of this school of thought, by far the most thorough student of Erasmus and the one who above all others concentrates on his religious thought is Augustine

---

[7] R. Bainton, *The Reformation of the Sixteenth Century* (Boston: Beacon Press, 1952), pp. 69–70.

[8] E. Harbison, *The Christian Scholar in the Age of the Reformation* (New York: Charles Scribner's Sons, 1956), p. 72.

[9] P. Smith, *Erasmus* (New York: Harper & Bros., 1923), p. 441.

[10] H. Hyma, "Erasmus and the Northern Renaissance," *Medievalia et Humanistica*, VIII, pp. 9–11.

Renaudet, who expresses the same doubts concerning his orthodoxy:

> Erasmus knows that human language cannot imprison the infinite; that dogma has developed from the beginning . . . and that this necessary adaption of dogmas to human history is both a development and an enrichment. Such a conception permits what must be called Erasmian modernism to escape the constraint of the Protestant criterion, which, posed in principle in his prefaces of 1516, rejects everything which does not seem exactly based on a primitive test, or in conformity with primitive usage. By it, Erasmus accommodates himself to the *provisional* shelter offered him by the Roman Church.[11]

In an illuminating study of Erasmus the outstanding Dutch historian Johan Huizinga maintains that Erasmus' classicism radically alienated him from traditional Catholicism and that his sensitive nature was truly unable to come to a final determination on the great doctrinal issues of his day. A disposition to interpret religious issues in a personal way blinded him to the cogency of his critics.

> Instinct did not deceive his adversaries when it told them that doctrine was at stake if the linguistic judgment of an individual might decide as to the correct version of a text. He was not aware of the fact that his conceptions of the Church, the sacraments, and the dogmas were no longer purely Catholic, because they had become subordinate to his philological insight.[12]

Like so many of his contemporary critics Huizinga pays virtually no attention to Erasmus' indebtedness to the Fathers and, apart from his evangelism, seems to view him exclusively as a disciple of the ancients. Owing to the great fondness of the "Hieronymi," as the Brethren of the Common Life were called, after the translator of the Vulgate, this would be a mistake even in evaluating Erasmus' earlier years, apart from his mature work, much of which is devoted to patristic studies. We see here the tendency reflected in all his critics to underestimate Erasmus' taste for allegory, which, rather than a

---

[11] A Renaudet, *Erasme, sa Pensée Religeuse et son Action d'Après son Correspondance* (Paris: 1926), p. 8.

[12] J. Huizinga, *Erasmus of Rotterdam* (London: The Phaidon Press, 1952), p. 136.

trifling aberration, is in fact one of the clearest testimonies to his debt to the Fathers. If his critics were more sensitive to Erasmus' consciousness of the patristic tradition, they would be less prone to interpret his distaste for many aspects of medieval Catholicism as an alienation from Catholicism as such. Those who see Luther, Calvin, or Loyola as representing the only genuine Christian alternatives of the early sixteenth century fail to see that between the fervor of alternatives of the Reformers and that of "le parti Catholique anti-Lutherien" there was room for an authentic Catholic irenicism. What they often call Erasmus' "velvet softness" was not the confusion of an undecided mind, but the sincere and consistent expression of Erasmus' conception of that peace that surpasses all understanding.

Erasmus was not a theologian in the ordinary sense of the word—he was not really interested in the importance of scientific theology—but rather he was a spiritual writer and the inaugurator of positive theology. As a Christian humanist he outlined what has been the only virtually complete system of a religious Humanism whose first component is an understanding of the psychology of Christ, as the hidden dynamic of history, consisting in the perfectibility of nature by grace.

It is to be hoped that more recent Catholic studies of Erasmus as evidenced in the works of Bouyer,[13] Etienne,[14] Auer,[15] and more recently Karl Oelrich [16] will gradually dissipate this century-old and ofttimes biased judgment on the great Humanist.

Those who seek to evaluate Erasmus' doctrinal orthodoxy usually err by taking little trouble to ascertain the exact state of orthodoxy on many points in Erasmus' time. But any attempt to evaluate Erasmus' theology almost exclusively in terms of its orthodoxy really misses the point, for the real significance of his attitude toward theological issues is his character as a *witness* to the necessity of Christian charity and peace in all things. It is quite evident that he insists too exclusively on the necessity of peace at all costs; that he is somewhat naïve in his estimate of the power of persuasion; and that he seems entirely unaware of the *credo ut intelligam* aspect, either of theology or of doctrine. But in view of the violent and abusive character of contemporary polemics, both Catholic and

[13] L. Bouyer, *Autour d'Erasme* (Paris: 1955).
[14] J. Etienne, *Spiritualisme Érasmien et les Théologiens Louvanistes* (Louvain: 1956).
[15] A. Auer, *Die volekommene Fromigkeit des Christen* (Düsseldorf: 1954).
[16] K. Oelrich, *Der Späte Erasmus und die Reformation* (Münster: 1961).

Protestant, one must admit that Erasmus was one of the few men of his time to guard the purity of the Christian ideal of charity.

Much of his theology—his insistence that the purpose of that science is to win men to Christ, and that this be done by gentleness and persuasion, not by force; his lack of interest in dogma, whether of the Church or of the schools—all these things are recapitulated, and more fully understood, in the consideration of Erasmus as a rhetor, or, as he more modestly says, a "rhetorculus." Erasmus' dislike of dogma, whether of the schools or of the Church, is a many-sided phenomenon, rooted partly in his own skeptical tendency, partly in his background in the undogmatic *Devotio Moderna*. But it is also expressive of his profound distaste for the whole trend of higher education in Europe since the time of Peter Abelard, that is, for dialectic.

Dialectic, he feels, has first of all subverted theology to a ludicrous and profitless concatenation of quarrels. Theology is far from *pure docere Christum* when it has become a prestigious intellectual gymnastic. Further, dialectic leads men to an obstinate pertinacity in their own opinions, dangerous to the peace and unity of the Church. This seems to be the meaning of Erasmus' criticisms of Luther on the grounds that he is just another scholastic. When speaking of practical moral counsels, Erasmus thinks that one should say, not, "This shall ye do," but, "This in my opinion were the better, this I suppose to be more tolerable." The same holds true *a fortiori* for questions of dogma that have little to do with piety.

Finally, the abstract and speculative character of dialectic theology is of no help for returning to the scriptural *fontes*. While St. Paul did not scruple to quote from the poets, there is nothing in his works that smacks of Aristotle or Averroes. More seriously, dialectical theologians are led to distort the meaning of Scripture to suit their own constructions, sometimes going to absurd lengths. Erasmus' own preference for rhetoric is likewise a complex phenomenon, partly explainable by his fondness for classic authors—it is interesting to note that Lucian of Samosata, whose works were the subject of scholarly labor by both More and Erasmus, was a rhetor [17]— and partly by his great attachment to the Fathers, so many of whom, like Augustine and Tetullian, were extensively schooled in classical rhetoric. Like the Fathers, and like popes and theologians generally, at least until Gregory IX, Erasmus justifies secular studies—which means rhetoric above all—as a necessary implement for scriptural study. Etienne points out

[17] A. Renaudet, *Erasme et l'Italie* (Geneva: 1954), p. 42.

Erasmus' full awareness of the need for a scientific interpretation of the sacred texts, for the meaning of Scripture is
not something plainly obvious to all good men. "As the
Saviour assumed the nature of man, so also He spoke our
language." Thus rhetoric, the study of the meaning and usage
of language, is necessary for an interpretation of Scripture.
Erasmus points out that St. Paul, when speaking of the Resurrection, does not use *Aristotelicis aut Platonicis enthymatics,*
but *similibus,* figures of speech. Unlike so many of his predecessors in the rhetorical tradition, Erasmus is quite aware that
modes of speaking peculiar to Latin cannot be transported en
masse into Greek, much less Hebrew. But nowhere does he
show himself more a continuator of the rhetorical, prescholas-
tic past of theology than in the *Enchiridion,* where he justifies
the use of secular studies for the interpretation of Scripture
by the timeless accommodated meaning of the spoils taken
from Egypt by the Hebrews.

By far the deepest significance of rhetoric lies for Erasmus
in its *persuasive* power. Christ's way of winning men to Himself was persuasion and love, and by imitating him to their
task, theologians are not only more efficacious in their task
of calling men to true Christian piety, but also promote the
blessed peace of the Church, so sundered by dialectical dispu-
tations. For Erasmus, the science to be conjoined with piety
is par excellence the science of eloquence, or persuasion. This
idea appears as early as the *Antibarbari Liber,* written at
Steyn, and shows that even then his concern for the classics
was not without Christian motivation:

> The man whose life is pure is great. But this grandeur
> serves only himself . . . If one is one of those who can
> express their thought finely and join eloquence to wis-
> dom, one aids not only his acquaintances, not even only
> his contemporaries, but strangers even to the ends of
> the earth, and men who will come after in future ages.[18]

The same idea appears later in a letter to Dorp: *Nihil enim
gloriosus inscitia cum scientiae persuasione conjuncta.*[19] This
is the deepest reason for Erasmus' polemic against contemporary theology. "What," he asks in the *Enchiridion,* "would the
Turks say if scholasticism were preached to them? The Turks
can only be won to Christ if they see that we seek nothing
else but only their soul's health and the glory of God." We

[18] Cited in F. Hermans, *Histoire Doctrinal de L'Humanisme Chrétien*
(Paris: 1948).
[19] *E. E.,* II, pp. 94–95.

might ask the same question in terms of the ideological conflict between the east and west of today.

Erasmus was a rhetor in practice as well as in theory.
While most of the men of his time, in their relations with
others and especially in their controversial writings, were concerned with proving to the world that their adversaries were
wrong, or wicked, or heretical, Erasmus, ever sensitive to the
human situation, was concerned with *winning* others to piety
and to Christ. On the feast of the Epiphany in 1504 Erasmus
delivered a panegyric to Prince Philip at the Burgundian
court, which some attacked as a piece of sycophantic flattery.
To such criticism Erasmus replies that "no other way of correcting a prince is as efficacious as offering the pattern of a
truly good prince under the pattern of flattery to them." [20]
Erasmus was not concerned with demonstrating immutable
truths, much less immobile truisms, but rather with bringing
about a change of heart in Philip. Here his sensitivity to the
personal and subjective dimension of reality appears as a con-
tinuation of the rhetorical tradition, possibly in this case guided
by his own experience or by counsel from his English friends.
Similarly, his anti-Lutheran *De Libero Arbitrio* was aimed,
not at crushing the dissidents by cold logic, but at persuading
them, if not Luther himself, then at least some of his followers. Some writers think that Melanchthon was himself convinced by the work, and even Luther, in the introduction to
his *De Servo Arbitrio,* testifies to the effectiveness of the work
in this regard.

> You have checked my zeal for battle and drained my
> strength before the fight began. This was due to two
> things; first, your skill in debate, for you discuss the
> matter throughout with quite remarkable restraint, by
> which you have prevented my wrath waxing hot against
> you.[21]

It is a measure of the failure both of his own generation and
of posterity to understand Erasmus that the *De Libero Arbitrio* was attacked by Catholics because of its very gentleness.

Perhaps the time is ripe for this gentleness of Erasmus to
bear fruit. Certainly those who hope for a Christian humanism
that can galvanize the disparate elements of society today, who

[20] *The Education of a Christian Prince,* trans. L. K. Born (New York:
Columbia University Press, 1936), p. 6.
[21] *Martin Luther on the Bondage of the Will* (*De Servo Arbitrio*),
trans. J. I. Parker and O. M. Johnston (London: James Clarke & Co.,
Ltd., 1957), p. 62.

believe that that which has fallen may be lifted up and that
which was old made new, can read this great spokesman of
Christocentricism with a realization that his failure is a warning and the sincerity of his effort an inspiration.

The selections which follow are taken from the *Erasmi
Opera Omnia,* edited by J. Clericus (Leiden: 1703–1706). As
in all translations, much of the richness of style has been sacrificed; in style Erasmus was the equal to the finest writers of
the golden age of classical Latin. Yet it is hoped that the
readings collected here, if they fail to convey his fine style, at
least will help to accomplish the great aim of Erasmus' life:
Christum ex fontibus praedicare.

The Life of Erasmus

Not unlike a number of other prominent Renaissance figures—Pope Clement VII, Leonardo da Vinci, Don Juan of Austria, to name a few—Erasmus' birth and early childhood are somewhat obscured by the unhappy fact that he was born out of wedlock. The several accounts of his early life that he himself wrote—one in 1516 [1] and another in 1524 [2]—are pathetic attempts to gloss over a situation that was, naturally enough, extremely distasteful to the great Humanist. The man who is generally believed to be his father, one Roger Gerard of Gouda, was already in orders when, probably in 1466, Erasmus saw the light of day in Rotterdam. His mother was the widowed daughter of a physician from the village of Severnbergen. If the great scholar found the circumstances of his birth an embarrassment that he later attempted to cover over by shifting the date of his birth, he also looked back upon the neglect and rejection experienced during his early youth with equal disdain.

At the age of nine he was sent to the well-known school of St. Lebuin in Deventer. For the next ten years, both at Deventer and later at Hertogenbosch, he came under the tutelage of the Brethren of the Common Life. Few movements in popular education have had such a profound influence in shaping the destiny of history as the pedagogical efforts of this remarkable group of teachers. Luther, Calvin, Loyola, and Pope Adrian VI were influenced at one time or another in their careers by association with the Brethren. Inspired by the *Devotio Moderna* of Gerard Groote and their founder Florent Radewijns, they were in many respects the precursors of those educational trends that developed later in the sixteenth century under the auspices of the newly

[1] *Opus Epistolarum Desiderii Roterdami*, ed. P. S. Allen (London and New York: Oxford University Press), Vol. II, p. 293.
[2] *Ibid.*, I, 47–52.

founded Jesuits and the disciples of Jacob Sturm. Combining a new methodology directed toward personal reform through a return to Christian inwardness and unfettered by religious vows or monastic traditions, the Brethren had established themselves as the leading educators in the Low Countries and throughout many areas of Germany.

Among his instructors in their schools were Johannes Synthen, famous classicist, Alexander Hegius, and the celebrated humanist Rodolphus Agricola, the latter two already in the forefront of the revival of letters that was sweeping northern Europe at this time. In later years Erasmus was to recall with acrimony the suppressive tendencies of the Brethren. They knew no other purpose, he wrote, than the destruction of natural gifts with blows, reprimands, and severity, in order to fit one's soul for the monastery.

Yet it was during these same trying years that Erasmus acquired those traits of study that were to distinguish him both as a writer and a religious reformer—a superb knowledge of classical Latin and a perduring appreciation of the fundamental ideal of the Brethren, an earnest and unswerving striving after Christ. If their strict discipline prepared one for the monastery, then there too they achieved at least a modicum of success. In 1487 the young scholar, bereft of parents and friends, entered the cloister of the Canons Regular of St. Augustine at Steyn. Although he later developed a deep-seated aversion to the monastic life—his famous phrase *monochatus non est pietas* engendered many a diatribe against the institution—there is little indication that his early years with the monks were entirely unhappy.

Freedom to pursue his craving for classical studies, the company of similar-minded humanists, and above all the security so singularly lacking in his early years provided a fertile soil for the seeds implanted by the Brethren, interest in the Fathers and a pursuit of that inner piety and spirituality that he was later to champion so forcefully. The *Antibarbari*, although it was not published until some years later, was written during these years at Steyn. Yet Erasmus gradually fell victim to that spirit of restlessness that pursued him for the rest of his life. The restrictions of the little monastery at Steyn, aggravated no doubt by the boorish company of his coreligious, many of them rustics from neighboring Dutch farms, eventually forced the delicate and sensitive scholar to seek an escape from the confines of an ill-chosen career.

In an age when monasticism attracted a far greater proportion of the faithful than its austere ideals warranted, and when the excesses resulting from failure to achieve these ideals was a commonplace, exclaustration, especially for talented young monks seeking secretarial work, was not uncommon. Illiteracy among prelates, then as now, often necessitated the talents of a reliable Latinist, and Erasmus was extremely fortunate in obtaining the patronage of Henry Bergen, Bishop of Cambrai, aspiring cardinal, and patron of the arts. The appointment of Erasmus as secretary to the bishop in 1493 was a step that not only enabled the young canon to make a dignified exodus from the monastery, but also provided him ample opportunity to move in some of Europe's finest society. Henry had just been appointed chancellor of the Order of the Golden Fleece and was thereby a link, not only with the elite of Burgundy, but also with the powerful and ubiquitous family of Hapsburg.

The final reward for his services to the bishop was a leave of absence to attend the University of Paris. Here at the recommendation of the good bishop Erasmus took up residence at the college of Montaigu, then under the supervision of the ascetical John Standonck, like Erasmus a product of the Brethren of the Common Life. If the monastery had been disagreeable to the young monk, studies at Europe's most famous university were equally distasteful. To the frugality of the college was now added an ingredient that the young scholar found absolutely revolting, the study of scholastic theology. The meaningless, mechanical ceremonies of the monastery had been an offense to his deep spirituality. Now he found their intellectual counterpart, the sterile quiddities and subtle formalities of Scotus and Ockham, an object of genuine scorn.

For almost four years Erasmus endured the poor climate and arid lectures of life in Paris. His stay was interspersed with returns to Holland to seek additional patronage. There were very few times in his career when he actually enjoyed any kind of financial security, a situation that his love for valuable manuscripts and his tastes in fine attire and good cuisine did little to alleviate. Although he failed to obtain a degree in theology, he did at least make some initial contacts with the world of humanism that he was soon to dominate—the French poet Robert Gaguin and the well-known author Faustus Andrelinus welcomed him to the circle of their friends, and he managed to have some of his writings published. More rewarding were his associations with a group of young English students whom he tutored in Latin: Thomas Grey, Robert Fisher, and William Blount, Lord Mountjoy. At the request of the latter he went to England in the summer of 1499, remaining there until the next year.

This first of several stays in England had a profound influence upon his future life. An immediate friendship with John Colet and Thomas More helped to direct his interests away from the classics and a career of tutoring toward a study of the ancient Fathers of the Church and the Scriptures. Theology, which had hitherto been a rather desultory sideline for him, now became a pervading preoccupation. A restoration of theology, not the conventional, hair-splitting dialectics of the schoolmen so devoid of life and inspiration, but rather a study of the very fonts of faith as interpreted by the wisdom of the early Fathers, now became his persistent ambition.

Returning once again to Paris, he busied himself with a critical study of the early witnesses of Christianity, St .Paul, St. Jerome, St. Augustine. The outcome was a work that contained in broad outline his program for the liberation of theology, the *Enchiridion Militis Christiani*. Here was a vision of the classical world preparing the mind for revelation, a practical Christianity based upon a knowledge of the Gospel, an ethical code founded upon a reverence for a divine Person.

Financial difficulties, accentuated by the death of his patron Henry of Bergen in October, 1502, forced Erasmus to change residence; he moved to the university city of Louvain. Although offered a professorship at the university by Bishop Adrian of Utrecht, later to become the last of the non-Italian popes, he preferred to continue supporting himself through patronage and the remuneration he received from the dedication of his works to men and women of high position. His dedicatory and eulogistic writings form a veritable "Who's Who" of the sixteenth century; popes, kings, cardinals, and queens were the flattered objects of his literary outpourings during these days. After two years in Louvain he returned once again to England. Having meanwhile mastered the Greek language, he was welcomed to the company of Linacre, Grocyn, and Tunstall, all of them excellent Hellenists. In January, 1506, Pope Julius granted him a long-sought dispensation that would enable him to obtain ecclesiastical benefices. The hope of financial independence through a substantial prebend, hitherto an impossibility due to his illegitimate birth and his monastic vows, now became a reality.

It was during this visit to England that his earlier dream of a trip to Renaissance Italy was also realized. As tutor to the children of Henry VII's court physician, Giovanni Barerio, he traveled for almost two years throughout the land that had grown so familiar to him through his deep knowledge of its ancient writers. In Turin he was given a degree as Doctor of Theology. He spent many months in Venice as the house guest of the great printer Aldo Manuzio, who published a new and elegant edition of his *Adagia*. While in Rome in 1509 he received word of the death of Henry VII and the accession of Henry VIII. He had met young Henry on several occasions, was greatly admired by him, and it was therefore with great expectations that he now made plans to return to England. The return journey through the Alps saw the incubation of his next great masterpiece, *Moriae Encomium, The Praise of Folly.*

The third visit to England, where he remained until 1514, was one of his most productive. He finished the final draft of *The Praise of Folly,* revised the *Adagia,* composed the *De Copia Verborum,* and continued his work on the New Testament. He also lectured on Greek and theology at the University of Cambridge.

In July, 1514, he returned again to the continent and soon thereafter received a delayed letter from his religious superior at Steyn, Servatius Rogerius, demanding that after all these years he return to the monastery. Erasmus, who had long since cast aside his monastic garb, replied emphatically that he had no intention of returning to a monkish incarceration. Neither his delicate health, his love of freedom, nor, above all else, his pursuit of true theology was compatible with a future in the cloister. It was not until 1517, however, that he was finally dispensed by the Pope from the religious vows that had been such an obstacle to his acceptance by a society still awed by the feudal stringencies placed upon religious. By this time he had become the unquestioned idol of Europe's literati, the most brilliant luminary in an age that perhaps as no other before or since appreciated the role of the intellectual. The agents of half a dozen printing houses clamored for his works; his letters were purloined and published; Wolsey coaxed him to England with promises of ecclesiastical preferment; Cardinal Ximenes invited him to the University of Alcalá in Spain. The previous year he had been appointed chancellor to the Prince of Burgundy, the future Emperor Charles V, and the King of France was urging him to take up residence at the royal court. The cities in the Rhineland welcomed him as a national hero wherever he traveled.

Yet Erasmus had dedicated himself to the task of renovating the Church and, through it, all of Christian Europe by urging a return to pristine Christianity, and he stuck doggedly to this for the remainder of his life. The events of 1517, the Lutheran affair, only confirmed him in this determination. Until 1521 he resided once again in Louvain, continuing his work on Jerome, Cyprian, and his Paraphrases on the New

Testament. His refusal to take up the cudgels against the reformer and his earlier identification with the movement gradually engendered a feeling of suspicion and outright animosity on the part of the Louvain faculty toward him. As life in that city became more and more intolerable, he decided to move to Basle.

It was in this city in the summer of 1513 that he had made his first acquaintance with the printer John Froben, and during the intervening years their close collaboration, crowned in 1516 with the publication of Erasmus' New Testament, became one of the most remarkable friendships of the Renaissance. The city itself, with its university, its libraries, and *sodalitates humanistae,* was known as the *domicilium musarum,* the home of the muses. Here in the friendly and international atmosphere that he loved Erasmus was to spend the next eight years editing his planned translations of the Fathers—Cyprian, Irenaeus, Athanasius, Augustine, and Ambrose—unconsciously providing the very arsenals from which the destroyers of religious peace would draw their ammunition. The storm that was now spreading all over Europe soon broke in upon this city at the source of the Rhine.

In 1524, pressured by Pope, Emperor, and princes, Erasmus finally broke silence and took a definite stand against Luther. The appearance of the *De Libero Arbitrio,* which he composed in the fall of 1524, marked a change in the direction of the entire reform movement. The revolutionary tendencies that Erasmus had hoped would be avoided, the peasant wars, the interference of politicians, gave a seditious character to what had hitherto been a genuine desire to reform the Church. Yet even in defending the freedom of the will against Luther, Erasmus continues to reflect his deep conviction that courtesy is necessary for effective discussion. Even in disagreement his moderation is overpowering. In the *Hyperaspistes,* which was his answer to the strongly worded rebuttal of Luther, he remarks, "The tyranny of princes, prelates, and monks, as you call it, you have not suppressed but doubled. Everything one says or does now serves as a pretext for suspicion."

Almost two years after Froben's death the suspicion of which Erasmus spoke finally forced him to leave the city that for eight years had been his home. As at Louvain, where he had refused to aid the Catholic party, so in Basle his determination not to become embroiled in a senseless struggle by supporting the evangelical cause once again forced him to move. This time he selected the Hapsburg city of Freiburg im Breisgau, where he arrived in April, 1529, a man broken in health and spirit, yet determined to carry out the great mission of his life, the restoration of Christian peace and tranquillity. It was during this final period of his life that he composed the treatise "On Ecclesiastical Concord," his work "On Preaching," and, perhaps sensing the close of his life, a beautiful meditation "On Preparing for Death."

Returning to Basle in 1535 in order to work with the younger Froben on his Latin edition of Origen, he was once again summoned by the Supreme Pontiff to help in a final attempt to bring peace and unity to the Church by an ecumenical council. In a letter dated May 31, 1535, the newly elected Farnese pope, Paul III, who had finally broken with the vacillating and deceptive policies of his predecessors and seriously taken up the matter of a reform council, summoned the aging scholar to Rome. The Pope wrote, "We especially exhort you, our son, whom God has adorned with so much talent and learning, to help us in this pious work, which is so much in keeping with your ideals, to defend the Catholic religion both in word and writing before and during the Council. In so doing you will not only crown in the best fashion possible a life of religion and literary productivity, you will also refute your accusers and rouse your admirers." [3]

Perhaps convinced that things had already gone beyond any real hope of reconciliation and sensing that the council would once again be postponed—it was delayed for another decade—Erasmus politely declined the invitation, which in all probability contained an offer of a cardinal's hat. Quite typically he continued his writing and produced his final work, "On the Purity of the Church." It is a measure of his greatness that he dedicated his last writing to an unknown customs officer in the little Rhenish town of Boppord who had befriended him fifteen years before and whom he had promised a work on the psalms.

The gentle scholar passed away in Basle on July 12, 1536, fortified by the sacraments of the Church and repeating as he expired, *O Jesu, misericordia, Domine libera me; Domine miserer mei.*

[3] *Ibid.,* XI, 137.

THE HANDBOOK OF
THE MILITANT CHRISTIAN

Although the fame of Erasmus as a scholar had been assured by the publication of his *Adagia* in 1500, it was the publication of the *Enchiridion Militis Christiani* in 1503 that called the attention of the literati of Europe to this brilliant spokesman of Christian Humanism. Mann Phillips remarks, "One cannot help regretting that this little book was not first written in a modern European language; it might have ranked beside the early masterpieces of the Renaissance."[1] Yet there is evidence for believing that if it was not one of the "masterpieces" of the Renaissance, it certainly proved itself one of the most popular works of its time. Between 1514 and 1518 some eight Latin editions of it appeared. It was translated into English in 1518, into Czech in 1519, German in 1520, Dutch in 1523, Spanish in 1526, and Polish in 1585. Professor Adrian Baarland of Louvain called it "a booklet of genuine gold" and recommended it as most useful for both lay and cleric.[2] A renowned preacher of Antwerp claimed that each page contained a virtual sermon.[3] It was especially in Spain that the enthusiasm for the book was unbounded.[4] The Council of Trent heard the suggestion that the book should be placed in the hands of all future priests.[5] The book has continued to exercise a lasting influence in the Church of England even to this day. The French Catholics in the seventeenth century relied upon its message to convert Calvinists to the ancient faith.

Yet strangely enough its message has been lost for centuries on

[1] M. Phillips, *Erasmus and the Northern Renaissance* (London: English Universities Press, 1949), p. 46.

[2] *E. E.*, II, p. 387.

[3] *Ibid.*, ". . . ex singulis pagellis singulas posse fieri et haberi contiones."

[4] J. Sellmair, *Humanitas Christiana—Geschichte des christlichen Humanismus* (Munich: 1948), pp. 335–350.

[5] *Concilium Tridentinum* (Freiburg: 1901 seq.), Vol. V, p. 117.

Roman Catholics who too often have seen it, as its author, under an enigmatic cloud of suspicion. The literary ecclesiastical campaign against Erasmus, particularly after the condemnation of certain of his teachings by the Sorbonne in 1526, was to continue for many centuries. The religious spirit of the Counter-Reformation had little time for a writer who preferred the Sermon on the Mount to papal decretals. The disciplined militance of the Jesuits was ill disposed to a man who held that the charity of the Christian must be free and spontaneous, unconstrained by external laws. Above all, the siege mentality that was to pervade Catholic thought for centuries to come, defending itself behind the walls of monasticism and scholasticism, had little sympathy for one of the severest critics of its defense. Nor did the fact that Erasmus was one of the idols of the Enlightenment enhance his chances for survival. Perhaps the deepest reason for the eclipse of his famous writings is the fact that the intellectual revival that he had hoped for, a Europe enlightened through a Christian Humanism, died an abortive death.

The wars of religion stifled all interest in a man who found peace and forbearance the highest expression of Christianity. The Tridentine seminary decrees, cutting off as they did the clergy from the mainstreams of intellectual life, the universities, destroyed that very inquisitiveness and open-mindedness fostered by the *philosophia Christi*. The reduction of theology to the sterile and defensive outlines of Bellarmine placed the clerical mind for centuries to come in a deep freeze, thawed only by an occasional ray of light filtered past the unwary censor. If a Toynbeean challenge and response theory can be applied to the Church's reaction to its critics, then surely it returned to those very devices that Erasmus so soundly exposed. So long as it defended a confined, extremely complicated, and long petrified philosophical system devoid of all operative vitality, the message of Erasmus remained unheard. For it stood too often in opposition to his oft-repeated purpose: "I have endeavored to recall theology that has fallen into sophisticated squabbling back to its source and original simplicity." (*Theologiam minimum ad sophisticas artutias delapsam, ad fontes ac priscam simplicitatem revocare conatus sum.*)

The *Enchiridion* begins with the impressive preface, "We must be watchful in life." Erasmus had no illusions about the strength of human nature. Neither the self-sufficiency of the Italian Humanists whom he knew so well nor the complacency of his contemporaries could delude him here. He knew human weakness only too well, and makes a point at the very outset of his treatise to warn his readers of self-delusion. Yet at the same time he is vitally aware that the power of evil in the world has been broken once and for all by the triumph of Christ and that, for this triumph to be effective in individual lives, the obligation of completing this victory is in-

cumbent upon all. Once he has indicated the perils that threaten
the spiritual safety of the Christian, and he does not euphemize
evil as a "mere absence of good," he indicates the means that are
to be used in escaping the omnipresent snares of the Evil One.
After prayer and an understanding of the Scriptures, nurtured by a
study of classical literature, Erasmus points to self-knowledge as
the first step in overcoming evil. Since its very beginning Christianity has posed the question: Does secular learning contribute to
spiritual growth or hinder it? The problem never, of course, assumed the magnitude that it now has, when scientific knowledge,
divorced from moral values, has reached a point where man's
growing mastery of the physical world carries with it a threat of
racial suicide. Yet the basic problem in the relation of learning to
the spiritual life is solved by Erasmus' belief that the literature of
the ancients offered a formative influence. The classics are recommended for the Christian, not only because they train his mind in
the art of appreciating the good and inculcate the principles of
self-knowledge, but above all because they have so much in them
conducive to righteous living.

Thus the first section of the *Enchiridion* lays the basis for Erasmus' teaching on the doctrine of piety. He points out that by nature
man is composed of both spiritual and corporeal elements and goes
to great length to prove this from the writings of Scripture, tradition, and philosophy. Once he has established this duality, he lays
down certain general norms or regulations that will be conducive
to piety. The Fourth Rule is concerned with the Christocentric
aspect of the spiritual life. Here he asks that "you set before you
Christ as the only goal of your whole life, to whom alone you
dedicate all zeal, all effort, all leisure and business." This is Erasmus' constant effort: to break through the narrow confinement and
isolation that keep religion out of the arena of public life. For him
bene agere is nothing other than to consider all in Christ (*in Christum spectare*). And yet the Christ who is to be the object and
model of all our earthly strivings is not merely Christ the Divine
teacher, or Christ the Divine exemplar, He is, above all, Christ the
Divine Redeemer.

In the Fifth Rule Erasmus lays bare the basic rule for genuine
Christian living: through visible things of the world to the invisible
(*per visibilia ad invisibilia*) life reaches its peak in this rule. In a
world not unlike our own, where religion had largely become a
matter of ceremonies and conventional observances, Erasmus endeavors to restate the essential character of religion, the cult of the
invisible.

The Sixth Rule brings out the image of Christ as the prototype
of genuine piety in every station of life. In the concluding section
Erasmus lists remedies against particular vices, and although there

is little original in the presentation, he nonetheless adds a concrete dimension to these remedies by situating them in the mainstream of daily events. The author makes the whole purpose of the little book clear from the outset; it is aimed not at making the reader learned but rather at making him pious. He will not preach retirement from the world but holiness in the world. He wants to present to the layman a simple, direct, and objective compendium of what it means to live a Christian life.

The aim of Erasmus' theology, so evident in the *Enchiridion*, was an interiorization, a spiritualization of religious practice, a more personal affair between the individual soul and God. Erasmus was above all a practical man, and thus the importance he attaches to rhetoric and eloquence in bringing warmth and color as well as transmitting the living ideals of the Gospel. The excessively rational and analytical theology of his day prevented the student and ultimately the Christian people from seeing theological realities as they actually are, i.e., in the living, breathing Christian.

We have an account of Erasmus himself as to the genesis of the *Enchiridion*. In a letter written to Botzhem in 1523 he has this to say:

> The *Enchiridion Militis Christiani* was begun by me nearly thirty years ago when staying in the castle of Tournehem, to which we were driven by the plague which depopulated Paris. The work arose out of the following incident. A common friend of mine and of Blatt's was in the castle—a man whose wife was a lady of singular piety. The husband was no one's enemy so much as his own, a man of dissolute life, but in other respects an agreeable companion. He had no regard for any clergyman except me; and his wife who was much concerned about her husband's salvation, applied to me through Blatt to set down some notes in writing for the purpose of calling him to some sense of religion, without his perceiving that it was done at the insistence of his wife. For even with her it was a word and a blow, in soldier fashion. I consented to the request and put down some observations suitable to the persons, and especially of Joannes Vitarius, a Franciscan friar of great authority in those parts. I finished the work at leisure, after the plague (then raging everywhere) had routed me out of Paris and driven me to Louvain.[6]

The present translation is based upon the Basle edition of 1518 and the *Erasmi Opera Omnia* of Leclerc (1704). There have been paraphrases and deletions to accommodate the modern reader.

[6] F. Nicholas, *The Epistles of Erasmus* (London: 1910), pp. 337–338.

The Handbook of
The Militant Christian

(ENCHIRIDION MILITIS CHRISTIANI)
1503

Non faciat ad disputationem theologicam, modo faciat ad vitam theologicam.

Let this book lead to a theological life rather than theological disputation.

Letter to Abbot Voltz
August, 1518   E. E. III, 363

I

You have requested, my dearly beloved in Christ, that I compose for you a kind of compendium, or guide for spiritual living, so that being instructed by it you may attain those virtues of mind that should characterize him who is truly Christian. In this request you have also indicated that your preoccupation with mundane affairs has forced you to perceive the need you have of abandoning worldly pursuits and turning your efforts rather to the attainment of virtue. Our own close friendship only adds to the joy with which I undertake this proposal, and I sincerely hope that He who is solely responsible for your decision will aid me in this endeavor. So that what I have to write will not in the end prove fruitless, let us begin by calling upon the kindly spirit of Jesus so that He will fill my mind with words of salvation, and that what I write will be for you a source of strength and determination.

1. In this life it is necessary that we be on our guard

To begin with we must be constantly aware of the fact that life here below is best described as being a type of continual warfare. This is a fact that Job, that undefeated soldier of vast experience, tells us so plainly. Yet in this matter the great majority of mankind is often deceived, for the world, like some deceitful magician, captivates their minds with seductive blandishments, and as a result most individuals behave as if there had been a cessation of hostilities. They celebrate as if they were assured of victory when, as a matter of fact, genuine peace could never be further away. It is amazing to see in what false security these people live and in what a complacent manner they close their minds to reality. In the meantime the vices, our armored enemies, attack us unceasingly; we are entrapped by their espionage and assaulted by their endless deceptions. If you but look around, you will see that regardless of where you go they are observing you. They are prepared to attack us with a thousand stratagems and, evil demons that they are, they concentrate on wounding our minds with inflammable and poisonous weapons. Unless we ward them off with the impenetrable shield of faith, they will prove to wield weapons of certain death. Nor is there any slackening in the manner of their attack, as it comes from all sides.

This is that world that St. John describes so well as being constituted entirely of vice. It is a world that is both contrary and hateful to Christ. It must be pointed out that the type of warfare it wages is anything but simple and straightforward. From time to time, especially in adverse circumstances, this raging world shakes the very walls of the mind. At other times it incites the mind to betrayal with vain promises. Or again, whenever it finds us unaware, in idle and false security, it unexpectedly and with secret contrivances captures the mind. Most important of all, that slimy snake, the first betrayer of our peace and the father of restlessness, never ceases to watch and lie in wait beneath the heel of woman, whom he once poisoned. By "woman" we mean, of course, the carnal or sensual part of man. For this is our Eve, through whom the crafty serpent entices and lures our minds to deadly pleasures. And yet, as if it were not enough that he threatens us from all directions on the outside, he also penetrates into the inner recesses of our minds. This is the ancient and earthly Adam, more intimate than our closest companions and more zealous than our deadliest enemy, since he cannot be contained by entrenchment or expelled with an army. He must be watched, then, with a hundred eyes, lest he expose God's fortress to demons.

Since it is quite plain that all of us are engaged in a major and difficult effort against an enemy who is numerically superior, better armed and more experienced than we are, are we not insane if we fail to take up arms against him? Are we not extremely foolish if we do not stand continuallyy on our guard and hold all things suspect? The fact of the matter is, however, that we slumber complacently through the whole siege. Indulgence in pleasure rather than hard work seems to be the norm. The self-interest we display would convince one that we are living in peaceful times. It seems that life is a drinking bout rather than a war. We clothe ourselves with boudoir trappings rather than armor. Ease and self-indulgence are everywhere preferred to the rigors of military preparedness. We practice on the peaceful harp rather than on the weapons of warfare, unaware that this sort of peace is the most terrible of all wars.

Anyone who concludes a treaty with vice violates the agreement made with God in baptism. You foolishly cry, "peace, peace," and at the same time treat as an enemy God, who alone is peace and the author of peace. He Himself has made it quite plain through His prophet: "There is no peace for the wicked." The condition that He lays down for peace is that we fight in the garrison of the body against all of our vices. If we compromise, if we consort with vice, we will make a foe of Him who alone, as a friend, is able to bless us, but who as an enemy will surely damn us. He will be our enemy for two reasons. First of all we will be siding with those vices that are diametrically opposed to the divine, for how can light and darkness be in agreement? In the second place, in so doing we ungratefully fail to abide by the pledge that we have made to Him, violating what we have solemnized with sacred ceremonies. Perhaps you are not aware, O Christian soldier, that when you were initiated into the mysteries of life-giving Baptism, you gave yourself by name to Christ as your leader. That is the reason you are doubly indebted to Him. He not only gave you life in the first place but He also restored it. You owe Him more than you could ever owe to yourself. If you break this contract, does it not occur to you that you are violating a pledge to such a kindly leader? Does it become quite plain to you that you have dedicated yourself in this sacrament to His most noble cause? Why did He see to it that you were signed on the brow with the sign of the cross unless He intended that you fight under His banner during this life? For what purpose were you anointed with sacred oils except to take up arms in this struggle against vice? What could be more shameful, more degrading, than to separate yourself from this princely leader? Is there any reason why you should hold Christ the King in derision? Does not the fact that He is God at least instill you with fear? Are you not moved by the love of Him who for your sake became man? Has no one ever warned you of the promise you once laid before Him? Will you actually betray Him who once redeemed you with the price of His blood?

Certainly you show the greatest impudence if you dare raise a hostile standard against a King who gave His life for your sake. He Himself has told us clearly that he who does not stand for Him stands against Him, and he who does not gather with Him, scatters. Not only do you fight under a disgraceful banner, but consider for a moment what your reward will be. St. Paul, the standard-bearer of Christian warfare, tells us "the wages of sin is death." Would anyone engage in warfare if death were the only reward? Death of the soul is hardly a reward. Look at the actual condition of misery that accompanies human warfare. What motivates the soldiers to endure such hardships and deprivation? Is it not the promise of booty, the dread of loss, and the fear of being accused of cowardice? If all they get is the praise of their officers or the hope of a little more pay, that is not much of a reward. Our motives can be neither the fear of shame nor the hope of reward. The same Person witnesses our struggle who will one day reward us. Our reward is that which "neither eye has seen, nor ear heard, nor has entered into the heart of man." I think this in itself ought to be of great consolation as we carry on the battle, for it is eternal happiness that will be ours.

In all earthly engagements a reputation for bravery is the goal, and even the material rewards are handed out by lot. With us in our struggle against vice the case is not quite the same. We do not fight for praise but for Life itself. And the very highest reward will go to him who perseveres, just as the most severe punishment will be meted out to him who deserts. Heaven itself is the promise we seek, and certainly the very hope of such a prize ought to encourage our efforts, especially when it is promised by Him who can neither deceive nor be deceived. Then, too, our struggle takes place before the all-seeing eye of God and is witnessed by the entire populace of heaven. The shame of defeat in the presence of such an audience ought at least to help inspire us to bravery. He will praise our effort whose mere approval alone is the equivalent of the greatest happiness. If the tepid mind is not aroused by the prospect of reward, it must be admitted that fear of punishment can awaken even the most indolent.

In ancient times it was customary in war to violate the corpses of the enemy. It was considered a great calamity if the body were separated by the sword from the soul. This enemy of ours is not only determined to destroy the body but he intends to cast both the body and the soul into hell. For this is actually what occurs when life, which is God Himself, is taken away from the soul. We know well enough that it is the nature of the body eventually to perish because, even though no one attempts to kill it, it cannot live on forever. But for the soul to die is another matter, one of extreme misfortune. I do not have to point out to you the great care and solicitude we exercise in caring for the wounds of the body; we doctor them with the greatest of concern. And yet at the same time we woefully neglect the wounds of the soul. All of us are horrified at the sight of a dying body because we are able to witness it with our bodily eyes. Yet, since the death of the soul is something we cannot witness, there are very few who believe in it and even fewer who are actually frightened at the thought of it. I might point out that the death of the soul is certainly more frightful than the death of the body. This is evident enough from the fact that the soul is something far greater than the body, and God, whose loss it entails, is greater than the soul.

Let me give you some signs, some evidence, whereby you can determine whether or not your soul is diseased or perhaps even dead. If you are troubled with indigestion, if it is difficult to retain food, it is quite apparent that there is something physically wrong with your body. Now the Word of God has been referred to as the food of the soul. If it is unpalatable, if it nauseates you, there can be little doubt that the palate of your soul is infected with diseases. If food is not retained, if it does not proceed along the digestive tract, it is pretty clear that your soul is sick. When your knees totter and it is only with difficulty that you drag your ailing limbs about, it is quite evident that you have an ailing body. Now you must certainly have a disease of the soul when the performance of an act of piety is done with great reluctance and hesitancy, when you have no strength to bear up under a slight rebuke, or when the loss of a few pennies makes you troubled and angry. There can be no doubt that after the sight leaves the body, when the ears fail to hear and the whole body loses its sensitivity, then the soul has departed. When the eyes of the heart are so obscured that you cannot perceive the brightest light (that is, truth), when you are no longer aware with your inner ears of the divine voice, do you think your soul is really alive? You see your brother suffering indignities. Provided your own affairs are not endangered, your mind is not in the least moved. Why at this point does your soul feel absolutely nothing? It certainly must be because it is dead. Why dead? Because God, its very life, is not present. Where

God is, there is charity, for God is charity. Otherwise, if you are a living member, how can any part of the body be in pain without your feeling anything?

Let me give you another sign that is even more certain. Supposing that you have deceived a friend, or that you have committed adultery; in other words, you should have received a major wound, and yet not only are you unaware of any pain, but you actually take pleasure in recalling your wickedness. Can there be any doubt that your soul is dead? We generally assume that the body is not alive if it is insensible to the prick of a pin. Can a soul be considered alive if it is unfeeling in this matter? Let us take another example. You happen to be in the company of someone who is using filthy language, who is raging in anger against his neighbor. If you think that his soul is alive, you are deceiving yourself. It is more like a stinking corpse whose foulness infects all who come near it. Christ referred to the Pharisees as whitened sepulchers. Why? Because they carried their dead souls about within themselves. The bodies of holy people are temples of the Holy Spirit. The bodies of evil men are sepulchers of dead corpses. No cadaver is so dead as that soul that has been abandoned by God. And certainly no corpse offends the nostrils of men to the extent that the evil odor of the buried soul offends the sensibility of the heavenly court. When dying words proceed from the heart, we can assume that a dead soul lies within. For, according to the saying of the Gospel, "the mouth speaks from the abundance of the heart," and if God, the life of the soul, is present, the soul will speak divine words.

If we read the Gospel, we find that the disciples once asked our Lord, "Whither shall we go? You have the words of life." Why "words of life"? The only answer to be found is the fact that these words flowed from a soul that was never for a moment separated from the divinity and that alone restores us to everlasting life. It is not a rare thing that pious men have recalled a dead body to life. But we must never forget that God does not revive a dead soul except by an extraordinary and gratuitous power, and certainly He does not resuscitate it if it is already dead when it leaves the body. I think that we can agree that the sensation of death in the body is very slight or, at least, very brief. The sensation of death in the case of the soul is entirely different; it is more than death itself, because it is everlasting.

With these remarks in mind need I point out further the tremendous powers of our adversary? It would be sheer stupidity not to be aroused to this fearful danger and to take the necessary precautions against it. On the other hand you must avoid the pitfalls of losing courage or feeling unable to cope with the situation. For we must never forget that regardless of the strength of the enemy we have an ever-present and an all-powerful auxiliary. "If God is for us, who is against us?" If He sustains us, what can be lacking? We must be ever inflamed with the hope and conviction of final victory. Let us not forget that our encounter is not with an undefeated enemy but with one who was once broken and who many years ago was overthrown, despoiled, and led captive by Christ our Head. This same Christ will unquestionably subdue him again in us. If we but remember to whose Body we belong, we will triumph in the strength of our Head. No man is strong in his own strength. In Him alone will we find our real worth.

This is the reason why I reiterate that the outcome of this war is not in the least to be doubted. Victory is not something that depends upon chance; it is entirely in the hands of God and, through Him, also in our hands. Anyone who has failed in this struggle was simply lacking in a will to conquer. The kindness of our Leader has never failed anyone. If you but listen to His call and do your part, you will be assured of victory, for not only will He fight alongside you, but His very liberality will be imputed to you as merit. At the same time you must thank Him alone for the victory. He alone is immune from sin and He alone first oppressed its tyranny. Yet this victory will not come without your own effort and diligence, for He who said, "Have confidence, I have conquered the world," does not want your confidence to be a matter of complacency. Profiting by His example, we will fight as He fought. We must steer a middle course between Scylla and Charybdis, neither acting too presumptuously because we rely too much on divine grace, nor surrendering in despair because we are disheartened by the difficulties of the war.

2. The weapons of Christian warfare

I think we can truthfully say that nothing is more important in military training than a thorough knowledge of the weapons to be employed and the nature of the enemy to be encountered. I would add to this that the need for preparedness, of having the weapons close at hand, is also of the utmost importance. In ordinary warfare it is customary that leave of absence or actual retirement to winter quarters brings about a cessation of hostilities from time to time. This is certainly not the case in the kind of warfare we are describing. We can never permit ourselves to be even a finger's length from our weapons. Since our enemy is incessant in his attacks, we must be constantly on the battle line, constantly in a state of preparedness. As a matter of fact, our enemy, when he appears peaceful, when he feigns flight or a truce, can at that very moment be assumed to be preparing for an attack. He is most dangerous when he appears peaceful, and it is during his violent attacks that we can actually feel most secure. It is for this reason that our primary concern must be to keep the mind armed. Our enemies are armed for no other purpose than to destroy us; surely we should not be ashamed to take up arms so as not to perish.

We will speak about Christian armor more in detail when we treat that subject later on. Meanwhile I would like to point out briefly two weapons that we should prepare to use in combating the chief vices. These weapons are prayer and knowledge. St. Paul clearly expresses the desire that men be continually armed when he commands us to pray without ceasing. Pure prayer directed to heaven is able to subdue passion, for it is, as it were, a citadel inaccessible to the enemy. Knowledge, or learning, fortifies the mind with salutary precepts and keeps virtue ever before us. These two are inseparable, the former imploring but the latter suggesting what should be prayed for. St. James tells us that we should pray always for faith and hope, seeking the things of salvation in Jesus' name. We may recall that Christ asked the sons of Zebedee if they really knew what they were praying for. We must always emphasize the dual necessity of both prayer and knowledge. In your flight from sin imitate Aaron as a model of prayer and Moses as an example of knowledge of the law. Neither allow your knowledge to lessen nor your prayer to become sterile.

Listen for a moment to what Christ has to say in Matthew's Gospel: "But in praying, do not multiply words, as the Gentiles do; for they think that by saying a great deal, they will be heard. So do not be like them; for your Father knows what you need before you ask Him." And St. Paul condemns ten thousand words spoken with the lips in favor of five uttered in understanding. Moses spoke nothing yet he heard the words, "Why do you call after me?" It is not the loud sound of the mouth, but rather the pleas of an ardent soul that reach the divine ear. Try to let this be a practice with you: When the enemy assaults you and the other vices give you trouble, lift up your mind to heaven and in your faith do not fail to raise up your hands also. Perhaps the best remedy in this matter is to be continually occupied with works of piety so that you will revert, not to worldly affairs, but to Christ.

You must believe me when I say that there is really no attack from the enemy, no temptation so violent, that a sincere resort to Holy Writ will not easily get rid of it. There is no misfortune so sad that a reading of the Scriptures does not render bearable. Therefore, if you will but dedicate yourself entirely to the study of the Scriptures, if you meditate day and night on the divine law, nothing will ever terrorize you and you will be prepared against any attack of the enemy.

I might also add that a sensible reading of the pagan poets and philosophers is a good preparation for the Christian life. We have the example of St. Basil, who recommends the ancient poets for their natural goodness. Both St. Augustine and St. Jerome followed this method. St. Cyprian has worked wonders in adorning the Scriptures with the literary beauty of the ancients. Of course it is not my intention that you imbibe the bad morals of the pagans along with their literary excellence. I am sure that you will nonetheless find many examples in the classics that are conducive to right living. Many of these writers were, of course, very good teachers of ethics. We have the example of Moses, who did not spurn the advice of Jethro. These readings mature us and constitute a wonderful preparation for an understanding of the Scriptures. I feel this is quite important, because to break in upon these sacred writings without this preparation is almost sacrilegious. St. Jerome assails the presumption of those who, even though they may be learned in other fields, presume to expatiate on the Bible. You can imagine the audacity of those who, having no preparation whatsoever, try to do the same thing.

We must not persist in clinging to the letter, and the reading of Homer and Virgil will be of no use unless we look to its allegorical side. If you like the classics, then you will understand what I mean. If the obscene passages in the ancients bother you, then by all means refrain from reading them. Of all the philosophical writings I would recommend the Platonists most highly. For not only their ideas but their very mode of expression approaches that of the Gospels. Of course they should be read in a cursory manner, and whatever is of real value in them should be applied and referred to Christ. If to the pure of heart all things are clean, then to the impure everything appears to be unclean. Whenever the reading of secular selections arouses your baser appetites, then leave them alone.

Reading the Scriptures with a clean heart is a basic rule.

It prevents what is intended to be medicinal from becoming noxious. You must maintain at all times a high regard for the revealed word. It is genuine because it has its origin in the very mind of God. If you approach the Scriptures in all humility and with regulated caution, you will perceive that you have been breathed upon by the Holy Will. It will bring about a transformation that is impossible to describe. You will perceive the delights of the Blessed Bridegroom; you will see the riches of Solomon. The hidden treasures of eternal wisdom will be yours. Yet I would caution you. The entrance to this abode of wisdom is narrow. The doorway is low, and there is danger in not stooping when you enter. There is nothing that you can believe with greater certitude than what you read in these writings. The senses themselves cannot offer greater certainty. Divine revelation has made it clear that heaven and earth will not pass away before all that is contained therein is fulfilled. Man may lie and make mistakes; the truth of God neither deceives nor is deceived.

Let me mention another requirement for a better understanding of Holy Scripture. I would suggest that you read those commentators who do not stick so closely to the literal sense. The ones I would recommend most highly after St. Paul himself are Origen, Ambrose, Jerome, and Augustine. Too many of our modern theologians are prone to a literal interpretation, which they subtly misconstrue. They do not delve into the mysteries, and they act as if St. Paul were not speaking the truth when he says that our law is spiritual. There are some of these theologians who are so completely taken up with these human commentators that they relegate what the Fathers had to say to the realm of dreams. They are so entranced with the writings of Duns Scotus that, without ever having read the Scriptures, they believe themselves to be competent theologians. I care not how subtle their distinctions are; they are certainly not the final word on what pertains to the Holy Spirit.

If your interest in sacred doctrine revolves more about what is vital and dynamic rather than merely dialectical, if you incline more toward what moves the inner man than to what leads to empty arguments, then read the Fathers. Their deep piety has withstood the test of time. Their very thoughts constitute a prayerful meditation, and they penetrate into the very depths of the mysteries they propound. I do not mean to condemn modern theologians; I am merely pointing out that in view of our purpose, namely, a more practical piety, they are hardly to be recommended. Let us not forget that the Divine Spirit has its own manner of speaking and its own figures of speech. Learn these from the very outset. The Divine Wisdom speaks to us and, like an attentive mother, adjusts Her language to our infancy. For the tiny infants She provides milk and for the sick, herbs. To receive solid food you must grow up spiritually. She lowers Herself to your humility. You must raise yourself to Her sublimity. To remain like an infant is unfortunate. Unending illness is reprehensible. Pluck the marrow from the broken bone: meditation upon a single verse gives more nourishment, brings more wisdom, than continued verbal repetition of the whole psalm.

I warn you with the more diligence because I know that this error has confused, not merely the crowd, but also those who in name and in garb claim perfect religion. These people believe the greatest piety is repeating as many psalms as possible every day, though they scarcely understand them. On every side monastic piety grows cold, languishes, and disappears because the monks grow old and gray in the letter of the Scriptures rather than maturing to a spiritual understanding. They fail to hear Christ proclaiming in the Gospel, "The flesh profits nothing, it is the spirit that gives life." We know the law is spiritual. Spiritual things should not be made carnal. In times past the Father was worshipped in the mountains. Now He wants to be worshipped in the spirit.

I do not want to be misunderstood. I by no means despise the weakness of those who, from feebleness of mind, do the only things they are able to do. Certain words in magic rituals are thought efficacious even when those who pronounce them do so without understanding them. Likewise, divine words, though little understood, should be believed beneficial for those who speak or hear them in sincere faith and pure affection. The angels who are present bring assistance. Nor, indeed, does Paul condemn those who sing in the spirit or those who speak in tongues. But he does urge a fuller use of graces. Of course there is no shame for those prevented from better things by vice, not of the mind, but of nature. As St. Paul has said, "Let not him who eats despise him who does not eat; and let not him who does not eat judge him who eats."

However, I do not want you who are better endowed to remain content with the barren letter. Rather, I want you to pass on to the more profound mysteries. Strengthen yourselves with frequent prayer, until He who holds the key of David, who closes and no one opens, will open for you the book sealed with the seven seals—the secrets of the Father, which no one knows except the Son and he to whom the Son deigns to reveal them.

But how should you pray? I intended to describe a way of

life, not a method of learning. Yet I deviated a bit to point out an arsenal of weapons that you could profitably use in this new type of warfare. So pick out from pagan books whatever is best. In studying the ancients follow the example of the bee flying about the garden. Like the bee, suck out only what is wholesome and sweet; reject what is useless and poisonous. Follow this rule, and your mind will be better clothed. Then you will enter into the battle of daily life better armed. Nonetheless, whenever you find truth and virtue, refer it to Christ. If you wish to consult the treasure house of Paul, that valiant captain, there you will discover "that the weapons of our warfare are not of the flesh, but are mighty before God for the destruction of fortifications, destroying counsels and every height that tends to bar the knowledge of God." You will find the weapons of God by which you can endure an evil day. On your right you will find the arms of justice, on your left the armor of truth, the breastplate of justice, and the shield of faith, a shield with which you can ward off the fiery darts of the devil. You will find also the helmet of salvation and the sword of the spirit, which is the word of God. Carefully fortified with these weapons, a man can fearlessly utter those courageous words of Paul: "Who shall separate us from the love of Christ? Shall tribulation, or distress, or famine, or peril, or persecution, or the sword?" See the many enemies the devil directs and how frightened they are at everything. But hear something stronger. Paul adds, "But in all these things we conquer because of Him who has loved us. For I am sure that neither death, nor life, nor angels, nor principalities, nor powers, nor things present, nor any other creatures shall be able to separate us from the love of God which is in Christ Jesus." What a happy confidence the arms of light give to Paul, an insignificant man who called himself a castoff of the world!

But to return to our original purpose. We must forge a handy weapon, an *enchiridion,* a dagger, that you can always carry with you. You must be on guard when you eat or sleep, even when you travel in the course of worldly concerns and perhaps become weary of bearing this righteous armor. Never allow yourself to be totally disarmed, even for a moment, lest your wily foe oppress you. Do not be ashamed to carry this little sword with you. For it is neither a hardship to bear nor useless in defending yourself. Though it is a small weapon, it will enable you, if you use it skillfully, to withstand the enemy's tumultuous assaults quite easily and avoid a deadly wound. Now is the time for us to teach ourselves a kind of "manual of arms." I promise that, if you diligently train yourself in it, our sovereign Lord, Jesus Christ, will transfer you, rejoicing and victorious, from this garrison to the city of Jerusalem, where there is neither tumult nor war at all, but everlasting peace and perfect tranquillity. Meanwhile all hope of safety should be placed in your arms and your armor.

3. The crown of wisdom is that you know yourself; and of the two sorts of wisdom, false and true

Peace is the highest good to which even the lovers of the world turn all their efforts. As has been said, however, their peace is a false one. It is this same sort of peace that the philosophers promise to those who follow their teachings. Christ alone grants that peace that the world cannot give. There is but one way to attain it; we must wage war with ourselves. We must contend fiercely with our vices. God, our peace, is separated from these enemies by an implacable hatred. His nature is virtue itself. He is the parent and author of all virtue. The dregs drawn from every kind of vice are called folly by the staunchest defenders of virtue, the Stoics. Scripture labels this folly malice. Among all these writers absolute probity is called wisdom. Does not the oracle of the wise man say "wisdom conquers malice"? The father and prince of malice is that ruler of darkness, Belial. Anyone who follows his leadership, walking in the night, hastens to eternal night. On the contrary, the author of wisdom, and Himself Wisdom, Christ Jesus, who is the true Light, alone shatters the night of earthly folly. He is the Splendor of paternal glory, who, as He was made the redemption and justification for us reborn in Him, so also was made Wisdom, as Paul testifies: "We preach Christ crucified, to the Jews a stumbling block, and to the Gentiles foolishness; but to them that are called, both Jews and Greeks, Christ is the Power of God and the Wisdom of God." Through this Wisdom, by His example, we are able to triumph over the malice of the enemy. If we are wise in Him, in Him also shall we conquer. Make the most of this Wisdom. Embrace it! You must set at naught the wisdom of the world, which bears a false title and shows itself only to fools. For St. Paul there is no greater foolishness in the sight of God than worldly wisdom; it must be forgotten by him who would be truly wise. If any man among you seems to be wise in this world, let him be known as a fool, for the wisdom of this world is foolishness with God. It is written, "I will destroy the wisdom of the wise, and the prudence of the prudent I will reprove." Where is the wise man, where is the subtle lawyer, where is the searcher of this world? Has not God made the wisdom of this world foolishness?

I doubt not that these wise fools now trouble you hatefully. These blind leaders of the blind shout that you are raving mad. They become hysterical because you are preparing to go over to Christ's side. Merely in name are they Christians. In all other respects they are first mockers and then attackers of Christ's teachings. Beware lest you be swayed by the blindness of those whose blindness ought to be pitied and deplored rather than imitated. For what is this preposterous kind of wisdom that is so cautious and skillful in worthless things and nothingness? Indeed, it is employed for wicked ends. Furthermore, it is no wiser than a dumb beast in those things that alone pertain to our salvation. Paul wishes us to be wise, but in what is good; simple in what is evil. These are wise that they may act evilly; they know not how to be good.

The eloquent Greek poet Hesiod judges those who, though they lack wisdom themselves, still refuse to accept good advice to be useless. In what class must we place those who, despite the fact that they are perniciously foolish themselves, never cease to disturb, to mock, and to hinder those who have recovered their senses? But shall not the mockers be mocked? He who dwells in the heavens shall mock them, and our Lord shall laugh them to scorn. We read in the Book of Wisdom, "They shall see and shall despise him, but God shall mock them." To be mocked by evil men is, as it were, to be praised. Their worldly wisdom leads inevitably to false presumption, which is followed by blindness of the mind, slavery to base appetites, and all other species of vice. The bad habits developed in this manner produce a dullness or insensibility of the mind, and the victim no longer considers himself a sinner. The climax of this gradual process of degradation is a sudden and unprovided-for death, which is followed by death everlasting.

But of the wisdom of Christ, which the world considers foolishness, we read, "All good things came to me together with her, and innumerable honors came to me through her hands. And I rejoiced in all of these for this wisdom went before me and I knew not that she was the mother of them all." She brings as her companions modesty and gentleness. Gentleness enables you to receive the divine Spirit, for the Spirit rejoices to rest upon a humble and gentle person. While there, it will imbue your minds with its sevenfold grace; it will produce an abundant crop of virtues that will bear blessed fruits—especially that inner or secret joy that is known only to those who have experienced it and that, in the end, neither vanishes nor is destroyed, but is gathered up into eternal joy. My brother, you ought, in accordance with James' admonition, to seek this wisdom from God with the most ardent intentions and, according to a certain wise man, to "dig it out" from the veins of Divine Scripture "like treasures."

The crown of this God-given wisdom is to know yourself, a maxim that the ancients believed sent from heaven and in which the great authors took enormous delight, holding it to epitomize the fullness of wisdom. However, let even this have little weight among you if it does not agree with Scripture. The mystical lover in Canticles threatens his bride, ordering her to depart unless she know herself: "If you know not yourself, O beautiful among women, go forth and follow after the sheep of your flock." No one should hold the fantastic opinion that he knows himself well enough. Might I not also question whether anyone knows his body completely or, indeed, whether anyone will truly recognize a habit of mind? Even Paul, whom God so loved that He revealed to him the mysteries of the third heaven, dared not judge himself. He would undoubtedly have done so had he known himself well enough. If such a man, a man so spiritual that he could judge all things without himself being judged by anyone, knew himself so little, in what are we carnal folk to put our faith? Surely a soldier who knows neither his own forces nor those of the enemy is quite useless. Yet our war is not between man and man, but within ourselves: The hostile battle lines spring forth in opposition to us from our very flesh itself. A friend is distinguished from an enemy by such a fine line that there is great danger of inadvertently defending an enemy as a friend, or attacking a friend thinking him to be an enemy. Our notorious enemy always takes on the appearance of an angel of light. We need always ask, "Are you one of ours or one of our adversaries?" Since you must war with yourself and since the first hope of victory lies in whether you know yourself as much as possible, I shall now put before you a kind of likeness of yourself so that you may plainly know what is within and what is merely skin-deep.

4. Of the outer and inner man

Man is a very complex creature composed of several contending parts: a soul, which may be likened to a sort of divine will, and a body, comparable to a dumb beast. Insofar as the body is concerned we do not surpass the dumb beasts; indeed, we are inferior to them in every bodily endowment. In regard to the soul we are capable of divinity, that is, we may climb in flight above the minds of the very angels themselves and become one with God. If you did not possess a body, you would be but a spirit; if you were not endowed with a mind, you would be but a beast. The greatest craftsman of all has joined together in happy concord these two diverse natures, but the serpent, hating peace, has split them in unhappy discord. Now they can neither be separated without the greatest suffering nor live together without constant war. Either of these natures might well say to the other, "I cannot live either with you or without you." They contend with one another to such an extent that one would think that they were utterly incompatible, but they are, in reality, one. Inasmuch as the body is itself visible, it delights in things visible; inasmuch as it is mortal, it follows things temporal; inasmuch as it is heavy, it sinks downward. On the contrary, the soul, mindful of its celestial nature, struggles strenuously against the weight of the earthly body to press upward. It distrusts things seen because it knows such things to be transient. It seeks only those things that are true and everlasting. The immortal loves things immortal; the heavenly, things heavenly. Like takes to like unless it be too deeply immersed in the sordid things of the body. The resulting contagion may cause it to lose its natural gentleness. Neither the fabled Prometheus nor nature itself has implanted this discord, but sin, evilly corrupting what has been well founded, has sown the poisonous seeds of dissension between these two natures that formerly dwelt together in peace. In the past the mind commanded the body without trouble, and the body obeyed freely and willingly. Now, with the natural order of things disturbed, the passions of the body seek to override the reason, and reason is compelled, in a sense, to forsake its direction.

Man, hampered as he is by this perplexing division, may be compared to an unruly state. Such a state is composed of various sorts of men whose dissensions create frequent disturbances and factions. To prevent strife the greatest power must be given to one supreme authority, and this authority must be of such a nature that it commands nothing that is not for the welfare of the state. To this end it is necessary for him who is wiser to govern, while he who is less wise ought to obey. No one is more lacking in sense than the lower classes, and for this reason they should obey the magistrate and not hold office themselves. The king, it is true, should consult the nobility, or the greater by birth, but the final decision must remain in his hands. He should sometimes be warned, but he should never allow himself to be forced or led.

In man, reason discharges the office of king. His nobles may be considered to be certain bodily, but not brute, affections. These include: true piety toward parents, charity toward brothers, benevolence toward friends, compassion for those who are afflicted, fear of dishonor, desire for an honest reputation, and like qualities. Consider the dregs of the lower classes to be those affections or passions that dissent as much as possible from the decrees of reason and that are least humble. These are lust, lechery, envy, and similar diseases of the mind, which we ought to resist as overseers restrain dirty, vile slaves so as to ensure that they perform the tasks assigned them by the master, or, at least, so as to prevent them from doing harm. The divinely inspired Plato wrote of all these things in his *Timaeus*.

The proper endowments of kings are: first, that they be as wise as possible so that they do not go amiss through error or lack of knowledge; then, that they do only those things they know to be good and right and that they do not will, falsely and corruptly, anything contrary to the dictates of reason. Whoever lacks either of these two qualities judge to be not a king but a usurper.

5. Of the diversity of passions

Though our king, reason, may at times be oppressed, he cannot be corrupted without protesting. He will be able to recover because of the eternal law that has been divinely engraven upon him. If the rest of the common people will obey him, he will do nothing either pernicious or that should be repented. He will do all things with the greatest moderation and the greatest calmness. While the Stoics and the Peripatetics disagree on the subject of the affections, they both agree that we should be guided by reason rather than by passion. The Stoics believe that, when those passions that are most closely connected with the senses have educated you to the point of being able to discriminate between what is to be avoided and what is to be sought, then those passions are to be discarded. They not only regard them as useless for the further pursuit of knowledge, but they consider them to be actually pernicious. For this reason they contend that the truly wise man must be free of all passions of this sort as diseases of the mind. Indeed, they scarcely wish to concede to the perfectly wise man those primary and more human impulses which precede the reason and which they call fantasies. On this point the Peripatetics disagree: they teach that the passions are not to be completely destroyed but merely subdued, for they consider them to be of value as incentive to virtue. Thus they regard anger as the incentive to fortitude and envy as the incentive to industry. Socrates, in the *Phaedo* of Plato, appears to agree with the Stoics when he says that philosophy is nothing more than a meditation upon death, that is, a withdrawal of the mind, as much as possible, from corporal and sensible things, and a dedication to those things that can be perceived only by reason.

Therefore, it is fitting, first, that we come to recognize the inclinations of the mind, and then that we realize that none of them is so violent that it cannot be restrained by reason or redirected toward virtue. Everywhere I hear the harmful opinion that men are compelled to vice. And there are others who, because of their ignorance of their own natures, follow those passions believing them to be the precepts of reason. Because anger or envy has prompted them, they think they have acted from zeal for God. As one state is more strife-ridden than another, so, too, is one person more prone to virtue than another. However, this difference proceeds, not from any mental differences, but either from the influence of heavenly bodies, or from their ancestors, or from their upbringing, or from the complexion of the body itself. Socrates' fable of the good and bad charioteers and the good and bad horses is no old wives' tale. There are some who are born with such a moderate temper and who are so easy to get along with that they incline toward virtue without any virtue at all. They even seem to hurry on of their own accord without any prodding whatsoever. For others the rebellious body can scarcely be subdued with the roughest rein, goad, or spur, so like to a ferocious, untamed, bucking horse is it. If such happens to be your lot, do not immediately abandon the struggle, but persevere with greater determination. Convince yourself, not that the path of virtue is closed to you, but that a richer means of virtue has been offered you. If, instead, you are endowed with a gentle mind, do not consider yourself to be better than another. You are merely more fortunate, and more fortunate in such a way that you are under greater obligation. Furthermore, who is so fortunate in disposition that there are not a great many things in which he needs to struggle?

Therefore, reason must especially guard that in which one feels most vulnerable. Certain vices appear to be most characteristic of certain nations. Thus deceit is a common vice among some people, gluttony among others, and lechery among still others. These vices accompany certain bodily habits, as for example, effeminacy and love of pleasure with the sanguine; anger, ferocity, and evil tongues with the quick-tempered; inactivity and sluggishness with the phlegmatic; envy, sadness, and bitterness with the melancholic. Some of these passions either slacken or increase with age. For example, in youth there is lust, prodigality, and rashness, while in old age there is niggardliness, moroseness, and avarice. There are also passions that seem to be related to sex. For example, men are characterized by ferocity; women by vanity and desire for revenge. Meanwhile, nature, as if to make amends, compensates certain diseases of the mind with certain virtues. Thus this person is prone to pleasure, but at the same time he is not at all irascible or envious; another person is of uncorrupted modesty, but is prouder, more irascible, and more worldly. Nor is there any lack of those who are troubled by such great and fatal vices as theft, sacrilege, and homicide. Every effort must be made to combat these, and a firm wall of definite purpose must be built against their exertions. On the other hand there are certain passions that are so similar to virtue that there is danger lest we be deceived by the doubtful distinction between them. These ought to be corrected in such a manner as to turn them toward the nearby virtue. To give an example, a person who is quite irascible should throw a rein over his mind, and he will be eager, not the least bit sluggish, and he will walk erect. He will be free and simple. Another person is somewhat grasping; let him exercise his reason and he will be frugal. Let him who is inflexible become constant. Let him who is sad become serious-minded. Let him who is tactless become courteous. Other light diseases of the mind should be directed to similar ends. We must be on our guard, however, lest we cloak a vice of nature with the name of a virtue, calling sadness gravity, harshness justice, envy zeal, niggardliness thrift, adulation friendship, scurrility urbanity.

This then is the only road to happiness: first, know yourself; do not allow yourself to be led by the passions, but submit all things to the judgment of the reason. Be sane and let reason be wise, that is, let it gaze upon decent things.

You say that it is difficult to put this advice into practice. Who denies it? Plato has a fitting saying: "Those things which are beautiful are also difficult." Nothing is harder than for a man to conquer himself, but there is no greater reward or blessing. St. Jerome expresses this thought very clearly, just as he does all others. No one is happier than the Christian to whom is promised the Kingdom of Heaven. No one is more burdened than he who must fear for his life every day. No one is stronger than he who conquers the devil. No one is weaker than he who is overcome by the desires of the flesh. If you carefully weigh your own strength, you will say that there is nothing more difficult than to subject the flesh to the spirit; but if you are mindful of God as your helper, there is nothing easier. Assume a perfect life as your goal; having done so, pursue it in a spirit of determination. The human mind has never strongly commanded itself to do anything it has failed to accomplish. One of the most essential elements of Christianity is a willingness to be and to act as a Christian. This rule of conduct may appear to be too difficult to accomplish at first, but in the process of time it will become easy and, with persistence, actually a pleasure. As the poet Hesiod declares, "The way of virtue is difficult at first, but after you have arrived at the summit there is perfect tranquillity." There is no beast so ferocious that he cannot be tamed by human effort. Can it be that there is no power to tame that agent that is the tamer of all things? In order to train the body you are able to abstain from overindulgence in drink and to give up the company of women for certain periods of time. Why, then, can you not sacrifice a few months to gain control of your evil inclinations? You must do all things necessary to save your body, as well as your soul, from eternal death.

6. Of the inner and outer man and his two parts as found in Holy Scripture

It is always a great source of embarrassment to me to realize that the great majority of those who bear the name Christian act for the most part as if they were dumb beasts. Most of them are such slaves to their baser appetites that in this spiritual combat they are unable to distinguish between the dictates of reason and the promptings of passion. They actually believe that they are behaving in a reasonable manner so long as they act upon what they feel or see. In fact, they consider that alone to have existence which is perceptible to the senses. Their only criterion for right or wrong is that which appeals to their desires. What they mean by peace is in reality a deplorable state of servitude. Entirely bereft of reason, they follow heedlessly wherever their selfish interests lead. This is that false and unhappy peace that Christ, the Author of peace, who will one day reward us, has come to do away with. He accomplishes this by stirring up a wholesome war between father and son, husband and wife, and between those things that weak arguments have attempted to reconcile.

I think it is agreed that the authority of the philosophers rests upon the fact that they state what is contained in a different manner in the Scriptures. What the philosophers term "reason" St. Paul calls either "the spirit" or "the inner man" or occasionally the "law of the mind." What they refer to as the "passions" he calls "the flesh," "the body," "the outer man," or "the law of the members." He says, for example, "Walk in the Spirit, and you shall not fulfill the lusts of the flesh. For the flesh lusts against the Spirit, and the Spirit against the flesh . . . so that you do not the things you would." And again: "If you live according to the flesh you will die; if, however, you mortify the flesh by the spirit, you will live." Certainly this is a new order of things; to seek peace in war, war in peace, life in death, death in life, freedom in slavery, slavery in freedom. Listen to what Paul says of freedom: "But if you are led by the Spirit, you are not under the law. We have not received the spirit of bondage in fear, but you have received the spirit of adoption, as sons of God." We read also in St. Paul concerning "the outer man who is corrupt and the inner man who is renewed from day to day." Plato distinguished two souls in one man. In the same way, Paul describes two men so joined in one that both of them will be together in eternal glory or eternal damnation. They cannot be separated. The death of one cannot be the life of the other. What Paul writes to the Corinthians is, I believe, also pertinent: "The first came from the earth and is terrestrial. The second came from heaven and is celestial." And to make this even more clear he applies this duality not only to Christ and to Adam but to ourselves as well. "As was the earthy man, such also are the earthy; and as is the heavenly man, such also are the heavenly. Therefore, even as we have borne the likeness of the earthy, let us bear also the likeness of the heavenly. This I say, brethren, because flesh and blood can obtain no part of the kingdom of God, neither will corruption have any part in incorruption."

I think you can see how evident it is that Paul, who elsewhere spoke of the "flesh" and the "outer or corruptible man," here calls him the "earthy Adam." This is certainly the "body of death" about which Paul so frequently speaks. "Unhappy man that I am, who will deliver me from the body of this death?" Pointing out a far different fruit of the flesh and spirit, he writes elsewhere: "For he who sows in the flesh will also reap corruption but he who sows in the Spirit will reap life everlasting." We know that a messenger of Satan came to trouble Paul in the flesh. When the tempter refused to leave him, God gave him this answer: "Paul, my grace is sufficient for thee." For strength is made perfect in weakness. This certainly is a new sort of remedy. Lest Paul be proud, he is tempted by pride. That he might be made firm in Christ, he is forced to be infirm. For he carried the treasure of heavenly revelations in a vessel of clay, that the sublimity might reflect the power of God, and not his own power. There are, of course, many other examples in the writings of St. Paul that indicate how we are to overcome temptation. Our first recourse in any kind of temptation is to implore the assistance of Almighty God. In fact, those who are well advanced on the road to perfection will actually welcome these temptations, for they guard virtue and, especially, form a bulwark against the danger of vanity that often lurks in the midst of the virtues. We might compare this vanity to the Herculean hydra because it is so difficult to destroy. Let us follow the example of the holy patriarch Jacob in this struggle against sin. He teaches us to persevere during the dark night of struggle until the dawn of divine assistance shines forth. Like him, let us say to God, "I will not let go until you bless me. . . ." The reward that this great wrestler with evil obtained contains a message for all of us. In the first place God blessed him on the very spot. This shows that after we overcome a temptation graces are immediately granted us so that we can resist the next attack. Furthermore, we read that God and the angel then smote Jacob so that henceforth he was lame in one foot. This was, of course, to show that God curses those who attempt to serve two masters. From that time Jacob walked only on the right foot, that is to say, he walked in the spirit. Even his name was changed, and from a highly active person he was transformed into a contemplative. In like manner, after you have overcome temptation and crucified your flesh with its evil desires, you will find true peace and tranquillity, and you will see that the Lord is sweet. God is never perceived in the midst of temptation, but once the tempest subsides, we will bask in the sunshine of spiritual consolation. Examine yourself in all honesty. If you are flesh alone, you will not see God, you will not be saved. Make it your determined effort, then, to become spiritual.

7. Of the three parts of man: spirit, soul, and flesh

In order to carry this comparison a bit further and to investigate it more fully, let us briefly refer to Origen and his treatment of the nature of man. Following St. Paul and those prophets of the Old Testament, Isaiah and Daniel, Origen speaks of a threefold division in man. The body or flesh is our lowest. Because of the original transgression Satan has, as it were, inscribed upon this part the law of sin whereby we are inclined to evil. Failure to overcome this inclination brings us completely under his control. The spirit, on the other hand, may be said to represent us as a reflection of the divine nature of our Creator. Here we find the original pattern of the divine mind wherein the eternal law is engraved by the finger of God, the Holy Spirit. This is that part of us that binds us to God and makes us one with Him. Finally, there is the third part, resting between the other two, which makes us sensual and subject to the terrible fate of those who live according to the flesh.

Let me sum up how we distinguish these various components of man. The spirit has the capacity of making us divine; the flesh tends to bring out our animal nature; the soul is what really constitutes us as human beings. It is the spirit that gives us the qualities of religion, obedience, kindness, and mercy. The flesh makes us despisers of God, disobedient, and cruel. The soul, on the other hand, is indifferent, neither good nor bad in itself. Let me show you how this threefold tendency operates in actual life. You respect your parents, you love members of your own family, your friends. Certainly we cannot honestly say that there is any real virtue in this. Yet not to do so would immediately be condemned as evil. Even those who are not Christians are expected to love those who are near and dear to them. This is found in the very nature of things and can hardly be imputed to meritorious action. But take a situation where reverence toward parents, or love of children, must be sacrificed for the love of God. Here the soul finds itself torn in two directions. The flesh beckons in one direction, the spirit cries out in the other. The spirit argues that you must obey God as you owe Him all you have. The flesh will answer, "If you disobey your father, he will disinherit you, you will be accused of disrespect and lose your good name. Besides, God will not notice this, and if He does, you can be later reconciled with Him." The soul begins to waver. If, holding the spirit in contempt, she turns to the harlot, that is, to the flesh, she will be one body with it. On the other hand, if, spurning the flesh, she rises to the spirit, she will be transformed into the spirit alone. How would you act in like circumstances?

I think it is a great mistake, indeed, to call virtuous those actions that proceed entirely from natural inclinations. There are even certain passions that some mistake for virtue. Take a judge, for example, who condemns a felon simply because this gives him a feeling of self-righteousness. Can you say that he acts in a virtuous way? If he upholds the law for his own evil purposes, for financial gain or personal reputation, his condemnation of the prisoner is tantamount to murder. If, on the other hand, his treatment of the criminal is motivated by personal concern and genuine equity, he acts according to the spirit. I feel that entirely too many people confuse what are really natural gifts or endowments with virtues. You will find that certain individuals are not in the least bothered by temptations of the flesh. Actually, this is an indifferent matter. We can speak of virtue in this regard only in the overcoming of an evil inclination. There are some people, too, who get a great deal of consolation out of attending divine services, Mass, vespers, and novenas. If they do this merely because they find pleasure in the ceremonies, because it is emotionally pleasurable or because it enhances their reputation, then they ought to examine their motives. They are in great danger of deceiving themselves. How many there are who, while in the very act of praying, pass judgment on those who are not naturally prayerful. Or again, in the matter of fast and abstinence, what virtue is there if, while you fast, you mentally condemn someone who fails to observe this regulation?

Too many feel that whoever does not carry out the same religious practices as they do is spiritually inferior. Take, for example, a case where your brother is in dire need of your help, and yet you go on mumbling your prayers, pretending not to notice his predicament. God will actually despise that kind of prayer. For how can He possibly listen to your petition while you cannot find it in your heart to help a fellow man? Take another example: You say that you love your wife simply because she is your spouse. There is really no merit in this. Even the pagans do this, and the love can be based upon physical pleasure alone. But, on the other hand, if you love her because in her you see the image of Christ, because you perceive in her His reverence, modesty, and purity, then you do not love her in herself but in Christ. You love Christ in her. This is what we mean by spiritual love, and we will say more about it later on.

II

SOME GENERAL RULES FOR LIVING A CHRISTIAN LIFE

Since we now have a general idea of what is to be accomplished by this little treatise, let us proceed lest this become a voluminous tome rather than a manual. It is my plan to propose a number of fundamental rules or norms that will guide us through the labyrinth of this world into the pure light of the spiritual life. If every other science has its own rules, then certainly the art of pious living must have some basic regulations. Leading a virtuous life is accompanied by a certain discipline that the Holy Spirit breathes into those who sincerely aim at godliness. Yet I feel that a certain predisposition is necessary, for a refusal to be willing to accept direction is a refusal of God's mercy.

The rules that I will suggest will be garnered from several sources, partly from the Person of God Himself, partly from the devil, and partly from ourselves. They will consist in an enumeration of both virtues and vices as well as components of these. They will be directed for the most part against the evil vestiges of original sin. For it is plain enough that although baptism has taken away the original stain, yet the remnants of this former disease remain. They are still with us so that our humility might be preserved and so that they might occasion the increase of virtue. We will call them blindness, the flesh, and infirmity or weakness. It is this blindness that dims our reason, resulting in ignorance. For there is very little of that divine light of God's countenance remaining in us. It was partially obscured by the sin of our first parents, and what remains has been completely enveloped through corrupt upbringing, evil companionship, and sinful habits. It is this blindness that drives us to seek after the worst instead of the best. It is this blindness that clouds our judgment, leading us to a false standard of values. It is the flesh that, through our passions, prompts us to cherish what is wrong, even though we know better. Weakness causes us either through tediousness or temptation to lose what virtue we may have already acquired. Blindness harms the judgment, the flesh weakens our will, and weakness destroys our constancy.

To counteract these three vestiges of original sin I would propose the following: First of all, to combat blindness we must develop a fine sense of discernment by investigating those things that are to be avoided. The flesh will be overcome if we immediately reject evil thoughts and desires and turn our thoughts to what is of God. Finally, we must acquire the habit of perseverance, so that abandoning the pursuit of virtue may appear to us more evil than never having pursued it. Ignorance must be remedied to give us a proper perspective. The flesh must be subdued lest it lead us from the straight and narrow into the alluring path of vice. And last of all, our weakness must be ever strengthened, so that, once putting our hand to the plow we refrain from looking back and advance like a giant, rejoicing until we receive the crown promised to those who persevere.

First Rule

Now since faith is the only gateway to Christ, the first rule I would lay down is that we ought to place great reliance on the Scriptures. This belief should not be, as is the case with most Christians, something cold, careless, and calculated, but rather should come from a fullness of heart. Be convinced that there is not a single item contained in Holy Writ that does not pertain to your salvation. The fact that the majority of mankind considers heaven and hell as some kind of legend or old wives' tale ought not to disturb you. Even if the entire world appear mad, even though the angels revolt and the very elements change, the truth cannot lie. What God has foretold must inevitably take place.

If you believe God exists, then you must believe that He speaks the truth. Convince yourself that nothing you perceive with your senses is as true as what you read in the Scriptures. The will of heaven, Truth Itself, has inspired it; the prophets of old have made it known; the blood of martyrs has proven it; and the constant belief of countless generations has testified to it. Christ Himself in His life here below has exemplified its pervading truth. Even the demons have confessed its veracity since they believe in it just as much as they fear it. Certainly the very beauty of the message it contains should in itself convince anyone who reads it. If such be the case, would it not be sheer madness not to believe? Take, for example, the many incredible things that were foretold by the prophets concerning Christ. Not one of them has not taken place. Do you think for a moment that He who did not deceive them would try to deceive others? If these prophets did not lie, certainly Christ, the greatest of all prophets, did not deceive us.

If, convinced of these truths, you ask God to increase your faith, it will indeed amaze me if you do not recoil from an evil life. I think anyone would change his life if he saw the eternal punishment and the torture of a guilty conscience that followed upon sin. Who could possibly exchange the joys of a clear conscience and the anticipation of an eternal reward for a moment of fleeting pleasure?

Second Rule

If our first rule demands that we doubt nothing in the divine promises, the second is that we act upon these promises without delay and hesitation. With resolute purpose we must be prepared to undergo loss of everything—property, life itself—

for Christ's sake. The kingdom of heaven does not belong to the lazy; it suffers violence, and "the violent bear it away." As you advance on the path to perfection, you must determine not to turn back. Neither the affection of your loved ones, the allurements of the world, nor the cares of domestic life should stand in your way. Whenever you cannot disentangle yourself from the affairs and business of the world, you must knife your way through them. The fleshpots of Egypt must be forsaken once and for all. We know what took place when Sodom was not forgotten at once. The woman looked back and was turned to a block of salt; Lot went on into the hills and was saved.

Looking back in this flight from the world will spell immediate defeat. I do not have to point out to you how many there are who delay in their flight from vice. They feel that if they immediately free themselves from this or that business they will not be able to finish it. Let them recall the words: "What if today I should require your soul from you?" I think it is apparent to all that business merely begets more business. One vice merely gives way to another. It is for this reason that I would advise haste in abandoning the world. Do it now— even a little recklessness would not be out of place. Forget about how much you are giving up or what you could have otherwise accomplished and realize that in Christ is the fulfillment of all things. Dedicate yourself to Him with your whole heart. Trust yourself no longer but rather cast yourself entirely into His care. Remember what the prophet said: "The Lord is my Shepherd and I shall not want." You must dare to believe in Him with your whole heart and to distrust yourself entirely. In other words get out of your own self and let Him support you. Give up this idea of trying to divide yourself between the world and Christ. "You cannot serve two masters." There is no compromise between God and Belial. Never forget for a moment that our God is a jealous lover of souls. He wants all for Himself. And rightly so, for did He not purchase all of us with His blood? Fellowship with Satan is out of the question, as Christ has completely conquered him by His death.

There are only two paths open to you: the one through gratification of the passions leads to perdition; the other, through mortification of the flesh, leads to life. Which one of these do you choose? There is no third way, and sooner or later you will have to make up your mind about one or the other of these. Yet let me remind you that this is a path upon which few men walk and that you yourself can walk only by exercising the greatest skill. Yet to say that it is beyond our capacities is ridiculous. Christ has trodden this same path, and since the beginning of time men pleasing to God have traveled it. You know well enough that if you desire to live with Christ, you must be crucified to this world. Then why delude yourself like a fool? Why, in such an all-important matter, are you so prone to self-deception?

There are all kinds of excuses, of course. Some will say, "I am a secular priest; I am obliged to live in the world." Some will reason, "Even though I am a priest, I have not joined a monastic order, I am no monk." They are in for a shock. And of course the monks easily delude themselves. "We do not belong to a strict order. This message is for others." The young, the rich, the generous, those in high positions reply that what was said to the Apostles can have no possible application to them. What a terrible delusion! Does the idea of living in Christ have any meaning at all? If you are in the world, you are not in Christ. Of course, if you mean by the world the earth, the sea, the atmosphere, the heavens, then obviously all of us are in the world. But if the world is for you ambition, desire for honor, promotion, or authority, if the world consists of pleasure and lust, then I doubt if you are even a Christian. Christ spoke indifferently to all men, that whoever would not take up His cross and follow Him would not and could not be His disciple. If living by His Spirit means nothing to you, then certainly to die with Christ means even less. If to be crucified to this world, to live for God alone, to be buried with Christ, to rise in His glory, have no meaning, then what does? If His humility, poverty, disregard of self, and incessant labors have no meaning, then neither does His kingdom.

It seems to me that nothing could be more lacking in justice than to offer the same reward to everyone while requiring a few to carry out the mandates upon which the reward is based. What could be more ridiculous than to desire to rule jointly with our Head and yet refuse to suffer with Him? Consequently, stop looking about you and trying to flatter yourself by comparison with others. I will grant that to die to sin is a difficult accomplishment. Even few monks ever actually achieve this. And yet at the same time we must agree that this is something that all of us without exception are sworn to do. When you were baptized, you took an oath to do just that. To my way of thinking there is no vow or no promise that is more religious or sacred than this. All of us, princes or paupers, are going to stand or fall on this one promise. There is really no other way of salvation. Even though all of us cannot reach this goal, cannot attain the perfect imitation of the Head, all of us must aim for this goal with all our efforts. The honest decision to become a Christian implies that one has already chosen the better part of Christianity.

Third Rule

I feel that fear is one of the real obstacles to the pursuit of virtue. This pursuit seems difficult because it involves relinquishing so many things we have come to love and because it demands incessant struggle against those three really formidable elements, the flesh, the devil, and the world. With that in mind I would like to propose a third rule. We must analyze these unfounded fears; when we do, we will find that they are not as bad as they appear. Even if we prescind from the notion of reward, the way of Christ is the most sensible and logical one to follow.

If you take a little time to think it over, it becomes quite apparent that there is no manner of life in this world that is not crowded with difficulties and hardships. Take a man in high political position. No one in his right mind would aspire to such a position if he were aware of the difficulties that beset such an office. What an endless parade of scraping and bowing to woo the good will of those above you! What an interminable suppression of disdain and concealment of despite for those with whom you must work! Need I mention the vicissitudes of the military life? The risks and dangers encountered by merchants and businessmen are well enough known. Take the state of matrimony. The cares and miseries flowing from domestic difficulties are incredible. Only those who are married can really appreciate and understand how real they are. Regardless of the vocation you may have chosen, there are difficulties on all sides. The life of man is filled from beginning to end with tribulation, and besides, the virtuous suffer right along with the guilty. If these are the difficulties you fear, you will find that they actually serve to increase your merit. Without virtue, you will have to put up with them anyway, and with greater trouble and no reward at all.

Let us take a look at those who have decided to fight for the world. In the first place, for how many years do they not endure all kinds of hardships and privations? And for what? For fleeting nothings, mainly. And is there any time during this relentless pursuit of pleasure that they can really be said to be hopeful of the outcome? The miseries that they incur are of such a nature that the longer they pursue false goals the greater is the pain. And what is the end of all this toil and anxiety? Eternal punishment! Now compare this with the life of virtue. To begin with, it becomes less and less tedious as we advance, and this increased pleasantness is further enhanced by the hope we have of eternal happiness. In other words the proportionately greater efforts of the wicked lead only to interminable labor, whereas the lighter efforts of the good culminate in eternal rest. The divine assistance offered to those who labor for God not only lightens the load but changes gall to honey. In the way of the world one care only adds to another, one sorrow gives rise to a second, and there is no peace whatever. Christ sums this all up, "Take my yoke upon you and you will find rest for your souls. For my yoke is easy and my burden light." To put it quite briefly, nothing is more pleasurable than a peaceful conscience, nothing more wretched than to have the mind tormented with a bad conscience.

Yet I would like to add that even were the rewards the same and the toil equal in this comparison, would it not be much nobler to fight and work under the banner of Christ than that of Satan? I think that it is quite obviously preferable to suffer awhile with Christ than to consort with the devil. No man in his right senses would take up arms, regardless of the reward, for so deceitful a leader. The rigors of the campaign are hardly worth such a fleeting recompense. Besides, can Satan be trusted to pay what he promises? The worry and concern resulting from this distrust would nullify any real anticipation of gain. If you lose in this gamble, you will be doubly miserable, since you were tricked out of what you hoped for, and your whole effort will be a miserable failure. Remember that Christ neither mocks nor is He mocked. When you abandon the world for Christ you do not give anything up—rather, you exchange it for something far better. You change silver into gold and rocks into precious gems.

Granted, your friends will be disappointed. Yet you will soon find more pleasant and reliable ones. You will have to give up some of the pleasures of the body, but they are not in the least comparable to those more certain and purer pleasures of the mind. This change will also bring about diminution of your material possessions, but here again what you will gain will be immune from moths and thieves. If your reputation in the world is not what it was, the friendship of Christ will more than make up for this. You will gradually come to realize the transparency of what you once cherished. Even those things that are of themselves quite harmless and licit you will come to regard with indifference. Good fortune usually comes to those who are not looking for it, and certainly if you are attached to absolutely nothing at all, what comes your way will be beneficial. Do not hesitate, then, to give up the devil and seek after Christ. For, regardless of how you estimate the situation, there is absolutely no comparison between the two.

Fourth Rule

In order to help you expedite this decision I am going to lay down a fourth rule: Make Christ the only goal of your life. Dedicate to Him all your enthusiasm, all your effort, your leisure as well as your business. And don't look upon Christ as a mere word, an empty expression, but rather as charity, simplicity, patience, and purity—in short, in terms of everything He has taught us. Consider as the devil, on the other hand, anything that deters us from Christ and His teaching. "When your eye is single, your whole body will be filled with light." Direct your gaze toward Christ alone to the extent that you love nothing, or desire nothing, unless it be either Christ or because of Christ. This way whatever you do, whether you sleep or wake, or eat or drink, or take your leisure, you will increase your reward.

Now since there are many situations where we have to decide whether or not a seemingly indifferent act leads toward or away from Christ, I am going to prescribe a threefold norm to determine our action in just such a situation. There are certain actions that can at no time be considered as other than intrinsically evil. To avenge a wrong, or to desire to injure your neighbor, are of this type. These must be shunned at all costs. There are other actions that by their very nature are so virtuous that they can never be really wicked—for example, wishing well to all men, helping friends with honest aid, hating vices, and participating in godly conversation. There are other things that of their very nature are indifferent, morally speaking. Among these we might list health, beauty, strength, eloquence, learning, and the like. Now none of these attributes should be used other than to aim at Christ. They should be evaluated in terms of how adequately they lead to this goal. This should be the criterion upon which we accept or reject them. I would say that among these things knowledge is the most to be valued. I would prefer it to beauty, strength of body, and riches. And although all learning is of great value, there is here again a certain priority. If you are interested in learning, certainly this is a fine quality, provided you turn your knowledge to Christ. If, on the other hand, you love letters only for the sake of knowledge, you have not gone far enough. You should go a step further. Let your study bring you to a clearer perception of Christ so that your love for Him will increase and you will in turn be able to communicate this knowledge of Him to others. However, I would admonish you to know your own limitations in this matter.

Of the other attributes I have mentioned, I would urge you to use them as the occasion presents, but in such a way that they do not form a hindrance to your spiritual progress. Suppose you come into money. If this does not harm your personal integrity, then by all means use it. But if you feel that it may be an occasion for dishonesty, then imitate Crates of old and throw your wealth away. You can do this rather easily if you accustom yourself to admiring nothing that is outside yourself, namely, things that do not pertain to the inner man. This way you will neither grow arrogant if fortune does smile on you, nor will you be greatly troubled if your wealth is taken away. It will help you in your conviction that Christ alone is the measure of happiness. If you feel that good fortune might be a real hindrance to your progress, then imitate Prometheus and leave the box alone. Anyone who actually admires money as the most precious thing in life and rests his security on it to the extent of believing that, as long as he possesses it, he will be happy, has fashioned too many false gods for himself. Too many people put money in the place of Christ, as if it alone has the key to their happiness or unhappiness.

What I say about money also applies to honors, pleasures, health—in fact, to the life of the body itself. Our determination to imitate Christ should be of such a nature that we have no time for these matters. St. Paul tells us, "The time is short; it remains that they who enjoy this world be as if not enjoying it." There is no doubt that this sort of reasoning is the object of scorn and derision in the world. Yet this is precisely the type of foolishness with which it has pleased God to protect those who believe. "For the foolishness of God is wiser than men." Let this saying be a guide for your every action. If you are a breadwinner engaged in supporting your family, then this is a noble end in itself. But do not forget that your household must be won over for Christ. Suppose you decide to fast. Certainly this has all the appearance of a virtuous act. But what is the motive for your fasting; to what do you refer it? Is it not perhaps that you might conserve food? Is it because others will then think you more pious? Most likely you fast in order to preserve your health. And why are you fearful of overeating? For the simple reason that this can interfere with your pursuit of pleasure. Perhaps you are concerned about your health so that you can continue your studies. And why, might I ask, are you so concerned about studies? In order to obtain the easy living of a clergyman, living that is for your own pleasure and not for Christ's. You have really missed the target toward which every Christian ought to aim. If you eat sufficiently and take care of your health so that you can take part in religious exercises, then you are hitting the mark. If your concern for health and gracious living is only to enable you to be more vigorous in lustful pursuits, you have fallen away from Christ and have made a god out of yourself.

Now there are not a few who are given over to the veneration of the saints, with elaborate ceremonies. Some, for example, have a great devotion to St. Christopher. Provided his statue is in sight, they pray to him almost every day. Why do they do this? It is because they wish to be preserved from a sudden and unprovided-for death that day. There are others who have a great devotion to St. Roch. Why? Because they believe that Roch can immunize them against certain physical ailments. Others mumble certain prayers to St. Barbara or St. George so they will not fall into the hands of the enemy. Still others fast in honor of St. Apollo so that they will not be troubled with toothaches. Others visit the image of holy Job to prevent boils. There are certain merchants who assign a portion of their profits to the poor so that they will not suffer a loss of merchandise in shipwreck. A candle is burned in honor of St. Jerome so that lost goods might be recovered. In short, for everything we fear or desire we set up a corresponding deity. This has gone to the extent that each nation has its own. Among the French St. Paul is esteemed, among us Germans St. Jerome has a special place. Certain areas hold St. James or St. John in lesser or greater esteem. This kind of piety, since it does not refer either our fears or our desires to Christ, is hardly a Christian practice. As a matter of fact, it is not a great deal different from the superstitions of the ancients. They pledged a tenth of their goods to Hercules that they might get rich, or a cock to Aesculapius to regain their health. A bull was sacrificed to Neptune to avoid mishap at sea. The names may have changed, but the purpose and intentions are the same.

You pray that you may not be overtaken by a premature death. Would it not be more Christian to pray that you might be of such a virtuous mind that wherever death overtakes you, it will not find you unprepared? You have absolutely no intention of changing your way of life, and yet you ask God that you may not die. Certainly the only reason you pray is that you may continue your life of sin as long as possible. You pray for the material things of this world and have not the slightest idea of how to use divine things. Are you not actually praying for your own ruin? You pray for good health and yet you continue to abuse it. Is not this rather a dishonoring than an honoring of Almighty God?

I am sure that these remarks will be disturbing to certain so-called saintly men who identify the worship of God with financial gain and who, with their sweet benedictions, deceive the minds of the innocent, serving their own bellies rather than Christ. They will protest that I am forbidding the veneration of the saints in whom God is also honored. I do not damn those who do these things with a simple and childish sort of superstition so much as I do those who, for their own advantage, magnify these practices completely out of proportion. They encourage these devotions, which of themselves are tolerable, for their own profit and thereby capitalize on the ignorance of the masses. What I utterly condemn is the fact that they esteem the indifferent in place of the highest, the nonessentials to the complete neglect of what is essential. What is of the smallest value spiritually they make the greatest. I will certainly praise them for seeking a healthy body from St. Roch, provided they consecrate their life to Christ. But I will praise them still more if they pray for nothing else than a love of virtue and of hatred for vice. As for dying or living, let them leave such matters in the hands of God, and let them say with Paul, "Whether we live, we live unto the Lord; and whether we die, we die unto the Lord." What would be ideal is that they desire to be dissolved from the body and be with Christ. It would be perfect if they, in disease and misfortune, make their real joy consist in this, that they have conformed their lives to Christ their Head. Accordingly, to practice these devotions is not so much to be condemned as is the danger inherent in them, namely, that of relying entirely or too much on them. I suffer from infirmity and weakness, but with St. Paul I show forth a more excellent way. Examine yourself in the light of these rules and you will not be content with these indifferent actions until all of them are referred to Christ; you will not stop midway but will continue so that all is aimed at serving and honoring God.

Fifth Rule

I am now going to add a fifth, subsidiary rule. You will find that you can best maintain this piety if, turning away from visible things, which are for the most part either imperfect or of themselves indifferent, you seek the invisible. We will follow the divisions we mentioned previously in discussing the nature of man. I am going to stress the difference between the visible and invisible because I find so many Christians, either out of neglect or sheer ignorance, as superstitious as the pagans. Let us suppose that there are two worlds, the one intelligible, the other visible. The intelligible or angelic world is that in which God dwells with the blessed. The visible world embraces the circle of heaven, the planets, the stars, and all that is included in them.

Now let us imagine that man is a third world participating in both of the others, the visible referring to his corporeal part, the invisible to his soul. In the visible world, since we are, as it were, mere sojourners, we ought to consider all that we perceive through our senses in terms of its relationship to the intelligible world. The sun, for example, in the visible world might be compared to the divine mind. The moon might be thought of in terms of the whole assembly of the angelic hosts and of the elect whom we call the Church Triumphant. These celestial bodies operate in relation to the earth as God does in relation to our soul. It is the sun that quickens, produces, matures, purges, softens, illuminates, brightens, and gladdens. When you are delighted by the beauty of the rising sun, consider the joy of those in heaven upon whom the divine light shines eternally. Paul tells us, "For God, who commanded light to shine out of darkness, has shone in our hearts, to give enlightenment concerning the knowledge of the glory of God, shining on the face of Christ Jesus." I suggest that you repeat over and over those passages from Holy Scripture in which grace is compared to the rays of the sun. If the darkness of night is oppressive to you, then think of how destitute is the soul without the light of God. If you find any darkness within your soul, then pray that the Sun of righteousness may shine upon you.

The things that we can see with our physical eyes are mere shadows of reality. If they appear ugly and ill formed, then what must be the ugliness of the soul in sin, deprived of all light? The soul, like the body, can undergo transformation in appearance. In sin it appears as completely ugly to the beholder. In virtue it shines resplendently before God. Like the body the soul can be healthy, youthful, and so on. It can undergo pain, thirst, and hunger. In this physical life, that is, in the visible world, we avoid whatever would defile or deform the body; how much more, then, ought we to avoid that which would tarnish the soul? I feel that the entire spiritual life consists in this: That we gradually turn from those things whose appearance is deceptive to those things that are real . . . from the pleasures of the flesh, the honors of the world that are so transitory, to those things that are immutable and everlasting. Socrates had this in mind when he said that the soul will leave the body at the time of death with little fear if, during life, it has rehearsed death by despising material things.

Now the cross to which Christ calls us and the death in which St. Paul urges us to die with our Head are of this earth. Once we have tasted the sweetness of what is spiritual, the pleasures of the world will have no attraction for us. If we disregard the shadows of things, then we will penetrate their inner substance. Sickness, for example, can be a means of advancing in spirituality. In fact, a little less care for physical well-being will give us more time to devote to the mind. If you fear the death of the body, then certainly you should fear the death of the soul. If lightning terrifies you, then think of that invisible lightning that is the wrath of God saying, "Depart ye cursed persons into eternal fire." Are you attracted by what is beautiful in the human figure? Think rather of the beauty of the soul that it conceals. You worry whether the drought will end. It is far better that you pray that God may water your mind lest virtue wither away in it. You are greatly concerned with money that is lost or being wasted, or you worry about the advance of old age. I think it much to be desired that you provide first of all for the needs of your soul.

Now this distinction that we make of body and soul can be applied also to what we read in Holy Scripture. Everything that is written has both an external, or, as it were, corporeal, meaning as well as a mysterious, or spiritual, significance. The Old Testament is filled with the accounts of events that would in no way edify us if we did not understand them in an allegorical manner, that is, by searching out the spiritual meaning. St. Paul, following the example of our Lord Himself, has used allegory as a means of better understanding the Scriptures. Origen, of course, is also a great advocate of the allegorical approach. Yet I think you will have to admit that our modern theologians either despise this method of interpretation or are completely ignorant of it. As a matter of fact they surpass the pagans of antiquity in the subtlety of their distinctions.

I find that in comparison with the Fathers of the Church our present-day theologians are a pathetic group. Most of them lack the elegance, the charm of language, and the style of the Fathers. Content with Aristotle, they treat the mysteries of revelation in the tangled fashion of the logician. Excluding the Platonists from their commentaries, they strangle the beauty of revelation. Yet no less an authority than St. Augustine prefers to express himself in the flowing style that so enhanced the lovely writings of this Platonist school. He prefers them not only because they have so many ideas that are appropriate to our religion but also because the figurative language that they use, abounding in allegories, very closely approaches the language of Scripture itself. The great Christian writers of the past were able to treat even the most arid subjects with a beautiful prose. They enriched and colored their sermons and commentaries with the constant use of allegory. Almost all of them were at home with the writings of Plato and the poets, and they used this literary training to the very best advantage in interpreting the words of Scripture.

It is for this reason that I would recommend that you familiarize yourself with the Fathers. They will lead you to an inner penetration of the word of God, to an understanding of the spiritual worth it contains. This is certainly to be preferred to the scholastic method that invariably ends up in useless disputation. In getting closer to the inner spiritual meaning you will find what is really most important—a hope for the unknown. We have already referred to the Old Testament as abounding in this sort of figurative writing. It is also to be found in the Gospel. For the New Testament has its flesh and its spirit. Paul tells us that we see not the thing itself, but that we see in an obscure manner. We see as through a mirror. We see but an image or a representation of the real object. Christ Himself tells us, "The flesh profits nothing; it is the spirit that gives life." He actually goes beyond what I am saying. As Truth Itself, He says that the flesh profits nothing. St. Paul reiterates the same point when he says that the flesh is actually fatal if it does not lead to the spirit. We have already explained that the body cannot even exist without the spirit. Yet the spirit is completely independent of the body.

If, then, the spirit is that alone which gives life, then it is obvious enough that our every action should tend toward the spirit. Time and time again in his Epistles St. Paul exhorts us not to place our trust in the flesh but in the spirit. Here alone is life, liberty, adoption. Everywhere he belittles and condemns the flesh. This is even more evident in the case of our Lord. By giving sight to the blind, by allowing men to eat with unwashed hands and, on the Sabbath, to lift the ass from the pit and to pick grain from the fields, He shows His disdain for the flesh. The parable of the Pharisee and the publican, the boastings of the Jews, the bringing of gifts to the altar, are all examples of His condemning the flesh of the law and the superstition of those who preferred to be Jews in public rather than in their secret selves.

He makes this very plain in the case of the Samaritan

woman: "Woman, believe me, the hour is coming, when you shall neither on this mountain nor in Jerusalem adore the Father. But the hour is coming, and now is, when the true adorer shall adore the Father in spirit and truth. For the Father also seeks the spiritual to adore Him. God is spirit; and they that adore Him must adore His spirit and truth." He meant the same thing when at the marriage feast He turned the water of the cold and insipid letter into the wine of the spirit. And just in case you feel that this was the limit of His disdain for those who seek the flesh and not the spirit, recall to mind what contempt He had for those who eat His flesh and drink His blood in other than a spiritual manner. To whom do you suppose He directed those words? It was certainly to none other than those who think their salvation consists in wearing a blessed medal or carrying an indulgenced relic. If receiving the very sacrament of His Body is nothing unless done in a spiritual manner, then I think it is plain enough that all other material things are useless unless they are spiritualized.

Perhaps you celebrate Mass daily. Yet if you live as if this were only for your own welfare and have no concern for the difficulties and needs of your neighbor, you are still in the flesh of the sacrament. The sacrifice of the Mass in this spiritual sense really means that we are of one body with the Body of Christ, we are living members of the Church. If you love nothing except in Christ, if you hold that all of your possessions are the common property of all men, if you make the difficulties and privations of your neighbor your very own, then you may say Mass with great fruit because you do so in a spiritual manner. I think there are far too many who count up how many times they attend Mass and rely almost entirely upon this for their salvation. They are convinced that they owe nothing further to Christ. Leaving church, they immediately turn to their former habits. I certainly do not hesitate to praise them for getting to Mass but I am forced to condemn them for stopping at this point. They have failed to let what takes place at Mass also take place in their hearts; the death of our Head that is there represented does not take place in their souls. Examine yourself and see if attendance at divine services renders you dead to the world. If you are filled with ambition and envy, even though you offer the sacrifice yourself, you are far from the real significance of the Mass. Christ was slain for you. Sacrifice yourself, then, to Him who sacrificed Himself to the Father. If you believe in what takes place at the altar but fail to enter into the spiritual meaning of it, God will despise your flabby display of religion.

Let us consider a moment the matter of baptism. Do you

really think that the ceremony of itself makes you a Christian? If your mind is preoccupied with the affairs of the world, you may be a Christian on the surface, but inwardly you are a Gentile of the Gentiles. Why is this? It is simply because you have grasped the body of the sacrament, not the spirit. The ceremony consists of washing the body with water, but for you this is not a cleansing of the soul. Salt is placed upon your tongue, but your mind remains uncured. The body is anointed with oil, but the soul remains unanointed. You have been sprinkled with holy water, but this accomplishes nothing unless you cleanse the inner filth of your mind.

Perhaps you are wont to venerate the relics of the saints, yet at the same time you condemn their greatest legacy, the example of their lives. No veneration of Mary is more beautiful than the imitation of her humility. No devotion to the saints is more acceptable to God than the imitation of their virtues. Say you have a great devotion to St. Peter and St. Paul. Then by all means imitate the faith of the former and the charity of the latter. This will certainly be more rewarding than a dozen trips to Rome. Do you really want to honor St. Francis? Then why not give away your wealth to the poor, restrain your evil inclinations, and see in everyone you meet the image of Christ? By avoiding contentions and overcoming evil with good, you will shine forth brighter in the sight of God than a hundred lighted candles. Do you value being buried in the Franciscan habit? The cowl of St. Francis will not benefit you after death if during your life you did not imitate his personal integrity. I have continually emphasized that the only complete example of perfect piety is to be found in the imitation of Christ. Yet I do not condemn the imitation of His saints; emulate them in such a way that each of them prompts you to eradicate one or another vice, and practice their particular virtues.

You may have a great veneration for the remains of St. Paul. If your religion conforms to this, then I cannot say that there is really anything wrong with it. But if you merely venerate the ashes of his remains and fail to imitate the resplendent image of him portrayed in his writings, you make your religion a ridiculous thing. You worship his bones hidden away and preserved in nooks and niches, but you fail to worship the great mind of Paul hidden in the Scriptures. A little fragment of his body seen through a glass covering evokes your admiration; why not marvel at his wonderful personality? The ashes you venerate are the very thing that vice will lead to. Let them evoke a feeling of sorrow. Our bodies will all one day be reduced to ashes. When you venerate the image of Christ in the paintings and other works of art that portray

Him, think how much more you ought to revere that portrait of His mind that the inspiration of the Holy Spirit has placed in Holy Writ. No artist could possibly have reproduced those words and prayers of Christ that represent Him so exactly in the Gospel. If our Father in heaven finds His perfect reflection in His divine Son, so the words of His Son are the closest image of His divine personality. No relic of our Blessed Lord can possibly approach the strength and beauty of His very self. You may gaze in silent amazement at the tunic that reputedly belonged to Christ, yet you read the wonderful sayings of that same Christ half asleep. You are convinced that it is advantageous to have a small particle of the true Cross in your home, yet this is nothing compared with carrying the mystery of the Cross fixed in your mind. If these external things were the true source of holiness, then certainly there could never have been any people more religious than the Jews. They lived with Him, listened to His words, touched Him—yet most of them rejected Him. What could be more envied than what Judas did, to press the divine mouth with his own? Even our Blessed Lady would not have been the great beneficiary of what Christ did unless she had conceived Him in the Spirit.

Let us carry this idea a bit further. The Apostles are a fine example of this failure of spirit. Even after all the miracles of Christ, after having listened to His teachings for so many years, after so many proofs of His resurrection, what does He say to them? As He is about to leave them He reproves them for their unbelief. Why was this? Surely it was because the flesh of Christ stood in their way. He tells them, "If I go not, the Paraclete will not come to you; it is necessary that I go." If the very physical presence of Christ is useless to salvation, how can you put your trust in corporeal things? St. Paul actually saw Christ in the flesh. Yet he says, "And if we have known Christ according to the flesh, now we know Him no longer." He meant by this that, in the spirit, he had advanced beyond this kind of knowledge.

Perhaps I am arguing with more verbosity than He who taught the rules. I have a reason for doing so. The attitudes I am talking about are, in my opinion, the worst plague of Christianity. This false set of values brings more ruin than any other because in appearance it is very close to godliness. There are no vices that are more dangerous than those that have the veneer of virtue. And it is precisely because of this fact that so many good people easily fall into this deception and that the uneducated faithful are led astray. Violent objections are made to anyone who attempts to point out these things. I care very little about objections to my criticisms so long as they have been approved by ecclesiastical authority. They are signs, supports of piety. And they are quite necessary for children in Christ, at least until they have become a little more mature. Even those more advanced in perfection should not scorn them, lest their scorn work great harm among the simple and uninstructed. My approval rests on the assumption that they are steps, or gradations, that lead to more appropriate means of salvation.

But to place the whole of religion in external ceremonies is sublime stupidity. This amounts to revolt against the spirit of the Gospel and is a reversion to the superstitions of Judaism. St. Paul was incessant in his attempt to remove the Jews from their faith in external works. I feel that the vast majority of Christians have sunk once again into this unhealthy situation. . . .

Charity does not consist in many visits to churches, in many prostrations before the statues of saints, in the lighting of candles, or in the repetition of a number of designated prayers. Of all these things God has no need. Paul declares charity to be the edification of one's neighbor, the attempt to integrate all men into one body so that all men may become one in Christ, the loving of one's neighbor as one's self. Charity for Paul has many facets; he is charitable who rebukes the erring, who teaches the ignorant, who lifts up the fallen, who consoles the downhearted, who supports the needy. If a man is truly charitable, he will devote, if needs be, all his wealth, all his zeal, and all his care to the benefit of others.

Just as Christ gave Himself completely for us, so also should we give ourselves for our neighbor. If the attitude of the religious were comparable to the attitude of Christ, the life of the religious would be much easier and much happier than we now know it to be. No longer would the religious be sad, weary, superstitious, and prone to many temptations; no longer would he fall a victim to the vices of the laity. You who are religious claim to be followers of the rule of Augustine; were he now to return to this life, I wonder if he would recognize as disciples you who turn not to the rule of the Apostles as Augustine desired, but to the superstitions of the Jews. Some among you attempt to justify the emphasis you place on little things by claiming that unless you are faithful in the less important matters you are opening the door to greater vices. This view deserves some commendation, but there is also a danger that in emphasizing the less you may forget the more.

In short, you must avoid the horns of the dilemma. To

observe these unimportant things is, of course, wholesome, but to make them the whole object of your devotions is extremely dangerous. St. Paul recommends ceremonies but he does not bind us to the law, since we are free in Christ. He is not opposed to good works (without them it would be impossible to be a good Christian), yet they do not make the Christian. Paul does not put great worth in the works of Abraham; why should you trust so in your works? Did not God chide the Jews of old for their empty sacrifices and fasts? He tells us that not every man who says "Lord, Lord" is saved and points out that the practice of charity is more important than empty ceremonies. Help him who is oppressed, aid the fatherless, the motherless, the friendless, defend the widow. He recommends that instead of fasting we cancel the debt of him who owes us, that we lighten the burden of him who labors, that we share our bread with the hungry, that we house the homeless and clothe the naked.

I am not advocating that you neglect the mandates of the Church or that you despise honorable traditions and godly customs. If, however, you consider yourselves to be good religious striving for perfection, let your acts be those of one who sincerely desires perfection. If there is a question as to what works should come first, there should be no doubt in your minds. I am not condemning manual works, but I am trying to impress upon you that such works are of little value unless they are accompanied by internal piety. God is a Spirit and is appeased by spiritual sacrifices. A little known poet once wrote, "If God is mind, in poems he's revealed; with a pure mind, then, you ought to worship him." Each one of us should meditate upon these words. While it is true that the author is a pagan and that he has no place of prominence in the world of letters, yet his message, which is read by few and understood by fewer, should not be despised. His advice is worthy of a great theologian. God is mind, the most pure and most simple mind of all; therefore, he must be worshipped with a pure mind.

You believe God to be greatly touched by such material things as a slain bull or the smell of incense; you think that burned wax is a sacrifice. Why, then, did David say, "An afflicted spirit is a sacrifice to God"? If God despised the blood of goats and bulls, he will not despise a contrite and humble heart. If you attend fervently to these things that men expect you to do, spend much more time on those things that God expects of you. Of what advantage to you is a body covered by a religious habit if that same body possesses a mind that is worldly? If your habit it white, should not your mind be white, too? If your tongue is at rest in public, should not your mind be also at rest? What does it profit you when you kneel to venerate the wood of the Cross and forget the mystery of the Cross? You fast and abstain from those things that do not pollute men, yet you do not refrain from obscene conversations, which are a cause of pollution not only to yourself but also to those to whom you speak.

Why do you feed the body and starve the soul? You keep the Sabbath outwardly, but in the secret recesses of your mind you permit all kinds of vices to run rampant. Your body does not commit adultery, but you make your soul to be an adulterer by your greediness. You sing psalms, but your thoughts do not keep pace with your tongue. You bless with the mouth and curse with the heart. You hear the word of God spoken to you, but you refuse it entrance to your heart. Listen closely to the words of the prophet: "Unless you hear within, your soul will weep." And again: "You hear, but you do not understand." Blessed are they who hear the word of God internally. Happy are they to whom the Lord speaks inwardly, for their salvation is assured. Do you wonder why the daughter of the king, she who was goodness itself, was ordered by David to listen within for the voice of God?

Finally, what does it mean if you do not do the evil things that your mind lusts after? What does it mean if you perform good deeds in public but allow evil deeds to dominate your mind? Where is the profit if you have the appearance of a Jerusalem but the character of a Sodom, an Egypt, or a Babylon? If it is to a man's credit that his body walks in Christ's footsteps, it is more to his credit that his mind has followed the way of Christ. If it is a wonderful thing to have touched the Lord's sepulcher, it is more wonderful to have learned the lesson of the mystery of the sepulcher. You who reproach yourselves when you confess your sins to a priest, how will you feel when God accuses you of the same sins? Perhaps you believe that by wax seals, by sums of money, or by pilgrimages your sins are washed away immediately. If you are confident that these are the ways of forgiveness, you are sadly mistaken. If you wish to be forgiven, you, who have loved what you should have hated and who have hated what you should have loved, must attack the enemy within.

Perhaps I am devoting too much time to discussing your external actions, but I will not be convinced of your sanctity until you begin to hate and to flee those things that you used to love. Mary Magdalene loved much, and many sins were forgiven her. The more you love Christ the more you will hate your vices, for just as the shadow follows the body, the hatred of sin follows the love of godliness. I would prefer that you really hate your evil deeds internally rather than enumerate them ten times before a priest.

Therefore, my brethren, put on Christ. Take as your rule that you no longer wish to crawl upon the ground with the beasts, but to rise upon those wings that sprout in the minds of those who love. Advance from the body to the spirit, from the visible world to the invisible, from things sensible to things intelligible, from things compound to things simple. If you come near to the Lord, He will come near to you; if you make a sincere effort to escape from the chains of blindness with which the love of sensible things has bound you, He will come to you, and you, no longer chained to the things of earth, will be enveloped in the silence of God.

Sixth Rule

From among the many thoughts that have entered my mind since I began this letter to you, I think it would be fitting to choose a sixth rule—a rule that, incidentally, is observed by too few of those who claim to be followers of Christ. If we would be holy, we must go to the sole archetype of godliness, Christ Himself. Anyone who refuses to do this is outside the pale. Plato in his *Republic* points out that no man can defend virtue unless he has trained his mind in opinions regarding the true nature of good and evil. We can see then how dangerous it is if false opinions of those things that pertain to well-being should sink deeply into the mind.

A man's actions are mere expressions of his inner convictions; for a man to live so as to always act well, he must be taught even from infancy the things that are of Christ. Since nothing takes root more deeply in a man's mind than that which is taught to him in his earliest years, children should always be protected from any vestige of evil example. A child, being what he is, is most susceptible to example; therefore let good example be given always so that no sinful errors may creep into the child's mind and so that salutary habits may take firm root. He who has such salutary habits will follow virtue of his own accord, and he will judge those who do wrong to be deserving of pity, and not of imitation. Socrates might be mentioned here, as he points out that virtue is nothing other than the knowledge of things that are to be sought after or of things that are to be avoided, with a distinction made between knowledge of goodness and love of it. Vice, then, can proceed from no other source than wrong opinions. Both he who loves Christ and follows Him and he who loves evil pleasures think that they seek something that is good for themselves. The world has never advanced in goodness to the point where common opinion does not still give its approval to what is basically evil. . . .

True pleasure consists in this, that out of love of Christ we are never moved by false pleasures. Take for example how the world abuses the expressions love and hate. When a foolish young man is completely out of his mind for the affection of a common wench, the common folk call this love. There is in fact no truer form of hate. True love looks primarily to the benefit of another. Whoever seeks after his own pleasure does not really love the object of his affections but rather himself. No man can hate except he first hate himself. Nonetheless, there are occasions when to truly love is to hate well, and to hate well is to love well. In the case of a young man about to seduce a girl with flattery and gifts, is this love or hate? What is more hateful than the action of those parents who, neglecting to discipline their children, pamper them to the point that they inculcate false values that will be detrimental to their eternal welfare? If you kill the sinner, you save the man. If you destroy what man has made, you will restore what God has fashioned.

Take, for example, power and weakness, courage and cowardice: what does popular error think them to be? Do they not call him powerful who can easily harm whomever he will? Although to be able to do harm, to inflict evil, is a power excessively hateful, it is common to cowardice, along with flies and scorpions, and the devil himself.

God alone is truly powerful, who could neither do harm if He wished nor want to do it if He could, for His very nature is to do good. But how, then, does this powerful One harm man? Will He snatch money away, will He strike the body, will He take away life? If He does this to a pious man, He has given good for evildoing; if He does it to a wicked man, He has but furnished the occasion—the man has harmed himself. For no one is harmed except by himself. No one prepares to harm another unless he has already far more gravely harmed himself. You prepare to cause me a loss of money, but since you have already lost charity, you have suffered the gravest loss of all. You cannot inflict a wound upon me unless you have already received at your own hands a much more frightful hurt. You will not deprive men of the body unless you have already safely slain your own soul. Yet does not Paul boast that he can do all things in Christ, for he is feeble in inflicting injury but exceedingly strong in bearing it? The crowd considers him strong and courageous who is fierce and of weak mind, who boils over with anger at any injury, however slight, who returns reproach for reproach, evil deed for evil deed. On the other hand they call him who disregards or conceals an injury that he has sustained cowardly, pusillanimous, spiritless. What is more foreign to greatness of mind than to be driven by a mere word from peace of mind, hence not to be able to condemn folly as alien, so that you do not think yourself to be a man unless you heap curse upon curse? Yet how much more manly, with full and lofty purpose, is it to be able to ignore an injury and, besides that, to return good for evil. . . .

Take care that you do not move the eyes of your heart away from your example, Christ. You will not err if you follow the leadership of the Truth. You will not cast yourself among the shadows while you walk after the light. You will not shudder when the light shines through if you distinguish the counterfeit good from the true, the true evils from the false. You will not imitate the blindness of the multitude, burning with desire for some Euripus or other with each of the passions in turn—anger, envy, love, hate, hope, fear, joy, pain. Brahmans, Cynics, Stoics fight for their doctrines. When the world loudly contradicts them, when everyone hisses and hoots at them, they pertinaciously urge what they have earlier persuaded themselves to be true. Dare likewise to fix the rules of your own sect deep within. Dare to adopt completely and firmly the views of your maker.

OPINIONS WORTHY OF A CHRISTIAN

Let these always stand before you as the paradoxes of true Christianity: that no Christian think himself to have been born for himself, nor wish to live for himself. All that he has, or is, he does not credit to himself; he gives credit to God as Author of all his goods and considers them to be the common property of all. Christian charity recognizes no property. Let him love the pious in Christ and the impious also for Christ's sake. Even when we were His enemies, He so loved us that He gave Himself wholly for our ransom. The pious He embraces because they are good. The impious He embraces equally, that He may render them good. He certainly hates no man, no more than a faithful doctor hates a sick person. Toward vices, however, He is unfriendly. The graver the disease, the greater the care that pure charity will bring to it. A man is an adulterer. He commits sacrilege. He is a Turk. Let the act of adultery be execrated, not the man. Let the sacrilege, not the man, be despised. Let the Turk be killed, not the man. Let him put forth effort that the impious man he has made of himself may perish. But let him also wish that the man whom God has made may be saved. Let him sincerely desire well of all men; let him pray well, let him do good. Nor let him harm the deserving and benefit the undeserving. Let him manifest as much joy over the good fortunes of all men as he does over his own. Let him be grieved over the ill fortunes of all men not differently than he is over his own. Doubtless this it is that the Apostles urged, to weep with those who weep, to rejoice with those who rejoice. . . .

In your defense against contempt and ambition place your reliance on good example rather than on the weapons of your guards. Let your rule of government be determined by the common good. The common people owe many things to you, but you in turn owe everything to them. In the face of ambition refer all to Christ. Let offenses against your person be considered as trifles. Let no man's injury infuriate you unless he acted against you as a private person. If you are talented in affairs of state and courageous in danger, be mindful not of these talents but of the responsibilities you carry. And in your governing let your guide be Christ rather than your predecessor in office! If you must imitate great rulers from the past, imitate only those virtues that in them are in agreement with the virtues of Christ. Let no empire be to you of such worth that you would deviate from justice for its sake. Christ will more than reward you for the loss of such an empire. Nothing is more admirable in rulers than their imitation of Christ. He was great in that He hid the secret of His kingdom here on earth. He denied that His kingdom was of this world, although He was in reality the king of heaven and earth.

It is always a source of amazement to me that popes and bishops so indiscreetly wish to be called lords and masters when Christ forbade His disciples to be called either. We must ever bear in mind that there is but one Lord and Master, Christ Jesus, our Head. The expressions apostle, shepherd, bishop, are terms denoting office or service, not dominion or rule. Pope, abbot, are terms meaning love, not power. Yet we are living in a world that has grown alien to the world of Christ both in doctrine and practice. There are too many who think that the expression "world" refers only to those who have embraced the monastic state. In the Gospels, for the Apostles, and for Augustine, Ambrose, and Jerome, the expression means the infidel, enemies of the faith and of the Cross of Christ. It consists of all those who place their care in tomorrow, who strive after riches and sensible pleasures. This world has not known Christ who is the true light of the world. It was from this world that Christ separated not only His Apostles, but all men who would be worthy of Him. How then can we say that this world, everywhere condemned in Scripture, should be associated with Christendom and in its name flatter and maintain our own vices?

Too many of our theologians and teachers only make this matter worse by adapting the words of Scripture to the justification of their own crimes. In truth Scripture should be a source of that norm of behavior that can correct them. Too often rulers today, reading that all power is from God, justify the perpetration of most horrible crimes. How many do not try to establish a new order of charity that engenders a greater regard for their own possessions than for their neighbor's, that sets their own life and fame over all others? Men will not defend the good name of their neighbor if by doing so they in any way tarnish their own. Who will not forsake their neighbor in time of danger, in order to save themselves? Pointing to the fact that many great saints were also great sinners is hardly a commendable thing. Out of fear of death, Peter denied Christ, yet he willingly died for Him later on. Do you think this is sufficient reason to deny Christ on so many occasions? Paul sinned in persecuting Christ, but once he was aware of this, he immediately changed his ways. Matthew was summoned but once and he immediately abandoned his position as a tax collector to follow Christ. It is indeed a sad state of affairs when we have given to vices the names of virtues, when we are more diligent in defending our vices than in correcting them, and when we even turn to Scripture to condone them. You have imitated David and Mary Magdalene as sinners; imitate them, also, in their repentance and love of God.

Keep all this in mind, my brother in Christ, and accept this advice: Have only contempt for the changeable crowd with its ways. To be holy, ignore the demands of your senses. Embrace Christianity with your whole heart. Adapt your personality to the men you deal with so that your inner heart may not lose its strength of resolution. Be friendly and affable, courteous and pleasant to these men so that no harshness of yours might keep them from Christ. Express your feelings with actions, not with angry words. Do not fear the crowd to the extent that you dare not defend the truth. Action of a humane kind ought to improve relations between men, and not lead to deception.

Seventh Rule

We are weak human beings and cannot attain fully to these ideals. This does not mean that we should stop trying; on the contrary, it means that we should come as close to them as we possibly can. The way to happiness is a rapid one, because all we have to do is turn our minds to things spiritual. Once this is done the love of Christ and things of the spirit will follow in exactly the same way as the shadow follows the body when the sun appears. The further you advance with your loving of Christ, the higher you will be able to rise above the transitory things of the world. The more you look to interior, spiritual things the less exterior, material things will attract you. Follow the example of the scholar seeking natural knowledge: he never lets any setback stop him in his quest.

To stay free of vice we have to be prudent. A person convalescing is closer to true health when the causes of his sickness are taken away. A soul is the same way: remove it from the habit of sinning and it will be more capable of receiving God's grace, even though it is not yet perfect. If the example of the saints is too much for us, we should at least have enough pride not to let ourselves be outdistanced by pagans. With little knowledge of God and less of hell many of them have managed to lead clean and upright lives. Some of them even suffered loss of property and of life for this. If your hopes of heaven or your fears of hell fail you, try to let your natural disgust for sin motivate you. Youths especially should be taught to learn about sin from the opinions of the informed rather than to say foolishly that they will learn what sin is from their own experience. If they follow the latter course, they will ruin their lives before they know what life is.

Avoid sin for the simple reason that Christ loves you. But if you cannot do this, try to avoid it merely for your own sake, because the possession of natural virtue, at least, is better than complete immorality. Furthermore, natural virtues form a good base from which to rise to higher spiritual things.

Eighth Rule

If you have frequent and heavy temptations, do not begin to worry that God feels you are not good enough for Him. Think of it this way: He is a loving Father teaching a future heir or punishing a beloved son. Or, He is a lonely man searching out a friend. Begin to worry when you do not have temptation, because that is a sure sign that you are outside the pale of mercy. Job, who was God's friend, the Church Fathers —Jerome, Benedict, Francis—all had terrible temptations. Follow their lead; let them help you. Be consoled that suffering is common to many great men. Try all the harder because when you conquer you will be in their company. "God will not forsake you and will not let you be tempted more than you are able to bear."

Ninth Rule

Careful generals set guards even in times of peace. You should be like a general and always look for the next assault of the enemy. "For he ever goes about seeking whom he may destroy." Prepare yourself for his attack and repulse him when he comes. Remember that evil is never either easily or totally conquered. Before the children of Babylon grow up, dash them on the rock that is Christ.

Tenth Rule

Here are some suggestions for handling temptation: Make a violent effort to put sinful thoughts out of your mind. Turn around and spit, as it were, in the face of the tempter. Or fasten your attention on some holy task and apply all your powers of concentration to it. Or pray with all your might. You might have some particularly stirring passages from the Bible ready to use to encourage yourself in time of particularly painful mental agony.

Eleventh Rule

You have two dangers to face: one is giving in; the other is becoming proud after a temptation has been conquered. To be always safe from temptation, remember that Christ will help His followers do all things, because He says to them, "Have confidence; I have overcome the world." After temptation has passed you, or while you are performing some worthy task, give all the credit to God's kindness. If you allow yourself to feel that you have done this on your own ability and merit, your mind, the inner shrine, will become filled with prideful pleasure. Keep yourself in check by remembering St. Paul's words: "What do you have that you did not receive? And if you received, why do you boast, as if you had not received it?"

There is, then, a double remedy for the double danger. During temptation, have distrust of your own abilities and ask God's help. Place all hope of victory in His benevolent kindness. After temptation remember your own unworthiness and immediately thank God.

Twelfth Rule

It is not sufficient for a soldier merely to repel an attack; he must also seize his attacker's weapons and turn them against him. Follow the example of the soldier and use temptation as a means to virtue. If your inclinations are to be greedy and selfish, increase your donations to charity. If you tend toward boasting, make a deliberate effort to be humble in all things. This way you can find in temptation a renewed determination to increase in piety. This procedure is the one that most galls Satan. It makes him afraid to tempt you because nothing is more hateful to the Author of Evil than that he should be responsible for some good.

Thirteenth Rule

Treat each battle as though it were your last, and you will finish, in the end, victorious. It is possible that God in His kindness might reward you for your virtue by freeing you from temptation. It has happened before. Origen is an authority to be respected, and he believed that when a Christian is victorious, the enemy's forces are lessened, and that once a Christian strongly defeats Satan, God will not again permit him to be molested. In temptation, then, train your mind on the hope of eternal peace. But when you conquer a temptation, think that the next one might come in the winking of an eye, and another immediately following that. As long as we fight in the garrison of the body, we should never put down our arms, never give up our post, never slacken our guard. We should always keep at heart the prophetic words: "I shall stand upon my watch."

Fourteenth Rule

We should not make the mistake of assuming that if we practice most of the virtues, it will then be permissible to have one or two small vices. The enemy you ignore the most usually is the one who conquers. I find that many people fool themselves this way. They think that as far as their standards are concerned it is perfectly all right to practice one or two of the lesser vices and be the last person to commit one of the remaining ones. Most of those whom people call good certainly would be the last to commit theft, or homicide, or adultery, or rape, or incest. Yet they might not be above an occasional fornication or some other pleasure. Or these same "good" people might from time to time overindulge, or use vile language, or boast. Now really, if one vice can fool us this way, why cannot the other ones? It is not that these "good" people permit themselves one vice and have all the other virtues, but rather that these "virtues" are really only virtuous-seeming habits that their personality or education has imparted to them. If a person, like a true Christian, detests one vice, he must, like a true Christian, detest all of them. If a person has true charity, he holds all the vices in equal abomination and does not let himself be fooled by any one of them, because he knows that the least of vices leads to the worst and that his negligence toward these least ones will lead him to destruction. It is impossible to root out all your bad habits at one time. But still, you ought to try each day to work on one bad habit and replace it with a good one.

Fifteenth Rule

If you are afraid of what you go through in overcoming a temptation, think along these lines. Do *not* compare the difficulties of combating temptation with the pleasures of the sin. *Do* compare the bitterness of the fight with the bitterness that sin brings. Before a sin is committed, the guilt in which the sin results has a sweet and comfortable air about it. But think of the sweetness and comfort that will come to you when you have won out, and you will have little difficulty making the choice.

Those who are not careful enough are fooled because they compare the difficulties of overcoming temptation with the pleasure of the sin. They pay no attention to the consequences of either. The man who gave in will be worse off than the man who did not because during the next trial his difficulty will be much harder to bear than that of the man who did not give in. The victor's pleasure will be far greater and longer-lasting than the sinner's pleasure. The man who carefully weighs both alternatives will see this easily. Every Christian should realize what follows when he overcomes temptation, and the more he does this, the more will his victory mean to him.

Sixteenth Rule

If you should be wounded when the enemy unexpectedly

attacks, do not give in. Many weak-willed and effeminate persons give up completely if they have been beaten once. They quit fighting, allow complete immorality to overcome them, and never even think of trying to regain their liberty. This faintheartedness is dangerous, and although it is not identified with hopelessness itself, it usually leads to despair, which is the most desperate of sins. A good soldier never admits defeat, even when he is in retreat. Imitate the soldier and do not despair if you have fallen into sin. The good soldier's temporary defeat and painful wounds seldom drive him from the field. They spur him to gather his strength and fight harder than before. We must be the same way. If spiritual disaster strikes us, we should quickly renew our courage. When sin disgraces us, we should find new resolution, new eagerness to live again a life of virtue. One wound is easier to take care of than many wounds; a recent wound is easier to heal than an infected one. Keep in mind and take courage from Demosthenes: "A fleeing man will fight again." The prophet David, Solomon the King, Peter the first pope, the Apostle Paul—all of these men sinned. Perhaps God let them sin so that you could follow their example and not despair. Stand up on your own two feet, and do it quickly and courageously. Return to the fight with fire in your heart. Control and caution are the watchwords. A pious man who overcomes great sin is all the more pious. What makes a man evil is not that he sins but that he *loves* his sin.

Seventeenth Rule

Each temptation has its own appropriate remedy. There is, however, one remedy that can be applied to any and all temptations, and that is the Cross, which is the example for those who fall, the refuge for those who toil, and the weapon for those in the fray. This is the one weapon you should use against the devil. The people have the Passion read to them and adore the image of the Cross. They strengthen themselves by hanging crosses about themselves and by keeping parts of the true Cross about their homes. They work themselves into veritable agonies as they meditate on Christ's Passion and cry tears of compassion for Him. This is all well and good for the ignorant. The true value of the Cross, however, is in profiting from its many examples. You cannot say that a person loves Christ if he does not follow His example.

If you want to meditate successfully on the Cross, you must have a plan of action, realizing that you are fighting a life-

and-death battle. Everything should be carefully figured out, so that when the time comes for you to make use of your plan, you will know exactly what to do. You must match the various parts of the Passion with the particular vices you are afflicted with and want to be rid of. There is no temptation or vice for which Christ did not furnish a remedy on the Cross. For example, when ambition pushes you to want to be great in the eyes of men, think, my suffering brother, of how great Christ is, and to what extent He lowered Himself to atone for your sins. When envy fills your mind, remember how gently and sincerely He poured Himself out for our benefit. He was good to the very worst of us. When gluttony is the problem, think of how He drank vinegar and gall. When lust tempts you, remember how Christ lived. All His life He denied Himself these pleasures and suffered discomfort, punishment, and misfortune. He will assist you, too, when anger burns inside of you. Think of how He stood like a lamb, silent before His shearers.

If poverty or avarice are your temptations, remember that God owns all things and that for your sake He became so poor that He did not even have a place to rest His head. If you follow this plan, it will not be painful to resist temptation. It may even be easy because you will know that you have conformed yourself to your Leader and even given, in a round-about way, thanks to Him for the agony He endured for you.

Eighteenth Rule

If, when passion stirs us to commit sin, we recall how loath-some, abominable, and detestable sin is, this will help to coun-teract the temptation. For those whose spiritual life is moder-ately comfortable this is the most effective remedy. It will also be of some help to those who are not so well off spirit-ually. We worry and scheme about trifling matters of no real importance. Before we sign up with the Devil by committing sin, should we not stop to consider our own worth as humans, seeing the terrible price that was paid for us? To consider that we, the most noble of God's creatures, were created for an end? That the marvels of the world were created for us? That we are of the company of the angels and heirs to immortality? That we are members of Christ's body and members of the Church; that the Holy Spirit dwells in us and that we are made in the image and likeness of God? Then, when we have weighed this side of the scale, should we not consider how sin is a sickness of the body, mind, and soul? That sin is the serpent's poison; that when we sin, we sign a contract to enslave ourselves to the Devil? Even in this age innocence cannot be willingly destroyed.

Having weighed both sides of the balance, ask yourself whether it is worthwhile to fall from such dignity for a pleasure that is gone in a second; to fall from such dignity into a trap where your own efforts to free yourself will be useless.

Nineteenth Rule

Compare the two opposing forces. You make God your enemy by sinning, and by sinning you set up for your master the Devil. Your innocence makes you God's friend, with the rank and privilege of a son. Your sin makes you a servant and son of the Devil. One is an eternal fountain, the Mount Ida of utter beauty and happiness. The other is the Father of Evil, of complete depravity, and of unutterable unhappiness. God does nothing but good for you; the Devil can only harm you.

God began your life by filling you with immeasurable goodness. He redeemed you with great mercy; He bestows riches on you with complete generosity. He helps you gently in your shortcomings; receives you joyfully when you come to your senses. But the Devil lays traps for you with perverse joy, bringing you nothing but misery. He tries every day to drag all of mankind down to the bottom of hell.

When you have considered all this, speak with yourself this way: Even forgetting where I come from and all that God has done for me, will I for the sake of a pleasure that will soon pass desert my noble, loving, and deserving parent and enslave myself to the most cruel of masters? Can I not be superior to the Devil, just as I am superior to a deformed dwarf? I will flee the Evil One who desires man's ruin.

Twentieth Rule

The rewards are as different as the givers. What can be further apart than everlasting death and everlasting life? What is more in contrast than the delightful companionship of the citizens of heaven and the horrible company of the damned? No Christian could have any difficulty in knowing which is better. He would have to be insane to make any mistake. The contrast is not only after death, but even during life. Virtue has its own reward, and once a person has it, he would not exchange it for anything in the world, because he has the peace of mind, the happiness, and heavenly joy of a pure conscience. The horrors of a troubled conscience are the worst consequence of all the things that come from sin. On the other hand peace is the hundredfold Christ promised in the Gospels. Peace is the preview of eternal happiness that He gives to us. This is the wonderful gift that the Apostle spoke of when He said that "neither eye has seen nor ear heard, nor has it entered into the heart of man what God has prepared for those who love Him," even in time. The worm eats the wicked even in the world; they already carry the flames of hell with them. The unending agony that haunts the habitual sinner is nothing less than hell.

Virtue is worth seeking for itself. Each virtue has an opposing sin whose very causes should be avoided. Keep this in mind if you want to take part in the glories of heaven.

Twenty-first Rule

Life is sad and miserable, short and quick. Death lies in wait on every side, haunting us. Since we do not know when death will come to us, how foolish it would be to continue living the kind of life that would damn us forever if we died unexpectedly.

Twenty-second Rule

The worst evil is hardness of heart. Those who do not repent, who deliberately remain in their habits of sin, have the most to fear. Careful thought about this will reveal how few there are who are truly converted from evil habits, especially among those who have prolonged their lives of sin right up to the end. The path down to evil is quick, slippery, and easy. But to turn and "to go forth to the upper air . . . this is effort, this is toil." Think of Aesop's goat before you descend and remember that climbing out is not easy.

SPECIAL REMEDIES FOR PARTICULAR VICES

So far we have been considering common remedies against vices in general. Now we will take up vices one at a time and point out particular means you should use to fight them.

Lust

Let us first consider lust. This is the first evil that attacks us. Its temptations are the strongest of all; its influence is the greatest. Lust drags more individuals to hell than any other

vice. When lust tempts you, fight immediately with these
weapons: First of all, think of how rotten, how unclean, how
utterly unworthy of human dignity lust is. It puts the divine
in us on a level with the animals. We are destined to be with
angels, to commune eternally with God. Remember how rotten and perverted, how momentary and fleeting, how pregnant
with remorse and guilt lust is. Think of how we have already
described the soul as noble and the body as beautiful. How
twisted it is to defile for a swiftly passing pleasure the soul
and the body. Christ consecrated with His own blood the
body that lust desecrates and pollutes. It brings nothing but
evil with it. No other vice brings bad reputation so fast and
so quickly. It depletes and weakens the great gift handed
down to us from our ancestors. It ruins mental alertness, destroys tact and consideration. It destroys the inclination to
serious study and healthy pursuits and plunges one into the
filth of moral degradation. It will deprive you of intelligence
no matter how great, and reason no matter how sound. It
drives youths out of their minds and forces wild lies into their
mouths; it makes old age filthy and detestable. You will find
that almost any evil you can think of has its roots in lust.
Look what lust has done to people you know. It destroys
health, brings on disease. It ruins youth before its time and
speeds the coming of a horrible old age.

Think of all the young adults, of all the charming virgins
who have remained pure, and they will motivate you in your
struggle for purity. If you follow their example, you will be
just as strong as they; the circumstances of their temptation
were much the same as yours. If they could do it, so can you.
Think how honorable and pleasant a pure soul and body are.
Purity in particular makes angels our friends and enables us
to receive the Holy Spirit. There is no vice the Holy Spirit
loathes more than impurity. He is the lover of purity. Clean
minds are the favorite abode of the Holy Spirit. Purity delights Him.

Think of the disgrace and madness that loving a prostitute
brings. Think of the mental torture, the endless and lying
protestations. There is nothing manly or virile about such a
relationship. There is no love; it can only be termed an emotional aberration. Think of all the social evil that uncontrolled
evil brings: mistreatment of parents and friends, waste of
wealth, rapine, murder, blasphemy, etc. Life is empty and
fleeting, like a passing cloud. Death sets his trap without regard to where you are or what you are doing. Think of all
your acquaintances and friends who died unexpectedly, especially those who used to be your partners in sin. The lightning-

fast judgment that followed their unprovided-for deaths sent them to hell, and all for the fleeting pleasures of a passing moment. It is not such a big thing to resist impurity for the sake of Christ who suffered the Crucifixion for you. Will you crucify Him again with your illicit pleasures and put Him again to torture? At the same time He has literally heaped benefits and blessings on your soul, although you deserve absolutely nothing. You can never repay Him, but you could make a start by imitating His goodness and purity. When a temptation comes to you, think of your guardian angel. He protects you and witnesses everything that you do. Think of your God, who sees even the most secret places of heaven and earth. Would you do in the presence of heaven's court what you would be ashamed to do in the presence of the lowest of human beings?

When temptation comes, think of your two alternatives. Either you will become so perverse and your mind so blind that impurity will become ingrained in you the rest of your life, or, by God's grace, you will see what you are doing and with almost endless suffering you will manage to rid yourself of this evil. Avoid the temptation immediately and you will avoid these painful alternatives.

Let your state of life motivate you. If you are a priest, remember that you are consecrated to God. Could anything be worse than to touch the rotten, stinking flesh of a whore with your mouth that receives the Body and Blood of Christ, or to handle loathsome filth with the same hands that execute the most beautiful and incomprehensible mysteries? Where is the consistency between oneness in body and soul with God and oneness in body with a whore? If you have a good education, think how poor it is for you to share divine thoughts with thoughts worthy of shame and rebuke. If you are of the upper classes, think of the example you give to others. If you are married, your marriage is the symbol of the union of Christ and His Church. If you are in the flower of youth, nothing will pollute you faster, nothing will haunt your memory more than this stupidity. Nothing is more painful than the stings of a sinful pleasure once gone. For a woman nothing is more noble than her chastity, nothing more shameful than the loss of it. If you are old, nothing is more monstrous, nothing more provocative of scornful laughter than impurity.

Here is a summary of suggestions that will save you from sins of the flesh: As fast as you can, flee from every occasion without exception. (This is good advice for *any* temptation. He who loves danger is likely to perish in it. The advice, however, is particularly good with regard to those sirens who cannot be avoided except in immediate flight.) Also, drink and eat with moderation. Be temperate even in pleasures that are allowed. Remember two things: that Christ died for you and that you will one day die. In view of these things have only pure and reliable individuals for companions, avoid corrupt and lustful conversations like the plague, flee idleness and occupy your thoughts with serious contemplation of things eternal. Especially, dedicate your whole heart to study of the Scriptures and to frequent and pure prayer, particularly during temptation.

Avarice

If you feel that your nature tends toward avarice, or if the Devil tempts you with that sin, put the above rules into action and think of the greatness of your value as a human being and of the end for which you were created and redeemed, because God wants you always to enjoy the highest good. The vast machine that is the earth was created to serve your ends. How narrow-minded and unthinking not to use it as a means but to be entranced with it as an end. This is man's error and is a stupid and worthless one. What are gold and silver but red and white earth? You are a disciple of Christ and are called to a far greater possession than that of gold. Even some of the pagan philosophers had only contempt for it. Forget gold and admire something truly great.

I am contradicted, however, by an argument full of vague generalities that even Christians use. Their only pleasure is in the deception of themselves. Their argument runs like this: "The more wealth one has, the easier one can take care of the necessities of life. One *must* lead a healthful existence, rear and educate one's children, be honored by one's fellow men. The more money the better. How can you live a good life any other way?" Nine out of ten Christians feel this way. They have cloaked their desire in necessity. Let me begin my answer by throwing back at them what Christ said about the lilies and the birds living each day and what He said about emulating them. Let me say that the Apostles carried neither wallet nor moneybag. Let me say that Christ told us that when we have forsaken all else, we should seek first the kingdom of heaven and all things will be added unto us. A person who strives to be godly will always have enough to get along. We really do not require very much. What we often do, though, is to set a limit on what we require on a basis of our own covetousness.

I am not greatly impressed with those who with one vow

dispossess themselves of everything they have and then run around for the rest of their lives begging shamelessly. It is not wrong to have money. It only becomes wrong when money is loved as an end instead of looked on as a means. If you should become rich, act like the generous steward; if you should become poor, do not feel robbed, but rather feel as though a friend had relieved you of a dangerous thing. A person who spends his whole life gathering wealth might be a good businessman but he can hardly be a good Christian. His very preoccupation with wealth betrays a lack of trust in Christ, who so liberally provides for the birds of the air.

Wealth is supposed to bring with it many good things. (Epictetus puts it lowest on the scale of things to be desired.) What does wealth contribute to your intelligence? You cannot say it brings wisdom or intelligence or understanding. Or that it brings health or beauty. You might say it brings honor. But I ask what kind of honor and reputation it brings. True honor can only come from Christ; it is a reward for virtue and not for money. If your *mental* poverty were exposed, you certainly would not be honored. No one can say a wealthy person has true friendship; the vast majority of his "friends" want his money and can hardly wait until he dies.

What wealth really brings is a host of evils. That is why Christ compares wealth to thorns that rip and tear all peace and quietness with a thousand never-ending cares. He tells us that it is easier for a camel to enter the eye of a needle than it is for a rich man to enter the kingdom of heaven. St. Jerome says that a rich man must be either dishonest himself or the heir of a dishonest man. You can neither keep nor get great riches without sin. Wealth robs one of a sense of value. St. Paul tells us that avarice and idolatry are the same things, while Christ says that we cannot serve God and Mammon at the same time.

Ambition

If your desire for things of this world ever becomes exaggerated, then following these suggestions will help you to put things in the proper perspective.

True honor is based upon virtue and upon nothing else but virtue. This comes from what we have said above and ought to be said before anything else. Even *true* honor is not an end in itself. Christ's example teaches us that Christians should go after only one kind of honor, that of being praised not by men but by God. The Apostle says, "He whom God commends is approved." If, for example, wicked men praise someone for something that is actually not true, this is not honor but a huge scandal. If honor comes for something shared by the honest and the dishonest—say, beauty, wealth, strength, birth—that is not really honor either. No one is praised for doing dishonorable things. On the other hand, when one is praised for an honorable thing, this is honor. But people who deserve honor do not seek it but are content with the basic goodness of the act that brings the honor. You can see now how the honors that most people desire so avidly are really empty and ridiculous. Because in the first place honor is bestowed by those who do not distinguish between honesty and dishonesty. In the second place it is usually bestowed for actions of dubious goodness, and sometimes even for bad actions. And in the third place it is usually given to an undeserving person.

Honor is bestowed for a number of reasons. Some people do it from fear. These people themselves are to be feared. Some do it so you can enjoy what they say to you. In this case you are being made fun of. Others bestow praise because they admire nothing, consider nothing honorable. These are to be pitied. Perhaps a sincere person will judge you to be truly worthy of honor. If he is not right about you, try to change yourself to live up to his expectations. If he is right about you, remember that God, not you, is responsible for your honorable traits. If you want to avoid honor that is false, avoid virtue that is false. Besides, what could be more stupid than to judge yourself by others' opinions of you? You know how changeable people are. They give you honor one minute and take it away the next. Nothing is more foolish than becoming proud of honor when you earn it or becoming angry when you lose it. Honor falls as often as not on unworthy people. How can honor have truth to it when people worse than you share the honor?

How peaceful is the calm of a modest and private life as compared to the lives of those powerful people always in the public eye. How difficult for the celebrity to keep his two feet on the ground and not fall on the slippery path. How difficult to keep perspective. The higher the pedestal, the more devastating the fall. Every honor brings responsibility with it. God's judgment will fall more severely on those who grab in all directions for honor, knocking everyone else out of the way. His mercy comes more easily to those who realize their weaknesses. Those who set themselves apart to receive honor from men also set themselves apart from the men who receive God's special graces. Follow Christ's example. According to the way men think, who was ever more despised and lower than Christ? He fled every honor offered Him—He was above honor. He accepted scorn riding on an ass. Recall to yourself the robe and the crown of thorns and how He was condemned. Recall the horrible way He chose to die. He scorned the world, *but* He was glorified by the Father. Christ's Cross will be your salvation—let the Cross be your honor. What good are honors if angels curse you and God looks in the other direction when you pass?

Pride and Haughtiness

Not to be a proud and haughty person, you have to follow the old proverb and "know thyself." That is to say, you must regard your special talents, whatever beauty or fame you have, as gifts from God, and not as things you earned for yourself. Whatever is low and mean is not God's doing, however. Here you can only blame yourself. Remember the squalor of your birth and how naked and poor you were when you crawled into the light of day like a little animal. Just think of all the disease and misfortune you were exposed to as a child. Little things could make you deathly ill.

Self-praise is ridiculous. If you flatter yourself for some inconsequential thing, you are foolish; if for some wicked thing, you are mad. And if you praise yourself for a good thing, you are ungrateful. Nothing is more stupid and unwise than to flatter oneself. Even if you are in a position to do what you will, your tendencies toward pride will be checked by recalling how great and powerful God is, how He could break you in two by snapping His fingers. If He levels the hills and did not spare the angels, will He allow you to raise your head in pride?

Comparing yourself to those better than you will also help you. If you think you are handsome, compare yourself to someone better looking than yourself. If you feel you can teach well, think of those whom you know you have taught nothing. Do not think of all the wonderful things you are, but rather of all the wonderful things you are not, and St. Paul's words will have meaning for you, too: "Forgetting those things that are behind, press toward those things that remain in front."

When pride tempts you, bring to mind those elements of your personality or behavior that embarrass you. Concentrate on your own obvious deficiencies. Never forget that pride was the vice Christ denounced the most and that, even among men, pride and arrogance meet with nothing but derision. A humble and gentle nature obtains not only God's favor but the good will and respect of your fellow man.

Briefly then, these two considerations will help you overcome pride: a realization of your own nothingness and a realization of the reward Christ has prepared for you.

Anger and Revenge

When resentment goads you to revenge, remember that anger is a false imitation of fortitude, and fortitude is the antithesis of anger. Nothing manifests a weaker will, nothing requires a feebler and weaker mind than enjoyment of revenge. In trying to appear brave by not allowing an injury to go unpunished, a person displays only immaturity, since he cannot control his mind in a particular situation. It is noble and generous to ignore someone else's mistakes and quite the opposite to imitate them. The more a person has done harm, the more violent and insulting he is—in short, the more wicked he is—the more should you be careful not to imitate him. To avenge someone else's corruption brings only self-corruption. If you are not a person given to violence, all the world will know that you have been unjustly injured. But if you are revengeful, you only offer reasons to be treated in the same way. An injury inflicted is not lessened, but only increased by revenge. There will be no end to mutual injury if revenge is reciprocated between the two injured parties. Enemies increase on both sides, the pain can only grow more severe. And the more ingrained the habit of revenge, the more difficult it is to stop. A gentle and tolerant nature sometimes even influences the wrongdoer and makes a good friend out of an enemy. Vengeance usually brings only an increase of harm.

If you bear in mind the scale of values we have worked out, you will remember that only the outer man can be harmed by other men. God alone can take away the worthwhile things of the inner man, and He usually does this only to unkind men. The only person that can harm a Christian is himself, and no injuries bring as much pain as self-inflicted ones. If you will use your intelligence concerning injuries, you will not make too much of them; you will also lessen their gravity by considering mitigating circumstances. You may have been injured, but you may also know it will soon be made up for. Or perhaps the person who did it was only a child or an inexperienced youth; maybe the person acted on someone else's advice, or maybe he acted with no previous reflection at all. He might have been drunk at the time. He is therefore to be forgiven. If the person is a member of your family or a close friend, he deserves to be forgiven because you love him or because you respect his authority. If the person has done you a number of good turns, take that fact into consideration. A liberal mind will not remember only the injuries and forget all the good things a person may have done. Lastly, when you fight your revengeful tendencies, think of how many times you have offended God. God will not forget the law He established, "to forgive us our trespasses as we forgive those who trespass against us."

You could rush off to Rome or Compostela and buy up a million indulgences, but in the last analysis there is no better way of reconciling yourself with God than reconciling yourself with your brother. It is really impossible to be seriously sinned against by your fellow man. Pardon your neighbor his offenses so that Christ might forgive you your countless thousands of sins. It is difficult, you say, to forgive when you are carried away with anger. Just remember what Christ suffered for you—remember the patience with which He allowed Himself to be insulted, chained, lashed, executed. And you were once nothing more than His enemy. Even now the infinitely gentle Christ tolerates you and your daily repetition of sins. Do not boast of the Head and refuse to take care of the Body. You will not be one of Christ's members unless you follow in His footsteps. The only praiseworthy anger is against vice, not against man.

How can you expect mercy for yourself and still be so unjust to your brother? Is it so much to expect you to forgive a sinner when Christ Himself prayed to His Father for those who crucified Him? Is it so difficult to be told not to strike back at the brother whom you are commanded to love? Are you really qualified to punish someone who hurts you? Let pity and not a desire to punish motivate you in your dealing with those who have harmed you. Be angry at the man's vice and not at the man himself. If your personality gives you a tendency toward anger, then prepare yourself for every contingency by repeating to yourself that you are determined to do or say nothing while you are angered. When you make a decision in anger, hold off putting it into effect until your anger subsides—even if it is a just decision. There is no difference between a person who has lost control of his mind and one who is unduly angered. Remember how often in the past you have regretted something you did or said in anger. Why not let reason, or pity, or at least Christ obtain what will come to pass anyhow? To overcome evil with goodness, malice with kindness, is to imitate Christ's perfect charity.

My dear friend, you can see what an immense number of

vices we still have to discuss in a similar fashion. But we will leave what remains to your own skill. When we started, it was not our intention to dissuade you from sin with an exhortation against each and every vice. All we wanted to do was familiarize you with this new method of warfare so that you would be better prepared to defend yourself against the attacks of temptation that stem from your past life. Thus we picked selected examples to show you how to act in particular instances, especially those to which we know your habits or personality incline. We described certain general rules you should fix in your mind and use to counteract temptation. To keep them effective, go over them frequently and renew often your resolutions against such sins as detraction, slander, envy, gluttony, etc. These are the Christian soldier's only enemies. Against them he should fortify his mind in advance, using prayers, the sayings of the wise, the teachings in Scripture, and the examples of holy men, especially of Christ.

CONCLUSION

Even if I had been sure reading Scripture were going to supply you with all the spiritual advice you need, my love for you as a brother would have prompted me to write this extemporaneous treatise to help you with your pious plans to improve yourself. I wrote this all the more speedily because I was afraid you might fall into the clutches of those superstitious religious who, partly for their own advantage, partly out of great fervor, but certainly not according to any definite knowledge, "wander about seas and deserts." If they ever get their hands on a man returning from vices to virtue, then by outrageous arguments, blandishments, even threats, they try to drag him into the monastic life, as if one were not a Christian without a cowl. They fill up his heart with unsolvable worries and his conscience with innumerable scruples, truss him up with a lot of meaningless human traditions, and finally drive the poor wretch into a sort of Judaism where he is taught not to live but to fear.

Monasticism is not holiness but a kind of life that can be useful or useless depending on a person's temperament and disposition. I neither recommend it nor do I condemn it. Let me warn you about it, however. Do not let your relationship with God depend on food, or on a particular form of worship, or on any visible thing, but only on those things we have already gone over. Whatever things you find Christ's image in, join yourself to them. If people do not think along lines that would make you better, withdraw yourself as much as possible from human companionship and take for companions Christ and His prophets and Apostles.

Make yourself completely familiar with Paul. Keep him in your heart at all times; "day and night he should dwell in your hand." Memorize what he has to say. It has taken a long time and many a battle to come to these opinions. It is perhaps a presumptuous thing to do. Nevertheless, we rely on God's assistance and carefully devote our attention to it. After Origen, Ambrose, Augustine, and so many more modern interpreters, we certainly shall not be alone in the task, and following them, we do not think that our effort will be entirely fruitless.

There are certain detractors who think that true religion has nothing to do with good literature. Let me say that I have been studying the classics since my youth. For me a knowledge of Greek and Latin required many a long, hard hour. I did not undertake this merely for the sake of empty fame or for the childish pleasures of the mind. My sole purpose was that, knowing these writings, I might the better adorn the Lord's temple with literary richness. Too many in recent years, through their ignorance and boorishness, have been doing the very opposite. Through this type of study a person's naturally generous qualities can be kindled to a love of the Holy Scripture. I have, however, set this work of translating the Fathers apart for a few days so that I could write this for you and point out for you a short-cut, as it were, to Christ. I pray that Jesus will bless your undertaking and that He will favor your whole project. I pray also that He will multiply and increase the grace He has already given you in helping you with your transformation. My purpose is that you may quickly grow great in Him and may hasten to a perfect manhood. In Him I bid you farewell, my brother and friend, who are ever beloved to my soul and who are now dearer than before, and more pleasing.

THE PRAISE OF FOLLY

The most celebrated and at the same time most controversial work of Erasmus, *The Praise of Folly,* continues to form the basis, probably because of its very popularity, of what many feel is an unfounded judgment on the very character of its author. For many this work confirms the suspicion that he is a man of no great personal integrity, the great spokesman for dissenters of all creeds, a John the Baptist and Judas Iscariot in one, the glory of the priesthood and its shame. There is an almost unanimous agreement in certain circles that he is at most a relativistic skeptic hiding behind a mask of erudition. Two recent critics of the great Humanist have taken up the theme of skepticism in evaluating him in terms of the theological problems of his day. He had, they contend, "a conservative turn of mind, for all his clearsightedness, and to him the revolutionary was more to be feared than the ignorant devotee of an old but corrupt system. His reforming ideals were based on an undogmatic Christianity, an eviscerated Christianity precisely because it was without Christ at its deepest level. The epigram is irresistible—Erasmus was shrewd but shallow, a man of cool calculation rather than of burning conviction." [1] These authors are not entirely wrong in stressing the primacy of Erasmus' concern for morality. But they are entirely wrong in assuming that because Erasmus does not have the burning convictions of a Luther, he has no convictions whatsoever. The incendiary character of Luther's convictions, and of others as well, is one of the major reasons for Erasmus' distinct lack of fondness of dogmatic disputes. This mistaken judgment, and it is widespread, makes the grave error of severing Erasmus' moral concern from its deep Christian roots in the New Testament, the Fathers, and the *Devotio Moderna.*

Huizinga, voicing another common position on Erasmus, gives

---

[1] *Martin Luther on the Bondage of the Will* (*De Servo Arbitrio*), trans. J. I. Parker and O. M. Johnston (London: James Clark & Co., Ltd., 1957), p. 19.

special attention to the unresolved classical-Christian tension in the great Humanist so evident in *The Praise of Folly*. "The foundation of his spiritual life was no longer a unity to Erasmus. It was, on the other hand, a strong desire for an upright, simple, pure, and homely belief, an earnest wish to be a good Christian. But it was also the irresistible intellectual need of the good taste, the harmony, the clear and exact expression of the ancients, the dislike of what was cumbrous and involved." [2] Huizinga lays a great deal of stress on what he calls the negative aspect of Erasmus' mind, as a consequence of which, "All symbolism and allegory were fundamentally alien to him and indifferent, though he occasionally tried his hand at allegory; and he was never mystically inclined." [3] Commenting on *The Praise of Folly* he states, "Only when humor illuminated that mind did it become truly profound." [4] He fails utterly to note in the work a deep respect for the suprarational, rather than the discursive. The true mystic is lost in contemplation to the common sense of the world. "Then the spirit will in a marvelous manner be absorbed by the Highest Mind, more powerful than the infinity of its parts," says *Folly* in the final section of the work. Here is a balanced contrast of a perfect suprarational mysticism with the earlier irrationality of the child or the lover. Such is the realism of Erasmus, who on the frontier of religion attempts to unite nature and grace. The remarkable equilibrium he establishes between what appears to be a disturbing mixture of skepticism and faith can only be the result of a man keenly aware of the need for an intensive interior spiritualism.

If the purpose of the *Enchiridion* was to foster the vision of a more practical Christianity embellished with the learning of the classics and based upon evangelical knowledge at work in a purified soul, then *The Praise of Folly* aims at projecting this program into a wider arena. Yet those who see in the latter a most improper and irrelevant tirade against monasticism and interpret his revolt against scholasticism as "a revolt against reason" will see in *Folly* only a livelier attack on the same institutions. For those who are still convinced that "he offered to an idle generation a short cut to truth and a dispensation from the tedious business of thinking" [5] we can only repeat what Erasmus wrote to Sylvester Gigli in 1521: "If you can't praise my wit and learning, at least give me credit for hard work." [6] Those who are impervious to his learning will

---

[2] J. Huizinga, *Erasmus of Rotterdam* (London: The Phaidon Press, 1952), p. 112.

[3] *Ibid.*, p. 101.

[4] *Ibid.*, p. 78.

[5] C. Hollis, *Erasmus* (Milwaukee: Bruce Pub. Co., 1933), p. 261.

[6] "Hic si nihil laudis debetur ingenio meo, si nihil eruditioni certe nonnihil debetur industriae" *E. E.* IV, 437.

certainly fail to see the basis of his effort to expose human foibles in terms of Menippean satire. The *ridendo dicere verum* employed by Erasmus may have exposed his works to the accusation of skepticism, yet on the other hand it had the happy effect of bringing the entire drama of human existence under his scrutinizing eye. It was above all the humor and guileless satire that he employed in *The Praise of Folly* that endeared him to all Europe of his day and has continued to endear him to all who appreciate good literature. Those who fail to perceive his piety will also undersell his humor because if rationality is denigrated, then surely risibility has no significance. There is an almost Chestertonean quality in his piety which fosters the belief that God sometimes smiles at mortal man. Whereas the *Enchiridion* criticizes the realm of religion and piety in its own intrinsic terms, *The Praise of Folly* exposes piety in a framework that critically analyzes all of mankind.

The years between the composition of the *Enchiridion* in 1501 and the return of Erasmus to his beloved England in 1509 were years of great maturation. Gone was a confidence in the spirit of the Italian Renaissance with its emphasis on the dignity of the individual and the autonomy of man. Travels in Italy had made Erasmus keenly aware of the decadence of the Italian Renaissance and the corruption of the Italian clergy. He began to realize that the breakdown of religion and morals had its basic cause in the narrow-mindedness and utter foolishness of humanity itself. Thus he expands his criticisms of piety to a critique of humanity itself, philosophers and poets, kings and merchants, wed and unwed, old and young. The humor, the satire, actually cloak his painful reaction to the degradation of life in a misguided world.

The composition was written, as he explains later, when the pangs of a physical ailment had confined him to his study at the home of Thomas More.

When I had returned from Italy and was staying at the home of my friend More, my kidney ailment kept me inside for a few days. My books had not yet been delivered and, even if they had been, sickness prevented me from doing any serious work. I began to amuse myself and pass the time with *The Praise of Folly*—with no intention of publishing it, but only to lighten the pangs of illness with this little diversion. When it was under way I showed some of it to several friends. They all laughed and were so pleased that they insisted I go on with it. I agreed and spent about a week at the job.[7]

The fact that the book was written in such a short period of

[7] *E. E.* II, 94.

time is in itself a tribute to his great genius, his restless pen, his power to improvise and extemporize. Yet this laughing parody of every form and rank of human life contains a logical development that is in agreement with his fundamental philosophy of restoring all to Christ. After introducing Folly as the symbol of all the good things of life, he proceeds to a severe criticism of those things that he feels are most responsible for the ills of humanity. A true appreciation of the final section exonerates Erasmus from the accusations of skepticism and relativism. The whole purpose of Folly is to lead the reader to the true notion of Wisdom, to God Himself. For wisdom is itself a kind of madness. It is a *sancta eruditio.* For Erasmus as for many of the Renaissance philosophers theology is not a *scientia* but rather a *sapientia,* not a systematic body of certain knowledge but a holy rhetoric in humble service of the sacred text of God's revelation.

The satire of so many ecclesiastical institutions must be understood in terms of the times in which it was written. For four centuries Christians of the West have exhausted themselves in attacking one another's theological positions, in many cases sacrificing truth in an endless effort toward protectionism. At a time when Europeans shared a certain universalism, a common *Weltanschauung,* the protectionist nerve of a later period was not quite as sensitive to criticism. Since the revival of letters in the Renaissance of the twelfth century the main brunt of satirical writings had been the most obvious institution in the pyramidal social structure of the Middle Ages, the Church. *The Carmina Burana* of the Goliards, *The Book of Burnel the Ass, The Decameron,* and *The Canterbury Tales* are but a few examples of the literary ridicule of the Church and its institutions. Works of this nature, for the most part products of *clerici vagabundi,* constitute a very substantial part of late medieval literature.

In Erasmus' time *The Ship of Fools* of Sebastian Brant had given rise to a whole family of navicular satirical literature. Jacob Winpfeling, Bishop of Strasbourg, had authored *Letters of the Seven Devils Plaguing a Country Pastor,* of which over 12,000 copies were circulated between 1489 and 1522. His fine humor ironizing the foibles of various classes of society is reflected in the works of Erasmus. The fool throughout the Middle Ages had retained a privileged place at the court and elsewhere; in the morality plays and satires his was the voice of bitter, unwelcome truth discoursing death and the folly of the wise. The Renaissance had put him in a different framework—man's weakness and absurdity, his dreams and illusions were given a more moralistic setting. *The Praise of Folly* must be contrasted with the nightmare hallucinations that crowd the canvases of Brueghel and Bosch or the Danse

Macabre of the period. For the reader who has no taste for banter or ridicule then there is little hope that the incongruities of human nature can lead to a better understanding of the Christian message.

The Praise of Folly

(ΜΩΡΙΑΣ ΕΓΚΩΜΙΟΝ)

Postermo opus hoc, qualecunque est, placet eruditis totius orbis omnibus, placet episcopis, archiepiscopis, regibus, cardinalibus, atque ipsi Leoni pontifici maximo, qui a capite usque ad calcem totum perlegit.

Finally this work, whatever else it may be, is pleasing to the whole community of scholars throughout the world, to bishops, archbishops, cardinals and even to the great pontiff Leo, who has read it entirely from beginning to end.

> Letter to Abbot Antonio de Bergis
> December 1517, E. E. III, 169

Dedication
Desiderius Erasmus of Rotterdam
to
Thomas More, his Friend

As I was traveling from Italy to England recently, I decided not to while away all the hours on horseback with useless talk and vulgar stories; I chose rather to think at times of the pursuits we have in common or to recall with relish the friends, both very learned and very enjoyable, that I had left in England. Among them you, More, came first to mind. So you see I enjoyed the memory of you just as much as I am accustomed to enjoying you in person, and let me be hanged if I have enjoyed anyone more in my life! Therefore, since I thought that something should be done about it and the time seemed little fit for serious thinking, I decided to have some fun with a praise of folly.

"How did the goddess Pallas put that into my head?" you ask. First of all, there was your family name of More, which is as close to the Greek word for folly as you are far from the meaning of the word. Then, too, I suspected that this playful exercise of wit would find your approval because you usually enjoy jokes of this kind that are not unlearned—unless I am mistaken—and yet not at all dull; and besides, you are a sort of Democritus amid the common run of mortals. Although you have, to be sure, a singular perspicacity that makes you accustomed to dissent sharply from the crowd, still, because of your incredibly affable and likeable ways, you can always get on well with all men, and enjoy doing it.

May you accept this little declamation, then, as a remembrance of a friend and may you undertake to defend it; for now that it has been dedicated to you, it is yours, not mine. No doubt there will be some querulous persons who will criticize on the one hand that these trifles are too frivolous for a Theologian and on the other hand too cutting for a meek Christian. They will complain that we are resurrecting the Old Comedy or Lucian and are sharply criticizing everything. Let those whom the whimsy and foolery of my argument offends remember that mine is not the first sample of such a work but that many famous authors in the past have written in the same vein. Homer, long ago, had his fun with a battle between frogs and mice. Virgil, the gnat and a salad; and Ovid, a nut. Polycrates eulogized Busiris; and Isocrates, a severe critic of Busiris, did the same. Glaucon praised injustice; Favorinus, Thersites and the quartan fever; Synesius, baldness; Lucian, the fly and the parasite. Seneca amused himself with a deification of the Emperor Claudius; Plutarch, with a dialogue between Gryllus and Ulysses; Lucian and Apuleius, with an ass; and someone else, as told by St. Jerome, with the last will and testament of Grunnius Carocotta, a hog.

Well, if it makes them any happier, let them think that all this time I have been playing checkers to refresh my spirits or, if they prefer, that I have been riding a hobbyhorse. For what an injustice it is that we allow to every other mode of life its diversions and then refuse any diversion at all to studies. Especially if these diversions may lead to serious results and if they are so structured that a reader who has any trace of a discerning eye at all may reap more from these literary trifles than he would from the pedantic and ornate arguments of some whom we know. As, for example, when one of these persons praises rhetoric and philosophy with a patched-up oration; another sings the laurels of a prince; another urges war against the Turks; another foretells the future; and still another invents a new set of petty discussions concerning a lock of goat's wool. Nothing is more nonsensical than to treat serious matters triflingly; but nothing is more entertaining than to treat of frivolous matters in such a way that you appear to have been nothing less than trifling yourself. Let others judge me as they will; yet unless self-love completely deceives me, I have praised folly and not altogether foolishly.

Now, in response to the charge of sarcasm, I reply that this freedom has always been permitted to men of wit, that in their satire they make fun of the common behavior of men with impunity, as long as this freedom does not go to an extreme. For this reason, I wonder at the present sensitivity of ears that are unable to bear anything except solemn addresses. Oh, yes, you will find some persons so perversely religious that they will listen to blasphemies against Christ more readily than the slightest joke about a pope or prince, especially if it pertains to money or revenue. Yet he that censures the lives of men without mentioning any names—I wonder if he does not teach and warn rather than bite. Indeed, if it is otherwise, how many topics could I write about? Besides, he who spares no class of men seems to be angry at the vices of men and at no man in particular. Therefore, if anyone claims to be injured, he betrays his conscience or at least his fear. St. Jerome indulged in this type of writing and with greater freedom and severity; sometimes he did not omit names. I have not only especially abstained from the use of names but I have also tempered my style so that the wise reader will readily see that my end is pleasure rather than pain. I also do not dip into the hidden cesspool of crimes as Juvenal did. Instead I have striven to bring forth the ridiculous rather than the foul. Finally, if there is anyone who is not satisfied with these reasons, let him remember that it is a noble thing to be scolded by folly. Since I have made her the narrator, it was necessary to maintain a sense of decorum in her character.

Yet, why do I say all this to you, a patron so singular that you defend in the best way causes not of the best? Farewell, eloquent More, and stoutly defend your Moriae.

From the Country,
June 9

Moriae Encomium
that is
The Praise of Folly
by Desiderius Erasmus

Folly Speaks:

No matter what people commonly say about me (and I am not ignorant of how bad the name of Folly sounds even among the most foolish people), I am still the one—the only one, I may say—whose influence makes both gods and men glad. As substantial proof for this argument witness that as soon as I began to speak in this crowded assembly, all your faces suddenly shone with a new and unusual cheerfulness. Your brows were enfurrowed, and you all applauded amid cheerful and frolicking laughter. Now as I look at all of you present here, you seem to me to be intoxicated with nectar, as the gods of Homer, and not without some nepenthe, also; whereas before you sat in a sorrowful and overwrought mood, as if you had recently returned from the cave of Trophonius. Just as it usually happens, when the sun first shows its brilliant and golden face to the earth; or when, after a particularly hard winter, the young spring breathes soft West winds, and a new appearance, color, and youthfulness come over everything; so at the sight of me your faces took on a different hue. And thus the banishment of cares that great orators are unable to effect with their long and carefully worked out speeches, I can bring about immediately just by my appearance.

The reason why I appear today in this unusual garb you will presently hear, if you listen to me with attention; not as you do in sermons, but as you do to salesmen in the market, to clowns and jesters, and as our friend Midas listened to Pan. For it is not my pleasure to play the rhetorician with you for a little while, not one of that type certainly who nowadays cram the heads of schoolboys with bothersome trifles and teach a more than womanish obstinacy in arguing; rather I imitate those ancients who in order to avoid the disreputable title of philosophers preferred to be called Sophists. These men labored studiously to celebrate the praises of both gods and brave men in eulogies. A eulogy, therefore, you shall hear not of Hercules, or Solon, but of myself, Folly.

I have no use for those so-called wise persons who say that it is absolutely stupid and insolent for a person to praise himself. Let them say it is foolish if they wish, but let them admit that it is proper; for what is more suitable than that Folly be the trumpeter of her own praises and αὐτὴ ἑαυτῆς αὐλή—"blow her own horn." Who can better describe me than myself? Unless by chance someone knows me better than I do myself. Besides, I do not think I am doing anything more shameless than that which many of our best citizens and scholars are continually doing. With a certain perverse modesty, they employ for a fee flattering speakers or vaunting poets from whose lips they listen to their own praises, which are nothing but pure lies. The blushing listener shows his feathers and spreads his plumes like a peacock while the brazen flatterer compares this good-for-nothing to the gods and proposes him as a paragon of all virtues. He himself knows, of course, that he is δὶς διὰ πασῶν, twice infinitely away from being such a person. Thus, this sycophant puts the beautiful feathers of other birds on a crow, makes the Ethiopian white, and finally makes an elephant out of a gnat. Lastly, I follow the well-known proverb of the common folk that says that he rightly praises himself who can find no one else to do it. At this point I wonder at the ingratitude or, should I say, slothfulness of men who assiduously cultivate me and freely acknowledge my benefits. No one, however, in all these ages has lived who would celebrate the praises of Folly in a grateful oration. However, there has been no lack of people to eulogize Busiruses, Phalarises, quartan fevers, flies, baldness, and pests of that sort, using up oil and losing sleep in the process.

My eulogy will be extemporaneous and simple, and for that very reason it will be so much the more true. I would not want you to think that it was composed to show forth my genius as is the case with the common run of orators. For they, as you know, work on a speech as much as thirty years, if it is theirs at all, and then swear they wrote it in three days or even that they dictated it.

On my part, however, I have always found it more agreeable simply to state what is on the tip of my tongue. Also, let no one expect me to explain by definition or even less by division as is the custom of common rhetoricians. For it is inauspicious to put limits on her whose influence is so widely spread, or to divide her whom all of nature has united in worshipping. Besides, what point is there for me to make a shadowy sketch of myself when you can all see me with your own eyes? I am as you see me, that true bestower of good things, in Latin called *Stultitia*, in Greek, ΜΩPIAN.

But what was the need to tell you that, as if my face and

visage, so to speak, did not tell well enough who I am. As if anyone who thought I was Minerva, or Wisdom, could not easily be convinced otherwise by only looking at me, even if I were not talking, though speech is the least deceptive reflection of the mind. I have no use for cosmetics. I do not belie the interior of my heart by my outward appearance. I am always myself and they who take for themselves the title and bearing of wise men are unable to disguise me even though they walk about like apes in purple robes or asses in lion skins. Even though they put on as much as they can, somewhere their oversized ears will give them away as Midases. An ungrateful class of men, by Jove! Even though they are most of my faction, they are so ashamed of my name when among people that they throw it up to others as a great reproach. Now, since they are μωρότατοι, "most foolish," and wish to be thought philosophers and Thaleses, would it not be especially fitting to call them μωροσόφος, "foolosophers"? For it seems best to imitate the rhetoricians of our time, who think themselves veritable gods if they can appear bilingual like a horse leech; and they consider it a notable accomplishment if they can subtly work into their Latin orations a few Greek phrases as embellishment even if there is no need for them in the speech. Then, if they want an exotic touch, they dig up four or five obsolete words from decaying manuscripts with which they becloud the reader; so that those who understand the words will be all the more pleased with themselves, and those who do not understand admire the more in proportion to their ignorance. Indeed, to revere especially that which is imported is a rather elegant pleasure of my followers. Those who are a little more ambitious laugh and applaud and, in the manner of the ass, prick up their ears in order to appear to others to understand, muttering the while, "Quite so, quite so." Now, I return to my outline.

You already have my name, gentlemen—what epithet shall I add? Why, what else but more foolish? For by what more honorable name could the goddess of Folly address her devotees? But since my ancestry is not known to many, I shall try, with the help of the Muses, to reveal it to you. My father was neither Chaos, Orcus, Saturn, Jupiter, or any other representative of the ancient and moldy gods, but Plutus, god of Riches, the Father of Gods and men, despite the opinion of Homer, Hesiod, and Zeus himself. At his nod, now as before, all things sacred and profane are turned topsy-turvy. By his judgment, war, peace, empires, plans, judgments, assemblies, marriages, treaties, pacts, laws, arts, sports, important matters (my breath is almost gone)—in brief, all public and private

affairs—are governed. Without his help that whole group of
deities of the poets' making and even—I will speak more boldly
—the most eminent gods themselves, either would not exist at
all or certainly would live very meagerly at home. Whoever
angers him cannot be helped by Pallas herself, but whoever
pleases him can order even mighty Zeus and his thunderbolt
to go hang himself. I glory to have such a father. And he did
not give birth to me from his brain as Jupiter begot severe and
gloomy Pallas; but rather from "youth," the most beautiful
nymph of all, and the gayest at that. Nor was this done in
confining wedlock—as that lame blacksmith was conceived—
but in the more pleasant manner of "extramarital love-mak-
ing," as our beloved Homer would say. It was not the Plutus
of Aristophanes, a man decrepit and going blind, that begot
me—do not make that mistake—but the god unimpaired and
still in the heat of youth, yet not heated by youth only but
also by nectar he had chanced to drink copiously and unmixed
at a gathering of the gods.

If you also want to know my birthplace (since that is considered in these times as an important mark of nobility—
where one lets out his first wail), I was not born in wandering
Delos, or the shimmering sea, or in deep caves, but in the Fortune Islands themselves, where all things grow without plow-
ing or planting. In these islands there is no labor, or old age,
or any sickness; nor does one ever see a daffodil, mallow,
onion, bean, or any other common thing. However, one's eyes
and ears are delighted at the same time by moly, panacea,
nepenthes, sweet marjoram, ambrosia, lotus, rose, violet, hya-
cinth, and the gardens of Adonis. Having been born amid
these delights, I did not begin life with weeping but straightway I smiled prettily at my mother. I do not envy great Jupiter
his she-goat nurse, since two charming nymphs nourished me
at their breasts—Drunkenness, the offspring of Bacchus, and
Ignorance, daughter of Pan. You see these two here in the
company of my attendants and followers. If you wish to know
the names of others, then, by Jove, you will have to listen to
them in Greek. This one whom you see with her eyebrows raised
so haughtily is Φιλαυτία (Self-love). The one with the laughing eyes clapping her hands is Κολακία (Flattery). The drowsy
one who looks as though she were asleep is Λήθη (Forgetfulness). She who is leaning on her elbows and has her hands
folded is Μισοπονία (Laziness). She who is wearing the wreath
of rose and smells of perfume is Ἡδονή (Pleasure). The one
rolling her eyes to and fro is Ἀνοία (Madness). Τρυφή (Sensu-
ality) is the one with the smooth skin and shapely body. You
see those two gods playing with the girls; one of them is named

Κῶμος (Intemperance), and the other Νήαρετος ὕπνος (Sound Sleep). With the help of this household, I say, I bring all things under my subjection, even emperors.

You have now heard of my birth, education, and companions. Now that it may not seem that I call myself a goddess without good reason, please give me your undivided attention while I tell how many advantages I bestow on gods and men alike. For if someone has written that to be a god is to help men, and if they have deservedly been admitted to the company of gods who show the use of wine or grain or some other commodity to men, then why cannot I be called and considered in truth the alpha of all the gods who alone am the dispenser of all goods to men?

In the first place what can be sweeter or more precious than life itself? And by whose assistance except mine is life conceived? Certainly not by the spear of potently fathered Pallas; not by the shield of cloud-gathering Jove is life propagated. Even the Father of the Gods and King of men who makes Olympus tremble by his least nod must set aside his three-pronged firebolt and that Titanic visage with which he terrifies the gods whenever he chooses, if he wishes to do that which he is forever doing, namely begetting children. Now, indeed, the Stoics think themselves very close to the gods; but give me a person who is Stoic three or four or even six hundred times over and see if he, though not putting aside his beard, an insignia of wisdom (but also common to the goat), will not surely put off his gravity, smooth his frowning brow, abandon his rockbound principles, and for a few minutes be silly and act the fool. In the end the wise man must come to me, me I say, if he wants to be a father; but why not speak more frankly, as I usually do? Now, I ask you, is it the head, the face, the breast, the hands, or the ear—all considered honorable parts—that bring forth gods and men? No, I think not; rather it is that foolish and ridiculous part that cannot even be named without laughter—the generative organ of the human race. It is the sacred fountain from which all things take life, more truly than from the tetrad of Pythagoras.

Tell me now, what man would wish to put himself in the trap of matrimony in the manner that these so-called wise men do, if he had considered beforehand the inconveniences of married life? What woman would give herself to a man if she pondered or foresaw the dangerous pangs of childbirth and the harassment of motherhood? Since you owe your existence to the marriage bed and marriage to my handmaid, you can now see how very much indebted to me you are. Then, too, would a woman who has gone through this experience repeat it again without the power and influence of Lethe? And Venus herself, Lucretius not withstanding, would not deny that without my powerful assistance her influence would be weakened and enfeebled. Thus from this silly and ridiculous game of mine come forth those supercilious philosophers (whose places have now been taken by those who are commonly known as Monks), kings in purple robes, pious priests, and thrice-holy Popes; also that whole company of the gods of the poets which is so numerous that Olympus itself, spacious as it is, can hardly hold the crowd.

However, let it be thought a small thing to be the cause of all life, if I do not show you that whatever good there is in life comes from me. Would life without pleasure be called life at all? You applaud! I knew that no one of you was so wise, or should I say foolish—no, wise is right—that you would err in that matter. The Stoics, however, spurn pleasure, or at least they carefully pretend to; they attack it assiduously in public but only so that they might enjoy it the more once they have deterred all others. But let them tell me, by Jove, what part of life is not sad, troublesome, graceless, flat, and burdensome unless you have pleasure, the seasoning of Folly, added to it. There is sufficient proof to this fact in that beautiful tribute given to me by Sophocles, a man not sufficiently appreciated, which states that ignorance is bliss—but come, let us take up the matter step by step.

First of all, who does not know that childhood is by far the happiest period of man's life and that it is much more pleasant for everyone? For what is there about little children that makes us kiss and hug and fondle them so that even an enemy would help someone of this age? The charm of folly, of course, that prudent nature bestows on the newly born. Does she not do this to dispel the troubles of bringing them up and to put them in the favor of their nurses? This age finally gives way to adolescence. How welcome and favorable this age is to everyone! How studiously everyone encourages it and gives it a helping hand! But what, I ask, is this gift of youth? Why, it is me, of course; whose favor youth knows so little; and for this reason is angry the least. And I am a liar if it is not true that as youth matures through experience and education the sparkle of its beauty begins to fade; its zest diminishes; its charm cools; and its vigor falls off. The farther one goes from me, the less and less he lives until he reaches that troublesome old age, which is not only hateful to others but even more so to itself.

No one would be able to tolerate old age at all if I, out of pity for its great troubles, would not stand at its right hand,

and in the same manner as the gods of the poets are wont to save by some metamorphosis those who are dying, so I recall those people near to death to childhood. Whence folk are accustomed to say that they are in their second childhood. If anyone would like to know how this transformation is accomplished, I will not hide it. I lead them to the spring of Lethe (for it arises in the Isles of Fortune and only a small stream flows through the Underworld) so that there they might drink deep draughts of forgetfulness and gradually, with the cares of the mind washed away, become young again. But now, you will say, they are merely foolish and doting. That is true, but to become young again is to do just that. For how else does a child act but foolishly and sillily? And is there not much delight in that age because it knows nothing? For who does not shun and abhor as a prodigy the boy with a man's wisdom? In the words of a proverb exchanged among common folk: I hate a boy with precocious wisdom. Who could carry on business or trade with an old man who would add to his vast experience an equally vigorous mind? So the old man dotes because of my gift.

Yet this doting old man of mine is free of those wretched old cares that trouble the wise men; and he is a good drinking companion to boot. He does not feel that dullness of life that a more robust age can hardly bear. Sometimes, like the old man in Plautus, he reverts to contemplating those three letters; then he would be the most wretched of men if he had his wits about him. Meanwhile, because of my gift, he is happy, a delight to his friends and the life of the party. Thus in Homer speech sweeter than honey flows from the lips of Nestor, while that of Achilles is bitter; and also in Homer the old men sitting by the wall exhibit flowery and elegant speech. By this trait old age even surpasses childhood, which is sweet but speechless and lacks the chief joy of life, garrulousness. Add to this the fact that old people delight in children and the children in turn delight in them. As the proverb says, "God brings like to like." What do they not have in common, other than the fact that the old man has counted more birthdays? Otherwise they are similar in all things: white hair, toothless gums, short stature of body, a thirst for milk, babbling, prattling, silliness, lack of memory, and thoughtlessness. Also, the older a person gets, the closer he gets to childhood, until, like a child, without tedium of life and sense of death, the person finally dies.

Let him who wishes compare my metamorphosis with that of the other gods. Those which they performed when angry are better not spoken about, but those persons to whom they were propitious they usually turned into trees, or birds, or cicadas, or even serpents, as if the land of metamorphosis were any better than dying. I simply restore a man to the happiest and best times of his life. But if men would abstain completely from any traffic with wisdom and live out their lives continually in my company, not only would there not be any old age but there would be perpetual youth. For do you not see that those gloomy people, engrossed in their study of philosophy or in other serious and difficult matters, grow old before they have even enjoyed youth—and this happens because their spirits have all the vitality sucked out of them by cares and the strict and assiduous application of their brains? While on the other hand, my morons are fat, sleek, and succulent like the hogs of Acarnania; they never suffer any of the discomforts of the wise unless, perchance, they contract something from some wise man. But then it is impossible for the whole life of man to be happy.

That proverb should not be taken lightly which says: "Folly is the only thing that makes fleeting youth linger and staves off ugly old age." And not rashly is it said of the Brabanters that while age brings prudence to other people, the closer they get to old age, the more foolish they become. Yet there are no other people more genial in everyday conversation or who feel less the sorrow of old age. Close to them in custom, as well as geography, are my Hollanders—and why should I not call them mine? They are such zealous followers of mine that they have merited a special name, and they are not ashamed of it either but bandy it back and forth between themselves. Go you foolish mortals and seek out your Medeas and Circes and Venuses and Auroras and the unknown fountain that restores youth! When I alone have and can use this power. With me is that miraculous juice with which the daughter of Memnon extended the youth of her grandfather Tithonius. I am that Venus by whose favor Phaon was made young again so that Sappho could fall in love with him. Mine the herbs (if any exist), mine the charms, and mine the fountain that not only returns lost youth but, what is even more to be wished for, preserves it forever. If you all give credence to the idea that there is nothing better than youth and nothing more detestable than old age, then I think all of you should realize how much you owe to me because I keep in existence such a wonderful good and keep away so great an evil.

But why talk about mere mortals? Survey the heavens and you may throw my name up to me if you can find anyone among the gods who avoids being harsh and unpleasant without my help. For why is Bacchus always young and curly haired? Because, wild and giddy as he is, he spends his whole life at parties, dances, revels, and games and he has no truck at all with Pallas. Finally, he is so far from wanting to be considered wise that he enjoys being worshipped in games and revels; nor is that proverb offensive to him which tabs him with the adjective, foolish. It goes like this: Μορύχου μωρότερος —"More foolish than Morychus." His name was later changed to Morychus because the sporting country folk used to smear his statue standing before the temple in the forum with new wine and figs. Then what insults were not thrown at him by the old comedy? "Oh stupid god," they would say, "who was more worthy to be born from a thigh!" But who would not prefer to be stupid and foolish when along with it one is eternally festive, eternally youthful, eternally bringing pleasure and gaiety to others? Better this than to be deep-minded. Jupiter, awesome to all; or Pan, spoiling everything with his tumults; or Vulcan, covered with cinders and always filthy from working in his shop; or even Pallas herself, with her Gorgon head, terrible sword, and even grim stare. Why is Cupid forever a boy? Why, but because he is a clown and cannot do or consider anything sensible. Why does the beauty of golden Venus forever retain its freshness? Doubtless because she is related to me; for this reason she bears the color of my father in her face and thus Homer calls her Golden Aphrodite. She also laughs continually if we are to believe the poets and sculptors. What divinity did the Romans worship more devoutly than Flora, the mother of all delights? If one desires to learn about the life of the austere gods from Homer and the rest of the poets, he will find out that it is full of folly. But why narrate all the deeds of the rest when you already know the loves and shenanigans of Jove, the Plunderer, and that chaste Diana, who, forgetting her sex, spent all her time in hunting—being all the while in love with Endymion?

I should prefer that their deeds be narrated by a certain Momus, by whom they used to be narrated often until recently when the gods angrily threw him down to earth for continually disturbing their pleasure with his sagacious interruptions. However, mortals do not think the exile worthy of hospitality, especially since there is no place for him at the royal court where my Flattery holds first place; and Momus could no more get along with her than a wolf with a lamb. So with him out of the way, the gods can play the fool more freely and pleasantly, doing what they please, as Homer says, without a censor. For what prank will not that rascally Priapus perform? What games will Mercury not play with his stealth and sleight of hand? Does Vulcan not usually provide humor for the company of gods and, partly by his lameness, partly by his taunts, and partly by his silly remarks, enliven the party? Even Silenus, that old lover, dances with Polyphemus and the bare-footed nymphs. Half-goat Satyrs leap obscenely and stupid Pan makes everyone laugh with some ballad the gods prefer to hear—even more than the Muses themselves—especially when they are getting drunk on nectar. Yet why should I go on to narrate what the drunken gods usually do after a banquet? They are things so foolish, by Jove, that even I cannot help but laugh. But it is wiser at this point to remember Harpocrates, lest some spy among the gods hear us telling the same things that Momus did not get away with.

However, now is the time to leave the heavens and, following Homer's example, return to earth where we again will see nothing joyous or fortunate except by my favor. First of all, you see how prudently nature, the mother and artificer of the human race, has taken pains to make sure that this race shall never lack its seasoning of folly. For, according to the Stoic definition, wisdom is nothing other than being guided by reason; folly, on the other hand, is to be swayed by the whim of passion. Now, in order that man's life should not be completely sad and gloomy, Jupiter put in much more of passion than of reason—about a five-to-one ratio. Because of this fact, he put reason in a narrow corner of the head and left the rest of the body to the passions. Finally, he instilled two violent tyrants, as it were, against reason, namely: anger, which occupies the fortress of the breast and therefore the very font of life, the heart; and lust, which rules a wide empire farther down even to the private parts. The ordinary life of man shows how good reason is in combating these two forces; for all reason can do is shout his prohibitions until he is hoarse and dictate formulas of virtue. These two forces simply tell their so-called king to go hang himself and become even more obstreperous; and finally the man, all tired out, gives up and yields to them.

Since man was made to handle affairs, he was given a little larger sprinkling of reason so that he could give counsel. But he soon brought me into the council chamber as in other places and I immediately gave him a piece of advice worthy of myself, namely: that he should take woman to himself, a stupid animal to be sure and a silly one, yet funny and attractive, so that by domestic familiarity her folly might soften and sweeten his harsh temperament. When Plato seems to hesitate about whether to place woman in the genus of brute animal or rational animal, he only wants to point out how outstanding is the folly of this sex. If a woman wishes to be considered wise, however, she only succeeds in showing herself as twice as much a fool. For it would be like taking a bull to a masseuse, a thing "quite against the grain," as they say. It is doubly sinful when against nature someone assumes a veneer of virtue and warps his true character in a different direction. For, as the Greek proverb has it, "An ape is always an ape, though dressed in purple," so a woman is always a woman—that is, a fool—no matter what she pretends to be.

Yet I do not think that the female sex is so foolish as to be angry at me because I myself attributed folly to them. For if they look at the matter in the right perspective, they would see that, thanks to folly, they are in many ways better off than men. First, they have the gift of beauty, which they rightly prize above everything else and by whose power they can be tyrannical with tyrants themselves. Where do men acquire that dreadful appearance, rough skin, forest of whiskers, and senility except from the defect of prudence? The cheeks of women, on the other hand, are always smooth, their voices gentle, and their skin soft as if taking part in eternal youth. Besides, what more do they want in life than to please men? Is this not why they use all their grooming, their cosmetics, their baths, their primpings, their creams and perfumes, their arts of making up, painting, and touching up their faces, eyes, and skin? Then under what better patron than Folly could they be better recommended to men? For what is there that men will deny to women? And for what return other than pleasure? Women delight for no reason other than their folly. The truth of this no one will deny who considers what absurdities a man tells to a woman and what trumpery he performs whenever he desires to enjoy the delights of feminine society.

You have now heard, therefore, where the first and chief pleasure of life arises. However, there are some, mostly old men, who are more interested in liquor than women and who take their greatest pleasure in drinking. Whether any party can be a success without women, let others decide. What always remains true is this: without folly, a party cannot be any fun at all. If there is lacking at a party one who creates laughter either by actual or pretended foolishness, then they send out and hire a clown; or they bring in some parasite who by his jests—that is, ridiculous sayings—drives silence and sorrow from the drinking party. For what good is it to load up the stomach with so much wine, sumptuous dishes, and rare meats, if the eyes and ears and whole mind are not fed by laughter, wit, and humor? And I alone am the cook of delicious dishes. Also, those other goings-on of banquets—choosing a king by lot, throwing dice, drinking good healths, sending the cups around, singing in rounds, dancing, and impersonating—were not found out by the Seven Sages of Greece but by me, for the welfare of the human race. The nature of all things of this type is such that the more they partake of folly the greater share of life they give to man, for that which is sad surely cannot be called life. Yet it cannot help but be sad, unless by diversions of this sort you chase away tedium, the brother of sadness.

Perhaps there will be some who do not care for this type of enjoyment but prefer to acquiesce in the good fellowship and company of friends. They declare that friendship alone should be placed above all other things as a thing more necessary than air, fire, or water; and so delightful that to lose it would be like losing the sun; and finally, so honorable (as if honor had anything to do with the matter) that the philosophers themselves did not hesitate to name it among the greatest goods. But what if I show myself to be the author and source of such a good? I will not demonstrate it by ambiguities, or dilemmas, or other types of dialectical arguments led by simple common sense (as the phrase goes). I will show it as plainly as I would with my finger. Look! Conniving at your friends' vices, passing over them, being blind to them, being deceived by them, and even loving these same vices as if they were virtues—does this not seem to be folly? The fellow who kisses the mole on his mistress' neck, the lover who is delighted with the growth on his dove's nose, the father who calls his son's crossed eyes gleaming—what, I ask, can this be except pure folly? You agree that this is folly three and four times over; but it is this same folly that makes friendships and keeps them after they are made.

I speak of mortal men of whom none is born without faults, and he is the best who has the least number of faults. Among the divinely wise Stoics, however, either there is no friendship at all or else it is a certain austere and cold type of friendship that does exist, and even this is very rare—I have scruples about saying that it does not exist at all. For most men are foolish, and everyone is foolish in many ways; and close friendship is contracted between equals. But whenever a mutual benevolence is struck up between these severe thinkers, it is not in any way stable or enduring. It is impossible among morose and sharp-eyed men who discern the faults of others with the keenness of the eagle or an Epidaurian serpent. Of course, they are blind to their own faults and do not see the packs on their own backs. Since it is the nature of man that no character can be found that is not blotted by great faults,

I add to this the great difference in ages and interests, the many lapses, errors, and misfortunes of mortal life—how could the joy of friendship exist for one hour among such argus-eyed people unless that were present which the Greeks so aptly call εὐήθειαν, which may be translated as "folly" or as "easygoing ways." Indeed, is not Cupid, the author and parent of all affection, afflicted in the eyes so that to him what is not beautiful seems so? Likewise, among you, what one has seems fair to him: the old man loves his old wife, the young boy his young girl. These things happen everywhere and are laughed at but, ridiculous as they are, knit and bind together our joyful social life.

What was said concerning friendship is even more true of marriage, which is nothing other than an indivisible joining for life. Indeed, what divorces or even worse things would come about if the domestic life of man and wife were not upheld and nourished by flattery, joking, compromise, ignorance, and duplicity—all satellites of mine? How few marriages would be contracted, if the husband inquired about what tricks his seemingly delicate and innocent little darling had played before the wedding? And once entered on, fewer still would last if the many tricks of the wife were not kept unknown through the negligence and stupidity of the husband. All this is a tribute to the worthiness of Folly. She sees to it that the wife pleases the husband, the husband pleases the wife, and that the marriage endures. A husband is laughed at, called cuckoo, and who knows what else when he kisses away the tears of his adulterous wife; but how much happier to be thus deceived than to wear himself out with an unresting jealousy and to disrupt everything with quarreling.

In short there is no society, no union in life that could be happy or lasting without me. A people will not long bear with its prince, nor a master his servant, nor a maid her mistress, nor a teacher his student, nor a friend his friend, nor a wife her husband, nor a landlord his tenant, nor a boarder his fellow boarder, unless they make mistakes together or individually, flatter each other, wisely overlook things, and soothe themselves with the sweetness of folly.

Now I know this seems to be the most that could be said, but there is still more to hear. I ask you: will a person love anyone else if he hates himself? Will he be harmonious with other people when he cannot get along with himself? Will he bring happiness to anyone else when he is sullen and grouchy with himself? I do not think anyone would say that this could be true unless he is more foolish than Folly herself. Now, if I were taken away, no man could get along with another, every person would despise himself and his possessions, and thus be hateful to himself. This is true because nature, in many things more of a stepmother than a mother, sowed into the hearts of mortals, especially in less prudent men, an evil seed so that they despise what is theirs and desire what is another's. With the result that all the gifts, graces, and charms of life are vitiated and destroyed. What good is beauty, the special gift of the immortal gods, if it is touched by the blemish of decay? What good is youth, if it is corrupted by the leaven of woeful old age? And, finally, what in the whole business of life, whether by one's self or with others, can be carried on with grace (for not only in art but in every other action as well the important thing is to act gracefully) unless Philantia (Self-Love), who is deservedly like a sister to me and everywhere plays my part energetically, is present at your right hand?

For what is so foolish as to be pleased with yourself? Or to admire yourself? But on the other hand, if you are displeased with yourself, what can you do that is pleasing or graceful or seemly? Take this seasoning from life and straightway the orator, like his gestures, will be cold and flat, the musician will please no one with his melodies, the actor will be hissed along with his character, the poet along with his Muses will be laughed at, the painter and his paintings will be considered cheap, and the doctor will starve amid his medicines. Without Self-Love, you will seem to be an ugly Thersites rather than a handsome Nireus, an old Nestor rather than an ever young Phaon, a sow rather than Minerva, tongue-tied rather than eloquent, and rustic rather than urbane. This is how necessary it is for you to be pleased with yourself and to commend yourself with a little applause before you can be commended by others. Finally, since happiness, for the most part, is to wish to be what you are, my Philantia brings it about in a short time, so that no one dislikes his features, talents, race, neighborhood, profession, or fatherland. For no Irishman would want to be an Italian, or a Thracian an Athenian, or a Scythian a citizen of the Fortunate Isles. Oh, the wonderful foresight of nature which makes all things equal in the midst of such diversity! Where she has kept back some of her gifts, she usually adds a little more Self-Love. . . . But what am I saying? Self-Love is the greatest gift.

May I not also affirm that you will find no great works embarked upon without my giving the impulse, no important arts discovered without my prompting? Is war not the seedbed and source of all deeds of praise? Yet what is more foolish than, for heaven knows what causes, to set up a battle line from which both sides reap more evil than good? For, like the

Megarians, of those who fall there is no mention. Also, when the two armored lines meet and the bugle sends forth its raucous cry, of what use, I ask, are those wise men who have been exhausted by their studies and have hardly any life in their thin, cold blood? In this business there is a need for the muscular and brawny who have a great deal of boldness but very little wit. However, someone might prefer to follow the military example of Demosthenes who, agreeing with the advice of Archilochus, at the first sight of the enemy dropped his shield and ran—as cowardly in battle as skilled in speaking. They say that wise planning is of extreme importance in war. I agree that it is for the general, but it is military not philosophical planning. For a war is fought by parasites, panderers, robbers, murderers, yokels, drunks, debtors, and the other scum of this type; not by the philosophers with their lamps.

These philosophers are useless for the work of real life; even Socrates, judged the wisest by the not so wise oracle, gives proof of this. When he tried to do something in public, he usually left amid the loud laughter of everyone present. Although it must be said that he was not altogether foolish, since he repudiated the title "wise" and gave it to God, he also held the opinion that a wise man ought not to meddle in affairs of state—perhaps he should have admonished us further and said that he who wants to be counted among men should abstain from wisdom itself. Finally, what made him drink the hemlock after he was accused except his wisdom? For while he philosophized about clouds and ideas, while he measured the feet of a flea and wondered at the voice of a gnat, he did not learn the common, ordinary things of life. From this teacher, in peril of death, comes his student, Plato, an illustrious advocate certainly, who, ruffled by the noise of the crowd, could barely speak out more than half a sentence. And what shall I say about Theophrastus? When he began to speak, he was suddenly struck dumb as if he had seen a wolf. Could he have inspired a soldier going into battle? Because of his timorous nature, Isocrates never dared to open his mouth in public. Marcus Tullius Cicero, the Father of Roman Oratory, used to speak with an awkward tremor, like a boy out of breath, which Fabius interpreted as a mark of a good orator conscious of the difficulty of his task. However, when he said this, did he not openly admit that wisdom stands in the way of the right performance of a deed? What would they do who fear so greatly when fighting with harmless words if they had to fight with swords?

After all this, God save us, that famous sentence of Plato

is brought up: "Happy is the state where philosophers are kings, or kings are philosophers." However, if you look into history, you will find that rulers have never been more injurious to the state than when the scepter has fallen into the hands of someone taken up with philosophy or *belles lettres*. I think the Catos are good enough examples of this. One of them disturbed the tranquillity of the state with his insane accusations; the other completely undermined the liberty of the Roman people while trying to defend it in a "wise" manner. To these two add Brutus, Cassius, the Gracchi, and even Cicero, who was not less injurious to the Roman state than Demosthenes was to the Athenian state. Then there is Marcus Aurelius, an example of a good emperor I have just recently dug up, who was oppressive and hateful to the citizens because of the very fact that he was so much of a philosopher. Even though he was a good emperor, however, he harmed the state more by leaving behind such a son as his than he had ever benefited it by his good management. As a matter of fact, this whole type of men who devote themselves to the pursuit of wisdom are unlucky in most other things and especially in the propagating of children. I think nature providentially ordains it so that the evil of wisdom will not spread widely among men. As a result Cicero had a degenerate son and the wise Socrates had children who "favored their mother more than their father," as one writer rather subtly put it; that is, they were fools.

It could be borne if philosophers only approached public affairs as asses do a lyre, but they have no dexterity whatsoever in any common function of life. Invite a wise man to a feast and he will spoil it either by a gloomy silence or asking a lot of bothersome questions. Ask him to a dance and you will see how a camel dances. Take him to a play and by his expression he will dampen the mirth of the people; and like Cato, he will be forced to leave the theater when he refuses to quit his superciliousness. Once entered upon a conversation, he will suddenly become dumb like the wolf in a fairy tale. If something is to be bought, or a contract to be made, or, in short, if anything is to be done without which this daily life is unable to go on, you would call this "genius" not a man but simply deadwood. He can be of no use to himself, his country, or his family because he is completely unskilled in the affairs of daily life and because he is so far removed from the common way of thinking and living; and for this reason he cannot help but be odious to the common folk because of the great diversity between their lives and his. For what of mortal things is not full of folly, done by fools, and in the presence of fools? If someone wishes to rebel against all this, then I would persuade him to imitate Timon and retire to some wilderness where he could enjoy his wisdom alone.

But let me return to my outline. What power drew those stonehearted, wooden, and wild people together into a civilized society except flattery? The lyres of Amphion and Orpheus mean nothing more than this. When the Roman people were plotting revolt, what brought them back to civil harmony? Was it a philosophical oration? Hardly. It was a ridiculous and puerile story made up about the stomach and the other members of the body. A similar story of Themistocles about a fox and a hedgehog had the same results. What oration of a wise man could have done so much as that fictitious white hind of Sertorius or that silly invention of the Spartan about the two puppies or the hilarious story about pulling hairs out of a horse's tail? Besides this, I have not said anything about Minos and Numa, both of whom ruled their foolish throngs by making up tall tales. By this sort of trivial device that huge and powerful beast, the people, is managed. Furthermore, what city ever accepted the laws of Aristotle and Plato or the doctrines of Socrates? What persuaded the Decii to give themselves to the gods of the underworld? What drew Quintus Curtius into that pit except glory, a very lovely siren who, for some strange reason, is condemned by wise men. For, what is more foolish, they ask, than for a political candidate to flatter the people, to buy their favor with gifts, to seek the applause of so many fools, to be pleased by their shouts of approval, to be led around in triumph as if he were some public spectacle for the people, and to have his statue placed in the market-place? Add to this the adoption of new first and last names, the divine honors paid to these nobodies, and the public deification of even the most evil tyrants. These things are all very foolish and one Democritus is not enough to laugh at them. Who denies it? But from this source spring the deeds of heroes that are borne to the very heavens by the writings of so many eloquent men. This same folly brought forth cities, maintained empires, authority, religion, governing and judicial bodies; nor is human life anything more than the play of folly.

However, let me now say something about the arts. What but a thirst for glory has moved men to think up and to pass on to posterity those talents they think are so great? Men are even so foolish as to believe that they will achieve success by sleepless nights and great exertion. At any rate you owe the greatest blessings of life to Folly; and what is sweeter still, you also enjoy the madness of others.

Now, since I have justified my praiseworthiness for courage

and resourcefulness, suppose I now try to lay claim to prudence also? Perhaps someone might say that this is like trying to mix fire and water. Maybe so, but I think I will be successful if you continue to favor me with the attention of both mind and ear as you have been doing. First of all, if prudence lies in experiencing things, to whom does the honor of that title more belong? To the wise man who partly because of modesty and partly because of timidity refrains from doing things, or to the fool who is not deterred from doing things either by modesty of which he has none or by danger he never thinks about? A wise man takes refuge with the books of the ancients, where he learns merely verbal shrewdness. A fool, however, reaps true prudence, unless I am deceived, from experiencing things at close range. Homer, even though he was blind, realized this fact, for he said: "Even a fool is wise after a thing is done." There are two main obstacles to gaining knowledge of things: shame, which clouds the mind; and fear, which, once the danger has been sighted, urges one not to perform the action. From both of these, Folly grandly frees us. Few mortals realize to what great heights being free from shame and fear could lead one.

However, if they prefer that prudence that relies only on the judgment of things, then listen, I ask you, to how far from this quality they really are who boast that they have it. First of all, all human affairs, like the Sileni of Alcibiades, have two very dissimilar aspects; so that what at first sight (as they say) seems to be death when looked into further becomes life, and vice versa. This is true also of what seems beautiful and ugly; rich and poor; disgraceful and glorious; learned and ignorant; robust and feeble; noble and base; joyful and sad; favorable and adverse; friendly and inimical; healthful and harmful—in short, you will suddenly find everything the opposite if you open the Silenus. If by chance this seems to have been said too philosophically, then come, I will make it clearer with the help of a fat Minerva (as the phrase goes). Who would not say that the king is a rich and powerful lord? Yet if a king is not furnished with the goods of the soul, he has nothing and is a very poor man indeed. Further, if he is given over to many vices, he is the cheapest of slaves. In this same way one could philosophize about other things, but let this suffice as an example.

"But what is it all about?" someone asks. Listen and we will develop the matter further. If someone should attempt to take off the masks and costumes of the actors in a play and show to the audience their real appearances, would he not ruin the whole play? And would everyone not think he deserved to be chased out of the theater with brickbats as a madman? For, suddenly, a new appearance of things would arise so that the player who played a woman turned out to be a man; who was before a young man is now old; who was before a king is now a slave; who was before a god now suddenly appears as a sorry little man. To destroy the illusion, then, is to destroy the whole play. The masks and costumes are what hold the audience's eye. For what else is the life of man but a kind of play in which men in various costumes perform until the director motions them off the stage. The director often orders the same actor to appear in different costumes. At one time he may be a king dressed in purple and at another a servant covered with rags. Everything is done under pretense, but this play could not be performed in any other way.

Suppose at this point some wise man, suddenly dropped from heaven, should confront me and exclaim that the person whom everyone looks up to as a god and master is not even a man because he is ruled by the passions of brute beasts and that, worse than the lowest slave, he willingly serves so many and such foul masters. Or, on the other hand, suppose he ordered someone mourning his father's death to laugh because only now has he begun to live—this life on earth being nothing but a kind of death. Again, suppose he called a person glorying in his ancestry ignoble and illegitimate because he is far from the practice of virtue, which alone is the source of nobility. If he continued in this vein, what else would happen, I ask you, except that he would be considered crazy and insane by everyone. Therefore, as nothing is more foolish than an absurd kind of wisdom, so nothing is more imprudent than an untimely prudence. He is all awry, therefore, who does not acclimate himself to the surrounding conditions, who does not follow the crowd, who does not keep in mind that law of conviviality—"Either drink or get out"—and, in short, who asks that the play no longer be a play. On the other hand, he is truly prudent who wishes to have no greater share of wisdom than is fitting for a mortal, who with the rest of the crowd is willing to let things go, or who sociably errs along with them. But that, they say, is folly itself. Indeed, I would scarcely disagree with them, but let them, in turn, admit that this is only acting out the play of life.

As for the next point, O immortal gods! Shall I speak or remain silent? But why should I remain silent when it is more true than truth itself? However, it might be fitting to have the Muses come down from Helicon whom the poets are accustomed to call on in the most trivial matters. Therefore, be present for a little while, daughters of Jove, while I show that no one can reach that excellent wisdom the wise call the citadel of happiness except with me, Folly, as his guide. First of all, there is no question that all emotion belongs to Folly. For by this fact a wise man is distinguished from a fool because emotions rule the fool, while reasons direct the wise man. Thus the Stoics exclude the emotions as if they were diseases from the wise man; but yet these emotions not only discharge the office of guides to those hurrying to the port of wisdom but they are even accustomed to be present as spurs and stimuli in every performance of virtue, as exhorters to well doing. However, that double-ply Stoic, Seneca, strongly denies this and strips all emotions from the wise man; but in doing this he no longer has a man but rather a new god or demiurge who never has nor ever will exist. Indeed, to speak more clearly, he makes of man a marble statue, dumb and completely devoid of all human feeling. But if this is what they want, let them enjoy their wise man and love him without any rival in Plato's republic, or if they prefer, in the realm of ideas, or in the gardens of Fontalus. For who would not be horrified at such a man and flee from him as from a bad dream or a ghost. He would be unaffected by all natural feelings, no more moved by love or pity than by hard flint or Marpesian marble. Nothing would escape him. He would make no mistakes. Like another Lynceus he would see everything. He would ponder about matters endlessly and would excuse nothing. He would be content with considering himself the only person who is rich, healthy, a king, free—in brief, singular in all things, but only in his own opinion. He would desire no friend and would not be one to anybody. He would not hesitate to tell the gods to go hang themselves, and he would condemn and laugh at as insane whatever life has to offer. This type of animal is the perfect wise man. Now I ask you, if it were put to a vote, what city would elect this kind of man as mayor? Or what army would choose him for a general? What woman would want such a husband? What host would want such a guest? What servant would choose or put up with a master with such qualities? Who would not prefer someone from the common lot of foolish men? He, being a fool himself, would be able to command or obey other fools; he would be able to please those like himself. Even more, however, he would be friendly to his wife, jolly to his friends, a gay companion, a good conversationalist, and, last of all, he would not consider any human thing foreign to himself. But this wise man has been boring me for a long time now, so let us turn this speech to other matters.

Suppose, then, that a man could look down from a great

height as the poets say Jove does, how many calamities he would see in man's life! How miserable and sordid his birth and how laborious his education! He would see the many injuries he is subject to in childhood, the laboriousness of his youth, the oppressiveness of his old age, and the hard inevitability of death for him. This man would observe the army of diseases man is plagued with; the misfortunes that wait for him at every turn; the inconveniences that assault him. He would see nothing without some touch of gall, and this is without mentioning those things man does to man. Things of this type are: poverty, imprisonment, disgrace, shame, torture, plots, slander, lawsuits, and fraud. In doing this, however, I am clearly trying to count the grains of sand. It would not be right for me to relate right now for what offenses men have deserved these things or to say what angry god caused them to be born into such misery. Yet will not anyone who ponders these things approve the example of the Milesian virgins, even if it is pitiable? But what kind of people have committed suicide because of the tedium of life? Were they not neighbors of wisdom? Besides Diogenes, Xenocrates, Cato, Cassius, and Brutus, there is Chiron who chose death above immortality. Now you see, I warrant, what would happen if all men became wise: there would be a need for new clay and another potter like Prometheus.

But with a mixture of ignorance, thoughtlessness, forgetfulness of evil, hope of good things, and sometimes a sprinkling of pleasure, I bring relief from troubles so that men are loath to give up their lives even when, their thread of life having been cut by the Fates, their lives are ready to leave them. The tedium of life is so far from touching them that the less reason they have for living, the more they enjoy life. Certainly it is because of my gift that you see those old men of Nestor's age whose appearance is hardly human: babbling, silly, toothless, white-haired, bald—or even better, let me describe them in Aristophanes' words: dirty, stooped, wrinkled, bald, toothless, and toolless. Yet they are so delighted with life and desire so much to be young again that one dyes his hoary hair, another covers his bald spot with a toupee, another uses false teeth he obtained from heaven knows where, and still another is desperately in love with some young girl and acts sillier than any adolescent. For it is becoming fashionable and the usual thing for these old sticks and dry bones to marry some tender young wife who has no dowry and is sure to be enjoyed by others in the future. However, it is even more hilarious to watch the old women, almost dead with age and so like corpses that they seem to have returned from the dead.

Still, they go around saying: "How good it is to be alive." They are always in heat, and they hire some Phaon to escort them about for a large sum. They painstakingly make up their faces. They can hardly pull themselves away from a mirror. They pluck out hairs from the strangest places. They show their withered and flabby breasts. And, with a quivering voice, they try to stir up a faint desire. They drink, go around in the company of young girls, and write love letters. They are laughed at by everyone because of their great foolishness. But they are pleased with themselves. They are bathed in delights and completely immersed in honey—all this happiness because of my gift! Of those who scorn this type of folly, I would only ask that they consider whether it is not better to lead a pleasant life of folly like this than to look for, as they say, the rope and rafters. Anyway, that their actions are scorned by people means nothing to my fools, for they either do not realize that anything is wrong or, if they do realize it, they easily shrug it off. If a rock falls on your head, that is certainly painful; but shame, disgrace, insult, and curses are only harmful in so much as they are realized. If there is no realization, there can be no harm done. What harm is done if the whole world hisses you, so long as you applaud yourself? Folly is what helps a person to do this.

However, I seem to hear the philosophers disagreeing. They say that it is misery itself to live in folly, to err, to be deceived, and to be ignorant. On the contrary, however, this is what it is to be human. I cannot see why they call this kind of life miserable when it is the common lot of all men to be born, brought up, and constituted in such a way. Nothing is miserable that is constant with its own nature. If so, then who would argue that man should be pitied because he cannot fly like a bird, walk on four feet with the rest of the animals, or be fitted out with horns like the bulls? In the same way the finest horse could be called unhappy because it is neither a grammarian nor a gourmet. Therefore, a foolish man is no more unhappy or ill-fated than an illiterate horse for the simple reason that each defect belongs to the particular nature.

The casuists argue next that men are naturally imperfect and support and strengthen themselves by the peculiarly human device of study. As if to make it appear that nature, who was so careful in making the flowers and herbs, should have dozed in making man so that he would need the sciences; but these were really thought up by Theuth, the evil genius of the human race, for the hurt of mankind. Instead of being instruments for the happiness of mankind, they hinder it. That is what that most prudent king of Plato also says about the discovery of letters. Therefore, studies crept in along with the other trials of men and from the same instigators who brought all the ills into man's life. Their name is "demons," from the Greek δαήμονας, which means "those who know."

The people of the golden age lived without the advantage of learning and lived under the influence of instinct and nature. What need was there for a grammar when everyone spoke the same language and speech was only needed so that one person could communicate with another? What use was there for dialectic when there was no conflict of opinion? What place was there for rhetoric when no one wished to take advantage of another? What need for skill in law since all those evil practices that brought forth our good laws were non-existent? Furthermore, they were too religious to peer with irreverent curiosity into the secrets of nature, to measure the size, movement, and influence of the stars, or to seek the hidden causes of things. They considered it a sacrilege for a man to try to know more than he should. That insane inquiry as to what is beyond the heavens never even came into their minds. However, man slowly fell from the innocence of the golden age and soon the arts were invented, as I have said, by evil spirits; at first there were only a few of them, and only a few people took them up. Later, hundreds more were added by the superstition of the Chaldeans and the idle speculation of the Greeks. This was simply looking for trouble, since even one grammatical system is enough to make life one endless moment of torture.

Among these arts the ones closest to common sense (that is, to folly) are valued most highly. Theologians go hungry, scientists are given the cold shoulder, astrologers are laughed at, and logicians are ignored.

"The doctor alone," they say, "is worth more than all the rest"; and to the extent that this doctor is unskilled, audacious, and ignorant, the more is he honored among the rich and noble men. However, medicine as it is now practiced by so many is no less a part of the art of flattery than rhetoric is. The lawyers take second place behind the doctors; perhaps they should even be first but I hesitate to join the philosophers who usually laugh at lawyers for being such asses. Their estates grow, while the theologian who has examined and pondered over trunkfuls of manuscripts lives on beans and wages an arduous war against lice and fleas. As those arts are more pleasant that have the greater affinity with folly, so those people are far more happy who abstain from any traffic with learning and follow nature alone as their guide. She lacks nothing, unless perchance man wants to overrun the boundaries placed for him. Nature hates counterfeits; the less something is touched by art, the happier it is.

For, do you not see that those species of living things are happiest that are the furthest away from any mental discipline and are led by no other guide than nature? What could be happier or more wonderful than the bees? They do not have all the senses of the body; but what architect can be found to equal them in building and what philosopher is there who could frame a republic to match theirs? The horse, on the other hand, does have some human senses and travels around with men and, and as a result, shares some of their ills. He feels ashamed if he is defeated in a race, and while seeking glory in war he is run through and bites the dust with his rider. Along with this he endures the hard bit, the sharp spurs, the prisonlike stable, the whips, the sticks, and straps, the rider—in short, all the tragedy of servitude that he adds to himself when he tries to imitate brave men and zealously seeks vengeance against the enemy. How much more desirable, except for the treacheries of men, is the life of flies and birds, who live for the moment and by the light of nature. Birds, however, if they are shut up in a cage and taught to sing, soon lose all the luster of their natural beauty. For in every sphere what is nature is happier than what is falsified by art.

Therefore, I can never praise enough that cock (really Pythagoras) who had been all things: philosopher, man, woman, king, subject, fish, horse, frog, and perhaps even a sponge; and who concluded that no animal was as miserable as man. All other animals are content with their natural limitations. Man alone tries to overstep his. Among men, furthermore, the foolish are in many respects placed before the learned and great. Gryllus was more wise than the crafty Odysseus when he preferred to grunt in a sty rather than to expose himself to further dangers. Homer, the father of fiction, does not seem to disagree with this, since he often observes that men are wretched and miserable and very often describes Ulysses, the exemplar of wisdom, as wretched, but he never speaks in this way of Paris, Ajax, or Achilles. The reason for this lies in the fact that sly and artful Ulysses never did anything without the counsel of Pallas, the goddess of wisdom. Is that not having too much wisdom and getting too far away from nature? Among men, those who seek wisdom are the furthest from happiness. They are fools twice over because they forget that they were born men and try to affect the life of gods, after the example of the giants. They use their arts as instruments with which to attack nature. It follows, therefore, that they are least unhappy who are closest to the folly of brute beasts and who never attempt anything beyond their capacity as men.

There is no need for us to argue this out of Stoic syllogisms, however, when we can prove it by an evident example. By the immortal gods, I ask you, is there anyone happier than that class of people who are commonly called morons, fools, nitwits, and simpletons—most beautiful names in my opinion? I may seem to be speaking foolishly and absurdly at first, but it is profoundly true. First of all they have no fear of death— not an insignificant evil, by Jove! They are free from the pangs of conscience. They are not terrified by stories of the dead nor frightened by ghosts and hobgoblins. They are not tortured by the fear of approaching evils nor filled with hope for future goods. To sum up, they are not troubled by the thousand cares this life brings to all men. They feel no shame, fear, ambition, envy, or love. If they were any closer to brute beasts, they would not even be able to sin—or so the theologians say. I would like you to count the cares that trouble your soul day and night, O foolish philosopher, and then you would understand how much I do for my followers. They are not only always rejoicing, playing, singing, and laughing but even spread these things wherever they go, as if they were given the favor of the gods to lighten the sadness of human life.

In a world where men are mostly at odds, everyone together recognizes, seeks out, feeds, favors, embraces my followers as their friends. They even permit them to do and say what they wish with impunity. No one wants to hurt them, not even the wild beasts who sense their harmlessness and do not attack them. They are certainly sacred to the gods, especially to me, and therefore everyone honors them. Why, kings cannot eat or travel or endure an hour without their fools who give them the greatest delight. In fact, they regard them more highly than the crabbed counselors whom they keep around for appearances. I do not think this preference is so strange, and it can easily be explained. Counselors, depending on their wisdom, bring to kings only the unpleasant truth, and they are not afraid of sometimes scraping the tender ears of princes. Fools, however, present only what the rulers want: jokes, laughter, scoffing, and other delights.

Fools also have this not insignificant virtue: they alone are candid and truthful. What is more praiseworthy than truth? Even though Alcibiades thought that only children and drunkards speak the truth, all the praise is really owed to me as is proved by this line of Euripides: "The fool speaks foolish things." Whatever a fool has in his heart shows itself in his expression and speech. A wise man, however, has two tongues, as Euripides mentions, one of which speaks the truth, the other speaking what happens to be expedient at the moment. He changes white into black and cold into hot in the same breath; and he speaks what is far from being in his heart. For this reason kings seem to me to be the most unhappy because they lack people from whom they can get the truth and are forced to have flatterers for friends. Someone might say that kings hate wise men and avoid them because they fear that one of them might dare to speak the truth rather than what is pleasant; and this is true, kings hate the truth. It is quite admirable, then, that kings will listen with relish to not only a truth but quite a sharp truth from my fools. If this same statement were spoken by a wise man, however, he would surely die. But coming from a fool, it gives great pleasure. A truth, if it gives no offense, has a certain genuine spirit of pleasure, but the gods give this power only to fools. It is for these reasons, too, that these same fools are taken up by women who are naturally inclined to pleasure and frivolity. Moreover, they can explain away whatever they do with these fools as good clean fun, even when the sport becomes serious; for this sex is ingenious, especially at covering up its own lapses.

Now let us return to the subject of the happiness of fools. They live a life filled with happiness, with no fear of death, or sense of it, and then go straight to the Elysian fields. There they entertain the pious and idle shades with their tricks. Let us now compare the life of a wise man with that of a fool. Think up some model of wisdom to oppose this fool, someone who spent his boyhood and youth laboring in the classroom, who dissipated the best part of his life with sleepless nights, cares, and worry and who never tasted a bit of pleasure for the rest of his life. He was always abstemious, poor, unhappy, and crabby. He is harsh and unjust to himself, oppressive and hateful to others. He is pale, emaciated, sickly, sore-eyed, prematurely old and gray, and dying before his time. What difference does it make when he dies, since he never really lived? This is your glorious image of a wise man for you.

Here, again, the Stoics croak at me. "Nothing," they say, "is more pitiable than madness; and exceptional folly is either near-madness, or, more likely, madness itself." For what else is insanity than a wandering of the mind? (But they wander the whole way.) With the help of the Muses, we will confute this line of reasoning. They are acute in their reasoning, but maybe they ought to distinguish two kinds of madness, in the manner of Socrates who teaches in Plato's *Dialogues* to divide Cupids and Venuses and one kind of madness from another—at least if they should wish to be considered sane themselves. Not every madness is a calamity. Otherwise, Horace would not have said: "A pleasant madness inspires me." Nor would Plato have placed the frenzy of poets and seers among the chief blessings of life; and the oracle would not have called the labors of Aeneas insane. There are two types of insanity. One is sent from hell by the avengeful furies, and as often as they unloose their snaky locks, they assault the hearts of men with a thirst for war, an insatiable greed, shameful and unspeakable lust, parricide, incest, sacrilege, or other evils of the same type. They also pursue the guilty and conscience-stricken soul with the fire of their terrible wrath. The second type of madness, which comes from me, is far different from this and should be desired above all things. It arises whenever a cheerful error of the mind frees the spirit from care and at the same time anoints it with manifold delight. Cicero, when writing to Atticus, expressed a wish for just this state of mind which would take away all sense of the great evils surrounding him. The Greek in Horace's *Epistle* had the right idea. He was so mad that he, all alone, would sit for days on end in a theater, laughing, applauding, and enjoying himself because he thought a play was going on when really there was no one on stage. In all other things he was sane enough, joyful with his friends, kind to his wife, and able to put up with his servants, who could even open up a bottle without his getting angry. When the care of family and physician had freed him from his sickness and he was himself again, he protested to his friends saying, "Why, you have killed, not cured me, my friends, since you have taken from me such great pleasure and destroyed my enjoyable delusions." He was right; for they were the mad ones and needed the medicine more than he, since they thought that such an enjoyable delusion was some sort of evil and should be cured by medicine.

I do not say, however, that every delusion or wandering of the mind should be called madness. A shortsighted man who thinks a mule is an ass is not considered insane; nor is someone who thinks that a trite poem is a very good one immediately thought to be insane. However, if a person is continually and extraordinarily deceived not only by his senses but even his judgment, then people will think him, at least, very nearly mad. For example, suppose he thinks he is listening to a symphony orchestra whenever an ass brays; or, if he is a pauper, suppose he believes he is Croesus, King of Lydia. This is surely insanity; but if it gives pleasure, as it usually does, it is extremely enjoyable both for those who are possessed by it and for those who watch it and are not mad in the same manner. For this type of madness is more widespread than the ordinary man realizes. One madman laughs at another, and they each give enjoyment to one another. If you watch closely, you will see that the maddest one gets the biggest laugh.

If Folly is any judge, that man is the happiest who is most thoroughly deluded. May he remain in that state which comes from me alone and is so widespread that I doubt whether there can be found one person in the whole race of man who has been wise for every moment of his life and has never been touched by some madness or other. The reason a person who believes he sees a woman when in reality he is looking at a gourd is called crazy is because this is something beyond usual experience. However, when a person thinks his wife, who is enjoyed by many, to be an ever-faithful Penelope, he is not called insane at all because people know that this is a common thing in marriage.

To this latter class belong those who sacrifice everything for hunting; for they swear that they experience an incredible joy whenever they hear the sound of the horn and the baying of the hounds. I understand that even the dung of the dogs smells like cinnamon to them. And what could be more enjoyable than the butchering of animals? Bulls and oxen are slaughtered, of course, by the common folk, but it is unheard of for anyone else except a nobleman to kill wild game. Bareheaded and kneeling, he solemnly cuts off certain parts with a special knife (it is a sacrilege to use any other). The crowd stands around in quiet awe as if it had never seen it done before (a thousand times at the least!); and if it happens that one of them gets to taste a piece of the meat, he thinks himself to have been lifted to the ranks of nobility. However, from this butchering and eating of animals nothing else is accomplished but that they degenerate into animals themselves, even though they think they are living royally.

A class similar to this is one composed of those persons who are afire with a zeal for building. They change round structures into square ones and then square ones back again to round ones. There is no end or method to this until they are reduced to such poverty that they have nowhere to live or nothing to eat. What of it? They enjoyed the greatest happiness while it lasted.

Next to these, it seems to me, are those who with new and secret arts try to change the appearance of things and search through sky and sea for some fifth essence. Lured on by sweet hope and sparing neither labor nor money, they always devise something, with marvelous ingenuity, with which to deceive themselves and produce their own delightful delusions. Finally, they run out of money and cannot afford even a little furnace. However, never stopping their pleasant dreaming, they continually urge others to enjoy the same happiness. When all hope is gone, they take great consolation in this one thought, "In great things, it is enough to have tried." They complain that life is too short for the magnitude of their undertaking.

I hesitate to admit gamblers to our fellowship, but some of these addicts are a rather foolish and ridiculous sight. When they hear the dice rattle, their hearts jump and beat faster. The hope of winning always lures them on until their means are gone, until their ship is shattered against the gaming table, which is not any less formidable than the Malean promontory. When they have lost everything, they cheat anyone except the winner in order not to appear to be men without honor. What about the old and near-blind fellows who have to play with glasses? When well-earned gout has stiffened their joints, they hire someone to put the dice in the box for them. It is a delightful game, except that it usually develops into a brawl and so belongs to the Furies rather than to me.

A group that does belong in our circle without a doubt is made up of those who enjoy either listening to or telling tall tales and strange stories. They never get enough of those fables that tell of unnatural happenings, ghosts, goblins, shades, and a thousand other strange things. They believe most readily and are more pleased with those stories that are furthest from the truth. These things not only alleviate boredom but they may even be a source of profit, especially to priests and pardoners. Very similar to these people are those who partake of the foolish but comforting belief that if they gaze on some carving or picture of Polyphemus Christopher, they will not die on that day; or that whoever says the right words to an image of Barbara will return safely from battle; or that if a person makes a novena to Erasmus with the proper prayers and candles, he will become rich in a short time. In St. George they have found another Hercules or Hippolytus. They all but adore his horse, which is piously adorned with ornaments and jewels; and they offer little gifts to obtain favors. It is even the custom of kings to swear by St. George's brass helmet. Then what shall I say about those who happily delude themselves with false pardons for their sins? They calculate the time to be spent in Purgatory down to the year, month, day, and hour as if it were a container that could be measured accurately with a mathematical formula. There are also those who think there is nothing they cannot obtain by relying on the magical prayers and charms thought up by some charlatan for the sake of his soul or for profit. Among the things they want are: wealth, honor, pleasure, plenty, perpetual good health, long life, a vigorous old age, and, finally, a place next to Christ in heaven. However, they do not want that place until the last possible second; heavenly pleasures may come only when the pleasures of this life, hung onto with all possible tenacity, must finally depart.

I can see some businessman, soldier, or judge taking one small coin from all his money and thinking that it will be proper expiation for all his perjury, lust, drunkenness, fighting, murder, fraud, lying, and treachery. After doing this he thinks that he can start a new round of sinning with a clean slate. How foolish, but, indeed, how happy are they who promise themselves something greater than the highest happiness for reciting daily the seven verses of the Psalms. These are the magic verses believed to have been pointed out to St. Bernard by the devil—a witty fellow but not very shrewd since he was tricked into telling by the saint's ruse. Things like this are so foolish that I myself am almost ashamed; yet they are accepted not only by the laity but even by theology professors. This same thing happens when certain regions of the country set up their own particular saint and attribute peculiar rites and powers to each one. One gives relief from toothache, another helps in childbirth, another restores things that are stolen, another brings help to the shipwrecked, still another guards the flocks, and so it goes down the line. There are some saints who can do many things, like the Blessed Virgin, whom the common folk honor more than they do her Son.

And what do people ask from these saints, except what is foolish? Among all the gifts hanging on the walls and even from the roofs of churches, have you ever seen one that was given in order to escape from folly or to become a little wiser? One is for escaping drowning; another for surviving a wound; another was lucky or brave enough to leave the battlefield while others were still fighting. Another was delivered from execution by the favor of the patron saint of thieves so that he could relieve those who are burdened with too much wealth. This one escaped prison; that one angered his doctor by getting well quickly. Another one was saved by a poison drink that loosened his bowels rather than killing him. His wife was very much displeased because she lost both the labor and the money. Another drove his horse home unharmed after his wagon had fallen over. This one's house fell in and he lived. This one escaped being caught by the husband. No one, however, gives thanks for warding off folly. There is so much enjoyment when one is not wise that mortals would prefer to give up anything except folly.

Why should I travel farther on this sea of superstition? "If I had a hundred tongues, a hundred mouths, a voice of brass, I could not describe all the forms of folly, or run through all its names." The life of Christians everywhere abounds with such nonsense. The priests allow and even encourage such things. They know that it brings in much profit. Imagine in the middle of all this some troublesome wise man speaking out the truth: "You will not die badly if you live rightly. You will be freed from your sins if you add to the payment of money, hatred for evil, tears, vigils, prayers, and fastings; and if you change your whole way of living. A saint will take care of you, if you imitate him." If a wise man said things of this type, I say, he would take all the happiness out of life and throw the world into a tumult.

To our company, also, belong those who, while still living, make elaborate funeral arrangements, going so far as to prescribe the number of candles, mourners, singers, and hired pallbearers. Perhaps they think that the sense of sight will be returned to them after death, or that, even though dead, they will be ashamed if they are not buried grandly. They work with such zeal that it looks as if they were planning a public show or banquet.

Even though I am trying to move this speech along, I can hardly pass over without a word those nobodies who take enormous pride in the empty titles of nobility. There is one who will trace his family back to Aeneas, another to Brutus, and another to King Arthur. They display everywhere the bust and portraits of their ancestors. They rattle off their grandfathers and great-grandfathers and know all the old titles by heart. Meanwhile, however, they are not far from being dumb statues themselves and are probably worth less than the statues they display. Sweet little Philantia, however, helps them to live a happy life; and there are always fools who regard strange animals like these as gods.

Philantia does, of course, make many other people happy in a variety of ways. This apelike fellow here seems handsome enough to himself. That other fellow drawing circles with his compass over there thinks he is Euclid. This ass of the lyre does not sound any better than this fellow with the rooster's voice who thinks he is as great a singer as Hermogenis the Satyr. The happiest fools, however, are those who glory in some talent they do not possess but have discerned in one of their followers. Of this type was that doubly-happy rich man about whom Seneca relates that he kept servants on hand to refresh his memory whenever he told stories. He was also so weak that he could hardly stand, but he did not hesitate to accept a fight for he kept at home some sturdy fellows whose strength he relied upon instead of his own.

It is really superfluous to mention the professors of the arts who are so horribly conceited that they would sooner lose the family estate than any part of their talent. This is especially true of actors, singers, orators, and poets. The worse they are, the more insolent, boastful, and conceited they become; and the more applause they receive. The worst always pleases the most because, as I have said, the majority of men are fools. If the poorer artist is most pleased with himself and admired by many others, why should he want to have true skill? It will cost him more, make him more self-conscious and uneasy, and please a much smaller audience.

I see that, as nature has endowed every individual with self-love, so she has given it to every city and nation. The British pride themselves on their good looks, their music, and their good food, among other things. The Scots boast of their gentility and royal lineage, as well as of their argumentative skill. The French think themselves remarkable for courtesy, and the Parisians regard themselves as the only ones who understand theology. The Italians claim eloquence and great literature for themselves and are pleased to admit that they alone are not barbarians. The Romans especially engage in this type of vanity, for they are still happily dreaming about those great conquests of old. The Venetians, meanwhile, are happy with their own notion of nobility. The Greeks, of course, are the discoverers of the arts and pride themselves on their great heroes of the past. Christian superstitions entertain the Turks and other actual barbarians who boast of their own religions. The Jews, moreover, still await the Messiah and hold as steadfastly to their belief in His coming as they do to their belief in the prophet Moses. The Spanish admit of no equal in soldiery, and the Germans take pride in their great size and knowledge of magic. Why should I go on? I think you see how much pleasure is brought to all men, individually and collectively, by self-love. Flattery, a subordinate of self-love, is another source of pleasure. Self-love is in fact, reversed and becomes χολακία, bile.

Nowadays this adulation has a bad odor, but only among those who are more concerned about the names of things rather than the things themselves. They are of the opinion that bad faith cannot be distinguished from adulation; but they could be proven wrong by the mere examples of dumb animals. There isn't a more fawning animal than a dog, and yet, what is more faithful? What is more appealing and lovable than a squirrel? And moreover, as a man's best friend, one can find none better. Unless, of course, you consider fierce lions, pitiless tigers, and fiery leopards as standing man in better stead. It is definite that certain traitors and mockers drive their victims to destruction by employing a baneful kind of flattery. But this flattery of mine stems from a certain kindness and candor of mind, and it approaches virtue more readily than does asperity, or what Horace calls "inelegant and burdensome sullenness." My flattery raises the dejected spirit, it soothes those who are in mourning, mollifies the angry, and permanently unites the bond of love. It attracts children to the study of literature, the elderly are cheered by it, and under guise of praise, it cautions and instructs princes in such a way so as not to offend them. In brief, it serves to make every man more pleasing and important to himself; this is truly the principal concept of happiness. What is more gracious than the way two mules scratch each other? But I shall not go on to tell you what a great part this flattery plays in your praiseworthy and forceful manner of discourse, in your medicine, and in the greatest part of all your poetry. In conclusion, it is the meat and spice of all human discourse.

But they say it is an unhappy thought to be deceived. To this I say no, for the unhappiest thought is not to be deceived. For those who think that the happiness of a man can be found in things as such could not be further from the truth; this resides in opinion. For nothing can be clearly known, since human affairs are so obscure and varied, a fact already stated correctly by my colleagues, the least impudent of the philosophers. Or if there is something that can be known, it is usually something that will hinder the enjoyment of life. Finally, the mind of man is so constructed that it is far more susceptible to accepting falsehoods than realities. If anyone wants to make a convincing and easy test of this, let him go to church and listen to the sermons. If something worthwhile is being said, everybody sleeps, or yawns, or is ill at ease. But if the bawler—I made an error, I meant to say prater—as often happens, begins some old wives' tale, then everybody awakens, straightens up, and listens attentively. Also, if there is a somewhat intriguing or poetical saint (you might include in this class George or Christopher or Barbara), you will see him honored in a much more devout way than Peter, Paul, or even Christ Himself. But these things are not relevant here.

Yet this addition to happiness costs so little! Whereas it is necessary to pay a much greater price for practically any of the worthwhile arts, even for the poorest of them—grammar, for instance. But public opinion spreads very easily, and in spite of this it is still far more conducive to happiness. Suppose a man is eating some rotten kippers, and the man beside him cannot tolerate the smell of them; still, they smell like ambrosia to the man who is eating them. Now I ask you, what is the consequence of happiness? On the other hand, if the best sturgeon upsets your stomach, what relationship does this have to the miracle of existence? If a man has a wife who is notoriously ugly, yet she seems, in the eyes of her husband, to be qualified to enter a contest with Venus, isn't this the same as if she were truly beautiful? If one viewed a canvas splattered with red lead and mud, and he thought it was a picture painted by Apelles or Zeuxis, would he not be happier than someone who buys a similar work at a ridiculously high price but derives no pleasure from viewing it? I know a man who has the same name as mine, who gave his wife some costume jewelry as a present, and convinced her—for he is a credible joker—that they were not only genuine and natural, but also of unique and inestimable value. Now tell me, what difference did it make to the girl, so long as she took great delight in having and looking at these imitations, and carefully kept these trinkets close to her person, at all times, and in a very safe place? Still, her husband had avoided a great expense, enjoyed his wife's delusion, and had strengthened their relationship just as though he had given her the most precious of gifts. In your opinion how do those in Plato's cave, who, quite satisfied with their existence, look contentedly at the shadows and likenesses of various objects differ from the wise man who emerges from the cave and looks upon reality? If Micyllus, in Lucian, had been allowed to go on dreaming that rich and golden dream forever, there would have been no reason for him to desire any other state.

Thus, either there is no difference or, if there is, unreality is the preferred state. First, their happiness is less costly, for the price to pay is only a bit of illusion. Secondly, they enjoy it in the company of so many others. To possess anything of value is useless unless you have a companion to share it with. The scarcity of wise men is well known to all, if indeed there are any to be found. The Greeks purported to have found but seven wise men throughout many centuries. Yet, believe me, if one were to canvass these centuries with care and accuracy, I would defy him to find so much as one half-wise man; indeed, he would not find so much as one third of one wise man!

You will remember that the chief glory of Bacchus was his ability to wash away the cares of the soul. Yet this cleansing only lasts a short time, for as soon as his magical effect wears off, the cares return to the soul with force and rapidity, riding four white horses, as it is said. How much more plentiful and prompt is my good fortune? For I place the mind in somewhat of a perpetual stupor. I fill it with joys, delights, and gay fancies, all without formality or difficulty. Gifts of the other gods are distributed with partiality, certain ones to certain people, but I have seen to it that no man alive shall go without my blessing. Rich and mild wine "that drives away cares and gives visions of profuse hope" is not to be found everywhere. Few possess facial beauty, which is a gift of Venus; eloquence, which is the gift of Mercury, still fewer possess. The rule of kingdoms is not haphazardly bestowed on anyone by Homer's Jupiter. Often Mars favors neither army. Many leave Apollo's tripod in great sadness. Apollo's arrows frequently bring pestilence, Neptune drowns more than he saves. And, of course, I must mention the anti-Joves of Pluto, Ate, Poena, Febris, and others like them—for these are not gods at all, but rather murderers. Only I, Folly, embrace all men without distinction in my provident goodness. Nor do I wait for prayers. I do not demand an apology if some ceremony has been overlooked, for I am not petty. If someone has issued an invitation to the other gods, but has not invited me, and thus does not allow me to participate in their rituals, I do not cause an unbecoming scene. The fact is that the critical nature of the gods is such that one would be better off, and even safer, if he would leave them alone entirely, rather than worship them as he should. There are people that are so hard to please and so easily offended that it is better to leave them alone entirely than to have even the slightest acquaintance with them.

But they say that nobody sacrifices or builds a temple to Folly. And I am truly amazed, as I said before, at such ingratitude. Yet I take this in good stride, in my own easygoing way, though I could scarcely complain, with any dignity, about these ingratitudes. For why should I demand incense, meal, a ram, or a sow when everywhere all men worship me with a kind of reverence that is highly approved by the fathers of the Church? Maybe I should envy Diana because she was appeased by human sacrifice. No, I shouldn't, for I feel that I am most reverently worshipped when all men contemplate me in their spiritual being, manifest me in their actions, and represent me in their lives. This type of worship of the saints is extremely rare among Christians. Many Christians will light a candle to the Blessed Virgin, even at noon when it is unnecessary. But how few have the ardent desire to imitate her in her chaste life, her temperance, and her love for spiritual things! For ultimately this is true worship and most pleasing to those in heaven. Besides, why should I want a temple when the whole world is my temple, and, if I am not mistaken, a wholesome one? Nor are gospelers lacking, except where men are lacking. I am not so foolish as to petition painted stone images; they would only detract from my worship, since only stupid and unimaginative people worship these idols, instead of the saints themselves. And the same thing would happen to me that happens to the saints—they are thrown out of doors by their substitutes. I feel that I have many statues erected in my behalf, as many as there are people who bear my living image on their faces, whether against their will or not. Therefore, I have no reason to envy the other gods, if one or the other is worshipped in some particular corner of the earth, and only on stated days at that, as for instance, Phoebus is worshipped in Rhodes, Venus in Cyprus, Juno at Argos, Minerva at Athens, Jupiter on Olympus, Neptune at Tarentum, and Priapus at Lampsacus, so long as I have the entire world fervently offering far greater sacrifices to me.

And if at this point I should appear to be speaking more rashly than truly, I suggest that for a moment we look into the lives of these men. It will be apparent how much they owe me, and how many, the most scholarly as well as the humble, follow me. We shall not look into everybody's life, as that would take too long, but only the most notable, and from these it will be easy to form an opinion about the others. For why should I spend my time on the common and humble people, when they are my followers beyond any doubt? Everywhere they throng in so many forms of folly and fabrication each day that a thousand Democrituses would not be sufficient for laughing at them, and even then there would be work for one more Democritus, to laugh at those who are laughing.

You would never believe the sport and entertainment that your human puppets provide daily for the gods. You are aware that these gods set aside their sober morning hours for composing quarrels and listening to prayers. But after that, when their minds are well clouded from the nectar and they have no desire to transact business, they search for some heavenly dignitary, and they sit there, gazing down at mortal men and watching them argue. There is no show like it. Good God, what a theater! How strange are the actions of fools. (I must admit that now and then I sit alongside the gods of the poets.) Here is a young man hopelessly in love with a sweet young girl, and the less he is loved in return, the more helplessly he is in love. This man marries a dowry, not a wife. He prostitutes his own wife, and another's jealousy hounds him like Argus. Here is a man in mourning, but forgive me, what foolish things he says and does, hiring mourners, as if they were actors, to play a comedy of grief! Another man squeezes out a tear at the tomb of his mother-in-law. This one spends whatever he can scrape together, by hook or by crook, on his stomach, but soon he will be just as hungry again. Another enjoys nothing better than sleep and idleness. Then there are those who get themselves into a predicament minding other people's business, while they neglect their own. There is also the broker who considers himself rich because he has other people's money, but is on the way to bankruptcy. Another thinks that happiness consists in living like a pauper so that his heir may be wealthy. Someone else, for the sake of a small and uncertain profit, sails the seven seas, risking his life, which no money could pay for, for the hazards of the sea and its storms. This one prefers seeking the spoils from war to passing a safe and quiet life at home. Some decide to most conveniently attain wealth by hypocritically catering to childless old men. There are even those would prefer this same procedure with rich old women. Both of these furnish a rare entertainment to those onlooking gods, because they are usually cheated by the people whom they set out to deceive.

But the most foolish and sordid of all are your merchants, in that they partake in the most illicit business by the most illegal means they can find. Sometimes they lie, they perjure themselves, they steal and cheat, and they impose on the public. Yet they consider themselves important men because they have gold rings on their fingers. Nor do they hesitate to flatter the friars who admire them and call them Right Honorable in public, with the purpose that surely a stipend from the ill-gotten gains may come into their possession. Elsewhere you will see certain Pythagoreans, who consider all things common to all——to such a degree, in fact, that whatever they pick up, lying around loose, they steal with no qualms of conscience, as if they gained it through inheritance. There are others who only dream that they are rich. They build beautiful air castles and they think that doing this is enough for happiness. Some delight in passing as wealthy men away from home, while they starve in their own homes. One man hastens to invest what money he has, while his neighbor hoards his at any cost. This man strives as a candidate for public office, and another finds his pleasure by his fireside. A large number of people file suits that are destined never to end; time and time again they eagerly strive to outdo each other, both in bribing the judge who sets the postponements and the advocate who colludes with him. One man zealously lives for revolutions, and another is laboring upon his unique subversive plot. And still another man leaves his wife and children at home and sets out on a pilgrimage to Jerusalem, Rome, or the shrine of St. James, where he has no particular business. In short, if you were to look down from the moon, as Menippus used to do, you would think that you were seeing a swarm of flies or gnats, quarreling among themselves, fighting, robbing, sporting, laying traps for each other, indulging in wanton practices, being born, growing old, and dying. One can hardly believe what commotions and tragedies this insignificant being, minute as he is and so soon to die, instigates. For at some time a trivial war or an epidemic of the plague will devastate and utterly wipe out thousands of them at a time.

But it would be most foolish for me, and worthy of the many-faceted laughter of Democritus, to continue naming types of folly and madness among the people. Let me direct my attention to those among men who show some indication of wisdom and, as the saying goes, search for the golden bough. Among these the grammarians hold first place. Nothing could be more disaster-stricken or more afflicted than this generation of men; none would show such a hatred toward God, if I were not present to mitigate the pains of their wretched misdeeds by a certain pleasing infusion of madness. For they are not only liable to the πέντε κατάραις, that is the five curses the Greek epigram mentions in Homer, but indeed to six hundred curses; as they are famished, and filthy in their schools or, even better stated, in their think-shops, or shambles, among herds of boys. There they grow old with their labors, they are deafened by the noise, and they become ill from the stench and filth. Nonetheless, because of my beneficence they see themselves first among their fellow man. They take such great pleasure in terrifying the fearful crowd by scowling or yelling at them when they beat the little wretches with rods, straps, or a punishing stick, fiercely storming around them in all directions, however they please, mimicking the ass in Aesop. And sometimes the filth seems like sheer elegance, the stench like the bouquet of marjoram, and the miserable servitude like unto a kingdom, such that they would not sacrifice their tyranny even for the empire of Phalaris or Dionysius.

But presently they are happy in their new dream world, thinking that they are learned men. Naturally they feed their pupils with utter nonsense; yet, good Lord, what Palemon or Donatus do they not scorn when comparing them to themselves! I don't know how they manage to fool people so well, but to the foolish mothers and ignorant fathers of their pupils they appear to be exactly what they are trying to be. And on top of this they entertain another pleasure; if they should have the opportunity to dig up out of some worm-eaten manuscript the name of Anchises' mother, or some obscure word, such as "bubsequa," "bovinator," "manticulator," or somewhere dig up a fragment of an ancient tombstone with an inscription that is difficult to decipher—holy Jupiter—you'd think that they had just conquered Africa or captured Babylon from the way they cheer and brag and eulogize among the people.

As for the stilted, insipid verses that they spout on most any occasion (and there are those who admire them), obviously the writer believes that the soul of Virgil has been transmigrated into his own being. But the funniest sight of all is to watch them praise and admire each other, trading compliment for compliment, and thus satisfying each other's ego. Yet if one forgets but a single word, another, more alert, sadistically pounces on the mistake. What a commotion, what hazing and insults, and what violent accusations occur. May the whole grammatical world frown upon me, if I am lying. At one time I knew a certain scholar who was versed in Greek, Latin, mathematics, philosophy, and medicine. When he was sixty, laying aside all other disciplines, he disputed and tortured himself with grammar for more than twenty years, estimating that he would find happiness if he were permitted to live until he had undoubtedly discerned how the eight parts of speech are to be distinguished, even though none of the Greeks or Latins had successfully completed the task. It becomes a matter of war when someone makes a conjunction out of a word that properly belongs under the heading of adverb. It is precisely because of this fact that there are as many grammars as there are grammarians—pardon me, there are even more, for my friend Aldus singlehandedly produced grammars on more than five different occasions. He has overlooked no work in this field, regardless of how barbarously or tediously written. He has expounded and criticized each work, jealous of anybody who may be even ineptly toiling in the same field, his great fear being, and pitiably so, that his labor over the years may go unrecognized should someone else outdo his efforts. Do you prefer to call this madness or folly? It does not matter to me; merely confess that it is done with my assistance, and in such a way that any man who otherwise is the most wretched of all men becomes so elated that he would not even wish to trade his place with that of the kings of Persia.

The poets owe me less, though they readily admit that they are extremely indebted to me, being a race of free souls (as the proverb has it); all of their efforts have no other intention than soothing fool's ears with inane quips and silly stories. Yet they rely so heavily on these things, strange as it may seem, that they not only promise themselves immortality and a life equal to that of the gods, but they also tell others that they will attain the same. Self-love and bile are more closely allied with this sect than with others, and no other tribe of men worships me with more sincerity or greater consistency. As for the rhetoricians, though they may play two ends against the middle at times and collude with the philosophers, they are in many ways in agreement with me, and this will definitely prove it: besides a great deal of other nonsense, they have written very critically and voluminously concerning the method of joking. Whoever it was that composed the art of rhetoric "ad Herennium," includes folly, itself, as one species of humor. Also, in the work of Quintilian, easily the greatest in his field, there is a chapter longer than the Iliad dealing with the art of making others laugh. Generally they attribute this much to folly, that many times what cannot be refuted by arguments can be parried by laughter. But you may think that arousing laughter with witty remarks, and so by a standard method, does not belong to Folly.

In the same realm are those who are authors of books. All of them are highly indebted to me, especially those who blacken their pages with sheer triviality. For those who write learnedly to be criticized by a few scholars, not even ruling out a Persius or a Laelius as a judge, seem to be more pitiable than happy to me, simply because they are continuously torturing themselves. They add, they alter, they cross something out, they reinsert it, they recopy their work, they rearrange it, they show it to friends, and they keep it for nine years; yet they still are not satisfied with it. At such a price, they buy an empty reward, namely praise—and the praise of only a handful, at that. They buy this at the great expense of long hours, no sleep, so much sweat, and so many vexations. Add also the loss of health, the deterioration of their physical appearance, the possibility of blindness or partial loss of their sight, poverty, malice, premature old age, an early death, and if you can think of more, add them to this list. The scholar feels that he has been compensated for such ills when he wins the sanction of one or two other weak-eyed scholars. But my author is crazy in a far happier way for he, without any hesitation, rapidly writes down anything that comes to his mind, his pen, or even his dreams. There is little or no waste of paper, since he knows that if the trifles are trivial enough, the majority of the readers, that is, the fools and ignoramuses, will approve of them. What is the difference if one should ignore two or three scholars, even though he may have read them. Or what weight will the censure of a few scholars carry, so long as the multitudes give it acclaim?

Actually, the wiser writers are those who put out the work of someone else as their own. By a few alterations they transfer someone else's glory to themselves, disregarding the other person's long labor and comforting themselves with the thought that even though they might be publicly convicted of plagiarism, meanwhile they shall have enjoyed the fruits and glory of authorship. It is worth one's while to observe how pleased authors are with their own works when they are popular and pointed out in a crowd—as celebrities! Their work is on display in bookstores, with three cryptic words in large type on the title page, something like a magician's spell. Ye gods! After all, what are they but words? Few people will ever hear of them, compared to the total world population, and far fewer will admire them, since people's tastes vary so, even among the common people. And why is it that the very names of the authors are often false, or stolen from the books of the ancients? One calls himself Telemachus, another Stelenus or Laertes, still another Polycrates, and another Thrasymachus. As a result, nowadays it does not matter whether you dedicate your book to a chameleon or a gourd, or simply to alpha or beta, as the philosophers do.

The most touching event is when they compliment each other and turn around in an exchange of letters, verses, and superfluities. They are fools praising fools and dunces praising dunces. The first, in the opinion of the second, is an Alcaeus, and the second, in the opinion of the first, is a Callimachus. One holds another in higher esteem than Cicero, the other finds the one more learned than Plato. Or sometimes they will choose a competitor and increase their reputation by rivaling themselves with him. As a result the public is split with opposing viewpoints, until finally, when the dispute is over, each reigns as victor and has a triumphal parade. Wise men deride this as being absolute nonsense, which is just what it is. Who will deny it? Meanwhile, our authors are leading a luxurious life because of my excellence, and they would not exchange their accomplishments for even those of Scipius. And while the scholars most certainly derive a great deal of pleasure from laughing at them, relishing to the utmost the madnesses of others, they themselves owe me a great deal, which they cannot deny without being most ungrateful men.

Among men of the learned professions, a most self-satisfied group of men, the lawyers may hold themselves in the highest esteem. For while they laboriously roll up the stone of Sisyphus by the force of weaving six hundred laws together at the same time, by the stacking of commentary upon commentary and opinion upon opinion regardless of how far removed from the purpose, they contrive to make their profession seem to be the most difficult of all. What is actually tedious they consider brilliant. Let us include with them the logicians and sophists, a breed of men more loquacious than the famed brass kettles of Dodona. Any one of them can outtalk any twenty women. They would be happier, though, if they were just talkative and not quarrelsome as well. In fact, they are so quarrelsome that they will argue and fight over a lock of goat's wool, absurdly losing sight of the truth in the furor of their dispute. Their egotistical love keeps them happy, and manned with but three syllogisms, they will unflinchingly argue on any subject with any man. Their mere obstinacy affords them victory, even though you place Stentor against them.

Next in line are the scientists, revered for their beards and the fur on their gowns. They feel that they are the only men with any wisdom, and all other men float about as shadows. How senilely they daydream, while they construct their countless worlds and shoot the distance to the sun, the moon, the stars, and spheres, as with a thumb and line. They postulate causes for lightning, winds, eclipses, and other inexplicable things, never hesitating for a moment, as if they had exclusive knowledge about the secrets of nature, designer of elements, or as if they visited us directly from the council of the gods. Yet all this time nature is heartily laughing at them and their conjectures. It is a sufficient argument just proving that they have good intelligence for nothing. They can never explain why they always disagree with each other on every subject. In summation, knowing nothing in general they profess to know everything in particular. They are ignorant even to themselves, and at times they do not see the ditch or stone lying across their path, because many of them are daydreamers and are absent-minded. Yet they proclaim that they perceive ideas, universals, forms without matter, primary substances, quiddities, entities, and things so tenuous that I'm afraid that Lynceus could not see them himself. The common people are especially disdained when they bring out their triangles, quadrangles, circles, and mathematical figures of the like. They place one on top of the other and arrange them into a maze. Then they deploy some letters precisely, as if in a battle formation, and finally they reverse them. And all of this is done only to confuse those who are ignorant of their field. These scientists do not like those who predict the future from the stars, and promise even more fantastic miracles. And these fortunate men find people who believe them.

Perhaps it would be better to pass silently over the theologians. Dealing with them, since they are hot-tempered, is like crossing Lake Camarina or eating poisonous beans. They may attack me with six hundred arguments and force me to retract what I hold; for if I refuse, they will immediately declare me a heretic. By this blitz action they show a desire to terrify anyone to whom they are ill-disposed. No other people are so adverse to acknowledge my favors to them, yet the divines are bound to me by extraordinary obligations. These theologians are happy in their self-love, and as if they were presently inhabiting a third heaven, they look down on all men as though they were animals that crawled along the ground, coming near to pity them. They are protected by a wall of scholastic definitions, arguments, corollaries, and implicit and explicit propositions. They have so many hideouts that not even the net of Vulcan would be able to catch them; for they back down from their distinctions, by which they also cut through the knots of an argument, as if with a double-blade ax from Tenedos; and they come forth with newly invented terms and monstrous-sounding words. Furthermore, they explain the most mysterious matters to suit themselves, for instance, the method by which the world was set in order and began, through what channels original sin has come down to us through generations, by what means, in what measure, and how long the Omnipotent Christ was in the Virgin's womb, and how accidents subsist in the Eucharist without their substance.

But those have been beaten to death down through the ages. Here are some questions that are worthy of great (and some call them) illuminated theologians, questions that will really make them think, if they should ever encounter them. Did divine generation take place at a particular time? Are there several sonships in Christ? Whether this is a possible proposition: Does God the Father hate the Son? Could God the Father have taken upon Himself the likeness of a woman, a devil, an ass, a gourd, or a piece of flint? Then how would that gourd have preached, performed miracles, or been crucified? Also, what would Peter have consecrated, if he had administered the Eucharist, while Christ's body hung on the cross?

Another thought: could Christ have been said to be a man at that very moment? Will we be forbidden to eat and drink after the resurrection? (Now, while there is time, they are providing against hunger and thirst!) These intricate subtleties are infinite, and there are others that are even more subtle, concerning instances of time, notions, relations, accidents, quiddities, and entities, which no one can perceive unless, like Lynceus, he can see in the blackest darkness things that aren't there.

We must insert those maxims, rather contradictions, that, compared to the Stoic paradoxes, appear to be the most common simplicity. For instance: it is a lesser crime to cut the throats of a thousand men than to sew a stitch on a poor man's shoe on the sabbath; it is better to want the earth to perish, body, boots, and breeches (as the saying goes), than to tell a single lie, however inconsequential. The methods that our scholastics follow only render more subtle the subtlest of subtleties; for you will more easily escape from a labyrinth than from the snares of the Realists, Nominalists, Thomists, Albertists, Occamists, and Scotists. I have not named them all, only a few of the major ones. But there is so much learning and difficulty in all of these sects that I should think the apostles themselves must have the need of some help from some other spirit if they were to try to argue these topics with our new generation of theologians.

Paul could present faith. But when he said, "Faith is the substance of things hoped for, the evidence of things not seen," he did not define it doctorally. The same apostle, though he exemplified charity to its utmost, divided and defined it with very little logical skill in the first epistle to the Corinthians, Chapter 13. And there is no doubt that the apostles consecrated the Eucharist devoutly enough, but suppose you had questioned them about the "terminus a quo" and the "terminus ad quem," or about transubstantiation—how the body is in many places at once, and the difference between the body of Christ in heaven, on the cross, in the Eucharist at the point when transubstantiation occurs (taking note that the prayer effecting it is a discrete quantity having extension in time)—I say that they would not have answered with the same accuracy with which the pupils of Scotus distinguish and define these matters. The apostles knew the mother of Jesus, but who among them has demonstrated philosophically just how she was preserved from the stain of original sin, as our theologians have done? Peter received the keys from One who did not commit them to an unworthy person, and yet I doubt that he ever understood——for Peter never did have a profound knowledge for the subtle——that a person who did not have knowledge could have the key to knowledge. They went everywhere baptizing people, and yet they never taught what the formal, material, efficient, and final causes of baptism were, nor did they mention that it has both a delible and indelible character. They worshipped, this is certain, but in spirit, following no other teaching than that of the gospel, "God is a spirit, and those that worship Him must do so in spirit and in truth." They seem never to have known that a picture drawn in charcoal on a wall ought to be worshipped as though it were Christ Himself, at least if it is drawn with two outstretched fingers and the hair uncombed, and has three sets of rays in the nimbus fastened to the back of the head. For who would comprehend these things had they not spent all the thirty-six years on the Physics and Metaphysics of Aristotle and the Scotists?

In the same way the apostles teach grace, and yet they never determined the difference between a grace freely given and one that makes one deserving. They urge us to do good works, but they don't separate work in general, work being done, and work that is already finished. At all times they inculcate charity, but they don't distinguish infused charity from that which is acquired, or state whether charity is an accident or a substance, created or uncreated. They abhor sin, but may I be shot if they could define sin scientifically as we know it, unless they were fortunate enough to have been instructed by the Scotists.

You could never persuade me to believe that Paul, upon whose learning others can be judged, would have condemned so many questions, disputes, genealogies, and what he called "strifes for words," if he had really been a master of those subtle topics, especially since all of the controversies at that time were merely little informal discussions. Actually, when compared with the Chrysippean subtleties of our masters, they appeared quite amateurish. And yet these masters are extremely modest; for if by chance the apostles were to have written a document carelessly or without proper knowledge of the subject, the masters would have properly interpreted what they wrote, they would not have condemned it. Therefore, they greatly respect what the apostles wrote, both because of the antiquity of the passage and their apostolic authority. And good heavens, it would almost be unjust to expect scholarly work from the apostles, for they had been told nothing about which they were writing by their Master. But if a mistake of the same kind appears in Chrysostom, Basil, or Jerome, our scholars would unhesitatingly say: "It is not accepted."

The apostles also defeated the pagan philosophers and the Jews in debates, and they are, by nature, the stubbornest of all. But they did this by using their lives as examples and by performing miracles. And, of course, they dealt with people who were not even smart enough to comprehend the most basic ideas of Scotus. Nowadays, what heathen or heretic does not immediately submit when faced with one of these cobwebbed subtleties? Unless, of course, he is either so stupid that he cannot follow them, or so impudent that he hisses them in defiance, or, possibly, so well instructed in the same ambiguities that the contest is a draw. Then it would appear that you had matched one magician against another, or two men fighting each other with magic swords. It would amount to nothing more than reweaving Penelope's tapestry. In my humble opinion it would be much wiser for the Christians to fight off the Turks and Saracens with these brawling Scotists, stubborn Occamists, invincible Albertists, and a whole band of Sophists, rather than with the undisciplined and unwieldy battalions of soldiers with whom they have been fighting for quite some time, and without any particular favor from Mars. Then I daresay they would witness the most onesided battle that they had ever seen, and one of the greatest victories ever achieved. Who is so impassive that the shrewdness of these fighters would not excite him? And who could be so stupid that these sophistries would not quicken him? And finally, who could be so alert that they would not cloud his vision?

But you think that I say all these things as a joke. Certainly, it is no wonder, since there are some even among the divines, instructed in aural learning, who are nauseated by what they consider the petty subtleties of the theologians. There are those who abhor speaking about holy things with a smutty mouth as a kind of sacrilege and the greatest impiety. These things are to be worshipped and not expounded upon. I am speaking of the heathens' profane methods of arguing, this arrogant way that they define things, and this defiance of the majesty of sacred theology by silly and sordid terms and sentiments. And yet, for all that, the others revel and even applaud themselves in their happiness, and they are so attentive about their precious trifles, both night and day, that they don't even have enough time to read a gospel or epistle from St. Paul. And while they waste their time away in school, they think that they are upholding the universal church, which is otherwise about to crumble to ruins, by the influence of their syllogisms, in the same way that Atlas supports the heavens on his shoulders, according to the poets. You can imagine how much pleasure they derive from shaping and reshaping the Holy Scriptures, as if they were made of wax. And they insist that their own conclusions, subscribed to by a few students, are more valid than Solon's laws and preferred before a pope's decrees; and as world censors they will force a retraction of any statement that does not completely adhere both to their explicit and implicit conclusions. And they announce these conclusions as if they were oracles. "This proposition is scandalous." "This one lacks reverence." "This one tends toward heresy." "This one does not have the right ring." The inference is that neither baptism nor the gospel, Peter and Paul, St. Jerome and Augustine, no, not even the great Aristotelian Thomas, himself, can convert a Christian, unless these scholarly men give their approval. And how kind it is of them to pass judgment! Who would ever have thought, unless these wise men had instructed us, that a man who approves of both "matula putes" and "matula putet," or "ollae fervere" and "ollam fervere," as good Latin, is not a Christian? Who else would have purged the Church from treacherous errors of this sort, which no one would have ever had the occasion to read if these wise men had not published them under the great seals of their universities? Henceforth, aren't they happy while they do these things?

And furthermore, they draw exact pictures of every part of hell, as though they had spent many years in that region. They also fabricate new heavenly regions as imagination dictates, adding the biggest of all and the finest, for there must be a suitable place for the blessed souls to take their walks, to entertain at dinner, or even to play a game of ball. Their heads are so stuffed and stretched with these and two thousand other trivialities of the same sort that I am certain Jupiter's brain was no more pregnant when he yelled for Vulcan's help to bring forth Pallas. Therefore, do not be astonished when you see one of their heads all wrapped up in swathes at a public debate, for if it wasn't, it would certainly fly into pieces. I often derive much pleasure myself when these theologians, who, holding themselves in such great esteem, begin speaking in their slovenly and barbarous tongues and jabber so that no one except a jabberer can understand them, reaching a high pitch—"highest acumen," they call it. This the common man cannot attain. It is their claim that it is beyond the station of sacred discourse to be obliged to adhere to the rules of grammarians. What an amazing attribute for theologians that incorrect speech be allowed them alone! As a matter of fact they share this honor with most intellectuals. When they are addressed as "Our Masters," they feel that they are in the proximity of the gods. They feel that the term has the same religious vigor as the unspeakable four letters of the Hebrews. They say it is sacrilegious to even write MAGISTER NOSTER in small letters, and should one mistakenly utter the term, he destroys in one stroke the sublimity of the theological order.

Those who are the closest to these in happiness are generally called "the religious" or "monks," both of which are deceiving names, since for the most part they stay as far away from religion as possible and frequent every sort of place. I cannot, however, see how any life could be more gloomy than the life of these monks if I did not assist them in many ways. Though most people detest these men so much that accidentally meeting one is considered to be bad luck, the monks themselves believe that they are magnificent creatures. One of their chief beliefs is that to be illiterate is to be of a high state of sanctity, and so they make sure that they are not able to read. Another is that when braying out their gospels in church they are making themselves very pleasing and satisfying to God, when in fact they are uttering these psalms as a matter of repetition rather than from their hearts. Indeed, some of these men make a good living through their uncleanliness and beggary by bellowing their petitions for food from door to door; there is not an inn, an announcement board, or a ship into which they are not accessible, here having a great advantage over other common beggars. According to them, though, they are setting an apostolic example for us by their filthiness, their ignorance, their bawdiness, and their insolence.

Moreover, it is amusing to find that they insist that everything be done in fastidious detail, as if employing the orderliness of mathematics, a small mistake in which would be a great crime. Just so many knots must be on each shoe and the shoelace may be of only one specified color; just so much lace is allowed on each habit; the girdle must be of just the right material and width; the hood of a certain shape and capacity; their hair of just so many fingers' length; and finally they can sleep only the specified number of hours per day. Can they not understand that, because of a variety of bodies and temperaments, all this equality of restrictions is in fact very unequal? Nevertheless, because of all this detail that they employ they think that they are superior to all other people. And what is more, amid all their pretense of Apostolic charity, the members of one order will denounce the members of another order clamorously because of the way in which the habit has been belted or the slightly darker color of it. You will find some among the monks who are so strictly religious and pious that they will wear no outer clothes other than those made of Cilician goat's hair or inner garments other than the ones made of Milesian wool; some others, however, will permit linen outer garments, but they again insist on wool underneath. Members of other orders shrink from the mere touch of money as if it were poison. They do not, however, retreat from the touch of wine or of women. All derive a great deal of joy in choosing the name of their order; some prefer to call themselves Cordeliers, who are subdivided into the Coletes, the Minors, the Minims, and the Crutched; others prefer to be called Benedictines or Bernardines; while still others prefer the names Bridgetines, Augustinians, Williamists, or Jacobines—as if it were not enough to be called Christians. In short, all the different orders make sure that nothing in their lives will be uniform; nor is it so much their concern to be like Christ as it is to be unlike one another.

Many of them work so hard at protocol and at traditional fastidiousness that they think one heaven hardly a suitable reward for their labors; never recalling, however, that the time will come when Christ will demand a reckoning of that which he has prescribed, namely charity, and that he will hold their deeds of little account. One monk will then exhibit his belly filled with every kind of fish; another will profess a knowledge of over a hundred hymns. Still another will reveal a countless number of fasts that he has made, and will account for his large belly by explaining that his fasts have always been broken by a single large meal. Another will show a list of church ceremonies over which he has officiated so large that it would fill seven ships, while still another will brag that he hasn't touched any money in over sixty years unless he wore two pairs of gloves to protect his fingers. Another will take pride in the fact that he has lived a beggarly life as exampled by the filthiness and dirtiness of his hood, which even a sailor would not see fit to wear. Another will take glory in the fact that he has parasitically lived in the same spot for over fifty-five years. Another will exhibit his hoarse voice, which is a result of his diligent chanting; another, a lethargy contracted from his reclusive living; and still another, muteness as a result of his vow of silence. But Christ, interrupting their otherwise unending pleas will ask to himself, "Where does his new race of Jews come from? I recognize only one commandment that is truly mine and yet I hear nothing of it. Many years ago in the sight of all men I promised, in clear language, not through the use of parables, the inheritance of My Father to those who perform works of mercy and charity—not to those who merely wear hoods, chant prayers, or perform fasts. Nor do I reward those who acknowledge their own good works too much. Let those who think themselves holier than I, dwell in those six hundred heavens of Basilides, if they wish, or let them command those whose fastidious customs they have followed in the place of my commandments to build them a new heaven." Having heard these words and seeing that even sailors and teamsters are considered better company than they are, it should be interesting to see what looks they give each other! Yet they are, in the meantime, with my assistance, contented with their present hopes of happiness.

No one, however, even though isolated from public life, will dare to rebuke one of these monks, because through the confessional these men acquire the secrets of everyone. To be sure, they believe it a crime to publish these secrets, but they may accidentally divulge them when drinking heavily or when wishing to promote amusement by relating funny stories. The names, of course, are not revealed, because the stories are told by means of implications in most cases. In other words, if anyone offends the monks, the monks in turn will take revenge against the offender. They will reveal their enemies in public sermons by direct implications, so that everyone will know of whom they speak. And they will continue this malicious chatter until bribed to stop.

Show me any actor or charlatan you would rather watch than these monks as they drone through their sermons, trying to exemplify all the art of rhetoric that has been handed down through the ages. Good Lord! How wonderfully they gesture with their hands; how skillfully they pitch their voice; how cleverly they intone their sermons, throwing themselves about, changing facial expressions, and in the end leaving their audience in a complete state of confusion by their contradictory arguments. Yet this "art of rhetoric" is handed down with much ceremony from monk to monk, as if it required the greatest skill, craft, and ingenuity. It is forbidden for me to know this art, but I shall relate what I think are a few of its foundations. First, each oration is begun with an invocation, a device they have borrowed from the poets. Next, if charity is to be their topic, they commence their sermon with a dissertation on the Nile River in Egypt. Or they are contented to begin with Baal, the Babylonian snake god, if they intend to speak on the mystery of the cross. If fasting is their subject, they open with the twelve signs of the Zodiac; if they wish to expound faith, they initiate their sermon with the problem of squaring the circle.

I know of one notable fool—there I go again! I meant to say scholar—who was ready to expound the mystery of the Holy Trinity to a very distinguished assembly. Wishing to exhibit exceptional scholarship and to please the Divine in a special way, he embarked upon his lecture in an unheard-of manner—that is, he began by showing the relation of letters, syllables, and words; from there, he explained the agreement between nouns and verbs and nouns and adjectives. At once everyone became lost in amazement at this new approach and began to ask among themselves the question that Horace had once asked, "What is all this stink about?" As his oration progressed, however, he drew out this observation, that through the foregoing elements of grammar he could demonstrate the Holy Trinity so clearly that no mathematician could demonstrate it more understandably through his use of symbols in the sand. This fastidious monk had worked so hard on this one sermon for the previous eight months that he became blind as a mole afterward, all the keenness of his sight having given way to the sharpness of his mind. This man, to this day, however, does not regret the loss of his sight to any degree, because he believes it to have been a small price, indeed, to pay for so much glory.

I know of another monk of eighty years of age who was so scholarly that it was often said that Scotus, himself, was reborn in him. He expounded the mystery of the name of Jesus, showing with admirable subtlety that the letters of the name served to explain all that could be understood about Him. The fact that the name can be declined in three different cases—Jesus, Jesum, and Jesu—clearly illustrates the threefold nature of God. In one case the name ends with "s," this showing that He is the sum; in the second case it ends with "m," illustrating that He is the middle; and finally, in the third case we find the ending "u," this symbolizing that He is the ultimate. He amazed his audience even more when he treated the letters of the name mathematically. The name Jesus was equally divided into two parts with an s left in the middle. He then proceeded to point out that this lone letter was ש in the Hebrew language and was pronounced Schin, or Sin, and that furthermore this Hebrew letter was a word in the Scottish dialect that means *peccatum* (Latin for sin). From the above premises he declared to his audience that this connection showed that Jesus takes away the sins of the world. His listeners, especially the theologians, were so amazed at this new approach that some of them came near to being overtaken by the same mysterious force that transformed Niobe to stone; as for my reaction, I was more inclined to imitate shoddy Priapus, who upon witnessing the nocturnal rites of Canidia and Sagona fled from the spot. And I had reason to flee, too, for when did the Greek Demosthenes or Roman Cicero ever cook up such a rhetorical insinuation as that?

These great rhetoricians insisted that any introduction that had no explicit connection with the matter of the oration was faulty, and was used only by swineherds, who had mere nature as their guide. Nevertheless, these eminent preachers hold that their preamble, as they have named it, contains its rhetorical values only insofar as it has nothing to do with the matter of the discourse, so that the listener will be asking himself, "Now what is he getting at?"

As a third step, instead of a narration they substitute the hasty explanation of some verse from a gospel, when in fact this above all other things is the part that needs to be dwelt upon. As a fourth rule, they interpret some question of divinity through references to things that are neither in earth or in heaven. Here is where they reach the height of their theological and rhetorical ability in that they astound their audience by flowering their speech, when referring to other preachers, with such illustrious titles as Renowned Doctor, Subtle Doctor, Very Subtle Doctor, Seraphic Doctor, Holy Doctor, and Invincible Doctor. Next, they mystify their uneducated audience by their use of syllogisms, majors, minors, conclusions, corollaries, conversions, and other scholarly devices, playing on the ignorance of the crowd. And they consider all these things necessary and unique to their art.

There remains, however, one more act in which they exhibit the highest artistry. In this fifth act they interpret a silly, popular tale drawn, I suppose, from the *Speculum Historiale* or *Gesta Romanorum,* allegorically, tropologically, and anagogically. It is with this that they bring their chimera, the likes of which are unapproached even by Horace's "Humano capito, etc.," to a fitting end.

They profess that the opening of a speech should be in a soft, relaxed tone rather than begin boisterously. This they have learned from some supposed authorities, although I do not know which ones. Thus the monks begin their sermons so softly that they are unable to hear their own voices, as if it were grand to speak what no one is able to hear. They have also been told that when they wish to emotionally stimulate their audience they should pitch their voice in a shouting tone and that they should use exclamations. Therefore, they will, every once in awhile, when droning through some statement in a low voice, suddenly raise their voice into a furious roar, even though there is no occasion to do so. One could almost swear that the man was in need of medical attention, except that from the way that he carries on it is plain that nothing would be able to help him. Moreover, because of their belief that as the sermon proceeds it should become more vehement, you will notice that they sometimes bring their voice to an almost shouting tone, no matter whether the subject is important or not or whether it has any direct connection with the preceeding matter or not. And so, many times when they close their oration, it is apparent that their only reason for closing is that they are too breathless to utter anything else.

The last step that is necessary to be a good rhetorician, according to them, is to be able to humor the audience. This they strive for by sprinkling jests throughout their speeches. O Golden Aphrodite! They inject these witticisms into their orations with so much grace, polish, and pertinence that, as some people would say, "The ass seems to be at the lyre!" They also try a bit of satire, but these attempts founder because they are amusing rather than piercing to the thing they are satirizing; nor do these men capture their audience in any greater degree when they pretend to speak with sincerity and informality to them. One further thing; their performances are such that it might seem that they have been taking lessons from wandering players, although it must be said that they fall far short of their teachers. Yet these players and preachers bear so many resemblances that there can be no doubt that one of the two learned his trade from the other, whether it be the players from the preachers or vice versa. And yet the preachers encounter some—and here I get into my own field —who believe, upon hearing them, that they are the likes of Demosthenes or Cicero. Most of these gullible people are, it must be said, either women or merchants. These the preachers especially wish to please; because the merchants, when pleased, will reward the preacher with a small sum of their ill-gotten wealth, and the women, although in many cases having betrayed the clergy, are accustomed to seek the advice of these men when they are at outs with their husbands. I am sure that you can now see wherein these men are indebted to me, who with their fastidious formalities and charlatan preaching command a sort of despotism over mortal men and believe themselves to be Pauls or Antonies.

In truth, I am happy to leave these actors and charlatans, who are as unappreciative for my succor as they are insincere in their false pretensions to sanctity. It now pleases me to expound kings and the nobility of their courts who sincerely and candidly, as becomes gentlemen, worship me. For indeed, if these men had any wisdom at all, they would see that their lives are as cheerless and as undesirable as the lives of the clergymen. For let anyone reflect upon how much responsibility would rest on his shoulders if he were to be a righteous king or prince, and he will conclude that it is not worth perjuring himself or poisoning someone else to become a sovereign. He will see that, on becoming a sovereign, he would no longer have any time to spend on his private affairs. All his time and efforts would, rather, be devoted to the general well-being of his public. He would have to be very careful to follow all the laws, of which he is the author and executor, to the very nth degree. Since he would be exposed to the public at all times and would more or less be their guiding light, upon his actions and conduct would depend the well-being and salvation of the society of his country. In other words, by his actions he could bring about the destruction of his state. Other men's vices are not so widely known or deeply felt as are a sovereign's, because the latter is in such a position that if at any time he lapses into immorality or dishonesty, his example will spread so that in a short time his vice will have grown so as to include all his subjects in its clutches. The possession of a princely title also brings with it vices such as pleasure, liberty, adulation, and excess; so that he must be all the more earnest and diligent toward these pitfalls, lest becoming beguiled by these, he fails in his duty. Finally, to say nothing of treasons, enemies, and other perils, there is always a higher sovereign, in this case the king, who is more powerful than he and who will call him to account for even the least of his breaches of duty. I hold that if any prince weighed these and many other things in his mind— and he would, were he wise—he would neither be able to rest nor eat with any security or serenity.

But as the fact is, kings, with my advice, leave all these matters to the gods and occupy themselves with living extravagantly, while granting audiences only to those people who wish to approach them on pleasant matters, for these sovereigns cannot afford to let fears get a hold on them. They believe that to play the part of a monarch to the hilt is to hunt diligently, raise fine horses, sell high offices so as to realize a profit, and to fashion new schemes of draining the wealth of the citizens into their own pockets. All these schemes are carried out in due form under various official titles so that even though unjust they will seem to have some appearance of justness; they also make sure that these schemes are applied appealingly, so that they can secure not only the wealth but also the hearts of their people.

Show me a man such as princes commonly are: a man ignorant of the laws; an enemy of the public; intent upon private gain; taken to pleasure; against knowledge, liberty, and truth; never occupied with the safety of the state; and finally measuring all things in terms of his own desire and profit. Now first seat him on a golden chair, the chair symbolizing the union of all the virtues; next give him a crown adorned with precious gems, this symbolizing that he ought to surpass all others in every heroic quality. In addition to these hand him a scepter, an emblem of justice and of a devoted heart and soul; and last of all place on him a scarlet robe, symbolizing the love and fervent respect that he ought to have for the realm. If any prince would try to uphold these symbols, even if it meant giving up his life, then I am sure that he would have the honor to be ashamed of his depravity. He would fear that some satirist might turn this whole solemn affair into ridicule and sarcasm.

Now what shall I say about the noble courtiers? These men desire to be likened as God's foremost creatures, yet the fact is that no group of men is more sordid, more obsequious, more idiotic, or more contemptible than this set of men. One point in which they are as unaspiring as one could be is that, while they are happy to wear gold, jewels, and scarlet on their bodies, they leave to others the virtues and wisdom that accompany these symbols. They are contented with being able to speak of the king as "our master"; in knowing how to return a compliment in three words; in knowing on which occasion to use the titles of "Your Grace," "Your Lordship," and "Your Majesty"; in not knowing shame; and in having mastered the art of flattery with exceptional success. For these are the skills that the nobleman and courtier take a great deal of pride in. As for other skills, if you examine their ways of life, you will surely find them "mere Phaeacious, suitors of Penelope"—and I imagine that you know the rest of the verse, from hearing it so many times, better than I do. These men are accustomed to sleeping till noon every day, at which time a hired priest comes to their bedside and quickly runs through the morning prayers before they awaken. After they awaken they set in on their breakfast, which is no sooner finished than dinner is served. After dinner they proceed to amuse themselves with dice, checkers, cards, clowns, fools, whores, and general horseplay and nonsense—scattered throughout which is a round or two of drinks. Next comes supper, after which is not only one but many toasts. In this way their hours, days, months, years, and lives are dwindled away. As for myself, I enjoy watching their extravagant lives almost as much as eating a good meal; observing how every one of the ladies thinks her closeness to the gods is measured by the length of the trailing train of her dress; how the noblemen pass one another in order to stand the closest to Jove; and how each of the nobles is exalted in wearing a heavier chain around his neck, as if they were demonstrating their strength rather than their wealth.

Our popes, cardinals, and bishops have, for a long while now, diligently followed the example of the state and the practices of the princes, and have come near to beating these noblemen at their own game. If our bishops would but stop and consider what their white albs signify—namely, sincerity and a pure life in every way untainted; what is signified by their two-horned miter, the peaks of which are joined by a common knot—a perfect knowledge and understanding of the Old and New Testaments; what is meant by their wearing of gloves—the immaculate administration of the sacraments, untainted by any selfishness or self-concern; what their crozier symbolizes—their diligent and protective watch of the flock that they are charged with; and what is signified by the cross that is carried before them in processions—the victory of spiritual charity over carnal affections. If they would but contemplate these and other virtues, I am sure that it would be safe to say that they would not lead such troubled and shameful lives. But as it is they are kept too busy feeding themselves to think on these things; as for the care of their sheep, they delegate this duty to one of their subordinates (suffragans, as they call them) or to Christ Himself. Nor have they stopped to contemplate the title that they bear or to examine its meaning; bishop, meaning labor, diligence, and solicitude. Yet when it comes to pecuniary matters they truly act the part of a bishop to the hilt overseeing everything—and overlooking nothing.

If, in a similar manner, the cardinals would stop and consider the fact of their succession of the Apostles, they would realize that the same good deeds are expected of them as were expected of their predecessors; that they are stewards, not lords of spiritual affairs; and that soon they will be held accountable for all those things in which they should firmly trust and believe. It would do them a great deal of good, also, to consider the significance of their vestments and to ask themselves these questions. Does not the whiteness of the upper garment symbolize the purity and stainlessness of the heart and of the disjunction of the wearer from human wants and selfishness? Is not the scarlet or crimson color of the lower garments an emblem of a burning love and desire of God? What is the significance of the outer robe of his Exalted

Reverence? Do not its abundant folds serve another purpose than just to cover the mule of his worship, although they could just as easily cover a camel? Is it not a symbol of a charity sufficient enough to receive all men by its helpfulness through teaching, encouraging, chastising, cautioning, settling wars, defying evil sovereigns, and freely spending blood—not money alone—for the advancement of the fold of Christ? And finally, "What need do I, a needy apostle, have for all this ill-gotten money?" It is my belief that if they would stop and consider these questions, then they would not clamor after the bishopric, or, if they did get the office, they would lead a weary and pious life of the sort lived by the ancient Apostles.

As to the Supreme Pontiffs, if they would recall that they take the place of Christ and would attempt to imitate His poverty, tasks, doctrines, crosses, and disregard of safety; if they were even to contemplate the meaning of the name Pope —that is, Father—or of the title of Most Holy, then they would become the most humble and mortified of men. How many would then be willing to spend all their wealth and efforts in order to procure this position? If someone were foolish enough to procure it in this manner, would they further be willing to defend their position by the shedding of blood, by the use of poison, or by any other necessary means? Oh, how wisdom would upset their nefarious plans if it were to inflict them! Wisdom, did I say? Nay! Even a grain of salt, that salt spoken of by Christ, would be sufficient to upset their plans. It would lose them all their wealth, their honor, their belongings, their powers won by victories, their offices, dispensations, tributes, and indulgences. They would lose a great many horses, mules, and carts. And finally, they would lose a great many pleasures. (See how I have comprehended in a few words many marketsful, a great harvest, a wide ocean, of goods.) These forfeitures would be replaced by vigils, fasts, sorrows, prayers, sermons, education, weariness, and a thousand other bothersome tasks of the sort. We should also mention that a great many copyists, notaries, lobbyists, promoters, secretaries, muleteers, grooms, bankers, and pimps— I was about to add something more tender, though rougher on the ears, I am afraid—would be out of jobs. In other words, that large group of men that burdens—I beg your pardon, I meant to say adorns—the Holy Roman See would be done away with and would have to, as a result, resort to begging as a means of making a living. Those who are even worse, those very princes of the Church and guiding lights of the world, would become nothing more than a staff and a wallet. However, this action would be barbarous and abhorred.

Under the present system what work need be done is handed over to Peter or Paul to do at their leisure, while pomp and pleasure are personally taken care of by the Popes. They believe themselves to be readily acceptable by Christ with a mystical and almost theatrical finery. Thus, they proceed with pomp and with such titles as Beatitude, Reverence, and Holiness—between blessings and curses—to execute the role of a bishop. Miracles are considered to be antiquated and old-fashioned; to educate the people is irritating; to pray is a waste of time; to interpret Sacred Scripture is a mere formality; to weep is distressing and womanish; to live in poverty is ignominious; to be beaten in war is dishonorable and not worthy of one who insists that kings, no matter how great, bend and kiss His sacred foot; and to die is unpleasant, death on a cross—dishonor.

The only remaining powers invested with the pontiffs are the sacred benedictions of which Paul speaks. The popes are certainly liberal enough with these interdictions; excommunications; re-excommunications; anathemas; edicts, vivaciously depicting damnation; and the terrific lightning bolt of the bull, which by merely flickering submerges the souls of men below the floor of hell. And these powers are launched against no one with more vigor than against those who, under the devil's tutorship, dispute and deny the heritage of Peter's throne. Although Peter has been recorded as saying in the gospels, "We have left all and followed Thee," the popes of our time still insist on profanely attaching Peter's name to territories, cities, taxes, wages, and all money. These are the things they fight to uphold with fire, sword, and blood—inflamed by a zeal for Christ, of course. Having thus fought, they believe themselves to be justly called defenders of Christ, bragging that they have routed the enemies of the Church—as if the Church had any greater enemies than these charlatan popes who encourage the disregard of Christ, who depict Him as mercenary, who corrupt His teachings by forced interpretations, and who scandalize Him by their infamous lives.

Now the Christian Church was founded on blood, built on blood, and strengthened on blood, and yet the belief that one should defend one's own property by one's own means has been abandoned. Instead of defending the Church in the way that is necessary, the popes, neglecting all their other functions, make war their only duty. War! Because of its barbarity, it is befitting of beasts, not men; it is so violent that many scholars say that it is sent with evil purposes by the Furies. It is referred to as pestilent because it is accompanied by a general disregard of morals; as iniquitous because the worst bandits usually are its leaders; and as hypocritical because of its discord with Christ's teachings and principles. In these wars even old and feeble men receive a great deal of pleasure and satisfaction by upsetting the established laws, religion, and peace—so much so, in fact, that they assume the vitality of youth and are not troubled by the waste of countless numbers of lives in the war or exhausted by the work involved. There are many learned sycophants who refer to this obvious madness as zeal, piety, or fortitude, thus making it legal for a man to draw his sword, kill his brother with it, and still be considered to be of the greatest charity—charity, which, according to Christ, is due every man by his neighbor. I find it hard to decide at this point whether certain German bishops set or followed the example of these popes. Because these bishops, putting aside their robes and forgetting about benedictions and other such formalities, personally acted as the heads of armies; as if they considered the battlefield the only place where they could do repentance for their blackened souls without shame and with a suitable amount of pomp and decorum.

The priests feel that it is sacrilegious to be in a lesser state of holiness than their prelates, so that they too go to war in the best military manner—with swords, spears, stones, and other weapons. They use their right to tax as an excuse in entering these wars. How ingenious these men are to interpret from the writings of the ancients an article by which they convince their appalled audience that they owe more than their just tithes! They never stop to consider those many teachings in Scripture by which they are indebted to perform certain duties for the people. Nor do they recall that their shaven heads are symbols of a priestly disinterest in worldly desires and a devoted interest in spiritual matters. On the contrary, these men insist that they have carried out their responsibilities when they have recited those little prayers. These, however, make me doubt whether even God hears or understands them, since they are barely audible to the priests themselves, who are still not able to understand them even though they repeat them constantly. The priests may also be paralleled with the ill-reputed in this way: they both anticipate profiteering and both remain up to date concerning the laws and restrictions on this subject. If there is any responsibility to be borne, they assign it to the shoulders of someone else, just as men toss a ball to one another. Or just as princes transmit to their ministers the ruling of some part of their realm, and these ministers, in turn, to one of their subordinates, so also do priests leave to the people the pursuit of piety. These common people then pass it back to those that they call the "ecclesiastics," as if they bore no moral responsibilities by merit of their baptismal vows in the pursuit of this virtue. The "ecclesiastics," who prefer to be called secular, as if dedicated to the world instead of to Christ, then delegate this burden to the regulars; the regulars to the monks; the more eminent monks to the less eminent ones; and both of these to the mendicants; and lastly the mendicants put it off to the Carthusians, among whom piety is such a hidden virtue that it is next to impossible to detect it in any degree. In this same manner proceeds the Apostolic responsibilities of the Pope, whose time is entirely engulfed in his personal pecuniary harvests, to the bishops, who in turn relegate them to the pastors, and thence to the vicars, from which they are laid upon the mendicant friars. These friars, however, return them to the shepherds of the fold, or to those who rob their people under the pretense of sanctity.

But I do not intend to expose fully the lives of the popes and priests, because I am afraid it would resemble a satire rather than a eulogy. And let no one think that I reproach good clergymen when I praise bad ones. I have briefly told of these things so as to illustrate that man can be happy only when he possesses my favor and has been admitted to my mysteries. This can be shown by the fact that Fortune, the directrix of human affairs, favors me while she has always been very hostile to the wise, because she gives all her rewards to fools, even while they are asleep. To prove this, you need only to have heard of Timotheus, of whom it is said in the proverb, "Fish came to his net when he was asleep." Or in the saying, "The owl flies." As concerns the wise, on the other hand, these proverbs are typical: "He was born in the fourth month," or "He has the horse of Seius," or "gold of Taulouse." But I shall now refrain from proverbializing for fear that I detract from the complications of my good friend, Erasmus.

I shall now get to my point. Fortune is rewarding only to those who are not sagacious, to those who are of the rasher sort, and to those who would rather live by the saying, "The die is cast." Wisdom commonly makes men scrupulous, which explains why these men are usually to be found in hunger, poverty, and smoke; they live unheeded and inglorious as hated men. The fool on the other hand, seems to live in a profusion of wealth, and sometimes as the head of state. In short it is the fools that flourish in every way. If we think ourselves fortunate, then, when we please princes or when we even come into contact with these such favorites of mine, then what should we think less of than wisdom? For, from the wise man's point of view, what could be more damning than such fawning? If a merchant wishes to be wealthy, how could he meet with success if he feels a distaste for perjury, if he becomes embarrassed when caught in a lie, or if he is in any way scrupulous concerning larceny or usury? How inconvenienced he would be if he were in such a situation! If anyone is in genuine want of wealth or ecclesiastical power, better he be an ass or a buffalo than a wise man. If you are in desire of a certain sort or pleasure, then let it be known that the young ladies (a very important and instrumental part of society) are much more inclined to give their hearts to fools than to wise men. They flee from these latter ones as if they were fleeing from scorpions. As a final point, whoever wishes to make life a bit gayer and livelier will exclude the wise man from his life and will rather admit any other animal than he. In short, whenever you mix among the popes, princes, judges, magistrates, your friends, your enemies, the great, and the humble, you will discover that all disputes and other matters are resolved through the exchange of money; since the wise have no regard for money, here is all the more reason to avoid them.

Although I could continue my praises indefinitely, it is necessary that my oration come to an end—sometime. And so I shall end it—but first let me show briefly how many authors have illustrated me in their writings (it could also be said in their daily lives), so that I can now infer that I please other people as well as myself. The lawyers will not be able to slander me now by saying, "nothing is alleged," because, following the lawyers' example, I shall free my proofs from legal difficulties by admitting that they contain nothing to the point but rather to the wit.

In the first place I think that everyone is in agreement with the familiar adage, "If you don't have a thing, then simulate it." Also, along this same line is the maxim that children are usually taught, "To pretend to be a fool is sometimes to be of the highest wisdom." The worth of folly can readily be seen in that the mere imitation of it (as seen above) is regarded of highly by intelligent men. But more clearly, does not the philosophy of Epicurus bid us "to mix in folly with our councils," although he rather disrespectfully adds the word brevem (a little)? In another place he declares, "It is sweet to play the fool in season." And in yet another place he affirms that he would rather "be giddy and taken as a dolt, than be wise and fret." We also find that Telemachus, in Homer, is praised in every possible way, except that he is now and then referred to as "silly"; or that many tragic dramatists refer to boys and youth in terms of this same word, as if it were a lucky omen. And again, is not the immortal Iliad a mere tale of the quarrels of foolish kings and their foolish peoples? Or is not Cicero's commendation, "Everything is full of fools," not worthy of consideration? Are we to also disregard what we have been taught, that as anything becomes more widespread, i.e. goodness, it becomes greater?

However, perhaps the authority of these writers is disregarded by Christians. We shall, therefore, illustrate our argument through the testimony of Sacred Scripture, as learned scholars frequently do to strengthen their points. Let us first say that we forge ahead in this way with the permission and good wishes of the theologians. Next, since we undertake such a difficult task and since it would not be worth having Muses travel all the way from Helicon to here, especially inasmuch as this business is out of their line, I think it suitable to call upon the soul of Scotus to depart from his beloved Sorbonne so that it can come and instill within me theological properties. I only ask that it remain for a season, after which it can return to wherever it pleases, even to the dog if such be its wish. I realize that to attempt to interpret Sacred Scripture without Scotus is to tread among thorns, while even with him the path will be pricklier than a porcupine or hedgehog, but such is my wish. My greatest boon, of course, would be if it were possible for me to assume the power, intelligence, and likenesses of God, so that my words would not be doubted. But as it is now I fear that you will profess me as a thief, charging that I have clandestinely plundered the private documents and papers of the Divine, because of the theological knowledge that I possess by virtue of the help of Scotus. I cannot, however, see why my knowledge of these theological answers should seem so strange, because I have been in closest contact with the Divine for a long time now. You may recall that the god Priapus learned Greek merely by listening to his master read; or that the cock in Lucian learned to speak by virtue of his constant proximity with men. Why should I not then be able to learn theology through my association with the Divine?

Now if the auguries are favorable, let us return to our discourse. Ecclesiastes writes in the ninth chapter: "The number of fools is infinite." By this expression does he not seem to include the generality of mankind, with a few exceptions whom I have never encountered? In his tenth chapter Jeremiah states this even more ingenuously when he says: "Every man is made foolish in his own wisdom." It is to God alone that he attributes wisdom, relegating foolishness to mankind. A little bit before this he says: "Let no man glory in his wisdom." Why, oh excellent Jeremiah, do you not wish man to glory in his wisdom? "Because," he would answer, "he has no wisdom." But let us turn again to Ecclesiastes. When he writes, "Vanity of vanities, all is vanity," what else does he mean other than what I have just told you, namely, that human life is nothing but a sport of folly? He reiterates the sentiment of Cicero, over whose great name is written, "Everything is full of fools." When the wise Ecclesiasticus said, "The fool is changed as the moon," but, "The wise man is permanent as the sun," what was his intention but to demonstrate that the entire human race is foolish, and the attribute of wisdom becomes God alone? Moon is always interpreted as meaning human nature, and the sun, the source of light, signifies God. Thus Christ in the Gospels forbids that anyone be called good other than God. If a man who is not wise is a fool, and whoever is good is thereby wise, as the Stoics maintain, it is quite obvious that folly embraces all mankind. Solomon in Chapter 15 states, "A Fool delights in his folly," thereby clearly acknowledging that without folly nothing in life is sweet. The other text points to the same thing: "He who increases knowledge, increases sorrow, and in much wisdom there is much grief." Does not the famous Preacher openly confess the same in Chapter 7: "The heart of the wise is the residence of sadness, but the heart of the fool pursues happiness." He did not consider it enough to have learned wisdom without a knowledge of me. If you cannot trust what I say, then look to what he wrote in Chapter 1: "I give my heart to know wisdom, and to know madness and folly." Note that the advantage is with Folly, since he places her in the last place. Ecclesiastes wrote that, and you are aware that in the ecclesiastical order it is for him who is first in dignity to take the last place. At least this is what the Gospel requires.

Ecclesiasticus, whoever he was, makes this quite clear in Chapter 44. However, I absolutely refuse to quote him unless you follow the Platonic method of dialogue and answer me. Or is it better to conceal precious things than things that are vulgar and cheap? Why don't you answer that question? Even if you are hedging, the Greek proverb, "We put refuse on the back porch," will answer for you. If you are inclined to turn up your nose at this quotation, know that Aristotle, the god of our masters, uses it. But which of you is such a fool as to leave gems and gold lying in the streets? None of you, I am sure. You keep them in secret corners and well-guarded chests. The filth you throw outside. If what is more precious is concealed and what is vile is put in the open, is it not clear that the wisdom which Ecclesiasticus forbids us to hide is worth less than folly, which he tells us to conceal? Now you are ready for his own words: "Better is the man who hides his folly than he who hides his wisdom." What about that section in the Scripture that attributes honesty of soul to the fool, while the wise man thinks there is no one like himself? This is how I understand what Ecclesiastes wrote in Chapter 10: "A fool walking along the way, being a fool, considers all men to be fools." Is this not an amazing kind of honesty, to hold all equal with oneself in a world where a person shares his compliments with all? It was for this reason that King Solomon was not ashamed of this name, when he said in Chapter 30, "I am the most foolish of men."

Paul, the teacher of the gentiles, in writing to the Corinthians openly admitted this name. "I speak as a fool," he said. And again, "I am more than a fool." This is as if it were a disgrace to be outdone in folly.

But meanwhile certain pedants raise a clamor, eager to pierce, as if they were crows, the eyes of theologians, covering with their annotations, as with smoke, the commentaries of others. Of this group I would mention, by way of honor, Erasmus. For if he doesn't stand in first place, he is certainly in second. What a foolish citation, worthy of Folly. The meaning of the Apostles is far from what you dream up. It was not his intention that these words be considered more foolish than the rest. When he said, "Are they ministers of Christ? So am I," he made himself equal to the others. Correcting himself, he adds, "I am more," and thus not only places himself on their level in the ministry, but a little above it. To avoid offending them with an air of arrogance, he uses the pretext of foolishness, meaning that it is the privilege of fools alone to speak the truth without offense.

I leave whatever Paul meant by this for the theologians to dispute. I follow the large, fat, crass theologians, approved by God, with whom the majority choose to err, rather than understand the trilinguists. Not one among them considers these pedants as more than crows. I especially say this since a certain well-known theologian, whose name I prudently omit lest the pedants continually gibe him with the reference to the ass and the Lyra, used the passage, "I speak as a fool; I am more," to begin a tract in a theological fashion. He used it to begin a new chapter in his book, and what only the highest dialect could accomplish, he began a new section with it. Here is how he interpreted the words: "I speak as a fool. That is, if I appear somewhat foolish in making myself equal to those pseudo-prophets, I must appear more foolish in making myself superior to them." A little later, as though he was oblivious to what he had said before, he comes up with another interpretation.

But why should I be so anxious to protect myself with the example of one person, when the theologians are allowed to stretch heaven, that is, the Scriptures, as a sheepskin. If we can give credence to Jerome, who knew five languages, there are some contradictory words in Paul. When he spoke to the Athenians, he twisted what he read on the altar into an argument for the Christian faith, omitting what was not for his purpose and selecting only two from the end, "to the Unknown God." The actual inscription reads, "To the Gods of Asia, Europe, and Africa, and to the Unknown Gods, and the Gods of Strangers." I feel that the sons of theologians follow his example today, when they accommodate for their own purposes four or five words out of context, or even change in meaning. They do this even though the words that precede and follow haven't the same significance, or are even opposite in meaning. Theologians do this with such impertinence that even our lawyers envy them. Following this great master of theology—I almost mentioned his name, but I fear the Greek proverb—there is no limit to their false exegesis. He has squeezed from Luke words so opposed to the spirit of Christ as fire is to water. Take the time when the final danger threatened, a period when clients are desirous of being especially close to their patrons, in order to defend them with all of their resources. Then Christ, attempting to dissuade his followers from any idea of such a defense, queried them concerning their needs when He had sent them forth unequipped for traveling, with neither sandals to protect their feet against stones and thorns, nor with money to keep from going hungry. Where they denied that anything was missing, He added: "But now whoever has a bag, let him take it and also a moneybag, and whosoever does not have a sword, let him sell his coat and buy a sword." Since the entire doctrine of Christ inculcates nothing but meekness, tolerance, and contempt of life, who cannot but see what He is saying here is that his representative should be even further disarmed, abandoning not only sandals and moneybags, but also their coats, in order to spread the Gospel, completely stripped and unimpeded. They were to equip themselves only with a sword, not that of robbers and parricides, but the sword of the spirit that enters the inmost recesses of the heart and severs from it all that is not of piety.

Now, I pray you, see how this renowned theologian twists these words. "Sword," he takes to mean a defense against persecution; "bag," to mean an adequate provision of supplies. It was as if Christ had sung a palinode of his former instruction, changing his mind and sending his emissaries out less royally equipped than they should be. Or it appeared that He had become oblivious to his earlier statements that they are blessed who are afflicted with reproaches, contumelies, and humiliations, and had forbidden them to resist evil since the meek are blessed. Or that he had forgotten also his call to the example of the sparrows and lilies and was now so opposed to their proceeding without sword that he urged them to purchase one, preferring their nakedness to the lack of a belted weapon. Just as the expression "sword" implies whatever is necessary to resist force, the expression "purse" is meant to include whatever is necessary for life. And in this way the interpreter of the Divine Mind has the Apostles go forth to preach the Crucified, armed with lances, crossbows, slings, and guns. He weighs them down with suitcases, satchels, and handbags, thinking they always depart from their lodgings without having eaten breakfast. It is of no concern to this interpreter that He who ordered that a sword be purchased a little while later rebukingly commanded that the sword be put up. Nor does it bother him that there is no record of the Apostles ever having swords and shields against the attacks of the pagans, although certainly according to his interpretation they would have done so.

There was another whose name, not really a bad one, I will nonetheless out of respect omit, who took the tense mentioned by Habakkuk, "The skins of the land of the Midians will be shaken," to mean the skin of St. Bartholomew who was skinned alive. Recently I was present myself at a theological discussion. (I attend them quite frequently.) Here the question whether a heretic should be burned or refuted by argument was posed. One old gent, whose arrogance identified him as a theologian, vociferously claimed that this matter is clearly stated by St. Paul, who says: "A person who remains a heretic after a first and second admonition, reject." After he had repeated this phrase a few times, it became apparent that he was taking *devita* (reject) to mean *de vita*, or remove from life. There was a ripple of laughter, but to some the answer seemed quite sound theologically. This lawyer of Tenedos, an unanswerable commentator, continued the argument. Take this case. The Scriptures: "Thou shall not allow a witch (*maleficum*) to live. Every heretic is a witch (*maleficus* meaning bad or evil), ergo . . ." His audience went along with him, admiring his mental gymnastics. It did not occur to any of them that this injunction is directed against sorcerers, enchanters, and magicians, whom the Hebrews in their language term מכשפים, which we translate as *malefici* or witches. If we interpret it as he did, we would be obliged to consider fornication and drunkenness as worthy of capital punishment.

However, it seems foolish to me to continue this; there are so many examples that the volumes of Chrysippus or Didymus could not contain them. At any rate, I hope you will consider that if such things are permitted among expert theologians, then I ought to be given a little leeway, being a kind of false theologian myself, in the matter of lack of precision in citations and quotes. Now I finally return to St. Paul. "Would to God that you could bear with some small amount of my folly." And again: "Accept me as a fool"; and "I do not speak according to God but as if in foolishness." In another place he says: "We are fools for Christ's sake." From a writer of this stature you hear so many great commendations of folly. What he actually does is openly to teach that folly is necessary for the good of the town: "Let him that seems to be wise among you become a fool, that he may be wise." And in Luke Christ calls the two disciples He met on the highway "fools." I do not find it out of the ordinary that Paul ascribes a certain foolishness to God Himself. "The foolishness of God," he says, "is wiser than men." It is true, Origen in his commentary disagrees that this foolishness is the same as the opinions of men as seen, for example, in the expression: "The preaching of the Cross is to them that perish foolishness."

Yet why should I be so anxious about this when Christ Himself in the mystical psalms gives evidences of this teaching? Addressing the Father, He says for all to hear: "Thou knowest my foolishness." I feel that is the real reason why fools are so pleasing to God. We see a similar situation reflected in the actions of great princes. They tend to look with suspicion and hatred upon those who appear too clever. Julius Caesar suspected and hated Brutus and Cassius, whereas he had no fear of the drunken Antony. Nero was suspicious of Seneca, Dionysius of Plato. The great take delight in the more stupid and simple souls. Thus Christ detests and condemns those wise men who depend upon their own prudence. Paul offers evidence of this when he says "God has chosen the foolish things of the world," and "It has pleased God to save the world by foolishness," since it could not be restored by wisdom. God indicates this clearly when He speaks through the mouth of the Prophet, "I will destroy the wisdom of the wise and I will reject the prudence of the prudent." Again, He gives thanks that the mystery of salvation is concealed from the wise but revealed to the children, that is to say, the foolish. For the Greek for children is νηπίοις, and is generally used in opposition to the "wise." We see the same thing frequently in the Scriptures when He attacks the Pharisees and the Scribes and the doctors of the law and defends the ignorant crowd. What else does the expression "Woe to you Scribes and Pharisees" mean other than, "Woe to you who are wise"? He seems to take His greatest delight in little children, women, and fishermen. In the animal kingdom he preferred those who were most removed in nature from foxlike cunning. Although He could have ridden a lion without danger, He preferred to ride upon a donkey. The Holy Spirit came down from heaven in the guise of a dove, rather than of an eagle or a hawk. The Holy Scripture gives ample mention to deer, fawns, and lambs. In addition, Christ terms those who are destined to immortal life "sheep." There is no other creature more foolish. Aristotle in his *History of Animals* writes of the "manners of sheep," which because of their stupidity has become a customary expression for the dimwitted and foolish. Yet Christ professes to be the shepherd and takes delight in having John point Him out as "the Lamb of God." The apocalypse has many references to this term.

What else do these expressions invoke other than the idea that mortals, even the pious, are fools? They point to the fact that Christ, although He was the wisdom of the Father, nonetheless was made foolish, taking on the nature of mankind, in order to save us from our foolishness. In the same manner He was made to be sin, in order to heal the sinner. No other means than the foolishness of the Cross was chosen by Him to heal. The Apostles whom He chose were weak and stupid and to them He recommended foolishness rather than wisdom. He called their attention to the example of children, lilies, mustard seed, and sparrows, things lacking in sense and foolish, existing on nature alone with neither art nor concern. He forbade them to worry about what they should answer to civil magistrates and to concern themselves with time and its changes. In short, He urged them to trust not in their own wisdom but to depend entirely upon Him. For the same purpose God the Divine Architect forbade eating of the tree of knowledge, as if knowledge were the poison of happiness. Paul disapproves of knowledge as something that puffs up and harms. St. Bernard follows him in interpreting *The Mountain of Knowledge* as the location of Lucifer's headquarters.

Certainly it seems that this argument should not be omitted, namely, that foolishness is so esteemed in heaven that it brings about a forgiveness of its errors, whereas nothing is forgiven wisdom. Thus it is that those who may have used prudence as an excuse for sinning find that foolishness is the excuse they use when begging pardon. If I recall correctly, Aaron in the book of Numbers prayed to God asking forgiveness of his sister: "I pray, my master, that you lay not this sin, which we have committed foolishly, to our charge." Saul says the same thing when asking pardon from David, "For it is evident that I have acted foolishly," as if his request would not be granted unless he pleaded folly and ignorance. This is borne out even more forcefully in the case of Christ praying on the cross for His enemies, "Father, forgive them for they know not what they do." No other excusing pretext was used but imprudence. Paul, in the same way, wrote to Timothy: "But therefore I have obtained the mercy of God, because being ignorant I acted in unbelief." "Acting in ignorance" means nothing other than "acting foolishly rather than maliciously." "But I obtained therefore the mercy of God" has no other meaning than "I should not have obtained it except that I was made pardonable by the excuse of folly." The mystical psalmist bears me out in this, although I forgot to mention this in the proper place: "Remember not the sins of my youth and my ignorances." You hear him speak of two excuses, youth, with whom I am a constant companion, and ignorance mentioned in the plural so that the tremendous power of folly can be understood.

But lest I pursue what is infinite, let me sum up. The whole of the Christian religion seems to have a certain relationship with some kind of folly but fails to agree at all with wisdom. If you would like proof of this, take a look at children, old people, women, and fools and see how they, more than others, take great pleasure in the things of religion. They seem to have a natural impulse to stand closer to the altar. Take the example of the first founders of religion. Embracing simplicity they became the most severe enemies of learning. And, finally, what fool could possibly act more foolishly than those whom the ardor of religion has totally consumed? They throw away their wealth, they neglect injuries, permit themselves to be deceived, fail to discriminate between friend and foe, shrink from pleasure, and cram themselves with hunger, vigils, tears, labors, contumelies. They prefer death to life and, in short, seem to have grown impervious to sensation and live as if their souls no longer dwelt in their bodies. What is this other than insanity? It gives credence to the fact that the Apostles appeared drunk on new wine and Paul seemed mad in the eyes of the Judge Festus. Now that I've played the lion, I'll point out also that the happiness of Christians sought after with so much effort is in effect nothing more than insanity and folly. God forbid that these words offend you. Give your attention to the main argument.

In the first place Christians agree in many respects with the Platonists in that they hold that the soul is submerged and tied down with earthly chains. It is so impeded by what is crass that it hardly has a chance to contemplate or enjoy the truth. It is for this reason that Plato defined philosophy as the contemplation of death, because like death it leads the mind away from visible and corporeal things. As long as the soul uses the physical organs only, it is called sane; when, however, breaking its bonds, it attempts to assert its liberty, breaking away, as it were, from its imprisonment, it is called insane. When this condition is due to some physical ailment, then there is no doubt that it is called insanity. Yet we see people so afflicted, predict the future, understand foreign languages hitherto unknown, and give every evidence of some divine quality. There can be no doubt that now that the mind is somewhat liberated from the contagion of the body it begins to exercise its native abilities. We see the same thing in the case of those who are near death. They speak, as if inspired, of things beyond the ordinary. If this happens as a result of studied piety, though not identical with insanity, it is nonetheless so close to it that most will consider it madness. This is particularly true since only a few unimportant individuals stand apart in this respect from the common herd in their way of life.

In my opinion, what happened in the cave of Plato's myth, where he who escaped told the others bound within that the outside held realities rather than shadows, is the fate of most men. Just as they continued to believe in the shadow, thinking him deceived, so he thought them mad to be captivated by such an error. The masses do the same thing in admiring only what is corporeal and holding all else as being almost lacking in existence. Religious individuals take the opposite position and are being wrapped up in the invisible to the detriment of the physical. The majority of mankind attributes the greatest importance to riches, bodily comforts, and finally the soul, which many of them do not even believe in, as it is not seen with the eyes. The pious agree in directing their efforts first toward God, the purest of all existence, and in the second place, in what comes closest to Him, namely the soul. The care of the body they neglect. Money they disdain as husks and avoid. If they are obliged to engage in money matters, they do so unwillingly, possessing as if they did not possess.

We might point to some particular differences in the levels

of difference between these two types of people. Although all the senses have a certain association with the body, some of them are more crass, as, for example, touch, hearing, sight, smell, and taste, while others are less closely tied up with the body, as the memory, intellect, and the will. Whichever of these receives attention grows accordingly. The pious, since they aim primarily at what is almost alien to the crass senses, are numbed and as it were stunned in what is sensual. On the contrary, the ordinary person gravitates toward them. Thus it is we read of holy men who have mistakenly drunk oil instead of wine. Considering once again the impulses of the soul we find that some have a greater contact with the body, as, for example, sex, love of food, sleep, anger, pride, and envy. These the pious wage a constant war against, whereas the vulgar crowd considers that without them life has no real existence. Then there are other affections that have a sort of middle classification, being sort of natural inclinations, as the love of parents, children, friends, or relatives. The ordinary person values these, but the pious attempt to banish them insofar as possible from the mind. They evaluate them only in terms of the higher part of the soul. They love a parent not as a parent, for he produced only the body and that through God, but rather as a good man impressed with the imprint of the Greatest Mind. This they call the highest good beyond which nothing is to be loved or striven after. With this as their rule, they evaluate all of life's other offices and either scorn that which is visible or prefer what is invisible to it.

They say that in the case of the sacraments and in other pious practices there are two elements, one physical, the other spiritual. In the case of fasting, for example, they do not follow the crowd in holding that the fast is just a matter of abstaining from food or flesh, but includes also a refraining from evil inclinations, pride, and anger. Thus the soul freed from the burden of the body will rise to a participation and enjoyment of celestial tastes. With regard to the Eucharist, they attach little value to its physical reception unless what it symbolizes takes place in the soul. The death of Christ that is represented must tame, extinguish, and, as it were, bury their evil inclinations so that they arise with a newness of life and become one with Him as well as with their fellow man. This is the meditation of the religious person. The common crowd, on the contrary, looks to the Mass only in terms of being close to the altar, hearing the words, and seeing the ceremonies. There are many other examples of this contrast wherein he who is spiritual abandons his association with the corporeal and is attracted to what is eternal, invisible, and spiritual. Because of this contrast between the pious and the vulgar, each appears to the other to be insane, although in my own opinion the insanity is better attributed to the pious. I think this will be more clear if I, as I promised, will demonstrate that their highest good is in itself a kind of insanity. Let us imagine that Plato had this in mind when he wrote that "the insanity of lovers is the happiest of all." He who loves vehemently no longer lives in himself but in what he loves, and his joy is in proportion to his withdrawal from self and his preoccupation with what is outside himself. When the soul meditates on traveling without the use of its limbs, this is certainly insanity. This explains the expressions, "He is not with us," "He has found himself," "He is himself again." The more perfect the love, the greater the madness.

Therefore, what is this future life of heaven toward which the pious aspire with so much endeavor? It consists in the first place of an absorption of the body by the spirit, accomplished the more easily as the spirit is now in its own kingdom and is furthermore by reason of its purgations during life adapted to this transformation. Then the spirit will be in a marvelous manner absorbed by the Highest Mind, more powerful than the infinity of its parts. In this way the entire man will be outside of himself, and his happiness will be due to no other fact than that, so placed, he will share in the Highest Good which draws all to Itself. Although this happiness is perfected only when the souls are rejoined to their bodies, yet since in this mortal life there is, for the pious, a meditation and foreshadowing of this, they occasionally have a foretaste of the reward to come. Even though this is but an infinitesimal drop by comparison with the flowing fountain of eternal happiness, yet it surpasses all corporeal pleasures even where they are combined into one vast pleasure. To this extent, does the spiritual surpass the corporeal and the invisible the visible? This is what the prophet refers to when he says, "Eye has not seen, nor ear heard, nor has it entered into the heart of man the things which God hath prepared for them that love Him." And this is certainly that part of Folly that will not be taken away by the transformation of life but will be perfected. And this is why those who are permitted to have a foretaste of this, and they are very few, suffer from something akin to madness. They speak in a manner that is not quite coherent, not in the ordinary manner but with meaningless sounds. Their facial expressions change from joy to sorrow, they weep and laugh and, in short, are outside themselves. When they return to themselves, they admit they have no knowledge of where they have been, whether in the body or out of it, whether waking or sleeping. They have no memory of what they heard or saw or did, as though in a dream, yet this they do know—that they were most happy in this ecstatic state. They regret this return to their senses and prefer nothing more than going back to this state of madness. And this is but a small sampling of the future happiness.

It seems that I have forgotten myself and transgressed the bounds. If anything I have said seems too impertinent or loquacious, consider that it is Folly and a woman who has spoken. Meanwhile, you may recall the Greek proverb, "Even a fool often speaks opportunely," unless you exclude women from this. I perceive you are expecting me to sum this up in an epilogue. I hope you are not so foolish as to suppose that after this mélange I can remember anything I have said. There is an old saying, "I hate a drinking companion with a memory." Here is a new one: "I hate a student with a memory." Therefore, to your health, cheers, live and drink, O most celebrated devotees of Folly.

Τέλος

THE COMPLAINT OF PEACE

Few of the works of Erasmus have enjoyed a more perduring popularity than *The Complaint of Peace*. Over the centuries wars and rumors of wars have enriched its significance. In a world of today that has more and more the aspects of an armed camp, when garrisons encompass the globe and the economy of every country is strained to the breaking point in the increased tempo of the arms race, its message is of even greater importance. Europe of the early sixteenth century, in spite of the optimism of the Renaissance philosophers, was as much preoccupied with war as any time in its history. Few men had a wider knowledge of this preoccupation than the mild scholar of Rotterdam, and few viewed it with greater anxiety. Travels and study in France, Italy, Germany, and England had brought him into personal contact with the elite of all the great powers. Few were more sincerely convinced that a universal peace based upon the spirit of the Gospels was necessary if Europe was not to be involved in a violent blood bath.

There is a prophetic note in Erasmus' unheeded plea for peace, as the religious strife of the following century was to prove. The antagonisms between Hapsburg and Valois that had been intermittently disrupting Europe for over a decade gave no indication of lessening. Maximilian's dream of a world monarchy uniting the papacy and the empire in a personal union was as fantastic and unrealistic as the French promise to lead a Crusade against the Turks. Spain was torn with rivalries between Castilians and Aragonese. England was on the verge of a continental war policy that was to eventually ruin its economy. The German Estates were disrupted with peasant revolts and a recalcitrant knighthood. In much of Italy the *condottieri* blocked any real hope for peace. Gone was the hope of neutrality that was born of the Alliance of 1513 between England, Aragon, and the Emperor. The Peace of Paris in 1515 had failed to terminate the troubles in the Netherlands. The Treaty of Noyon in the summer of 1516, although it involved all of the important nations of the West, including the papacy, depended upon conditions that few of the participants had any intention of fulfilling.

This was the political situation that formed the background for *The Complaint of Peace*. It can be listed along with the *Institutio Principis Christiani* as the most important political works that Erasmus composed during the period he enjoyed the title of Councilor to Prince Charles, later Emperor of the Holy Roman Empire. A comparison of either of these works with the contemporary *Prince* of Machiavelli is extremely revealing. Unlike the famous Florentine, who assumes that politics is an end in itself, Erasmus continually reiterates the conviction that the whole purpose of political science is ethical. He follows the great tradition of Aristotle, Plato, and Aquinas in placing its chief concern at the moral level of individual and collective action. The common good is the determining factor for all public effort on the part of princes. Few writers were more aware of the miseries of the common man as the result of the personal greed of princes than Erasmus. His famous Horatian passage to the French humanist Budaeus, "when the kings go mad, the people are smitten," [1] epitomizes his position on tyranny. Whereas Machiavelli writes entirely of the mechanics of government whereby states may be strong, Erasmus speaks of the inner spirit of society, comparing it to the relationship between the soul and the body. The inequality of man and the resulting need for cooperation creates a demand for peace and concord as an integral element in the structure of society. If for Machiavelli political and military interests are entirely divorced from religious, moral, and social considerations, Erasmus finds that these represent the entire aim and purpose of political activity. In assigning a sacral function to the political order, Erasmus sees its chief purpose as the mtaintenance of peace in civil society, a peace that in turn abets the members of Christ's Body, the Church.

The reader will no doubt be struck by the repeated attacks in the *Querela Pacis* on the militarism of certain of the higher clergy. It is one of the great ironies of history that the Church, whose advent was announced with an angelic proclamation of peace, had in the course of the Middle Ages become identified with the great military movements of the age. The Crusades were inspired, directed, and fostered by the papacy, and the idea of a *bella cruciata* lingered on under papal direction well into modern times. It was, in fact, this papal direction that gave the Crusades their specific character, and it was largely the members of the mendicant orders who, century after century, stirred Christians to armed intervention in Moslem territories. Nor was the audience of

[1] "Τῶν μωρῶν βασιλέων καὶ λαῶν" [Horatium Ep. 12, 14], *E. E.* III, p. 559.

Erasmus totally oblivious of the great deeds or the warrior bishops of Imperial Germany's past, men like Renald of Dassel and Dietrich of Weid. One of the essential elements of early feudal warfare had been the levies of troops supplied by monastic foundations, and the liturgical veneer that the Church had given chivalry encouraged rather than diminished the pursuit of arms. The recent memory of the armored figure of the late Pope Julius II personally leading his troops to the attack had more of the elements of a tragedy than a comedy.

While Eramus personified peace, Cardinal Ximenes of Spain directed his galleys to the coasts of Africa and Italy and the wily Cardinal Wolsey of England plotted a war policy for England that was to bring its very economy to its knees. The "Church militant" had acquired a meaning quite alien to the original significance of the term.

The little work was first printed in 1517, and although Erasmus could not have had knowledge of the fateful events in the realm of religion that that year introduced, yet there is little doubt that had its maxims been listened to, the upheaval that was to involve Europe in a series of religious wars for a century might well have been avoided. There is a note of the prophetic in Erasmus' pointing to the dangers of politically motivated matrimonial liaisons. They disturbed Europe until recent times. The list of foreign cardinals who directed the armies of Bourbon France for two centuries to come reads more like a consistory than the bellicose policymakers of the eldest daughter of the Church.

In short, the *Querela Pacis* finds Erasmus centuries ahead of his time in condemning the terrible evil of international homicide, the participation of Church leaders in war, and above all in voicing the belief that no Christian should remain indifferent to the problems of justice, peace, and freedom among nations. There is the same recurring theme of his earlier writings—a blending of the peace ideals of Hellenic and Roman society with the Christian love ethic of the Sermon on the Mount. Yet as far as his final aims were concerned it was beyond the grasp of most of his readers.

The Complaint of Peace

(QUERELA PACIS)
1517

Summa nostrae religionis pax est et unanimitas.

The whole purpose of our religion is peace and unanimity.

Letter to Archbishop Carondelet
Jan. 1522, E. E. V. 177

Peace Speaks:

If mankind had rejected me for its own advantage, I would, it seems, have sufficient reason to regret both an undeserved injury and an injustice. However, since men have cast me out, who am the source of all their happiness, and in doing so have brought down calamity after calamity upon themselves, this situation becomes more an object of pity than of resentment on my part. My inclination toward angry retaliation gives way to one of sympathy. To repel one who loves you is certainly a breach of kindness, yet to act in this manner toward one who is the protector of the entire race is an out-and-out crime. Consider the insanity of those who deem themselves unworthy of the advantages I offer and exchange them for increasing evils. Evil in itself is worthy of any kind of suppression, but what can we do other than lament the fate of those who are completely obsessed with evil? Their failure to recognize their own unhappy lot only increases the need for such lamentation. One of the surest signs of convalescence is the recognition of the seriousness of the disease. Even this they fail to do.

As Peace, am I not praised by both men and gods as the very source and defender of all good things? What is there of prosperity, of security, or of happiness that cannot be ascribed to me? On the other hand, is not war the destroyer of all things and the very seed of evil? What is there of prosperity that it does not infect? What is secure or pleasant that it does not undermine? No greater enemy of goodness or of religion can be found. Though nothing is more odious to gods and harmful to man, yet it is incredible to see the tremendous expenditure of work and effort that intelligent beings put forth in an effort to exchange me for a heap of ruinous evils.

Actually it would be much easier for me to be rejected by wild beasts. This I could forgive on the grounds that they are lacking in intelligence. But we are dealing with men endowed with reason and enriched with the gifts of the Holy Spirit, which should incline them toward love and concord with their fellow men. It is a strange situation, indeed, that I should prefer to take up my abode among beasts rather than men.

If we look at the various solar systems and the stars in the firmament, we find, although there is a diversity of motion and power, one continuing harmony. The very forces of the elements about us, although often ranged in opposition to one another, actually through a shifting of pressures bring about and facilitate a great concord. If we turn to animal life, we see that there is here every evidence of agreement and collaboration for mutual ends. What can be more dissimilar than the body and the soul? Yet nature has bound them together in such a marvelous manner that only death can adequately illustrate it. Life itself is nothing other than a union of body and soul, and health is based upon a working together of the various parts of the body. The various species of the animal kingdom live everywhere in peaceful communities. Take, for example, the behavior of elephant herds, of swine and sheep pasturing together. Cranes and jays flock together. Storks noted for their parental care have their well-known roosts. Dolphins are known to defend one another, bees and ants demonstrate great community efforts.

Thus far I have spoken of creatures that lack intelligence but are nevertheless equipped with sense perception. Yet even members of the vegetable world, trees and herbs, show an attraction toward others of the same species. Vines embrace elms, peaches welcome the encirclement of vines. The world of the insensible appreciates the benefits of peace. Possessing life, they come close to the power of sense perception. Lifeless stones have a sense of peace and concord, as for example the magnet attracts and holds metal. Among themselves wild beasts exhibit basic agreement. Lions are wont to act civilly toward fellow lions, a boar will not threaten one of his own kind with its tusks, there is peace in the lynx family. Dragons refuse cruelty to fellow dragons, and the behavior of wolves has been praised in proverbs. It may amaze you to note that even the diabolic spirits who first broke the peace and continue to create discord among men and angels are joined together in an effort to defend their tyranny.

Unanimity is of absolute necessity for man, yet neither nature, education, nor the rewards of concord and the disadvantages of disunity seem to be able to unite mankind in mutual love. Man possesses a unifying principle in the fact that he is molded to the same figure and form and endowed with the same power of speech. Whereas beasts differ in the variety of their shapes, man is identical with fellow man in possessing speech and reason. It is this that distinguishes him from the beast. His ability to speak enables him above all to cultivate friendship. We find in him the seeds of all virtue, a ready disposition toward mutual benevolence, and a delight in helping others. Yet he appears to have been corrupted and to be prone to fall to the very level of beasts. What the common people call humanness and gentility we prefer to term benevolence. To all of this nature has added the gift of tears. Should any offense be committed or friendship darkened, the shedding of tears often rectifies the situation. Although nature has provided so many means for securing concord, she has not done so merely to afford pleasantries but rather because amity is of necessity as far as man is concerned. The very makeup of man is such that regardless of how well he may be endowed with various gifts of mind and body, he still requires the aid and assistance of his inferiors. This very fact that various men have diversified gifts indicates the need for mutual love and friendship. The variety of products of different nations lends itself to this need for reciprocity. Whereas nature has equipped the animal kingdom with various sorts of armor and means of defense, man's lack of these means necessitates mutual assistance. Necessity has invented cities, constructed for the purpose of repelling the attacks of beasts and brigands through the combined efforts of its citizenry.

The nature of things is such that were it not for the concord of the matrimonial state man would perish at birth without the care of his parents. As a matter of fact he would not have been born at all without parental effort and care. His infancy is a period demanding the solicitude of nurses and midwives. To this nature adds the love of children for their parents as it supports them in a mutual way during their helplessness. This the Greeks call ἀντιπελάργωσις, or mutual compensation of benefits. We can add to this the bonds of kinship and affinity. Some display a similarity of natural dispositions, similar tastes and interests that are a sure means of mutual love. Many possess a certain unanimity or mutual attraction that the ancients were wont to consider a special gift of God.

Thus we see that nature has amply provided man with inducements to peace and concord. With how many different arguments does she not attract us? With how many means does she not actually compel us to concord? Yet it appears that some diabolical fiend has taken over the very heart of man and forced him to reject and destroy these inclinations to tranquillity with an insatiable desire for fighting. Had not continual strife and discord dulled our sense of concord, who could believe that man endowed with reason could perpetrate with continual strife such crime, bloodshed, and destruction of places sacred and profane? No combination of efforts, however holy, is able to prevent them from destroying each other. If affairs were as they should be, the very nature of mankind would be sufficient to bring some kind of agreement. Yet as things now stand, nature, such a force in the animal world, is of no avail among men. But can we say that Christ is of no consequence among men? Why is it that his most cogent doctrine, that of peace, has no effect among men? If nature is inadequate, then why is the more powerful teaching of Christ also ineffective? Why does his urging to mutual benevolence not deter them from the madness of war? When I hear the expression "man," I run joyfully to his company since it was for him that I was created and I hope to find an abode in his midst. This is particularly true in the case of Christian men. Yet I find that Christians are actually worse than the heathen. Things are actually so bad that whereas in former times lawyers were the bane of the ordinary man hauled into court, they are now the least of the evils he has to encounter facing trial.

I see a city and hope that there at least a single wall enclosing a common code of laws might govern a society peacefully and with cooperation. Yet the city is so filled with dissension that it appears that here I have been completely proscribed.

I take my leave of the common people, who are as turbulent as the stormy seas, to go to the courts of the princes. Here I expect to find a sure haven since princes are wiser than the common people, and they have received a commission from the Prince of Peace, Who sends peace to all men but especially to princes.

Everything appears in order here, kind greetings, embraces, merry banquets and all of the amenities. Yet it is all a façade, a mere shadow of true peace and concord. Peace is but a pretense covering factions and secret dissensions. The courts of princes are not the home of peace but rather the real source of war.

Where shall I turn? Hope has too often deceived me! Princes display brawn rather than intelligence and are led by cupidity rather than reason. I will join the company of scholars. Good letters produce men; philosophy, more than men; theology, gods. I will be able to rest with these men after having been driven from all other areas. What a disillusion!

Here is a new kind of warfare, not as bloody but just as foolish. As if the truth were changed by its location, some doctrines do not cross the sea, do not pass the Alps, or do not swim the Rhine. In the same university logicians war with rhetoricians, theologians dispute with lawyers. In the same profession the Scotist fights with the Thomist, the Nominalist with the Realist, the Platonist with the Peripatetic. They disagree on the smallest matters and are frequently incensed over nothing at all. They fight until the heat of argument leads to slanders and to blows. Their weapons are not daggers but venomous pens. They tear one another with taunts. They attack the reputations of their opponents with the deadly darts of their tongues. After this deception where shall I turn? What remains but religion? Though religion is common to all Christians, the clergy, as their title, apparel, and ceremonies indicate, are more completely committed to it. Their profession of religion gives me hope of finding a haven among them. Their garments are of white, my own color, a fact that pleases me. I perceive crosses, the symbols of peace. I hear the name of brother, a sign of love. I hear salutations of peace happily pronounced. I see all things held in common, a united chapter, a single Church, a common set of laws, and daily exercises. Who would not expect to discover good here? Yet the chapter rarely agrees with the bishop. This would not matter so much if the chapter members agreed among themselves. How many priests are there who do not tangle with fellow priests? Paul says that Christians should not take fellow Christians to court. Should a priest wage war with a priest or a bishop with a bishop? Perhaps these men should be forgiven because custom has brought them into the company of laymen who have corrupted them. Let them defend what has by now become their right.

There is one type of man who is bound to religion as closely as a turtle is to its shell. The tie is permanent. I had hoped to find a place among these, but my hopes again proved false. They were included since I did not wish to leave any stone unturned. I departed from nowhere more gladly than from the abode of the monks. What could I hope for when one order does not agree with another? There are as many factions as there are communities. The Dominicans wrangle with the Minorites; the Benedictines with the Bernardines. Community practices and ceremonies are as different as their purposes. Pleased with their own, they condemn all others. The same communities are divided into factions. Observants speak evil of Coletani, and they both attack the Conventuals. There is absolutely no agreement among them.

No longer trusting anything, I decided to hide myself in some little monastery that I felt was truly peaceful. What I found was most unpleasant. Would to God it were not true! I found no monastery that was not infected with hatred and disorder. Older men, revered for their wisdom, excited unprofitable debates on trifles. Yet in their own eyes they were fonts of wisdom and piety. A fading hope remained that perhaps in marriage I might find an abode. For do not a common home, a common bed, and common children promise peace? Certainly a union that binds two bodies into one promises it. Yet strife creeps in. Disagreement in outlook soon divides those otherwise so closely bound. Yet it would be more likely for me to find a place of abode among these than among those who with so many ceremonies profess absolute charity. Finally, desiring a place in at least one individual, I failed to discover even one who did not fight within himself. Reason wars with inclinations; inclination struggles against inclination; piety goes one way, cupidity another; lust desires one thing, anger another; ambition wants this, covetousness that.

Men who are not ashamed to be called Christians act in total disagreement with what is most important to Christ. Consider His life. What is it other than a doctrine of concord and love? What do His commandments and parables teach? Peace and charity. Did the prophet Isaias, when he foretold of the coming of Christ, promise that He should be a ruler of cities or a warrior? No! What then did he promise? A Prince of Peace. Isaias named Him after what he judged to be best since he wanted Him to be understood to be the finest of all things. It is not marvelous that it should seem so to Isaias, when Silius, the pagan poet, wrote of me: "Peace is the best of all things, which nature gives to man." The Psalmist agrees, "His seat is made in peace." He said, "In peace rather than among armies. He is a prince of peace and loves peace. He is offended by discord."

Isaias calls peace a work of justice, meaning what Paul, the once turbulent Saul made peaceable, also signified. This doctor of peace, who preferred charity to all other gifts of the spirit, eloquently thundered out my praise to the Corinthians! Is it not to my glory to be praised by so laudable a man? Sometimes he calls Him the god of peace, sometimes the peace of

God. He declares that these are so closely united that there can be no peace where God is not present, nor God where peace is not to be found.

We read in Holy Scripture that the angels of peace are called meek and the ministers of God. It is quite evident whom we understand by the angels of war. Under whose banner do these warriors fight? Under his who first sowed discord between God and man. Man should therefore ascribe every calamity he suffers to the devil's dissensions.

It is beside the point that some argue that God in Holy Scripture is called the God of armies and the God of vengeance. There is a great difference between the God revealed to the Jews and the God revealed to the Christians, though in nature He is one God. If we wish to retain old titles, let Him be called the God of armies if you understand armies to mean virtues united together with good men for the destruction of vice. Let Him be the God of vengeance if you take vengeance to be the correction of vice, and if you understand the bloody slaughters of men that fill the books of Hebrews, not as the tearing of men into pieces, but as the tearing of wicked affections out of their hearts.

To return to my topic. As often as Holy Scripture indicates absolute happiness it does so under the name of peace. Isaias says, "My people shall sit in the beautifulness of peace." The psalmist says, "Peace upon Israel." Isaias marvels at the beauty of the feet of the messengers who announce peace and salvation. Whoever brings tidings of Christ brings tidings of Peace. Whoever proclaims war proclaims him who is most unlike Christ.

Did not the Son of God come to earth to reconcile the world to the Father, to join men by indissoluble bonds of charity, and to make man His friend? He was an ambassador for me; He did my business. Solomon prefigured Him. Regardless of David's greatness, because he was a warrior defiled with blood, he was not permitted to build the House of God. He did not deserve in this to be a figure of a peaceable Christ.

Consider, O soldiers, if wars undertaken on the command of God profane, what is the result of wars undertaken for ambition or anger? If pagan blood pollutes the meek king, what does Christian blood do? I pray the true Christian prince to behold the image of his chief Prince. If he observes how Christ entered His Kingdom and how He departed the earth, he will understand how He would have him rule. Peace and concord should be the goal.

Did the angels sound military trumpets when Christ was born? The Jews, who were permitted war, heard the sound of such trumpets; they were allowed to hate their enemies. The angels of peace sing a different song to the people of peace. They do not call men to war. They proclaim peace and the oracles of the prophets. They proclaim peace, not to murderers and warmongers, but to those who in good will are inclined to concord.

Let men pretend what they will about their own injuries. If they did not love war, they would not war continually among themselves. What did Christ teach besides peace? What did He express Himself on besides peace? He saluted His disciples with, "Peace be to you." He prescribed it as the only worthy form of greeting for Christians. The Apostles, mindful of this, begin their Epistles with wishes of peace to all and with peace to those whom they particularly love. He desires an excellent thing, who wishes for good health; but he who desires peace wishes the very totality of happiness.

Notice the care with which He, in departing from this world, commended the peace He frequently commended throughout His life. He said, "Love ye one another as I have loved you," and "I give you My peace, I leave you My peace." Do you hear what He leaves us? Does He bequeath horses, an army, an empire, riches? No, none of these things. What then? He leaves peace—peace with His friends, peace with His enemies.

Consider His prayer to the Father at the Last Supper, when death was imminent. One would suppose that He would ask for something extraordinary since He knew that whatever He asked for He would obtain. He said, "O Holy Father, keep them in My name that they may be one as We are one." See what a noble union Christ asks for us. He said not that they might be of one mind but that they might be one, and not one in any manner but, "As We are one." We Who are one in a most perfect and ineffable manner. He declared that men could be saved only by nourishing among themselves peace and concord.

The princes of this world give a distinctive uniform to their men, particularly in time of war, that they may be distinguished from others. Take a look at the badge with which Christ has marked His followers. It is none other than the badge of mutual charity. He said, "By this sign shall men know that you are My disciples," not if you wear such a uniform, or if you eat this or that food, or if you fast, or if you read psalms, but "if you love one another as I have loved you." The precepts of philosophers are innumerable, and the commandments of Moses and of kings are many; but He said, "My precept is but one: that is that you love one another."

In prescribing a form of prayer, does He not even at its

beginning urge a remarkable concord? "Our Father," He says. It is the common petition of all men; they are all one household, one family, dependent on one Father. How is it then that they make continual war amongst themselves? With what audacity do you call upon the common Father while thrusting your sword into your brother's vitals. This is the one thing He would have uppermost in the minds of His followers. In so many signs, parables, and precepts He emphasized this zeal for concord. He called Himself a shepherd and His servants sheep. Who has ever seen sheep fighting with sheep? What will the wolves do if the sheep tear at one another?

When the Vine calls Himself the roots and calls His followers the branches, what is He expressing but unanimity? It would be amazing for one branch of a vine to fight with another. Is it not a more monstrous thing for a Christian to fight with a Christian? If anything is sacred and holy to Christians, it should be Christ's last commandments. His last will and testament, so to speak, gave us what He wanted and hence should never be forgotten. What did He command if not mutual love among His followers? What does the communion of holy bread and cup decree but a new and indissoluble concord? When He perceived that peace could not stand up against competition for position, riches, glory, and the desire for vengeance, He forbade such aspirations to His followers. He called on them not to resist evil. He commanded them to do good even to those who did not deserve it and to pray for and wish well to those who were malevolent. Can we call them Christian who for every light injury plunge the greater part of the world into war?

He commands the prince to play the role of minister among his people, not to be superior in just anything but to surpass others in aiding those who need help. Yet for small territorial gain they are not ashamed to stir up widespread dissension. He teaches us to live without possessions like birds or lilies. He forbids us to be concerned about the morrow. It is His will that we all should depend upon heaven. Yet some men do not hesitate for the sake of a little unpaid money to shed much human blood even before payment is due. In these days this appears an extremely justifiable reason for declaring war.

Christ does nothing but command them to learn one lesson from Him: meekness and placidity. When He commands that the gift to be left before the altar be not offered until you are in friendship with your brother, is He not teaching us that concord is to be preserved above all other things and that no sacrifice is pleasing to God if offered in discord? God refused the Jew's gift, a sheep or a kid, if offered by those in disagreement. Dare Christian men while making war offer the Holy Sacrifice?

When He likens Himself to a hen gathering her chickens under her wings, how apt a symbol He uses to depict concord. He is a gatherer. Is it proper that we Christians should act like hawks? He is called the cornerstone. Is it right that His vicars should move the world to battle? Those who boast that they have that supreme moderation as their Prince cannot be reconciled to themselves. He reconciled Pilate and Herod, yet He cannot bring His followers to agreement. Peter, still half Jew, was ready to defend his Lord at the risk of his life; Christ rebuked him and told him to put up his sword. Yet among Christians the sword is drawn against Christians for any light matter. Would He be defended with the sword Who prayed for the authors of His death while dying?

All Christian doctrine in both the Old and New Testament calls for peace, yet Christian life is filled with warfare. What evil is there that cannot be overcome? Let them either relinquish the name of Christian or give expression to the doctrine of Christ by concord. How long shall theory and practice disagree? Adorn your house and your clothes with the image of the cross as much as you please; Christ will never acknowledge any other sign but that which He Himself prescribed—concord.

The Apostles were commanded to wait for the Holy Spirit when they saw Christ ascending. He promised that He would be continually present among those of His followers who were assembled. Hence no man should expect Christ to be present in war.

What was that fiery and flaming Spirit but Charity? Nothing is more common than fire. Fire is kindled with fire, just as the Spirit is the parent of concord. Yet look at the result. Christ claims that they were all of one heart and mind. Remove the spirit from the body and it decays. Take Peace away from the Christian life and it perishes. Many theologians affirm that the Spirit is infused by the Sacraments. If they preach the truth, where is the effect of the Spirit—one heart and one mind? If these are fables, why do they pay such great honor to them? I write this in order that Christians might be ashamed of their lives, not that I would dishonor the Sacraments.

Christians are called the Church. Does this not admonish us to unanimity? What agreement can there be between military forces and the Church? One points to dissension, the other to togetherness. If you take pride in being a member of the Church, what have you to do with war? If you are outside the Church, what have you to do with Christ?

Are you not received into the same household? Have you not the same Prince? Do you not strive for the same goal? Are you not consecrated by the same sacraments? Do you not enjoy the same gifts? Are you not nourished by the same food? Do you not desire the same reward? Then why do you cause such a disturbance? We notice agreement among mercenaries hired to slaughter because they wage war under the same banner. Cannot the benefits just mentioned unite pious men? Are so many sacraments able to accomplish nothing?

Baptism is the sacrament common to all. By it we are born again to Christ, cut off from the world and grafted as members of Christ. What can be as much itself as the members of a body? There is neither bond nor free, barbarian nor Greek, man nor woman. All are identical in Christ, Who reduces all things to concord.

A little blood tasted on both sides joins the Scythians so that they do not hesitate to die for their friends. Amity is a sacred and holy thing among pagans when a common table unites them. Shall not that Heavenly Bread and that mystical cup unite Christian men in charity when Christ has ordained it and they renew that sacrifice daily? If Christ has accomplished nothing, why these ceremonies? If He did something really important, why do we neglect it as if it were trivial? Does any man dare be so bold as to come to that table, the banquet of peace, who prepares to war against fellow Christians, who prepares to destroy those for whom Christ died, who prepares to draw that blood for whom Christ shed His?

O hard hearts! In so many things there is fellowship, yet in life there is inexplicable tension. All men are born, must grow old, and die. We are all of the same species. Our religion is the work of one man. We are redeemed by the same sacrifice and nourished by the same sacraments. Whatever gifts come from this come from one source to all equally. We have one Church. All men will have the same reward. The Celestial Jerusalem Christians desire is called the vision of peace. The Church on earth is its prototype. How is it then that the Church differs so greatly from its exemplar? Has industrious nature accomplished so little? Has Christ with His commandments and mysteries accomplished nothing?

Vicious things, according to the proverb, attract to themselves more evil. What is more fragile than the life of man? What is shorter? How many infirmities is it not subject to? Being burdened themselves with more evil than they can bear, these madmen call down upon themselves the worst part of all evil. Blindness clouds their minds, and driven headlong, they break the bonds of nature, Christ, and every organization. They fight everywhere endlessly and without measure, nation against nation, city against city, one faction against another, one prince against another, continually destroying one another. For the foolish ambition of two men, who will shortly perish, human affairs are turned upside down.

I will not recall the tragedies of antiquity. Let us look at the last ten years. What land or what sea did not witness warfare? What region was not soaked with Christian blood? What river was not dyed with human blood? The cruelty of Christians surpasses that of heathens and beasts. The Jews' wars were against strangers and at God's command. Christians should war against vice. Yet they ally themselves with vice to war against men. All pretense aside, ambitions, anger, and the desire for plunder are at the base of Christian wars. The Jewish wars were against foreigners, yet Christians have allied themselves with the Turks to war with fellow Christians.

A desire for glory aroused heathen tyrants to war. When they subdued the barbarians, they treated them well and endeavored to make the victory as bloodless as possible, thus increasing their own fame and rendering defeat more bearable.

It shames me to recall the vain and superficial reasons whereby Christian princes provoke the world to war. This particular prince finds or feigns an old title as if it mattered who ruled a kingdom so long as the welfare of the people was seen to. Another finds a trifling fault in some neighboring confederation. A third is privately offended over some slight to someone's wife.

The most criminal of all causes of war is, of course, the desire for power. When certain princes see power slipping from them because a general peace has rendered them expendable, they stir up war in order to remain in power and oppress the people. Others are unable to find a place in peaceful society. What diabolical agents could have put such poison into Christian hearts? Who taught Christians this tyranny? No Dionysius or Mezentius can answer this. They are beasts, not men, and are noble only in tyranny. Their wisdom leads only to harm and misfortune. They are in agreement only to oppress the common good, yet they who do these things are accepted as Christians. Thus polluted they enter holy churches and approach our altars. They should be exiled as diseased persons to some remote corner of the globe.

If Christians are members of one body, why does not every man rejoice at another's fortune? Yet if a neighboring kingdom is prosperous, this is considered a just cause for war.

What has moved or will move so many to tear at the kingdom of France except that it is prospering? There is no larger kingdom. Nowhere is there a nobler senate. No other country has such a famous university. Nowhere is there greater concord and therefore greater power. Nowhere is the law more respected. Religion itself is pure and free from corruption. It is not infected by the proximity of Turks or Moors as is Hungary or Spain. Germany (excluding Bohemia) is divided among so many princes that there is not even the semblance of a kingdom. France is the undefiled flower of the Christian commonwealth. Should a storm arise, France stands as a strong castle to be attacked with cunning and deceit, and this very fact other Christians delight in. They use their own title as an excuse for wickedness. They enlarge the empire of Christ. Nonsense! They believe the common good is not well provided for unless they overthrow the most beautiful and most fortunate part of Christendom.

Indeed, in doing these things they surpass beasts in cruelty. Not every kind of beast fights. The conflicts of animals are against other beasts. This we cannot overemphasize. A snake does not bite a snake nor a lynx tear a lynx to pieces. When beasts fight, they use their own weapons. Nature has armed them, but man she has left defenseless. O God! With what weapons does anger not arm mankind? Christians attack Christians with the very weapons of hell. Who could believe that man invented explosives?

Beasts do not fight collectively. Who has ever seen ten lions fight ten bulls? Yet how often do 20,000 armed Christians fight 20,000 armed Christians? Is it such a pleasant affair to injure your fellow man? Beasts fight only when motivated by hunger or when fear for their young has enraged them. Actually, what injury is there important enough to cause war between Christians?

The vulgar crowd can claim ignorance for acting thus; the young, lack of knowledge, criminals, their delinquency. However, the seed of war actually springs from those who by age, experience, and wisdom should overcome the ignorance of the common people and the inexperience of the young. The common people construct excellent cities, rule them peacefully, and enrich them. Governors and rulers, like wasps and drones, creep into those cities and secretly steal that which was provided by other men's industry. What many have gathered is wasted by a few; what was well constructed is ruined. If you will not remember things long past, remember the battles and the wars fought during the past ten years. You will find that they were fought for causes that did not concern the common man.

Among the heathens it is a shameful thing for an old man

to be obliged to go to war. Among Christians it has become praiseworthy. An old soldier is a shameful thing for Naso. Yet today we praise men in military service who are over seventy.

The priests, who in times past under the bloody law of Moses were not permitted to be defiled with blood, are no longer ashamed to fight. Theologians, masters of the Christian life, are not ashamed, nor are religious, bishops, and even cardinals. The vicars of Christ do not hesitate to instigate that very thing that Christ so detested.

What do miters and helmets have in common? What has a crosier to do with a sword? What has a Bible to do with a shield? How can one reconcile a salutation of peace with an exhortation to war; peace in one's mouth and war in one's deeds? Do you praise war with the same mouth that you preach peace and Christ? Do you herald with the same trumpet both God and Satan? Do you, wearing a cowl, incite the simple to murder, believing you are preaching the Gospel? Do you in the place of the Apostles teach what is contrary to the precepts of the Apostles? Are you not afraid that what was spoken of by Christ's messengers—how good the seat of those who spread peace and salvation—will be contradicted? What filth is the tongue of a priest who exhorts war, evil, and murder!

Among pagan Romans, whoever became Pontifex Maximus took an oath to keep his hands free from blood and, if he should injure anyone, never to excuse his action. Titus Vespasian, the pagan emperor, kept the oath constantly and was praised by pagan writers. Yet priests dedicated to God as well as monks, who should be even more holy, now inflame men to murder. They make the trumpet of the Gospel the trumpet of Mars. They forget their dignity and stop at nothing in their warmongering. Through these clergy normally peaceful princes are incited to war by the men whose duty it is to divert them from warfare. Priests fight for things condemned even by the pagan philosophers, a contempt that should be strongly evident among followers of the Apostles.

A few years ago, when the world was violently drawn into war, those gospel preachers, the gray and black friars, stirred up to a greater tempo men already so inclined. They encouraged Frenchmen against Englishmen; Englishmen against Frenchmen. Only one or two, whom I cannot name for fear of causing them great difficulties, fought for peace. Holy bishops, forgetting their dignity and calling, ran hither and thither vexing an already troubled world. On the one hand they urged Pope Julius to war and on the other they pressured

the national leaders, as if kings were not of themselves bellicose enough. All this madness we cloak with fine-sounding
terms.

For purposes of war, not only laws, the writings of pious
men, but the Scriptures themselves are compromised. It has
come to the point where it is considered folly to express yourself against war or to praise what Christ Himself praised.
Whoever gives advice to the common people appears to neglect the rulers in recommending what is salutary.

Priests follow the armies. Bishops leave their diocese to
perform the business of war. Mars consecrates priests, bishops,
and cardinals. The honorable title of military legate is esteemed as a term indicating a successor of the Apostles. Any
attempt to remedy this situation is concealed under the guise
of piety. Their standards are adorned with crosses, and mercenaries hired to murder carry before them the same symbol.
That alone which can dissuade men from war has become its
banner. O wicked soldiers! What have you to do with the sign
of the cross? Your actions are more in line with those of
ferocious beasts. This is the sacred symbol of Christ whose
triumph was in death rather than war. The cross is a warning against your real enemy and a means of victory over him.

You soldiers with the sign of salvation emblazoned on your
banners hasten to destroy those who were saved by the very
same sign of the cross. What a terrible thing it is that men
receive the sacraments now administered in the camps and
then rush out to combat. The sacrament is the principal symbol of Christian union. Yet Christ, if He is present, is made
to witness swords drawn against fellow men in a demonstra-
tion that is above all acceptable to the forces of evil. And,
finally, what is more horrible than the fact that the cross
is honored in both camps and in both lines of battle. Does
the cross fight the cross, and does Christ fight against Christ?
The sign of the cross once terrified its enemies. Why do men
now fight against that which they adore and worship? What
is the prayer of the soldier during the service? "Our Father."
How can you dare to call Him Father as you go forth to slay
your brother? "Hallowed be Thy name." How could the name
of God be more dishonored than by your fighting? "Thy
kingdom come." Are you praying that so much shedding of
blood aid tyranny? "Thy will be done on earth as it is in
heaven." His will is to preserve the peace and you prepare for
war. You ask for daily bread from our Father and at the same
time you destroy the crops of your brother and hope their
destruction will hasten his death. How can you repeat, "and
forgive us our trespasses as we forgive those who trespass

against us," when you rush out to slay your brother? With danger to yourself and your neighbor you ask to avoid the dangers of temptation. You ask deliverance from evil and yet at the instigation of the Evil One you prepare evil for your brother.

Plato in the *Republic* denounces any war of Greek against Greek and calls it sedition. Christians consider war to be sacred even when the causes are not proportionate to the means used. The pagans of old were wont to sew into a bag anyone who had bloodied his sword with the blood of his brother and cast him into the water. What is the difference between blood brothers and those who are brothers in Christ? In this case both the victor and the vanquished are guilty of parricide. Such is the misery of war.

In spite of this they detest and curse the Turk as foreign to Christ. They do this because they assume themselves to be Christian. Yet what could be more pleasant in the sight of the Turk than to see Christians engaged in internecine warfare? The Turk offers sacrifice to Satan, but the behavior of Christians toward Christians must certainly fulfill the same purpose. In this case there is a double sacrifice. The excuses that are made to explain warfare are well known to me. They protest that their action is not in the least voluntary. It is high time they threw aside the mask and dropped their pretenses. If they examined their consciences, they would find that the real reasons are anger, ambition, and stupidity. If these constitute necessity, you ought to reevaluate them.

The populace ought to be reminded that God is not mocked, nor is He deceived with pretenses. Meanwhile solemn prayers and processions are undertaken and peace is prayed for with loud supplications. "Grant us peace, we beseech Thee, hear us." God can justly answer us with, "Why do you laugh me to scorn? You ask me to avoid what you yourselves are the authors of." If each and every offense is a sufficient cause for war, then who is there who has not been offended? How often are not offenses between husband and wife condoned that mutual love be preserved? If offense be given to this or that prince, is this cause for war? There are laws, learned men, pious abbots, and reverend bishops whose mature counseling can bring these matters to a peaceful solution. Let these be the arbiters, and even though the decisions arrived at be somewhat unjust, they are much to be preferred to the evil of war. No peace, regardless of the injustice it involves, should be passed over in favor of war. A sober consideration of the results of any war will weigh the scales in favor of peace. The pope would be an excellent authority in this matter. But when man has been engaged for so long a time in violent struggle, what happens to his authority? Where is that power that is, after Christ, the most potent? In this matter it would be demonstrated were it not hampered by worldly considerations. When the pope issues a summons to war, men obey. Why is it that they cannot exhibit a similar obedience when he calls for peace? If they prefer peace, why did they obey Pope Julius, the author of war? Hardly anyone has obeyed Pope Leo in his exhortation to peace. If the pope's authority is sacred, then certainly it should be obeyed whenever it is voiced. This is especially true when it voices what Christ most particularly exhorted. Those who listened to Julius' war cries explain that they cannot hear Leo's proposals of peace under the same false guise of religion. Under pretense of serving the Church they have satisfied their own malicious ambitions.

Let me give a few words on the defense of peace and concord to those of you who actually despise war. Peace is not to be found in various leagues or confederations of men, which are ofttimes the very source and cause of wars. We must look for peace by purging the very sources of war, false ambitions and evil desires. As long as individuals serve their own personal interests, the common good will suffer. No one achieves what he desires if the methods employed be evil. The princes should use their wisdom for the promotion of what is good for the entire populace. The measure of their majesty, happiness, renown, and riches should be what actually makes great men outstanding. Let their attitude toward the common good be that of a father toward his family. The mark of a great and noble king is that he so acts and governs as to make his subjects honest, content, and wealthy. In this he should respect the wealth of his richer citizens, the freedom of his citydwellers, and above all he should take care that peace flourish in all places. His subordinates should imitate their king and take special care that the common good of all be protected. In this way they will insure their own office of state. Will a king that is of this mind hand over the money of his subjects to strange and barbarous mercenaries? Will he expose them to famine and hunger to provide pay for hired captains? Will he risk the lives of his people with many dangers? We do not think so.

In his performance of kingly duties let him bear always in mind that as a man he is dealing with fellow men, that as a free citizen he is dealing with free citizens, and above all that as a Christian he is dealing with fellow Christians. The citizenry on their part must act in such a manner that their respect for the king be motivated also by the interests of the common good. No ruler can expect more than this. Consent and approval on the part of the citizens will be a curb to the aspirations of the prince. For both the ruler and the subject private gain should not be a consideration. Those who make it their purpose to do away with war and who extend every effort to secure peace and concord rather than mobilization should be shown the greatest honor. In this matter the case of Diocletian should be recalled to mind.

If war is unavoidable, then it should be conducted in such a way that the misfortunes resulting from it be dropped at the door of those who occasioned and caused it. In most wars the safety of the heads of government is assured and their captains stand to gain. It is the poor farmer and the common people who bear the brunt of the destruction, and they have hardly any interest in it and were certainly not its cause. Any prince is lacking in wisdom if he does not take this into consideration. Some kind of plan ought to be devised that will terminate this constant change of empire. Any kind of innovation or renewal brings in its wake uprisings and wars. One suggestion in this regard would be to have royal families marry within their own realms or at least within adjoining territories. This would lessen the problem of royal succession. It should be illegal to sell or alienate territories, as if free cities were up for sale. Kingship does not imply absolute ownership. This continual intermarriage between royal families could produce a situation similar to an Irishman ruling in India or a Syrian becoming king of England. Thus neither of them will have an adequate ruler for the one realm is abandoned and the other is in the hands of one from another world. While such a king is attempting to establish his regal right through conquest and bargaining, he wastes the resources of his former kingdom. Trying to rule two areas he loses both of them. There should be some kind of an agreement that once the borders of an empire have been determined they must remain inviolate and no alliance can be allowed to alter or destroy them. Once this has been established, each rule shall be expended toward the improvement of the realm to the end that the ruler's successors shall find it a richer and better place in which to dwell. In this way each and every territory will prosper. Among themselves their alliances must be based, not on covenants and federations, but on a sincere friendship that shares in efforts toward the common good of all. The question of succession should be determined either by blood or by a general election of the people. Honesty and personal integrity should be the criterion of promotion to lesser offices. Personal interests should in no way determine the preferences of the ruler but rather the common good. He should especially avoid traveling about and should confine his peregrinations to his own kingdom. Let him bear in mind the age-old adage: "The forehead is more excellent than the backside."

Let him consider himself enriched only when he amasses wealth of his own and not of his neighbors. When confronted with the decision to declare war, he should have as his consultants neither young men, whose inexperience finds war attractive, nor those who stand to profit by public disturbance, nor those who fatten their purses at the expense of civic disasters. Rather let him choose older men renowned by their mercy and benevolence. In no case should war, such a terrible thing once begun, be instigated because of the disagreement of one or two men. The common consent of all must be obtained.

A certain frankness must be observed in pointing to the causes and occasions for war. Yet there are certain incidents that must be overlooked, for forbearance generates forbearance. There are times when peace must be purchased. If one considers the tremendous destruction of men and property that the purchase avoids, it is cheap at any price. Meanwhile let bishops turn again to their obligations and let the clergy act in a priestly manner. Monks should be cognizant of their profession. Theologians should concern themselves with what is worthy of Christian study. In every area let there be a combined effort to establish peace. This should be the aim of preaching and teaching. It should preoccupy them privately and publicly. If these efforts fail, at least let them show their disdain and disapproval by keeping themselves aloof from any association with its agents. It would be a good thing to prohibit the burial of those killed in battle in consecrated ground. Should there be any innocent in this group, this will hardly detract from their final reward. Such a prohibition would certainly have an effect on warmongers.

Of course I am speaking of those wars that Christians conduct among themselves. It is not our intention to condemn those who undertake legitimate war to repel barbarous invasions or defend the common good. Nowadays the trophies and souvenirs of their battles, dyed and stained with the blood of those for whom Christ shed His own blood, are exhibited in our churches along with relics of the Apostles and martyrs, as if it is a work of religion not only to be martyred but to perform the martyring. I feel it would be preferable to hang these trophies either in the courthouse or in some armory. The church is hardly the place to exhibit anything that has been defiled with blood. Priests especially should do everything in their power to dissuade men from war. If they attack it with greater effort, there is no doubt their endeavors will bear fruit.

If, however, the disease of war is a malady of such a nature that it cannot possibly be extricated from men's minds, then let them expend their warlike efforts toward the extermination of the Turkish menace—although here again it would be much more in keeping with Christian principle to convert them with honest doctrine and good example. Would that there were some simpler means of solving disagreements among Christians. Certainly if mutual charity does not unite them, then some common enemy may perhaps do so. Yet, should this be effected, it can hardly be said that this concord would be the ideal.

Nothing is more conducive to genuine peace than a sincere desire that comes from the heart. Those who really favor it make it their duty to promote it at every opportunity. The obstacles to their endeavor they either circumvent or remove, even though this involves concessions on their part. Others not of this mind look for causes and excuses for war. The things that pertain to peace they either make light of or actually conceal. Whatever seems to promote war they advocate and favor with every assistance. It shames me to point out the trivial things they exaggerate and the conflagrations they enkindle. Once the flames of dissent appear, it is amazing the amount of forgotten injuries that are heaped upon it. So forgotten are the good deeds and blessings of the past that all seem to desire nothing other than war. How often it is that very insignificant matters of petty rulers are the causes of conflict, their true nature being withheld from the public. Lacking causes they use false propaganda to stir up the populace, nursing their grievances with all sorts of falsehood for no other purpose than personal gain. In this matter the clergy are not entirely blameless.

The English despise the French for no other reason than that they are French, the Scots are disliked because they are Scots, and the German is at odds with the Frenchman and both oppose the Spaniard. What can be more perverse than peoples being opposed to one another simply because of a dissimilarity of names? There are so many things that should bring them together. Why as men are they not benevolent to man, as Christians well disposed toward fellow Christians? Why is it that what is really of no great significance can dominate the minds of these men when the stronger forces of nature and of Christ seem to be powerless? Space can separate men's bodies but it cannot separate their minds. In previous centuries the Rhine separated the Gaul and the German, but it cannot be said to separate Christian from Christian. The Pyrenees divide the Spanish and the French, yet they do not divide the communion of the Church. The North Sea divides the French and the English, but hardly the society and fellowship of religion.

The Apostle Paul was disturbed to hear the early Christians say, "I am Apollo's, I am a follower of Cephas," or "I am Paul's disciple." He violently opposed evil language as contrary to the mind of Christ. Yet empty words are today the reasons why nations turn against one another. Others, not finding this sufficient reason, seek even more subtle means of causing division. They partition France as neither the sea, the mountains, nor its natural provinces divide her. They disseminate the seeds of dissension so that friendship between France and Germany may not be based upon their common inheritance.

If judges in matters of divorce deliberate long and seriously, why do they not realize the seriousness of hasty judgment in affairs more grievous? Let them examine the self-evident fact that this world of ours is the fatherland of the entire race. If the same nationality binds together those born of the same forebears, if blood relationship fosters amity, if the Church is a great family common to all men, and if the same household can produce concord, is it not foolishness not to accept it everywhere? You can put up with your father-in-law because he is the parent of your wife. Then why not tolerate a little from him who is your brother in religion? The fellowship of Christ is the strongest bond of all.

Why do you dwell only on those things that embitter the heart? If you are seriously desirous of peace, let this be your manner of thought. "Although he has offended me in this particular case, nevertheless on the other occasions he has been a real friend to me," or "He did not harm me of his own accord but rather because someone else put him up to it." In the case of the dissension between Agamemnon and Achilles the blame was laid at the feet of the goddess Ate. In these matters where we cannot find a real excuse, then let us blame it on Destiny, an evil god, and transfer our anger to this.

Why do men feel that wisdom lies in the self-destruction of their own faith, rather than in its defense? Why is evil, rather than the common good, such an obsession among men? Wise men deliberate when confronted with a personal affair. But these men charge aimlessly into war. They do not consider the fact that once a war has been viciously ignited, terminating it is a very difficult matter; evolving from insignificant skirmishes, it matures to full-scale battles, at the expense of many lives and much bloodshed.

It is the crucial duty of the prince and his nobility to perceive these possibilities if their subjects should overlook them. It is also the obligation of the clergy to continually promulgate and firmly insist upon these facts, regardless of the people's attitude. If the above method is diligently adhered to, there should be no fear concerning their effectiveness.

Are you preparing to wage war? The task is to define peace and war, carefully calculating the profits of peace and the chaos of war. If destruction and good sense require a war rather than peace, this will be evident. Consider for a moment a kingdom flourishing in every aspect, well-constructed cities, ruled by conscientious lawmakers, well-cultivated fields, honest industry, and a pervading pious spirit. Consider this thought thoroughly: "If I involve myself in war, I will inevitably disrupt this present concord." Then consider the ruin of cities, the destruction of thoroughfares, the desolation of fields, and the insidious annihilation of churches. Seriously consider this: these are the fruits of war. If you are repulsed at the thought of bringing into your country wicked and filthy mercenaries whom you must support at the expense of your own people and at a great loss to yourself personally, then consider this as the price of war.

If you abhor theft, war necessarily demands it. If you detest parricide, it is readily accepted in war. Can someone be even minutely sensitive about killing one person when mass murder is his profession? If laws are totally neglected in peacetime, they are completely abolished in a time of war. If adultery, incest, and other insidious immoralities are wantonly favored by you, then war is the answer to your desire. The tempests of war completely disregard piety and religion, as impiety and neglect of religion are the roots of all evil.

If you perceive the state of your country to be such that evil conditions prevail, and men of questionable character are forcefully controlling the country, then you are in a condition of war, as under this condition the most deplored men rule. Those whose action would be staunchly condemned in peacetime are highly regarded in time of war. Who could more skillfully infiltrate a town with an army than one dedicated to theft and stealing? Who could with greater facility contemptuously pillage houses or destroy churches better than a professional soldier? Who will more maliciously smite his enemy and terminate their lives than someone skilled in weapons and

all types of cold-blooded murder? Who is better qualified to reduce cities to mere ashes than someone experienced in the use of incendiaries? Who will better escape and unjustly survive the perils of floods and the sea than a well-seasoned pirate? If you desire fully to comprehend the destruction and agony of war, then consider well those who wage it.

Accepting the fact that a pious leader is primarily concerned with the safety and welfare of his people, he will most assuredly despise war. If the chief happiness of a ruler is that of his subjects, he must embrace peace. A good leader with the best interests of his subjects always in mind must vicariously detest war, which is the cesspool of all impiety. Since he will accept the possessions of his subjects as his own, he is morally obligated to make every attempt to prevent war. Otherwise the results of honest industry will be wasted on public executioners.

They must realize that every man's cause is a flattering of self and thus deceives him, especially when the cause is an evil one. But let us assume that the cause is a just one and the end victorious, then we must carefully weigh the advantages and the disadvantages involved and attentively judge whether the means justify the end.

Bloodless victories are few and far between. Your men will inevitably be contaminated with the blood of others. And at the same time earnestly consider the moral degeneration and absence of public discipline, whose restoration will be a very tedious matter. Your spoils are slothfully gluttoned; you pamper your people; those who are just are burdened; the malicious are enticed further, and after a victory their appetites are not easily quieted. Skilled labor, art, and commerce rapidly decay. The banks are closed. To contain the enemy, it is necessary to exclude yourself from many regions. Before this malignant conflict commenced, all territories adjacent to you were unrestricted, for peace made all things common by their exchange.

Behold what you have done; the territory that was yours is impossibly restricted. Debate the quantity of war materials necessary just to besiege a small town. In order to overthrow a town you must erect another, a sham town; yet you could erect your own town, a better town, with less labor and bloodshed. In order to prevent an enemy ambush you must uncomfortably camp in the open air. It would be cheaper to erect new walls than madly to batter down old ones and rebuild them elsewhere. I bring this to your attention, completely disregarding the graft that has fallen into the hands of the tax collectors, receivers, and captain's purses.

Consider then what you would expend on war and if you find that peace would have cost you more than a tenth of that expense, then I will willingly allow you to do away with me wherever you will. Yet if you remit even a small injury, you feel you are lacking in courage. There is no greater proof of a small mind than to seek revenge. You feel that it is an embarrassment to have to make some small allowance to a neighbor, or possibly a relative who once did you a favor. But you will humiliate yourself even further when you fill the pockets of the lowest dregs of society with gold that will never be repaid, or when you fawningly send ambassadors to the filthy and obnoxious Carians, entrusting the lives and possessions of your people to those who are absolutely lacking in trust and holiness.

If peace seems to be iniquitous for you, avoid thinking in this way, "This I lose," but think instead, "I buy peace for so much." A more subtle approach would be, "If it were mine, I would grant it, but I am a prince and rule a commonwealth." No leader whose primary consideration is the public welfare will unwittingly enter in a war. Beyond all doubt quite the contrary is evident, and war is spooned by the food of wretched inhumanity. Will you defend to the death any portion of your country? What does his country hold for a man? Will you seek revenge on the one who has forsaken your daughter? What does revenge hold for the commonwealth? The consideration of these facts is the supreme proof of a very wise man and a noble prince.

Who has ever ruled more successfully than Octavius Augustus? He sought to give up his empire if he could find some other prince more deserving and in the better interests of the commonwealth. Many literary men have praised the one saying of an emperor, "My children be lost to me if any other can better govern and counsel the commonwealth." These well-meaning heathens demonstrate interest for the commonwealth. On the other hand, Christian leaders show little or no respect for their fellow man. They choose either to satiate their own cupidities or childishly pamper their egos by exacting the most grotesque violence on those who have slighted them.

I hear others say that their only safety lies in barbarically encountering the evil schemes of the wicked. Why were the Antoniones, the meek, and the philosopher the sole emperors of Rome not attacked? It was because no man rules more efficiently and confidently than one who is prepared to give up his throne, contrary to his own interests, if it is for the common good of his people. If neither an earnest interest in

humanity, nor a respect for piety, nor any calamity will move you, certaintly the ill repute of a Christian name will shame you to human harmony. I ask you, what percentage of the world do Christians possess? This is the city situated well in the view of all and sinfully exhibited as a yardstick of human peace and tranquillity. How shall we interpret what the enemies of Christianity voice? What blasphemies will they spew forth before Christ, when they observe Christians bickering among themselves about more trivial matters than even the heathen, with more cruelty than the wicked, and with what machines of war?

Who invented artillery? Was it not Christians? They dedicate these inventions to the Apostles and carve their images on them so as to make them seem less treacherous. O cruel, contemptuous ridicule! Shall Paul, the faithful exhorter of peace, turn hellish war machines against the Christians?

If it is our aim to convert the Turks, we must first be Christians. They will inherently rebel against what we are trying to inculcate in them if they observe what Christ detests above all things thriving more among the Christians than any other people in the world.

Homer marveled at satiability in such desirable things as sleep, meat, drink, dance, and music, but saw that war could never be satisfied. This stands out among those who ought to abominate war. Rome, the mighty conqueror of past centuries, would frequently bolt up the temple of Janus. Why is it that among us war never takes a recess? How can you dare to spread the Word of Christ, the Author of peace, when you constantly war among yourselves in perpetual dissension? Doesn't anyone realize that this chaotic spirit will give the Turks courage? Nothing is easier to defeat than a group divided amongst itself. If you wish to inspire them with fear, be at peace.

Why do you estimate yourselves so unworthy of life's pleasures? Will you retreat from the peace and contentment to come? Man encounters many misfortunes in a lifetime. Harmony softly displaces trouble and grief, so that if all are earnestly striving for harmony, one will be able to aid the other in a time of need. Whenever anything righteous and just occurs, greater concord is emanated. A faithful companion not only rejoices when his comrade is at peace, but he also grieves in the same way when his friend is grieved.

These incidents that arouse such great conflict among you are so petty and vain. Death continually threatens king and subject alike. What subversions shall an enemy of the state viciously incite, only to vanish shortly thereafter, as smoke

from fire? Eternity is awaiting us. What point is there in grappling uselessly for these phantoms of the present as though this life were an eternity?

O pitiful mortals, you neither believe nor confidently aspire to the tranquil life of the righteous—foolish boasters who mistakenly promise themselves a peaceful way of life. The life of the just is really nothing other than an unspeakable gathering of happy souls who have a foretaste of that union that Christ requested in terms of the union between Himself and His Heavenly Father. How can you prepare for this final concord unless you now meditate upon it? As an angel is not abruptly transformed into a stinking glutton, so a companion of martyrs and saints is not suddenly transformed into a bloody warrior.

More than enough Christian blood has been shed. We have aimed furiously at destroying each other. We have unwittingly offered sufficient sacrifices to hell and the furies, and we have sufficiently nourished the appetites of the Turks. This beastly fable is through. Now that we have taxed the miseries of war, let us at least grow discreetly in wisdom. Whatever has been done foolishly in the past, let it willingly be imputed to destiny. Let Christian men happily rejoice, as did the pagans, that the past evils of life lay buried forever in time. Faithfully give your attention to the study of peace, that it may fittingly be bound, not with weak hemp, but with a lasting cohesiveness.

I beseech you, princes, upon whose nod mortal affairs depend and who, among men, bear the image of Christ, willingly acknowledge the voice of your Creator, endlessly summoning you to peace. The whole world, wearied from war, mournfully petitions you to heed this cry for peace. If any single person is displeased with this, let the common good prevail. It is of the utmost urgency that we all undertake this project, rather than shunning it for more insignificant matters.

I beseech you, consecrated priests of God, unflinchingly promulgate that which you most certainly know to be most pleasing to Christ and exorcise that which is most hateful to Him.

I beseech you, theologians, fervently preach the gospel of peace, and unceasingly exhort the people to live by it.

I beseech you, bishops, who excel all others in ecclesiastical dignity, see that your authority is properly exercised to eternally bind peace to all. I beseech you, magistrates, to be uncompromisingly faithful to the wisdom of kings and the mercy of bishops. Now with no exceptions I beseech all Christians unselfishly to consent to universal peace and fervently to obey those who govern it. Illuminate the power of

peace and tranquillity among all men, so as finally to terminate the tyranny of nobles.

For this purpose let everyone muster all that he possesses. May eternal concord, already established by nature, and more wondrously reestablished by Christ, unite all things. And finally, let every man zealously aspire to that which pertains to the concord of all men. Every evidence points to peace: in the first place the very meaning of nature and humanity; secondly, Christ, the Prince of human concord; finally, the many fruitful advantages of peace and the many destructive disadvantages of war.

It is to this cause that the minds of princes, divinely inspired, beckon you. Behold the meek and peaceful Leo, piously reigning as the Vicar of Christ, who has set forth his ensign of peace, inviting all who join in its glory. If you are true sheep, follow your shepherd. Francis, most Christian king of France, not only in title, fraternally beckons you. He does not believe the peace negotiations to be nonsense. He is not at all concerned with his own well-being, which would selfishly prevent him from providing for the common good, but declares it to be a noble effort to propagate the common peace. The most noble Prince Charles, a young man of incorruptible disposition, convincingly summons you to peace. The Emperor Maximilian is abundantly in favor of it. King Henry of England does not refuse it. It is compelling that all men should follow the eminent example of such noteworthy princes.

Most people detest war and piously pray for peace. A few, whose wicked happiness thrives on public chaos, loathfully wish for war. Conscientiously judge whether it is right or wrong that their dishonesty should so heavily outweigh the earnest will of all good men.

Nothing is accomplished by confederations, alliances, violence, or revenge. On the other hand, be consciously aware of what placability and benevolence can do. War incessantly sows war, vengeance seethingly draws vengeance, kindness generously engenders kindness, favors will be abundantly returned by other favors, and he will humbly appear most righteous who, at all times, considers the rights of others first.

What is limitedly pursued by human effort does not succeed. Christ shall divinely occasion good counsel to prosper. He will make His presence overwhelmingly known, and most favorably so. He will favorably breathe upon those who cherish what He most favors. Public welfare will shadow private interest.

While peace is fervently adhered to, every man's fortune

will be increased. Princes' kingdoms will be carefully amplified if they conscientiously rule their subjects by laws rather than arms; the dignity accorded noblemen will be increased in sincerity; the leisure of priests more tranquil; the contentment of the people more productive and their productivity more quietly directed; the name of Christ will be more formidable to the enemies of the Cross; and finally everyone shall be fraternally affectionate to his fellow man and, above all, pleasing to Christ, the pleasing of Whom constitutes the greatest happiness. I rest my case.

AN INQUIRY
CONCERNING FAITH

Although *An Inquiry Concerning Faith* is one of the least known and briefest of the colloquies, its appearance six months before the well-known *De Libero Arbitrio,* which marked as it were a definite break on the part of Erasmus with the Lutheran movement, gives it a special interest. Whereas his treatment of the freedom of the will demonstrates a rejection of Luther's basic doctrines, the *Inquisitio de Fide* shows a remarkable sympathy, if not a friendly agreement with the doctrines of the great reformer. The little work, basically an exposition on the Apostles' Creed, is an imaginary dialogue between Barbatius (Luther) and Aulus (Erasmus), with the latter sounding very Erasmian and the former speaking for the most part as a Lutheran. It is obvious the purpose of the work is to show that in essential doctrines, as contained in the New Testament and the writings of the Fathers, there is no great difference between Catholics and Lutherans.

Recent Reformation studies have shown that the lines of demarcation between Catholic and Protestant were not as marked as once assumed. In fact, the ambivalence evidenced in many doctrinal issues often seems to defy delineation. The current interest in dialogue has more than borne this out in our own day. Quite overlooked in the treatise are the more immediate causes of disagreement between the religious parties of the time, freedom of the will, indulgences, and the authority of the pope. The crucial problem of justification by faith is almost totally ignored. Actually the problem of justification was no new problem. Since the days of Augustine and his struggle with the Pelagians the theme had continued to occupy the great minds of Latin Christendom. Luther had merely proposed a new solution to a problem that in itself was ancient. Furthermore, with a few exceptions the question of justification by faith was one that was deliberately toned down by the theologians on both sides during the critical years between

1520 and the opening of the Council of Trent in 1545. Melanchthon clearly aimed at keeping it in the background in the *Confessio Augustana* of 1530, and in spite of the tremendous popular interest in the problem, its discussion was at least officially avoided.

Much later Erasmus was to write Pope Paul III that the definition of dogmas should be reserved to a council ("Dogmatum definitio synodo reservetur"),[1] and that pronouncements should be limited to essential matters. The seemingly latitudinarian treatment of dogma has led some to believe that Erasmus is more interested in the superiority of religion over theology. And there is certainly no doubt that he was opposed to whatever speculation that was not aimed at genuine piety. Parenthetically, the *Inquisitio* touches upon the perennial question of whether there is salvation outside of the Church. Although Erasmus appears to give an affirmative answer, yet his general attitude toward God's mercy and the universalism of the Christian message implies a humanitarian belief that there are anonymous Christians who have made a personal surrender to the truth of an "Unknown God." A. N. Whitehead feels that Erasmus, like Origen, has grasped the central importance of treating popular religion in such a manner as to keep a proper balance between its divine sources and their adaption to what is important in a given time and place.[2]

Erasmus perceived in the paganistic trends of the Renaissance a greater threat to religion than the theological squabbles he was so reluctant to participate in. We cannot agree with Renaudet's criticism of Erasmus that his neglect of dogma was indicative of a desire to reduce the essential dogmas of Christianity to mere symbols and thereby disengage its essential elements.[3] The *Inquisitio* surely bears out this often-misunderstood aspect of Erasmus as a theologian. We see here also that sense of history that accords development to revelation. The spirit of Christ, as Erasmus sees it, was not a total and complete manifestation to the Church in one instant of history. If its roots lay deeply hidden in the Old Testament, its growth, like that which preceded, required the maturing process of time. The Gospel had to be adapted to human weakness and the circumstances of time and place. If we detect a note of liberalism, he is merely following the example of the majority of the ancient Fathers of the Church, among others Athanasius and Basil.

More recent students of Erasmus credit him with a fairly well thought out notion of the development of dogma. In defending

---

[1] *E. E.*, XI, 62.

[2] A. N. Whitehead, *Religion in the Making* (New York: The Macmillan Co., 1926), p. 144.

[3] A. Renaudet, *Erasme, Sa Pensée Religeuse et Son Action d'après Son Correspondance* (Paris: 1926), p. 55.

what he had written in his preface to the 1516 edition of the New Testament, where he suggested that the laws of the Church on divorce might be liberalized, he explains that Christ's teaching might be better understood if the condemnation of divorce be interpreted as a condemnation of Jewish divorces obtained on frivolous grounds. Though he defers to the final judgment of the Church, he urges that this interpretation be accepted because by it, *saluti multorum consulatur*. His is basically a belief in progressive understanding of the sacred Message. The most notable aspect of the progressive changes is that through them the cause of salvation is furthered. In other words dogmatic development means that the Church has better understood the teaching and correctly adapted it to the moral needs of her members here and now. This dogmatic development exhibits both a progress in the sense of biblical interpretation and a deterioration in the loss of evangelical vigor. These apparently contradictory aspects of dogmatic development seem to result from Erasmus' exclusively moral valuation of dogma and especially his conception of Church history. To a certain extent one meet a similar approach in the better through-out position of Cardinal Newman.

That Erasmus was ever loyal to the Catholic Church, the Universal Church of the ages, cannot be doubted. Writing to his Franciscan friend, Conrad Pellican, who later defected from the Church, he continually reiterates his conviction that the Church of Rome is the one and only Church.[4] The same protest of his loyalty to Rome is seen in his letter to Bishop Marlianus in Galicia: "Christum agnosco, Lutherum non novi; Ecclesiam Romanam agnosco, quam opinor a Catholica non dissentire."[5] This letter, which so clearly expresses his views on the Lutheran question, is of interest, for Marlianus had recently penned an anti-Lutheran tract that had implicated Erasmus. Anyone reading his lengthy answer to the bishop can have no doubts as to Erasmus' position.

In his *De Libero Arbitrio* he reiterates this conviction:

> Granting that the Spirit of Christ could have let his people fall into error on some secondary point, with no immediate repercussions for the salvation of men, how can you admit that He left His Church in error for 1300 years, and that from among this crowd of holy men, He could not find one to whom He should show what we late-comers pretend constitutes the very depth of the whole Evangelical doctrine?[6]

---

[4] "Scis me in nullo dogmate per omnia sentire cum Luthero, nisi quod nimium, vere taxat corruptos hominum mores." *E. E.*, VI, 211

[5] *E. E.*, IV, 459

[6] *De Libero Arbitrio*, trans. (into French) P. Meanard (Paris: 1945), p. 91

What is contained in the *Inquisitio* is what constitutes for Erasmus the depth of the Christian message, for it is the belief to which every Christian subscribes when he is incorporated by baptism into the Body of Christ. Here is the basic contract whereby the Christian vows himself to the fundamental elements of faith.

An Inquiry Concerning Faith

(INQUISITIO DE FIDE)
1524

Quin et illud, mea sententia, complures populos conciliaret Ecclesiae Romanae, in quam nunc velut in caput quoddam colliguntur omnes, si non passim quaelibet sic definiantur ut velimus ad fidei negocium pertinere: sed ea duntaxat quae evidenter expressa sunt in sacris litteris, aut sine quibus non constat ratio salutis.

But it is my opinion that many would be reconciled with the Roman Church, in which all have been gathered as in one head, if instead of wishing to fix and define every little detail, we were to let suffice what is clearly contained in the Scriptures and is indispensable to salvation.

Letter to John Slechta
November 1519, E. E. IV, 118

Aulus. Saluta libenter is a book of Latin poems for young boys, but I question whether it is all right for me to wish you well!

Barbatius. Frankly, I would rather have you make me well than wish me well. But why do you say that, Aulus?

Aulus. Why? Well, if you must know, you smell of brimstone or Jupiter's thunderbolt.

Barbatius. They are malevolent gods, and there are senseless thunderbolts that differ greatly in origin from those that are ominous. I suspect you are thinking about excommunication.

Aulus. Exactly.

Barbatius. I have heard the thunder but never felt the bolt.

Aulus. How so?

Barbatius. Because I do not suffer from indigestion and can sleep soundly.

Aulus. But sickness is generally so much more dangerous the less it is felt. And as for these so-called senseless thunderbolts, why, they strike even the mountains and the seas.

Barbatius. True, but they have no effect there. But there is lightning that comes from a glass or a vessel of brass.

Aulus. And that, too, is frightening.

Barbatius. Yes, but only to children. Only God has thunderbolts that strike the soul.

Aulus. But suppose God is in His vicar?

Barbatius. I wish that He were!

Aulus. Many are amazed that you have not already been reduced to ashes.

Barbatius. Suppose I was. Then according to the gospel my salvation would be much more desired.

Aulus. We should not speak of such things but, rather, hope for them.

Barbatius. And why?

Aulus. So he who has been struck may be ashamed and repent.

Barbatius. If God had done this, we would have all been lost.

Aulus. I don't follow you.

Barbatius. Because when we were enemies to God, and worshippers of idols, soldiers in Satan's camp, that is to say, most excommunicated, then in a special manner He spoke to us by His Son, and by His speech restored us to life when we were dead.

Aulus. What you say is true.

Barbatius. It would be very hard on a sick person if a doctor would only examine him when he was well, for he doesn't need a doctor when he is well.

Aulus. But I am afraid that you will infect me with your disease before I shall cure you of it. It sometimes happens that he who visits a sick man is forced to be a fighter instead of a physician.

Barbatius. Indeed it sometimes so happens in physical illness; but in the diseases of the mind you have an antidote ready against every contagion.

Aulus. What's that?

Barbatius. A strong resolution to stick to your opinion. And besides, why do you fear fighting when this business is managed by words?

Aulus. There is something in what you say, if there is any hope of doing good.

Barbatius. It is said in the proverb that, "While there's life, there's hope"; and according to St. Paul, charity cannot despair, because it "hopeth all things."

Aulus. Your admonition is not ill advised, and with this in mind I will carry on this discussion with you a little; and if you'll permit me, I'll be a physician to you.

Barbatius. Do.

Aulus. Inquisitive persons are commonly hated, yet physicians are allowed to inquire after every particular.

Barbatius. Ask me what you will; the sky's the limit.

Aulus. I'll try. But you must promise you'll answer me sincerely.

Barbatius. I promise. But let me know what you'll ask me about.

Aulus. The Apostles' Creed.

Barbatius. I hear a military word. I will be content to be looked upon as an enemy of Christ if I shall deceive you in this matter.

Aulus. Do you believe in God the Father Almighty, who made heaven and earth?

Barbatius. Yes, and whatever is contained in heaven and earth; as well as the angelic minds.

Aulus. When you say God, what do you understand by this?

Barbatius. I understand a certain eternal mind, which neither had beginning nor shall have any end, than which nothing can be either greater, wiser, or better.

Aulus. You believe indeed like a good Christian.

Barbatius. Who by His omnipotent nod made all things visible or invisible; who by His wonderful wisdom orders and governs all things and by His goodness feeds and maintains all things; and who freely restored fallen mankind.

Aulus. These are indeed three special attributes in God; but what benefit do you receive by a knowledge of them?

Barbatius. When I conceive Him to be omnipotent, I submit myself wholly to Him, in comparison with whose majesty the excellence of men and angels is nothing. Moreover, I firmly believe whatever the Holy Scriptures teach to have been accomplished by Him, and also that what He has promised shall be done, since He can by His will do whatever He pleases, however impossible it may seem to man. And therefore, distrusting my own strength, I depend wholly upon Him who can do all things. When I consider His wisdom, I attribute nothing at all to my own, but believe all things are done by Him righteously and justly, although they may seem to our way of thinking absurd or unjust. When I consider His goodness, I see nothing in myself that I do not owe to His free grace, and I think there is no sin so great but that He is willing to forgive a true penitent, nor nothing that He will not freely bestow on him who asks in faith.

Aulus. Do you think that this is a sufficient belief?

Barbatius. By no means. But with a sincere affection I put my whole trust and confidence in Him alone, detesting Satan and all idolatry and magic arts. I worship Him alone, preferring nothing to Him, nor equating anything to Him, neither angel, nor parents, nor children, nor wife, nor prince, nor riches, nor honors, nor pleasures. For this I am prepared to lay down my life if He demands it, assured that one cannot possibly perish who commits himself wholly to Him.

Aulus. Then you worship nothing, fear nothing, love nothing but God alone?

Barbatius. If I reverence anything, fear anything, or love anything besides Him, it for His sake I love it, fear it, and reverence it, referring all things to His glory, always giving thanks to Him for whatever happens, whether prosperous or adverse, life or death.

Aulus. Certainly your confession is very sound so far. What do you think about the Second Person?

Barbatius. Try me.

Aulus. Do you believe Jesus was God and man?

Barbatius. Yes.

Aulus. How could it be that the same should be both immortal God and mortal man?

Barbatius. That was an easy thing for Him to do who can do what He will. And by reason of His divine nature, which is common to Him with the Father, whatever greatness, wisdom, and goodness I attribute to the Father I attribute the same to the Son; and whatever I owe to the Father, I owe also to the Son, except that it seemed good to the Father to create all things and bestow all things on us through the Son.

Aulus. Why then do the Holy Scriptures more frequently call the Son Lord than God?

Barbatius. Because God is a name of authority, that is to say, of sovereignty, which in a special manner belongs to the Father, who is absolutely the origin of all things, and the fountain even of the Godhead itself. Lord is the name of a redeemer and deliverer, although the Father also redeemed us by His Son, and the Son is God, but of God the Father. But the Father alone is from no other and obtains the first place among the divine persons.

Aulus. Then do you put your confidence in Jesus?

Barbatius. Why not?

Aulus. But the Prophet says he is accursed who puts his trust in man.

Barbatius. But to this Man alone has all the power in heaven and earth been given, that at His name every knee should bow, both of things in heaven, things in earth, and things under the earth. Unless He were God, I would not, as they say, make Him the sacred anchor of my faith and hope.

Aulus. Why is He called Son?

Barbatius. So that no one would imagine Him to be a creature.

Aulus. Why an only Son?

Barbatius. To distinguish the natural Son from the sons by adoption, the honor of which surname God imputes to us also, that we may look for no other besides this Son.

Aulus. Why would He have Him who was God become man?

Barbatius. That being man, He might reconcile men to God.

Aulus. Do you believe He was conceived without the help of man, by the operation of the Holy Spirit, and born of the undefiled Virgin Mary, taking a mortal body of her substance?

Barbatius. Yes.

Aulus. Why did He wish to be born in this way?

Barbatius. Because it so behooved God to be born. It behooved Him to be born in this manner Who was to cleanse away the filthiness of our conception and birth. God was willing to be born the Son of man that we, being regenerated in Him, might be made the sons of God.

Aulus. Do you believe that He lived upon earth, performed those miracles, taught those things revealed in the Gospel?

Barbatius. Yes, more certainly than I believe you to be a man.

Aulus. I am not an Apuleius turned inside out, that you should suspect that an ass lies hidden under the form of a man. But do you believe this very person to be that Messiah whom the prototypes of the law delineated, whom the oracles of the prophets promised, whom the Jews expected for so many ages?

Barbatius. I believe nothing more firmly.

Aulus. Do you believe His doctrine and life are sufficient for perfect piety?

Barbatius. Yes, perfectly sufficient.

Aulus. Do you believe that He was really apprehended by the Jews, bound, buffeted, beaten, spit upon, mocked, scourged under Pontius Pilate, and finally nailed to the cross, and there died?

Barbatius. Yes, I do.

Aulus. Do you believe Him to have been free from all sin?

Barbatius. Yes, why should I not? A lamb without spot.

Aulus. Do you believe He suffered all these things of His own accord?

Barbatius. Not only willingly, but even with great desire; and according to the will of His Father.

Aulus. Why would the Father have His only Son, innocent and most dear to Him, suffer all these horrible things?

Barbatius. That by this sacrifice He might reconcile to Himself us who were guilty, we putting our confidence and hope in His name.

Aulus. Why did God allow all mankind so to fall? And if He did allow them, was there no other way possible to repair our fall?

Barbatius. Not human reason but faith has persuaded me that it could be done in no better way nor more beneficially for our salvation.

Aulus. Why did this kind of death please Him best?

Barbatius. Because in the estimate of the world it was the most disgraceful; its torment was cruel and lingering. It was appropriate for Him who would invite all the nations of the world to salvation to stretch Himself out toward every region on the earth. To summon men, attached to earthly cares, to heavenly things. Finally He did this that He might represent the brazen serpent that Moses erected, that whoever should fix his eyes upon it should be healed of the wound of the serpent and thus fulfill the Prophet's promise, "Proclaim to the nations, God hath reigned from a tree."

Aulus. Why was He buried also, and so carefully anointed with myrrh and ointments, enclosed in a new tomb cut out of hard and living rock, the door being sealed, and public guards being placed there?

Barbatius. That it might be more apparent that He was dead.

Aulus. Why did He not rise again at once?

Barbatius. For the very same reason: for if His death had been doubtful, His resurrection would have been doubtful, too; but He wanted that to be as certain as possible.

Aulus. Do you believe His soul descended into hell?

Barbatius. St. Cyprian affirms that this clause was not formerly inserted either in the Roman creed or in the creed of the Eastern churches; neither is it recorded in Tertullian, a very ancient writer. And yet I do firmly believe it both because it agrees with the prophecy of the psalm, "Thou wilt not leave my soul in hell," and again, "O Lord, thou hast brought up my soul from the grave"; and also because the Apostle Peter, in the third chapter of his first epistle (whose authorship has never been doubted), writes in this manner: ". . . being put to death in the flesh, but vivified by the Spirit, by which also He went and preached unto the spirits in prison." But I believe He descended not to be there tormented, but that He might destroy for us the kingdom of Satan.

Aulus. Well I hear nothing yet that is impious; but He died that He might restore us to life again who were dead in sin. Why did He rise to live again?

Barbatius. For three reasons particularly.

Aulus. What are they?

Barbatius. First of all, to give us a certain hope of our resurrection. Secondly, that we might know that He in whom we have placed the safety of our resurrection is immortal and shall never die. Finally, that we being dead to sin by repentance, and buried together with Him by baptism, should by His grace be raised up again to newness of life.

Aulus. Do you believe that the very same body that died upon the cross, that revived in the grave, that was seen and touched by the disciples, ascended into heaven?

Barbatius. Yes, most certainly.

Aulus. Why did He leave the earth?

Barbatius. That we might all love Him spiritually, and that no man should appropriate Christ to himself upon the earth, but that we should all equally lift up our minds to heaven, knowing that our Head is there. For if men now take such pleasure in the color and the shape of garments, and boast so much of the blood or the foreskin of Christ, and the milk of the Virgin Mary, what do you think would have happened had He abode on the earth clothed, eating, and discoursing? What dissensions would those peculiarities of His body have not occasioned?

Aulus. Do you believe that He, being made immortal, sits at the right hand of the Father?

Barbatius. Yes, as Lord of all things, and partaker of His Father's kingdom. He promised His disciples that this should be, and He presented this vision to His martyr Stephen.

Aulus. Why did He show this?

Barbatius. That we may not be discouraged in anything, knowing what a powerful defender and Lord we have in heaven.

Aulus. Do you believe that He will come again in the same body to judge the living and the dead?

Barbatius. As certain as I am that those things the prophets have foretold concerning Christ have come to pass, so certain I am that whatever He would have us expect for the future shall come to pass. We have seen His first coming, according to the predictions of the prophets, wherein He came in humility to instruct and save us. We shall also see His second coming, when He will come on high, in the glory of His Father, before whose judgment seat all men of every nation and of every condition, whether kings or peasants, Greeks or Scythians, shall be compelled to appear; and not only those whom at that coming He shall find alive but also all those who have died from the beginning of the world, everyone in his own body. The blessed angels also shall be there as faithful servants, and the devils who are to be judged. Then from on high He will pronounce that unavoidable sentence that will cast the devil, together with those that have taken his part, into eternal punishments, that they may not afterward be able to harm anyone. He will translate the godly, freed from all trouble, to the company of His heavenly kingdom; although He wishes the day of His coming to remain unknown.

Aulus. I hear no error yet. Let us now come to the Third Person.

Barbatius. As you please.

Aulus. Do you believe in the Holy Spirit?

Barbatius. I do believe that It is true God, together with the Father and the Son. I believe those who wrote the books of the Old and New Testaments were inspired by It, without whose help no man attains salvation.

Aulus. Why is He called Spirit?

Barbatius. Because as our bodies live by breath so our minds are vivified by the secret inspiration of the Holy Spirit.

Aulus. Is it not lawful to call the Father Spirit?

Barbatius. Why not?

Aulus. Are not the persons confounded?

Barbatius. No, not at all, for the Father is called Spirit because He is without a body, which is common to all the persons according to their divine nature. But the Third Person is called Spirit because He breathes out and transfuses Himself insensibly into our minds, even as the air breathes from the land or the rivers.

Aulus. Why is the name of Son given to the Second Person?

Barbatius. Because of His perfect similarity of nature and will.

Aulus. Is the Son more like the Father than the Holy Spirit is?

Barbatius. Not according to the divine nature, except that He resembles the property of the Father the more in this, that the Holy Spirit proceeds from Him also.

Aulus. What, then, hinders, the Holy Spirit from being called Son?

Barbatius. Because, as St. Hilary says, "I have read nowhere that He was begotten; neither do I read this of His Father; I read of the Spirit, that He proceeds from!"

Aulus. Why is the Father alone called God in the Creed?

Barbatius. Because, as I have said before, He is simply the author of all things that are, and the fountain of the whole Deity.

Aulus. Would you clarify that?

Barbatius. Because there is nothing one can name that has

not its origin from the Father. For in this very fact, that the Son and Holy Spirit is God, they acknowledge they receive from the Father. Therefore the chief authority, that is to say, the cause of beginning, is in the Father alone, because He alone is of nothing. But yet in the Creed it may be so interpreted that the name of God may not be proper to one person but used in general, since it is distinguished afterward by the terms of Father, Son, and Holy Spirit into one God, which expression includes the Father, Son, and Holy Spirit; that is to say, the Three Persons.

Aulus. Do you believe in the Holy Church?

Barbatius. No!

Aulus. What? Don't you believe in it?

Barbatius. I believe the Holy Church, which is the body of Christ, that is to say, a certain congregation of all men throughout the whole world who agree in the faith of the Gospel, who worship one God the Father, who put their whole confidence in His Son, who are guided by the same Spirit of Him; from whose fellowship he is cut off who commits a mortal sin.

Aulus. But why do you shrink from saying, "I believe in the Holy Church"?

Barbatius. Because St. Cyprian has taught me that we must believe in God alone, in whom we absolutely put all our confidence. Whereas the Church, properly so called, although it consists of none but good men, yet consists of men, who may become bad, who may be deceived and deceive others.

Aulus. What do you think of the communion of saints?

Barbatius. This article is not touched on at all by Cyprian when he particularly shows what in such and such churches is more or less used. For he thus connects them: "For there follows after this saying, 'the Holy Church, the forgiveness of sins, the resurrection of this flesh,' and some are of the opinion that this part does not differ from the former, but that it explains and enforces what previously was called the Holy Church, so that the Church is nothing else but the profession of one God, one gospel, one faith, one hope; the participation of the same Spirit and the same sacraments, in short, a kind of communion of all good things, among all pious men from the beginning of the world to the end, just as the fellowship of the members of the body is between one another. So that the good deeds of one may help another so long as they are living members of the body. But in this society even one's own good works do not further his salvation, unless he be reconciled to the holy congregation; and therefore follows, 'the forgiveness of sins,' because outside of the Church there is no remission of sins, though a man should pine himself away with repentance and perform works of charity. In the Church, I say, not of heretics, but the Holy Church, that is to say, gathered by the Spirit of Christ, there is forgiveness of sins by baptism, and after baptism by repentance and the keys given to the Church."

Aulus. Thus far those are the words of a man who is sound. Do you believe that there will be a resurrection of the flesh?

Barbatius. I should believe all the rest to no purpose if I did not believe this, which is the most important of all.

Aulus. What do you mean when you say the flesh?

Barbatius. A human body, animated with a human soul.

Aulus. Shall every soul receive its own body that it left dead?

Barbatius. The very same from which it left, and, therefore, in Cyprian's Creed it is added, "of this flesh."

Aulus. How can it be that the body, which has now been so often changed out of one thing into another, can rise again the same?

Barbatius. For Him who could create whatever He would out of nothing, is it a hard thing to restore to its former nature that which has been changed in its form? I don't dispute anxiously how it can be done; it is sufficient to me that He who has promised that it shall be so is so truthful that He cannot lie, and so powerful as to be able to accomplish with a nod whatever He pleases.

Aulus. What need will there be of a body, then?

Barbatius. That the whole man may be glorified with Christ, who in this world was wholly afflicted for Christ.

Aulus. What does the addition of "and life everlasting" mean?

Barbatius. That no one should think that we shall so rise again as the frogs revive at the beginning of the spring, to die again. For here is a twofold death: of the body, that is common to all men, both good and bad; and of the soul. And the death of the soul is sin. But after the resurrection the pious shall have everlasting life, both of body and soul. Nor shall the body then be subject again to diseases, old age, hunger, thirst, pain, weariness, death, or any inconvenience, but being made spiritual it shall be moved as the spirit will have it; nor shall the soul be any more perplexed with any vices or sorrows, but shall forever enjoy the greatest good, which is God Himself. On the contrary, eternal death both of body and soul shall seize upon the wicked. For their bodies shall be made immortal, for everlasting torments; and their souls forever distressed by the torments of their sins, without any hope of pardon.

Aulus. Do you believe these things from your very heart, and truthfully?

Barbatius. I believe them with greater certainty than that I am now talking with you.

Aulus. When I was at Rome, I did not find all believing with equal sincerity.

Barbatius. No, but if you look about more thoroughly, you'll find a great many others in other places, too, who do not firmly believe these things.

Aulus. Well, then, since you agree with us in so many important points, what keeps you from joining completely with us?

Barbatius. I thought that you would ask that. I believe I am orthodox. Although I will not risk my life for it yet, I endeavor at all times to fulfill the obligation of my profession.

Aulus. Why, then, is there so great a war between you and the orthodox?

Barbatius. Do inquire into that. But listen, Doctor, if you are not displeased with this introduction, have lunch with me, and after dining you may inquire of everything at leisure. I'll give you both arms to feel my pulse, and you shall see both stool and urine; and after that, if you please, you shall anatomize this whole chest of mine, that you may make a better judgment of me.

Aulus. But I make eating with you a matter of religion.

Barbatius. Physicians are accustomed to do so, that they may better observe their patients and study their ailments.

Aulus. I am afraid lest I should seem to favor heretics.

Barbatius. No, there is nothing more religious than to favor heretics.

Aulus. How so?

Barbatius. Did not Paul wish to be made anathema to the Jews, who were worse than heretics? Doesn't he who attempts to improve a bad man and revive a dead man help him?

Aulus. Yes, he certainly does.

Barbatius. Well, then, do me the same favor and you need not fear anything.

Aulus. I've never heard a sick man answer more to the purpose. Well, come on, let me dine with you, then.

Barbatius. You shall be entertained in a medical way and as it befits a patient to entertain; and we will refresh our bodies with food that the mind shall be nevertheless fit for disputation.

Aulus. Yes, let it be so, we shall dine on good birds.

Barbatius. You had better make that bad fish, unless you have forgotten that it is Friday.

Aulus. That is something outside our creed.

CONCERNING THE IMMENSE
MERCY OF GOD

One of the constant aims of Erasmus' reform endeavor was to make the message of the Gospel a more vital factor in the lives of his contemporaries. His cultural ideal of *eruditio* and *pietas* is perhaps best summed up in the preface he wrote to the first edition of the Greek New Testament (1516). It was "to lead the way back to the original source of God's word instead of drawing it from conduits of stale water." Although not a preacher himself, he was deeply aware that the ministry of proclaiming the Gospel was one of the most important means of making the message of Christ more palatable to the indifferent and often apathetic congregation of his time. His work in translating the homilies and sermons of Augustine, Ambrose, Basil, and Chrysostom had attuned him to the need of a more dynamic portrayal of the doctrine of Christ. The aim of their sermons had been to convey the greatness of Christ, not by means of an abstract list of divine attributes, but by concrete examples. They vividly present the conviction that because Christ is truly God, He surpasses our most daring hopes. Because He is man, blood of our blood, we believe in His understanding of our weaknesses and miseries and in His great mercy, which bridges the bottomless abyss separating the divine from the human.

Compared with contemporary methods of preaching, these great masterpieces make him painfully aware of a need for revitalizing the great mysteries of Christianity in the spoken word. The mediaeval sermon, overloaded with scholastic subtitles and more often than not a stereotyped version of a sermon written centuries before, had grown distasteful to the enlightened citizen of the Renaissance. Filled with sophisms, it failed to touch either the current problems of the day or to present the basic beliefs of religion in a living fashion. What little reference there was to the Scripture was culled from the *catena aurea* and, completely out of context, was aimed more at proving irrelevant theological propositions than conveying the thought of Christ. Since the mendicant orders, particularly the Franciscans and Dominicans, monopolized the pulpits in most European churches, the sermons were for the most part filled with those same emotional and rabble-rousing cliches that one associates with the mission sermon of our own day.

Erasmus was in a certain sense a pioneer in the reform of hermeneutics. His work, *On the Method of Preaching* (*De Modo Conciendi*), originally dedicated to Bishop John Fisher, revolutionized preaching methods, not only by providing doctrinal subject matter drawn from Scripture that bore on the more fundamental elements of Christian belief and practice, but above all because it outlined a more inspiring mode of presentation. His last work on preaching, *Ecclesiastes*, which he completed in 1535, is a serious study on the preacher's need to understand the language of the people. The popular misconception that Erasmus spoke only Latin is still widespread. In the *Ecclesiastes* he urges that a knowledge of the vernacular is a requisite for the polished speaker.

> The first requisite is to associate with people whose speech is pure and polished. The second is to listen to preachers of refinement. The third is to study the books of those who have attained to eloquence in the vulgar tongue such as Dante and Petrarch among the Italians. Indeed there is no tongue so barbarous but that it has some elegance and expressiveness of its own if it is properly developed. . . . The learned will think Latin and Greek more agreeable, but the true Christian will find no tongue barbarous by which he can win his neighbor for Christ.[1]

His constant advice to the preacher is to aim at moving his hearer to some kind of personal involvement and action, rather than a cold, impersonal intellectual presentation. It is interesting to note that the Council of Trent recommended the Erasmian approach to improved preaching and many bishops insisted that his works on preaching be placed in every rectory library.[2]

The sermon, *On the Immense Mercy of God* (*De Immensa Dei Misericordia*), was written in 1524 on the occasion of the consecration of a chapel and is dedicated to Erasmus' friend and patron Bishop Christopher von Utenheim of Basle. Erasmus begins the sermon with an explanation of why he does not offer a prayer to the Blessed Virgin. Few theologians were more keenly aware of

---

[1] Quoted in P. S. Allen, *Erasmus Lectures and Wayfaring Sketches* (London: Oxford University Press, 1934), p. 79.
[2] *Concilium Tridentinum*, ed. S. Eheses (Freiburg: 1911), Vol. V, pp. 147–148.

the deteriorating effect of the extreme mariology of the late Middle Ages. The cult of the Mother of God was in his eyes one of the abuses that needed toning down if Christ was to regain the central position that was his in both dogma and the prayer life of the Church. A generation earlier the area had witnessed the execution of several friars for their extreme position on the role that Mary played in the redemption, and throughout all of Europe what has been termed "mariolatry" was reaching a peak unequaled even in our own times.

Erasmus introduces his subject in terms of the great need that all of us have for the virtue of hope. Certainly the troubled times of the early sixteenth century, with so much disruption in religion as well as politics, explain the timeliness of this exhortation. For Erasmus Christian hope not only looks to the loftiest goal, the possession of God, but it relies directly upon the infinite and unconquerable mercy of God for its attainment. It trusts God's omnipotence, which surpasses all created forces. Following the ancient Fathers, he describes the justification effected by the communication of God's mercy as a miracle of greater importance than the creation of all other wonders occurring in the material and spiritual world. Following St. Augustine, he assigns that mercy whereby sinners are saved to a world order that has its immediate cause in God Himself.

The beautiful sermon is replete with an intermingling of examples from both the Old and the New Testaments proving the mercy of God. The writers of the Old Testament, differing in time and place, contributed to the unfolding of a divine place of mercy that centers in the work of Christ. The words of those who lived before Christ are meshed with those of the Apostles in a striking fulfillment of God's promise of divine mercy. One is forcefully reminded throughout the work of Augustine's sermon *De Patientia*, which Erasmus had translated:

So, before the Incarnation of the Word the just of old were justified in the faith of Christ or in this true justice, which for us is Christ, for they believed that this would occur which we believe has occurred. . . . Their good works did not anticipate the theory of God but fulfilled it. Surely, they themselves heard, they themselves wrote long before Christ had come in the flesh: "I will have mercy on whom I have mercy and I will show pity to whom I will show pity." From these words St. Paul was to say much later: "So then there is question, not of him who wills nor of him who runs, but of God showing mercy." There are also the words of those who spoke long before Christ had come in the flesh: "My God, his mercy shall prevent me." How can they by whose charity Christ was foreannounced to us be aliens to the faith of Christ, for without faith in Him there never was nor can there be any just man.[3]

The recurring identification of God's mercy with justification is of great significance in the sermon. Seldom had men been more preoccupied with the Pauline doctrine of justification than in the early sixteenth century. All over Europe during these years theologians as well as laymen took up the study of St. Paul and the Fathers, especially St. Augustine, and experienced in themselves the meaning of redemption in Christ and justification by faith in Him. This stirring was in evidence not only in Germany but in France, Italy, and Spain as well.[4] The question raised by Luther on *sola fide* was but a partial aspect of a movement that Imbart de la Tour has termed *evangelisme*. Ochino, Seripando, and Giberti in Italy shared an interest in this searching question with such diversified personalities as Lefèvre, Margaret of Navarre, Alfonso Valdes, and Reginald Pole. Even Aquinas' Commentary on the Pauline epistles went through three editions between 1522 and 1532. Hence it is that Erasmus, aware as he was of the deep current of interest in "the religion of justification," injects into his sermon the compromise elements of relating justification and good works to the immense mercy of God. This he accomplishes with a remarkable blending of his biblical exegesis without prejudice to the traditional scholastic approach. Dividing mercy into *gratia praeveniens, sublevans, consolans, medicans,* and *ignoscens,* he follows the time-honored approach of the schoolmen but happily avoids the arid distinctions of overconceptualization. Erasmus and Aquinas are in agreement in concluding that the "work of divine justice always presupposes the work of mercy and is founded upon it."[5] For Erasmus mercy is justice in a higher form. We are saved because we believe willingly in the promises of God, because we love these promises in themselves, because we are already in harmony with the Source of these promises, Who is love. To choose mercy is to rejoice in the fact that everything depends on God's good pleasure.

[3] *The Fathers of the Church,* ed. R. J. Deferrari (New York: 1952), Vol. 16, pp. 256–257.
[4] Imbart de la Tour, *Les Origines de la Reforme* (Melum: 1946), II, pp. 570–571.
[5] "Opus autem divinae justitiae semper praesupponit opus misericordiae et in eo fundatur," *Summa Theologiae,* I, 21, 4.

Concerning the Immense Mercy of God

(DE IMMENSA MISERICORDIA DEI)
1524

Nullum enim argumentum magis congruebat vel isti tuae pietati, qua vehementer cupis universos mortales per Dei misericordiam salutem consequi, vel huic saeculo longe corruptissimo nimirum, in tanto miseriarum diluvio conveniebat omnes ad asylum Divinae misericordiae cohortari.

There is no subject better suited either to your piety whereby you earnestly desire the conversion of all mankind through God's mercy, or more needed for the depraved world of today. For certainly in this flood of present miseries it is most fitting to call all men to the haven of divine mercy.

Dedication to Bishop Utenheim
August, 1524, Op. V. 558

It is our purpose here today, my dearly beloved brethren, to speak to you of the magnitude of God's mercy without the protection of which our human weakness is of no avail. Therefore let us beseech His mercy so that it may so guide my tongue that we may depart enriched by His divine grace and may thus be more merciful toward our fellow man. Some of you here would perhaps wish that I begin with a prayer to the Virgin Mother, whom we must agree is worthy of the highest honor. Yet in view of the subject matter, I feel that it would be more suitable for you to repeat this little prayer with me.

O Jesus Christ, Almighty Word of the eternal Father, Who has promised that where two or three are gathered together in Thy name, Thou wilt be in their midst, behold how many of us have gathered here together. Vouchsafe, therefore, in keeping with Thy promise, Thy Holy Spirit being poured forth in the hearts of all, that we may more fully understand the greatness of Thy mercy. Grant that at the same time we may ren-

der thanks for this mercy so often experienced by us, that
we may earnestly implore it in all our necessities, and finally
that in our dealings with our fellow men we may emulate it.
Amen.

I will expect that each of you, following the dictates of the
orators, will listen attentively to these matters that concern
you so deeply. Let none of you fall asleep during the course
of this sermon, since your very salvation depends upon the
mercy of the Lord. No one, whether young or old, king or
commoner, rich or poor, learned or unlearned, sinful or
righteous, has not experienced the Lord's mercy; for he needs
the Lord's mercy in everything he does. Is there any topic
more worthy of our discussion than that through God's mercy
eternal salvation is prepared for all men? Therefore, all of you
present here should be not only attentive, but eager and willing
to listen to this address. For whoever is well disposed to this
exhortation will be well disposed to himself.

There are two main evils, among the many that bring the
human race to eternal perdition, of which the pious soul must
beware if he wants to share in God's happiness. They are self-
confidence and despair. One is brought about by a mind re-
sentful of God, blinded by self-love. The other arises from
weighing the magnitude of the sins committed on the one hand
against the severity of divine judgment on the other, forgetting
God's mercy. Both evils are so deadly that many have questioned which of them is the worse.

What could be more insane or more deplorable than that a
man, who is made of dust and ashes and who owes everything
that he is or can do to the divine goodness, should make
insurrection against Him? Against Him, by Whom he was
made, by Whom he was redeemed, and by Whom he is so
often bidden to share eternal life. It is the height of ingratitude
to despise Him, who has given you so much. It is madness
willingly to rebel against Him, Who can destroy at His nod. It
is impiety not to recognize your Creator, not to fear your
parent, or love your Saviour.

Lucifer did this. He claimed as his own what God had given
him and said in his heart, "I will scale the heavens; I will lift
my throne higher than God's stars, take my seat at His
trysting-place, at the meeting of the northern hills; I will soar
also above the level of the clouds, the rival of the most High."
I hope that his unhappy downfall might, at any rate, deter
mortals from following such an example, that is if the very
impiety of it does not. For God did not spare the angels who
sinned, but cast them down into hell, into the chains of darkness, to await their judgment on the last day.

What, then, will be man's punishment? He is a mere worm, crept forth from the earth, soon to be returned, if he lifts up his head against God. We are told of a sedition that once arose among the gods. Jupiter himself was compelled to leave heaven and flee to Egypt, and lie hidden there in a strange form. Having conspired together against Jupiter, they piled mountains upon mountains in an attempt to storm heaven and hurl Jupiter down from his stronghold. You laugh, and rightly so; but nevertheless the wise men of old wished to teach us the ways of men with stories of this kind. Salmoneus was cast down into hell because he mimicked the thunder and lightning of Jupiter: a fable, of course, but there have been many miserable little men who have claimed divine honors for themselves. God changed Nebuchadnezzar, who deemed himself a god, into a brute beast, afterward turning him into a man again. Alexander the Great wished to be thought of as the son of Jupiter and allowed himself to be worshipped at his banquets. Domitius Caesar desired to be styled God and Lord in all his letters rescripts, and even when spoken to in person. Adrian paid divine honors to his favorite Antinous.

Why do I mention these cases when it was a Roman custom to make their emperors gods, after they had ceased to be men? Divine honors were even paid to some during their lifetime, though to accept them would have been madness, and to assume them, blindness. If you take the authority of history lightly, listen to what the Apostle Paul writes to the Thessalonians about Nero, for some so interpret it: "This is the rebel who is to lift up his head above every divine name, above all that man holds in reverence, till at last he enthrones himself in God's temple, and proclaims himself as God." But perhaps it does not seem strange that men who worshipped oxen, apes, dogs, vile creatures, and even stones as gods would gladly be looked upon as gods themselves. For they were without doubt superior to those things they worshipped.

Herod was well aware that there was only one God, whose honor was incommunicable, yet in the Acts of the Apostles he allowed himself to be acclaimed thus: "It is the voice of a god, and not of a man." Immediately smitten by the avenging angel, that god perished by insanity, the most painful of all forms of death. And I wish there were no Christians who imitated, I will not say surpassed, the wickedness of Lucifer. Would you have me betray the secrets of the confessional? There is no need to do so, since in certain parts of the market-place, in the churches, at feasts and games—everywhere, in fact—we hear the name of God taken in vain. And what is more, we hear God's name abjured and the holy name of

Christ openly reviled. Men bite their fingers, utter threats against God, put their thumb between their fingers insulting their fellow man in spite of God. There are among Christians, if such men are still to be called Christians, those who desert their Prince for the sake of riches they must soon leave behind; for foul bodily pleasure; or transitory honors. They make a treaty with Satan, abjuring once and for all and in set terms whatever treaty had previously existed between them and Christ. These men have pledged their souls to hell. These things, when discovered, are punished with public execution.

What did Lucifer do that was similar to this? The Son of God had not died for him, and yet not even he blasphemed God, but only claimed equality of honor.

That region where five cities once flourished is now a noxious lake, yielding reeking pitch in place of the sweet Jordan. Inhabited by men ruined by debauchery and lust, the memory of its dreadful doom persists through all generations. We do not read that any of these men were impious enough to make bitter accusations against God, or to curse and threaten Him, yet they all perished beneath a rain of fire and brimstone.

It is worse that among those who profess the name of Christ there are men who dare to do what Lucifer and Gomorrah dared not. To these evils they add blasphemy as well! I see, my brethren, that you shudder at the mention of these things, and no wonder, since I myself shudder in body and soul as I tell them.

But nevertheless, the purpose of this sermon is to set forth the foolishness of despair of forgiveness, as well as the immense mercy of God. For it is God's mercy we will speak about today, as it endures with such men and moves them to repentance. Perhaps you think that examples of the crimes I have just mentioned are rare among us? What is the difference if you do not blaspheme, when your whole life is one long act of blasphemy against God? For some are slaves of gluttony, whose god is their stomach. They are forever eager to accumulate wealth, by fair means or foul; gaining honor by means of murder or treachery, tyrannously oppressing the poor, setting the world ablaze to gratify their ambitions, persevering in their sin neither ashamed nor repentant, enjoying the vilest of things like brazen-faced harlots, making a mockery of the life of the good. These men, by their very deeds, say that there is no God and that His promises are vain, his threats empty. They say also that the Gospel is false when it claims the blessings of heaven will be bestowed upon those who mourn, hunger and thirst after righteousness, who are meek, suffer persecution, and have all manner of evil said against them for righteousness' sake.

Only despair could be worse than this blasphemy. A sinner, since he is able to do as he pleases, becomes elated with his success and cries, "There is no God, neither is there knowledge in the most High, nor does He care for the things of men." He who does not believe God exists is less insulting to his fellow man than he who believes God is cruel or vain. In the same way, to deny God altogether is not as bad as to believe that he is inexorable, for this robs Him of that which makes kings kings, rather than tyrants.

He who gives up hope of forgiveness and throws himself into the pit of despair does not believe there is an almighty God. Not only that, but if he supposes there is any sin that God cannot wipe out, he also makes Him a liar. He has promised, through the prophet, that He will immediately forget all transgressions as soon as the sinner repents. The offspring of Cain, on the other hand, says, "My sin is so great that I do not deserve forgiveness." How foolish is this? If God, overcome by the greatness of sin, cannot forgive, you detract from His omnipotence if He will not do what he can. He is a liar and his word is vain, because He refuses to do what He so often promised to us through his prophets.

Whatever is in God is infinite. There are three chief qualities in Him: supreme power, supreme wisdom, and supreme goodness. Although power is generally ascribed to the Father, as his particular property, wisdom to the Son, and goodness to the Holy Spirit, each of these attributes is equally common to all three persons.

He declared His supreme power when he created this marvelous world by His will alone. Every part of it is filled with wonders, for even the gnats and spiders proclaim the boundless powers of the Creator. He showed Himself to be nature's Lord when he divided the water of the Red Sea; when He held back the water of the Jordan and allowed the people to go through the dry riverbed; when He made the sun and moon stand still while Joshua fought; when He healed the lepers with His touch; and when He brought the dead back to life with His voice. As He governs those things, which His ineffable power has created, He, with equal wisdom, proves He is no less wise than omnipotent.

His goodness is evident everywhere. It was an act of goodness to create the angels, since He required nothing to complete His own happiness. Yet He created the human race so that he might use His goodness and mercy even better than before. In this way God wished to be worthy not only of our love, but our amazement as well.

A king's power and greatness are sometimes admired by those who hate or envy him. But clemency and beneficence are also loved by those who have no need of them——even considering human fortune, which can place any of us in need. However, there is not, nor ever was, nor ever will be any man who does not need mercy. According to the Old Testament, not even the stars are pure in the sight of God, and He discovered iniquity in His own angels. For Paul cried to the Romans: "There is no distinction, all have sinned and need the glory of God." Listen to how the mystic harpist agrees with this. He exhorts all men to celebrate the glory of God with a spiritual lute, a ten-stringed psaltery, a new song, and a mighty shout. "The Lord," he says, "loves mercy and judgment, the earth is full of the Lord's mercy." While judgment is only mentioned once, mercy is mentioned again and again, with the eulogy that the earth is full of it.

Relying on the authority of holy Job and the Apostle, I would venture to add that not only the earth is full of the Lord's mercy, but heaven and hell also. For Psalm 35 says, "Lord, thy mercy is high as heaven; thy faithfulness reaches to the clouds." Hell perceived the mercy of the Lord when, having broken through the gates of darkness, He led those who were detained into the kingdom of heaven.

If anyone considers His works, which according to Moses' account were completed in the first six days, he cannot help but wonder at His power and ineffable wisdom. He should exclaim, "Heaven and earth are full of Thy glory," and sing the Hymn of the Three Children: "O all ye works of the Lord, bless ye the Lord; praise him and magnify him forever. Whatever has been created in heaven and above the heavens, in the earth and under the earth, in the waters and in the air, displays constantly the glory of the Lord."

Psalm 144 says, "How gracious the Lord is, how merciful, how patient, how rich in pity! Is he not a loving Lord to his whole creation; does not his mercy reach out to all that he has made?" Consider how wonderful is the creation of the heavens, with all the light from the stars. Consider also the creation of the earth, with its variety of trees and animals and other creatures, or the creation of hosts of angelic intelligences. Who would dare to affirm this if the prophet did not proclaim clearly that the Lord's mercy surpasses all of His works?

And yet no one will doubt the truth of this if he considers how much more wonderful the work of redemption is in comparison to creation. It is more marvelous that God was made man than that He created the angels. That He wailed in a stable, wrapped in swaddling clothes, rather than that He reigns in the heavens He created. It was here that the angels sang Glory to God in the highest, as at the most amazed work of God. They behold lowliest humility and recognize the highest sublimity. This plan to redeem the human race is Christ's life, Christ's teaching, Christ's miracles. It is His passion, cross, resurrection, appearance, ascension, and the descent of the Holy Spirit—the transformation of the earth by a few humble and ignorant men. It is a plan, replete with miracles, that even the angelic spirits could not fathom.

The evil spirits see and understand the fashion of the world's creation, but the plan of the world's redemption was hidden from them. Here art outwitted art; the art of mercy outwitted the art of malice. The creation of the world was a work of power, but the redemption of the world was a work of mercy.

"He has horns," says Habakkuk, "coming out of his hand, where his power is hidden." What could be more contemptible than a cross, what weaker than one crucified? But beneath that weakness was hidden the immense power of the divine mercy, which broke, overcame, and crushed the whole tyranny of Satan.

The same prophet was frightened when he had his eyes enlightened by faith and the world's proclamation of God's greatness. He considered his words and was amazed. And, as if God's greatness was manifest too little in all of these things, he added something to surpass all of these works: "In the midst of two animals you will see his work." In the confines of the Old and New Testaments He was made man and demonstrated that miracle of His mercy.

We say of those who have done great things: "In all else he surpasses others, in this he surpasses himself." With all reverence we may say something of the same about God: In all His deeds, God is incomparable and matchless. In His mercy He excels Himself. Holy Writ extols God's mercy more than any other virtue. It calls it great, then exceedingly great, and magnifies it even more by speaking of its multitude. The prophet king combines the greatness and the multitude of the divine mercy in one passage: "Have mercy upon me, O God, according to thy great goodness: according to the multitude of thy mercies, do away with my offenses."

Where there is great misery, there is a greater need for mercy. If you consider David's sin, you will perceive the greatness of His mercy. If you consider the number of ways David sinned in a single crime, you are able to see the multitude of

His mercy. A sin is never committed alone. Guilt follows guilt, like the links of a chain. In the first place David combined murder and adultery, two deadly offenses. Either of these is more heinous when committed by a king since it is his duty to punish these crimes in others. The more impudently princes sin among men, the more seriously they offend God. David carried a sword for the purpose of punishing murder and then committed murder himself. Adulterers were handed over to him to be stoned, and he himself compelled a woman to adultery. Furthermore, he increased the guilt of that adultery since he already had a large number of wives and concubines at home. Yet he coveted another man's wife, not because he had none of his own, but because he was possessed by lasciviousness to the extent that he seems to have delighted in rape rather than mere lewdness.

The man who, impelled by poverty, steals something from a rich man has not committed the same crime as the man who steals the only tattered garment of another when he himself has enough at home. Nathan, the prophet, drives home the atrocity of this crime with the parable of the rich man who despoiled and the poor man whom he robbed. The worst kind of murder is that which is not committed by chance, or a sudden fit of passion, but one that has set purpose and is planned beforehand. Uriah had done no wrong; the king knew he was faithful, and yet he abused the man's uprighteousness for his own destruction. He refused to go into the tent to sleep with his wife because the ark of God dwelt in a tent and because Joab, the leader in the war, slept upon the ground with the people. But Uriah's magnanimity did not divert the king's mind from evildoing. The following day he invited him to dine and made him drunk, planning to kill him if he said anything imprudent. But even when he was intoxicated, Uriah refused to go into his house with his wife. So another method was devised to bring about the death of this brave and loyal soldier. A letter directing his murder was sent to him. He suspected nothing, for the king knew because of his tested uprighteousness that he would not open it.

Joab, the leader, shared the guilt of that murder, just as David shared the adultery with Bathsheba. Uriah did not perish alone. In order to conceal the plot, many lives were risked, so that one innocent person could be destroyed to satisfy the king's lust. So you see, therefore, how many crimes one crime involves.

If there had been only one crime, even though a very serious one, then there would have been need for great mercy. Now David, seeing that his sins were many and varied, prayed for many mercies. Psalm 35 declares the extent of God's mercy. "Lord, thou dost give protection to man and beast," it says, "so rich is thy divine mercy." God not only saves men but promises to save cattle for men's sake as well.

The prophetic spirit says, "I will sing the mercies of the Lord forever." Therefore the mercy of the Lord must be praised with hymns in heaven also. Another psalm says: "O give thanks unto the Lord, for he is gracious and his mercy endureth forever." It might be supposed that the singing of God's mercy would end when all misery had ended. But what the righteous enjoy in heaven is the gift of mercy, for it was His mercy that tempered their torments.

But when one's whole life is corrupted by countless sins and a whole brood of vices, what then? Then we must cry with Asaph: "O remember not our old sins, but have mercy upon us, and that soon, for we are to come to great misery." Again, "Thy mercies are many, O Lord; enliven me according to thy word." And David, as if expostulating with God, cries: "Where are thy old mercies, O Lord?" And in Psalm 106: "Praise they the Lord in his mercies, in his wondrous dealings with men." This verse is repeated again and again as a kind of burden. Also in the psalm immediately preceding: "In his great mercy he would relent; their very captors should be moved to pity." He said mercy because he had mentioned several things that had provoked the Lord to anger. And when David is threatened with evils from many sides, he says, "It is better for me to fall into the hands of the Lord, for very many are His mercies, than into the hands of men."

As one crime contains many crimes, so one mercy contains many mercies. For consider how many mercies it took when He redeemed the human race once and for all. Isaiah the prophet, foreseeing this, speaks in the person of God, when he promises the Saviour Jesus: "I will make an everlasting covenant with you, even the sure mercies of David." God, when appeased, uses a similar figure of speech in Jeremiah: "I will show mercies unto you and have mercy upon you." When many evils threaten, many mercies are promised. In like manner, being reconciled to His people after many afflictions, God says in Zachariah, "I will return to Jerusalem with mercies and my house shall be built." Why do we recount these things from the Old Testament, where the word mercies is so often used? Because that law, though coming from a just and not a good God as some heretics believe, talks of hardly anything but the mercies of the Lord.

It is less amazing, then, if the Apostle Paul, in the second epistle to the Corinthians, writes things according to the prophets in the following manner: "Blessed be God, even the Father of our Lord Jesus Christ, the Father of mercies, and the God of all comfort; who comforteth us in all our tribulation." The Apostle has added something to mercy. It is the office of mercy to pardon wrongdoings. Here there is something greater, since God is made the comforter instead of the avenger. We have repeated these things from the Old Testament so that we may understand the immense and ineffable mercy of God that is signified to all men in this way.

The same thing is shown by another figure, which is either anadiplosis, which you call conduplication, or similar to anadiplosis. What is remarkably good the Hebrews call good, and what is notably evil, evil evil. Likewise in Holy Writ God is often said to be merciful and compassionate because of the excellent greatness of His mercies. You read in Psalm 144, "How gracious the Lord is, how merciful": and, as if this were too little, the writer has added, "how patient, how rich in pity!" Again in another psalm, "The merciful and compassionate Lord hath so done His marvelous acts, that they ought to be held in remembrance." Likewise in Joel, "Rend your hearts and not your garments; for the Lord is compassionate and merciful and repenteth him of evil." And in Jeremiah, "Therefore my heart is troubled for him; in compassion I will have mercy upon him, saith the Lord." What does to have mercy in compassion mean, other than to have immeasurable mercy? It is due to the same cause, namely, since whatever is in God is infinite, Holy Writ seems to ascribe an excessive and immoderate mercy to Him, a thing that passes for a vice among men.

Being persuaded that there is nothing in God that is liable to any vice, you will understand that the Scripture, in adapting itself to human comprehension, uses this figure to express an incredible hyperbole of divine mercy. In order to understand this more clearly consider this carefully: A king has enacted severe laws against murder. It might be called clemency if he pardoned a murderer once. But if the man committed murder ten times or even more and the king pardoned him each time, then the people would cry that the king's clemency was immoderate, since it impaired the force of the law and encouraged sin by the impunity it allowed. A father might be said to be lenient and kind if he was understanding when his son squandered his money once or twice. But if he went on trusting his son with money, though he squandered it again and again, it would be said that he was immoderately lenient and ruining his son with his indulgence. The same could be said with much more justice if he did the same to a slave. Moreover, if a husband caught his wife in the act of adultery and forgave her, he would be admired in that he considered such a woman worthy of his bed. But if his wife broke her marriage vow again and again and had intercourse with several men, and he still took her back, then people would say he was either remarkably stupid or his wife's pimp.

God, who is our King, our Father, our Spouse, makes no exception to any kind of sin and prescribes no number of sins. As often as we repent, He remits the penalty that His eternal law has promised. He receives us back into His family and allows us to lie in the bed of His love. He not only receives us, but forgets all our sins as well. He carries the lost sheep on His shoulder and brings them back to the fold. He calls upon the church of the saints to share His joy with Him, He runs to meet the prodigal son when he returns from the far country, brings forth the robe and ring and bids the fatted calf be butchered.

If I may say so, this must mean only an excessive and immoderate mercy on the part of God. It would certainly seem less wonderful if a man forgives a fellow man who sins since he himself has on occasion fallen into that sin, or someday may fall into it, or if a king pardons someone who has served him well, or a father condones a fault in a son whose company makes his old age easier, or if a master shows grace to a slave whose labor has helped him, or if a husband forgives an adulterous wife whose company he has sometimes enjoyed.

Occasionally a person fears the one he has pardoned and cannot punish him even should he want to. But God, who needs nothing and who can destroy at will if He wishes, bears with us, calls us to Him, and receives and embraces us, although He is so often scorned, abandoned, and denied by us.

There is no greater love nor closer union than that between husband and wife. Likewise there is no greater wrath than that felt at the breach of conjugal fidelity. And yet in Jeremiah the lenient Lord says to His adulterous spouse, who had had so many lovers, "Let wife that has been put away by her husband marry a second, can she afterward return to the first? That were shame and defilement. And thou with many lovers hast played the wanton; yet come back to me, the Lord says, and thou shalt find welcome." If a man throws out his wife, and after the divorce she marries another man, he does not take her back. Married love cannot be shared with another mate. But, although God's spouse, for whom He died and purified with His own blood, willingly flees from Him and prostitutes herself, he does not turn from her in disdain when she comes back. It is so strange that He who has exceeding mercy has exceeding love toward us.

Paul is not afraid to write this to the Ephesians: "We were by nature children of wrath, even as others. But God, who is rich in mercy, for His exceeding love wherewith He loved us, even when we were dead in sins, hath quickened us together with Christ." John expressed the Father's love toward us more clearly in his gospel. "God," he says, "so loved the world that He gave His only begotten Son, that whosoever believeth in Him should not perish but have everlasting life." Paul agrees with this entirely when he writes to the Romans, "He that spared not His own Son, but delivered Him up for us all, how shall He not with him also freely give us all things?" This great love and great mercy must seem immoderate when compared to human love and mercy. This will appear even truer if we consider the nature of the One who loves us so and pursues us with His mercy, and what manner of men we are to whom God promises such honor.

Each man should consider, in terms of the name he took in baptism and his renunciation of Satan and his pomps, how often he has been false to his vow and sided with the enemy of Him to whom he has sworn allegiance. Also, after receiving absolution from the priest, how often have you committed even worse sins? How often have you committed a sin on the same day that you have solemnly renounced it? Let no man fool himself, my brethren; whoever steals or commits adultery, envies or slanders his brother, or covets the honors of the world has deserted Christ, to Whom he has sworn allegiance. He has turned from his Father, revolted against his King, and fled from his Master. Perhaps a more convenient occasion for saying these things will be given later.

In order to better understand the scope of God's immense mercy you must know how the word is used in Holy Scripture. It sometimes means munificence, sometimes prevenient grace, occasionally uplifting grace, very often consoling grace, healing grace, pardoning grace, or even punishing grace. For in my opinion, at any rate, what the Lord says in Luke refers chiefly to kindness: "Be ye merciful even as your Father is merciful." For kindness is perfect, if a man is kind to his enemies. Matthew has said this more clearly in a similar discourse by our Lord: "Be ye perfect, even as your heavenly Father is perfect, who makes His sun to shine upon the evil and the good, and sends rain upon the just and the unjust." Since we have nothing we did not receive from God, whatever we can do or are, whatever we possess is God's mercy. If He had created them for Himself, His power and wisdom might be lauded, but now, since He has created all these things for us, we must recognize God's immense mercy.

For whom do the heavenly bodies revolve, and for whom do the sun and stars shine, if not for mankind? For whose enjoyment were all these things created when there were none? What about running rivers, gushing springs, the ebbing and flowing of the seas, the pools lying stagnant? For whom then does the fruitful earth bring forth so many living creatures and so much wealth if not for mankind? For in all nature there is nothing that is not subject to man. God wished only that man be subject to Him. Paul witnesses this when he writes to the Corinthians, "All things are yours and you are Christ's, and Christ is God's."

The eighth psalm repeats what Moses relates in Genesis, marveling at God's goodness, who has bestowed so much mercy on man. "What is Adam's breed," it says, "that it should claim thy care? Thou has placed him only a little below the angels, crowning him with glory and honor and bidding him rule over the works of thy hands. Thou hast put them all under his dominion, the sheep and the cattle, and the wild beasts besides; the birds in the sky, and the fish in the sea, that travel by the sea's path." I will say what is even more sublime: we even owe the angels of heaven to the Lord's mercy.

My word would carry little weight, if Paul did not teach this clearly when writing to the Hebrews. Speaking of the angels he says: "What are they, all of them, but spirits apt for service, whom he sends out when the destined heirs of eternal salvation have need of them?" Frequently in both the Old and New Testaments we read of the ministry of the angels reviving the hungry, setting the captives free, defending countries, averting evils, and refreshing the righteous with glad tidings. Not only that but the Lord himself says in the Gospel, "These angels continually behold the face of my Father who is in heaven." What is more wonderful than the condescension that children should have angels as their guardians?

Therefore whatever you have is due to His mercy, and as long as you remain with Christ you have all things. Paul cries aloud, "What hast thou, O man, that thou didst not receive?" Now, if you have received, why do you glory, as if you had not received? Whatever evil you see in others, recognize the prevenient grace of God. David speaks of this in many places: "And thy mercy shall go before me." You were not born illegitimate, lame, or blind, or poor, you were not slow-witted, as many are born; so give thanks to His prevenient grace. The misfortunes of other men might have been yours also, if God's mercy had not preserved you. You are not an adulterer, a perjurer, a murderer, or a blasphemer as many men are, therefore you should recognize God's mercy, for you would have been these things if God's mercy had not protected you. Physionomous accused Socrates of excessive and immoderate lust. Some of Socrates' students who knew of his extraordinary moderation laughed at Physionomous, while others were indignant. Socrates restrained them by saying: "He has spoken the truth. All of these I was, if philosophy had not taught me moderation."

What Socrates ascribed to philosophy, Francis ascribed more correctly to the divine mercy. For once when, at his request, his companion insulted him as he would a criminal, calling him a parricide, a sycophant, a ravisher, and a poisoner, he bore it patiently and lamented his sins. When his companion asked why he had been compelled to tell so many lies about an innocent man, when none of it applied to him, Francis replied: "You have in no way lied; all this I was and much more, had not God's grace saved his servant from these ills."

God's mercy not only incites us to piety, but also helps us in our endeavors. It accompanies us when we begin and helps us to accomplish what human strength alone could not. The Apostle Paul seems to refer to this kind of mercy. When invoking grace and peace in his salutations in the epistle to Timothy, he adds mercy also. For, without prejudice to a better opinion that others may have, it seems to me that grace refers to vocation, and we are called by faith, that is to say by readiness, to believe.

The faith is a free gift of God, and on that account those who have it owe it to the divine mercy. Mercy refers to the gifts that are apportioned to each of us according to the measure of our faith. Peace refers to the innocence of the whole life, without which there can be no friendship with God or true concord with our brothers. Therefore attribute it to God's mercy when you are saved from evil, not to the stars, or fortune, or your own prudence. No one entangled in the bonds of sin can be freed if the divine mercy does not come to his aid. The one hundred and twenty-ninth psalm teaches us this: "Patient as a watchman at dawn, for the Lord Israel waits, the Lord with whom there is mercy, with whom is abundant power to ransom. He it is that will ransom Israel from all his iniquities." Paul declares, when he writes to the Philippians, that God's mercy saves us from sickness. "Epaphroditus was sick unto death; but God had mercy upon him; and not only on him but on me also, lest I should have sorrow upon sorrow." Nor is there any difference between sustaining mercy and consoling mercy, except that we are sustained when our troubles are taken away, while consoling mercy is with us during our time of trouble so that we may be able better to bear it, as Paul says. Often these evils are sent by a merciful God, so that He may cleanse us from the sins we have committed, or keep us from committing them, or so that we may have an opportunity of practicing virtue.

Abraham was tempted in this way, and Job was tried by various evils. All men who have lived holy lives in Jesus Christ have been tested by various trials in this world, just as gold is tested by fire. Those who blame God when sickness or death strikes their wife or family, or when their property is lost, or when their crops fail, do not understand that these are the most infallible signs of our merciful God.

Hear how Solomon admonished us: "My son, despise not the chastening of the Lord; for whom the Lord loveth, He correcteth; even as a father the son in whom he delighteth." Paul repeats the same aphorism when he writes to the Hebrews, only in different words: "For whom the Lord loveth He chasteneth, and scourgeth every son whom he receiveth." Therefore, my brethren, when the storm of adversity strikes, persevere in Godly discipline, according to Paul's counsel, knowing that God offers Himself to us as His sons.

In the eighty-eighth psalm God corrects His sons: "Do his children forsake my law, to follow paths not mine; do they violate my decrees, leave my will undone? Then they shall feel the rod for their transgressions, I will scourge them for their sin, but I will not cancel my gracious promise to him; never will I be guilty of unfaithfulness, never will I violate my covenant, or alter my decree once spoken." Paul also threatens the sons whom he loves, "What will ye? Shall I come unto you with a rod, or in love, and in the spirit of meekness?" And again, "What have I to do to judge them also that are without?" Nothing is more bitter to a son than when he hears his father say, "Do what you wish, it matters nothing to me." These are the words of a man who is giving up. This meekness on the part of the parent is harder to bear than any rebuke.

Therefore, while indulgence is cruel, correction is merciful. Let the righteous correct me in mercy and reprove me, but do not let the oil of the sinner anoint my head. The Roman general Aemilius, having achieved remarkable success, foresaw that some disaster was menacing him. When the ill will of fortune perpetually smiled upon Polycrates, the tyrant of Samos, he tried to avert it by the loss of a precious ring. Therefore, if we live sinful lives, how frightened should we be if the just vengeance of God menaces us whenever prosperity smiles upon us. For in the book of the prophets, when God wishes to express His implacable wrath, He threatens to take away the rod from them and not heal their sins by afflictions.

If we are not so fortunate, my brethren—that is, if our Father's mercy grants us fair weather—let us give thanks to Him by being careful never to abuse His loving kindness. But if we are threatened with storm and stress, let us give Him thanks and resign ourselves wholly to His will. You put yourselves in the hands of a physician so that he will restore your health, and you trust a surgeon to bind and cut; therefore, trust yourself to your Creator, Lord, Father, and Saviour. You dare not tell a physician how to cure you, therefore do not tell God how to further your salvation. The Apostle Paul permits Satan's angel to menace him. "When I am weak," he says, "then I am strong." He is glad of his infirmities, in order that he may possess the power of Christ.

To whom are we to pray to be released from this mercy of God? He procures our salvation through these afflictions, as if they were bitter drugs. When common people see a man born into an illustrious family, blessed by health and wealth, laden with honor, they say, "How much he owes to God!" Men judge this way, appraising good fortune by that which is obvious. But if you consider the matter in the light of God's judgment, an obscure, needy, sickly person, the scorn of men, often owes more to God's mercy than those whom the ignorant multitudes see as peers of God. Take as much as you want of what the world calls unhappiness. You are immensely happy if, by this temporal unhappiness, you achieve eternal happiness.

Everyone, except the hypocrite who believes himself free of sin, knows of pardoning mercy, which is also called clemency. But the Apostle John says, "If we say that we have no sin, we deceive ourselves, and the truth is not in us." If the stars are not clean in the sight of God, and if He finds iniquity in His angels, if no one is pure in the sight of God, not even a babe one day old, which of us will boast that he has an unpolluted heart? Many are thought to be righteous by men, but before God no one is actually righteous. But all our righteousnesses are filthy rags, defiled by menstruous discharges. Paul cries, "O wretched man that I am! Who shall deliver me from the body of this death?" Job is called righteous, but from what God says, he is not completely faultless. Even the Prophet David dreads God's judgment, unless it is tempered by mercy: "Enter not into judgment with thy servant, for in thy sight shall no man living be justified."

Let each of you consider truthfully how many times, in how many ways, and how badly you have offended God. How often have your good deeds been blemished. In this way each of you shall know how much he owes to God's mercy. For God calls us to repentance on so many occasions and graciously remits all guilt to those who are contrite.

I will add to this what some may think not altogether probable. When God destroys the wicked who are sunk in the depths of iniquity and casts them into hell, even then He is not unmindful of His mercy. He sets the Hebrews free by dividing the waters of the sea and then drowns the Pharaoh and his followers. There was mercy on both sides. Sustaining mercy was shown toward His people, and punitive mercy was shown toward the king. For if the king continued sinning, he would be forced to endure the worse pains of hell. It was an act of mercy that he called him to repentance when he was guilty of so many sins. Already broken by misfortunes, he had begun to show a contrite heart, but then he repented wickedly of his wholesome repentance, saying, "I know not the Lord, neither will I let the people go." He could not be kept from pursuing them even by this great miracle, but blinded by wrath, he boldly entered the sea. God mercifully put an end to an iniquity that was past remedy. Although he could not be healed, he at least perished by a less fearful death. It was the same way with all other instances of severity given in the Old Testament, such as in the case of those consumed by fire, swallowed up by the earth, those who were slain by the sword and the serpent.

In the Gospel instances of vengeance are very few; mercy predominates. For it was a lenient reprimand when Elymus was suddenly struck blind and taught not to resist the preaching of the Gospel. Paul delivered only a few to Satan, so that their souls could be saved on the day of final judgment, and thus they would be shamed into mending their ways. The greatest instance of mercy ever recorded was that of Ananias and Sapphira, who suddenly fell down at Peter's rebuke. Yet it is uncertain whether their souls were saved by the destruction of their bodies.

Finally, the damned souls in hell suffer less than they deserve. Some believe the divine mercy to be so efficacious that they hold that even the damned and the demons are restored to mercy after a long time. This opinion, although it rests on high authority, was nevertheless condemned by the orthodox fathers. They only quoted it to show us what an eminent opinion of God's mercy was held by very learned men, who constantly study the sacred volumes which contain hardly anything else than the mercy of God.

It has now been sufficiently demonstrated that whatever we are and whatever good we possess is all due to the divine mercy. This is why we are protected from menacing evils, saved from oppressors, made brave and cheerful during illness, guided to repentance, trained in perfect virtue, and forgiven our frequent offenses.

In order that you may be able to understand the immense height, breadth, and depth of the divine mercy, regard yourselves with me awhile. First consider in what respect you are most worthless, secondly that in which you excel, and finally consider the evils that menace you. Then consider the blessings, the hope of which has been set before you. The contemplation of these things will show us the fullness of the divine mercy, of which there is truly neither measure nor number. Let us consider our own body, the dwelling place of the soul. There is hardly any weaker, more worthless, or more wretched creature. If you ask its origin, the author of our race was made of the dust of the earth. Consider how void of dignity that small amount of fluid is, the human sperm from which the human offspring is created.

I shall not mention the squalor of human birth here but only ask you to think about the ugliness of it all—the long efforts of those in labor, their piteous cries. Finally the child is born and revived, whimpering. Nature provides other creatures from the moment of their birth with some covering or protection—shells, bark, hide, thorns, hair, bristles, down, feathers, scales, fleece, a trunk, and even shelters some trees with two layers of bark. Only man does she cast upon the earth, naked from the day of his birth. Even a chick coming forth from its shell would seem more fortunate in this respect. Further we see in humans the swaddling clothes, the speechless tongue, the eyes unused to light that seem to regret leaving the dark womb, the throbbing head, indicating the greatest weakness in all living creatures. In this entire weak, puny body no part is sure of its function. Most other living creatures possess their instincts from birth. Horses are given swiftness; the butterfly can flit the moment it emerges from its cocoon; the lion cub is dangerous soon after birth; fish can swim when they emerge from their eggs; tadpoles twist before they become frogs. What does nature allow man to do but whine? He must learn to walk, to become a two-footed instead of a four-footed creature. He cannot even eat until he is taught. Then there are the innumerable diseases, with new ones constantly springing up. There may be no cure for these new ones, just as there is no cure for some of the old. These attack the newborn. Some are already born with diseases such as leprosy and epilepsy, from which many die at an early age. I hardly need to mention abortions and deformed babies. Consider the injuries childhood is liable to, the evanescence of youth, the anxiousness of the prime of life, the misery of old age. How short the whole of life is. How few men actually reach its fulfillment.

Each of you who has attained the prime of life should think of the perils and diseases you have escaped and give thanks to the divine mercy. On my part I hold that the most serious evils are those whose seeds are implanted within us. From our birth we are prone to wrath, lust, greed, envy, avarice, and rapacity, while other creatures, by nature, keep within their limits. It is a difficult struggle with these remnants of the old Adam. Few are successful. The soul is weighed down with the earthy mass of the body, and the weak-willed plunges into sin. Consider how many hazards surround us and you will see that many more die from accidents than from disease. Many have been wiped out by lightning, earthquake, landslide, flood, hurricane, poison, plague, falling buildings, and unskilled physicians. But there is no greater disaster than that caused by war.

These hazards, however, threaten only our bodies. How many hazards menace the soul? There is constantly an enemy in our midst. We are flattered in the hope that we will be unwary and shown rage in the hope that we will be overwhelmed. There are evil spirits that change themselves into angels of light. Who would not shudder if confronted with a multitude of these? They are full of strength, cunning, malice, and destruction. Amid all this there is the thought of death, the severity of the last judgment, the never-ending torments of hell. Death must come to all, though its coming is known to no man.

I see you tremble at the mere mention of all this, and not without cause. The more evil and danger you behold, the more you owe to the divine mercy, which not only protects those who believe in it amid these things, but also makes them all more pleasant. We owe all these calamities to the old Adam, but in turn there is a happiness paid with interest that we owe to the new Adam, who is Jesus Christ, to be lauded by men forever.

Satan drove men from paradise. Christ, instead of an earthly paradise, has opened the kingdom of heaven to us. The serpent involved us all in the many pains of life; Christ gave back to us the joy of immortal life. Satan, by his subtlety, won eternal death for us; Christ, by His mercy, bestows eternal life upon us. He who sincerely surrenders to God has no need to fear the number of his enemies. He has broken all of Satan's tyranny, He has overcome the world, and has changed flesh into spirit.

Let us worship His merciful power and enjoy His powerful mercy. Through Him, who gives us strength, we can do all things, if we only abide in Him. We possess all things through Him, for in God is the sum of all good things, protecting, sustaining, comforting and enriching us with His mercy.

Those who put their trust in their own talents, in health, in chariots, horses, worldly prudence, and their own deeds are exposed to a great deal of evil. But under what protection are the righteous safe? "But as for me," it is said, "I will come unto thy house in the multitude of thy mercy." And a little later, "O Lord, thou hast crowned me with the shield of thy favor." When natural strength fails and merit is of no use, then mercy comes to our aid. Whereas a warrior's shield protects only part of his body, the shield of the divine spirit protects us on every side—from spiritual wickedness from above, from the serpent at our heels, from the danger facing us, from the danger threatening from behind, on the right so that prosperity may not make us arrogant, on the left so that adversity may not defeat us. Relying upon this shield, the psalmist cries, "The Lord is on my side, I will not fear what man doest unto me." And elsewhere, "I will not be afraid for ten thousands of the people that have set themselves against me round about."

The Apostle Paul even more boldly writes to the Romans, "If God be for us, who can be against us?" That warrior uses faith and trust in the divine mercy for his armor. With this equipment he despises not only hardship, hunger, nakedness, peril, and persecution, but also the tyrant who threatens instant death. Human cruelty can do nothing when the protecting mercy of God is present. Still bolder, Paul despises, besides life and death, angels, principalities, powers, things present, things to come, courage, height and depth, and anything created in heaven or hell. This is the man who, aware of his own weaknesses, calls himself an earthen vessel: "We have this treasure in earthen vessels." Where does this fragile pitcher get such strength? "By the mercy of God," he says, "I am what I am." The grace of God is then God's mercy. Then let us rejoice with Paul in our infirmities, that the power of Christ may dwell in us.

It is more fitting that we glorify the mercy of God through

the contemplation of our infirmities. And yet at the same time a man will contemplate himself in those areas where he excels every living creature. For if you compare only your body to that of the beast, you can readily see how many of the latter are superior: the camel in size, the tiger in speed, the bull in strength, the swan in color, the peacock in grandeur, fish in health, and you will believe the proverb: "Almost all surpass you, lynxes and eagles in keenness of vision, vultures in smell, stags and crows in liveliness."

Yet if you consider the endowments of the human body, you will also find cause to praise God's mercy. What keenness of perception, what symmetry of limbs, what adaption of organs to so many uses. Lactantius, a man of remarkable eloquence, has published a book concerning these matters called *Of God's Handiwork*. It would be profitable to read it. Anything good in the body comes from God's mercy, and therefore must be attributed to His loving kindness.

He who is proud of the endowments of the body will hear it said, "Mortal things are but grass, the glory of them is but grass in flower; grass that withers, a flower that fades, when the Lord's breath blows upon it." Again, "Why are earth and ashes proud?" Man has no cause to be arrogant in the endowments of the body. He who created the body created the soul as well. He fashioned the body from clay and breathed the breath of life into his nostrils. Because of this, while the soul of other animals perishes with their body, ours survives its body, until it is received back at the resurrection as we are promised. Even death itself shows how powerful the soul is, for as soon as it departs, the body becomes a useless corpse. It has no heat, color, motion, or senses. The soul is held captive in the body and can do nothing except through the bodily organs, which often hinder it from putting forth its native force. Yet the soul is so swift and clever. What a great gift memory is. There is nothing hidden so deeply in nature, either in heaven or earth, that man cannot observe it, apprehend and understand it. From the position and movement of the stars, many men can foretell things that will happen in the future. Better yet, the virtue and divinity of the great Craftsman is understood from the things created. Human thought is rapid; a man can survey a great many things in a short space of time. The force of memory is immense; it unerringly retains the forms and names of so many things that were given to it by the senses. I will not speak of those who learn many difficult sciences and languages and remember these well. Think how many faces and names, animals, trees, herbs, and so many other things each of you can recognize and name from memory. Common people call these natural endowments, although they are really gifts of the divine mercy. We receive these things, not because we deserve them, but because of the goodness of the divine mercy.

When the prodigal son abused these things at the expense of human will, what he had been given was not taken away and even more was added. He has trained us by the law, through His Son, whom He gave wholly for us, who has taught us the mysteries of God. Through His spirit He enriches our minds with endowments that surpass human strength. He enables us to understand the Scriptures, to know the future, to speak to overcome the gates of hell, to become members of Christ, sons of God, to inherit the kingdom of heaven, of which there is no end.

Consider now what you have been created of—one half of you is dust, and sin has degraded you below the beasts of the field. Still, great dignity and happiness await you. The Lord's mercies are without number or measure. What could be more contemptible than a beetle? But the beetle is pure compared to the squalor of sin. What is more sublime than the angels? What if He made an angel of a beetle? As it is He has made man, who is more worthless than a beetle, greater than an angel. I would venture to say He has made him a god. Holy Scripture says this also: "I have said, you are gods; and all of you are children of the most High."

Whatever is born of God to some extent becomes God. Whatever is joined to the body and spirit of Christ comes into fellowship with His name. If there are none of these things here that you deserve, then worship and extol His great mercy. If anyone attributes these things to what he deserves, the Apostle Paul will cry out that they are all due to the divine grace. All his letters ring with the word grace. As often as you hear it, remember that God's mercy is being commended to you. For it is by grace that we are cleansed from our sins, it is by grace that we believe, it is by grace that, through His Spirit, charity is diffused in our hearts, in the virtue of which we do righteous deeds. For we are not sufficient to think anything of ourselves; but our sufficiency is God.

According to Paul, there exist shameless people who sell their good works to anyone who will buy—as if they had such superfluity that they could make others rich. These people must be wretched, and those who would buy their services are cursed. Of this, the Apocalypse says to the Laodicean church, "I am rich, thou sayest, I have come into my own; nothing, now, is wanting to me. And all the while, if thou didst but know it, it is thou who are wretched, thou who art to be pitied.

Thou art a beggar, blind and naked." But those who promise riches to others from their own abundance sin even more. Does the Holy Spirit counsel anything of this sort? "I counsel thee," He says, "to buy me of gold tried in the fire, that thou mayest be truly rich."

You who are aware of your poverty, why do you beg from beggars? "Is there one of you," says James, "who still lacks wisdom? God gives to all, freely and ungrudgingly; so let him ask God for it, and the gift will come." Why do you want to become clothed in the works of man when you become more naked the better you think you are clothed? If you recognize your own misery, mercy is right at hand. Among men who exact payment for a favor and claim a loan with usury, nothing costs more than that which has been bought with prayer. Nothing is more freely given by God than that which is bought with the two coins of prayer and trust, for He who is willing to sell this mercy has paid the price himself.

We have already dwelt for some time on God's mercy, my brothers, but there is more that remains to be said, if we would recount all those passages in the Scripture that refer to the divine mercy. All that remains is for me to exhort you to show that you are worthy of the ever-ready mercy of God. This will be the culmination of our discourse, if the Lord's mercy promises to be with us while we speak. Above all, may God keep pride away from us, for He resists the proud and gives grace to the humble.

Many are led by success in temporal affairs into the blind madness of pride, so that they live according to the lust of their own minds. Unmindful of the Creator, they are so far from repentance that they enjoy evil. "They rejoice to do evil and delight in the boldness of wickedness." Solomon writes this about them: "When the wicked cometh, then also cometh contempt, and with ignominy, reproach." Paul says also, "God abandoned them to passions which brought dishonor to themselves." Some of these despise admonition and assure themselves of perpetual impunity. They refuse anything that may move them to repentance, saying let God keep His heaven to Himself and leave the earth to us. Moses spoke of them in his song. When he had told how much God had given to the Israelites, he said, "Jeshrun grew fat, and kicked: thou art grown fat, thou art grown thick, thou art covered with fatness"; and then he forsook God. Then Psalm 72 describes these men: "Not for these to share man's common lot of trouble; the plagues that afflict humankind still pass them by."

This is why they are so proud and overwhelmed with cruelty. They do whatever they desire. They have conceived iniquity and spoken against God. But what follows this felicity? They are cast down and destroyed. They shall vanish as quickly as a dream vanishes upon awakening. Those who follow Lucifer's example shall suffer what the Lord threatens in the Gospel: "I beheld Satan, as lightning, fall from heaven." Corozain, proud of her transitory possessions, was told, "Woe unto thee, Corozain! For thou who are exalted to heaven shall be brought down to hell." Paul, too, was once arrogant, and threatened the disciples of the Lord. He was suddenly cast down to earth by God's right hand and heard these words spoken to him: "It is hard for thee to kick against the goad." But in his case it was error and not perversity, so he was forgiven. He soon realized that God forgave his sin, and not only forgave him but transformed a wolf into a sheep, a tyrant into an apostle. Malediction awaits those who say to God, Depart from us, we will not have knowledge of thy ways. They have hardened their hearts and refused to realize that they may do well.

In Isaiah, when the Lord calls the people to weeping and mourning, they continue eating the oxen and the sheep, saying, "Let us eat and drink, for tomorrow we shall die." In the same prophet they mock the threatenings of the Lord when He calls them to repentance. They say in another place, "We will not hear the Lord, but will die in our sins." According to the old proverb patience too often abused becomes fury. When the Lord's mercy is scorned, it becomes severe condemnation. The Lord, when scorned, says in Isaiah, "And the word of the Lord shall be to them precept upon precept, line upon line, here a little, there a little, and they may go and fall backward, and be broken, and snared, and taken." These men, left to their own desires, go from bad to worse, passing their days amid good things, and then in a moment they go down to hell. They are wretched men, devoted to destruction, who are fattened for the slaughter. Nothing softens them to repentance.

God's clemency is with us often enough to enable us to amend our lives. He grants you time for penitence and does not take His loving kindness from you at that time; He gives you good health, wealth, and the other blessings of life, heaping them upon you as He would coals upon a fire.

If you cannot hate your sin because hate itself is heinous, then you should hate it because it displeases a Father who is so loving. Aeschinus, the young man in the comedy, found that his father was tender toward him even when he was wrong. This moved him to treat his father more reverently in the future. He says, What can be the meaning of this? Is this being a father, or is this being a son? If he had been a brother or a familiar companion, how could he have been more complaisant? Is he not worthy to be loved? Is he not imprinted in my very bosom? His kindness imposes upon me the obligation to considerately avoid whatever he dislikes. Through this we see that the tenderness of parents teaches the noble mind to hate sin.

You should not harden your hearts against the goodness of the Lord, but listen to Paul when he seeks to win you back from your madness. Do you despise His goodness and the forbearance of His suffering? God's goodness leads you to repentance. There is no beast so savage that it cannot be tamed by man's kindness, yet when God graciously calls upon you, you rage against Him. Nothing is so hard that it cannot be softened by human art. Copper is melted in the furnace, iron is softened by fire, adamant can be softened by goat's blood. Yet some men have hearts that neither the fires of hell nor the loving kindness of a tender Father can soften. These men should rejoice, for they have conquered the divine skill and have won a luckless victory. "Luckless is the land," as Paul says, "and near to malediction, which though it has oftimes received showers from heaven, brings forth nought but thorns and thistles." But how luckless are they who, so often watered with the rain of the divine mercy, harden into stone so hard that even the divine mercy cannot make an impression. God wrote the law for Moses on stone tablets. Therefore your heart must be harder than stone, for God can write nothing of the Gospel on it. Only He who rent the rocks so that the dead could come out of their tombs can rend our stony hearts. Only the Word of God, who was made flesh for us, will give us a heart of flesh.

Even more incurable than these are they who spread blasphemies, saying that there is no God and that He is not concerned with the affairs of men. They say that there is no life after death; that those who live good lives in Christ will not have everlasting life; that those who follow Satan need fear no hell; that the threats of the Scripture are empty; that the promises of the Gospel are vain; that those who interpret the Scripture to defend their sins do rightly. They constrain the word of God when they ought to amend the lusts of their mind. They make heresy the basis of their other crimes.

Your pale faces and tremors at the mention of this shows how much you abhor what you have just heard. I hope there are none of these here among you who profess the name of Christ.

I have shown you Scylla. I will now show you Charybdis,

who is even worse. Some men choose to follow the examples of Cain and Judas, despairing of pardon and plunging into everlasting perdition. The destruction is the same; only the manner of perishing is different. Pharaoh hardens his heart and says, "I know not the Lord, neither will I let the people go." What did Cain say? "My sin is greater than I can bear." And Judas: "I have sinned in that I have betrayed the innocent blood." Each recognized the magnitude of his sin, each repented of what he had done, each departed from the face of the Lord, with whom alone there is mercy and redemption from sin. You can read this about Cain: "And Cain went forth from the presence of the Lord and dwelt in exile on the land to the east of Eden."

Judas left the supper of the saints and did not return. He left this mercy that he did not see again. This, I think, is what Jeremiah had in mind when he said, "Not for the dead your tears, not for him bow your heads; if weep you must, weep for him that must go and come again no more, never again to see the land of his birth." He does not want us to weep for the dead, for they shall live again. But rather he who turns away from God and never repents should be the object of our lamentations.

The prodigal and spendthrift son left the home of a loving father for a faraway country, but he returned. Peter had ceased to follow the Lord when he was denied three times, but he soon returned. When he remembered Jesus' words, he began to weep bitterly. He had been untrue to himself, but when he returned to his right mind, he returned to Jesus. For Isaias says, "Remember this, and be confounded, and return to your right mind, you transgressors." Peter remembered and returned to his right mind. His stony heart, from which a teardrop could not be squeezed, was replaced with a heart of flesh. Tears then gushed forth, bitter because of the pain of his repentance, but wholesome because of his restored innocence. Judas did not return to Jesus. He went away to the priests and Pharisees and brought back the fatal money.

The Lord permitted these things among His own disciples so that we could learn from them. You can see how differently the two Apostles who sinned came to their end. Judas, who was called to repent so often, persisted in his sin. But Peter remembered his Master's words, when Jesus looked upon him, and remembered what he was. He had recourse, not to the noose, but to tears; that is, not to despair, but to healing. Judas imitated Cain, the author of this evil, and recognized the magnitude of his sin. But he did not remember the words of God that ask men to repent, promising them mercy.

There is no page in the Bible that is not replete with God's mercy. This includes both the New Testament, which is the law of grace, and the Old Testament, which is supposed to be more inflexible.

In Jeremiah the Lord calls His people to penitence, as a husband would his spouse who had deserted him and slept with several men. "Turn ye, turn ye," saith the Lord; "for I am married unto you." And in Job: "The Lord openeth the ears of sinners to rebuke them and commandeth them to return from iniquity." The man who will not hear the Lord is more deaf than the viper, which deliberately stops its ears so that it cannot hear the charmer. "Today," says the psalm, "if you will hear His voice, harden not your hearts."

As long as we are on this earth, the Lord speaks to us, calling us to penitence, offering us His ready pardon. Did I say pardon? The mercy of the Lord is greater. The book of Job says this: "Fall in with the Lord's ways, and be his friend; thou shalt be rewarded. Let his lips be thy oracle, his words written on thy heart. Turn back to the Almighty for thy healing, and rid thy dwelling place of guilt." In Isaiah the Lord's mercy is shown: "If ye will inquire, inquire ye: return, come. If ye seek an end of evils, seek it not from the sons of men, in whom there is no safety, nor from evildoers, nor from the noose, but seek it from me, who alone am both ready and able to pardon. Only turn away from those things which ye have shamefully loved, and turn and come to me." In the same prophet He calls the whole race of mortals to Him, saying, "It is the Lord that speaks, and there is not one to rival me, no God but I; I, still unknown to thee, was fain to make thee strong, to what end?"

God says these things to idolatrous nations, murderers, the sacrilegious, parricides, the incestuous, and blasphemers: "And do you, wretched man, turn from the Lord in despair?"

In ancient times, when sin reigned without constraint among the nations, God's mercy seemed to be confined within the narrow limits of Judea. But through the Gospel mercy was extended to all ends of the earth. In Jeremiah He threatens the proud but offers ready pardon to those who repent. "If that nation, against whom I have pronounced, turn from their evil, I will repent of that evil I had thought to do unto them." He Who had shortly before threatened to destroy promises better things and says, "I shall speak concerning a nation, and concerning a kingdom, to build and to plan it."

In Ezekiel He promises mercy to those who return to Him, and also that amnesty celebrated in the Greek adage, forgetfulness of all past evil. For after having mentioned all kinds of sin, He adds, "It may be the wicked man will repent of all his sinful deeds, and learn to keep my commandments, and live honestly and uprightly; if so, he shall live on; life, not death, for him. All his transgressions shall be forgotten, and his uprightness shall bring him life." "What pleasure should I find in the death of a sinner," the Lord says, "when he might have turned back from his evil ways and found life instead?" And a little further on: "Come back, and make amends for all this guilt of yours, that shall else be your undoing; away with them, your defiant rebellions against me; a new heart, a new spirit! Why must you choose death, men of Israel?" "Die who will, his death is none of my contriving," says the Lord; "come back to me, and live." No doubt he is himself the mercy of God, when the psalmist refers to him; "We have thought of thy loving kindness, O Lord, in the midst of thy temple. Let him be in the temple and embrace mercy." He says again, "I would not the death of a sinner, but rather than he should turn and live."

Listen to these words, O sinners, and follow Christ so that you may live. For He lived again so that we could be saved from the death of sin. The clemency of God is ready for all, not just those who have committed a few venial sins. For the Lord clearly promises: "Whosoever the sinner bewails his sins, I will not at all remember his iniquities." He does not make exception to any particular type of crime, nor to the number, nor the magnitude. Only repent of your sins and forgetfulness of all past crimes awaits you. For more venial offenses, from which no mortal is free, we call upon the Lord's mercy every day, saying, Forgive us our debts, as we forgive our debtors. We are forgiven only if we forgive our neighbor.

There is a kind of order in deadly sins, just as some men sleep more lightly than others. A whisper will awake some, others need a shout, and a pinch will barely rouse some. Likewise, in the sight of God some are more dead than others. But there is no kind of death so hopeless that He cannot banish it with His voice; for even those in the tomb rise at His voice.

The Scriptures tell of three dead people whom Jesus Christ called back to life, signifying that there are three degrees of death. First He revived the twelve-year-old daughter of the ruler of the synagogue. He allowed only a few people to witness this and forbade them to repeat what they saw. This typifies the people who have sinned either because of their youth, or because of human weakness, but had not planned the sin beforehand. These men have not yet become criminals. The Lord easily revives these.

The widow's child, however, was more difficult to bring back. The body was being carried to the tomb when the widow's tears moved Him to stop the procession and call the child back to life. The child first sat up, then spoke, then leaped from the coffin. This typifies those who have sinned enough so that public penitence is required to bring them back. For, ceasing to sin, the sinner may sit up insofar as he decides to lead a better life. And he who confesses and recognizes God's mercy may speak. Being completely cured, he is restored to the communion of the Church.

Lazarus, however, was already rotting in the tomb. All his sisters and friends could do for him was weep. Jesus, having been shown the tomb, had the stone removed. He called Lazarus out of the tomb, and Lazarus came out bound. He was unbound and given back to his sisters.

It was not difficult for the Lord to raise up one who had been dead for four days. It is a more difficult matter to raise up someone who has lived in sin all his life and has become rotten as well. "The child," He says, "shall die a hundred years old; but the sinner being a hundred years old shall be accursed." And the Lord will promise to bring him back to life if all he does is hear Him this time. Every day He calls, "Maiden arise!" "Young man, arise!" "Lazarus, come forth!" But there are many who are more than dead, who do not hear Him when He calls them back to life.

But hearing is believing. The wicked do not hear the Holy Scripture so therefore do not listen to it. Let us implore God's mercy so that He will say to these men, "Thou deaf and dumb spirit, I charge thee, come out of him and enter no more into him." Now that you can perceive the mercy that awaits those who repent, listen to what David says. "I here confess to the Lord; and with that thou didst remit the guilt of my sin." If you are only meditating confession, then mercy will only meet you halfway; but to confess your sins will bring the presence of the Lord.

Many men confess and lament their sins before men. If this is done before God, that is to say, with an unfeigned heart, the Lord's mercy will follow swiftly. "It is your hearts," He says, "not the garments you wear, that must be torn asunder." For God will not despise a humble and contrite heart.

"Let us lament," says the psalmist, "before the Lord who made us." Many fast, but fast improperly. Many change their clothing but not their hearts. These things should be done before men as well, for our penitence may make those who sinned because of our sin repent. But it is useless to do these things before men if they are not first done in the sight of God. For Judas confessed his sin, but to the Pharisees. If he had confessed to the Lord, he would have been shown mercy.

The prophet Hosea prescribes the form of confession to be used: "Come back, men of Israel, with a plea ready on your lips: Pardon all our guilt, and take the best we have in return; the praises we utter shall be our victims now." Let us turn to Him, who alone can take away our sins and who shed His blood for our sins, and say to Him, "Take from us all the evil we have committed." Give thanks to His mercy, for any good you do after your fall you owe to this.

In Joel God has threatened those who condemn His mercy. He expresses the same idea as Hosea but in different words: "Come back to the Lord, your God; he is ever gracious and merciful, ever patient and rich in pardon; threatens he calamity, even now he is ready to forgive," or as the Greek texts have it, is Μετανοῶν, that is, repentant for evil.

The magnitude of your sin is matched by the magnitude of the divine mercy. The prophet insists upon this. He is gracious, for the Septuagint has it ἐλεήμων, that is, compassionate. Although that should be enough to keep us from despairing of forgiveness, He adds merciful also, which the Septuagint translates σίκτίρμων. From this we see that the Lord not only forgives our sins, but grieves over them as well. Not content with this He adds long-suffering, expressed Μακρόθυμος, of gentle mind, and by no means swift to vengeance, whereas human mercy is easily turned into indignation.

And do you still despair, sinner? Then listen to the kindness that is in the Greek πολυέλεος. If your sins are numerous, do not be anxious, for His mercies are also numerous. Why not convert and repent now? You fear threats of punishment. Then listen again: "And He is able to do you evil." Evil here means the pain due to our sins. Now there is nothing left except to recognize the mercy of God. This is what follows in Joel: "And he will leave a blessing behind him, even a meat offering and a drink offering unto the Lord your God." This must be what Hosea meant by the calves of our lips and the sacrifice of praise and thanksgiving.

Reconciliation is difficult when one offends a fellow man. Anger subsides slowly, and any excuse is enough to bring back the old grudge. Yet men are called kindly when they make amends. God, who is offended so often, remits His threats, does not inflict the punishment of hell, and offers His good will instead of punishment. When the sinner is repentant, He meets him halfway, as the saying goes, with open arms. He has promised this in Zachariah: "Turn ye unto me, saith the Lord of hosts, and I will turn unto you." What does turn unto Me mean? Recognize your misery, and seek mercy from Me. What do the words "I will turn unto you" mean? This: Becoming a helper instead of an avenger, I will help you in your endeavors, so you may have My strength to help you accomplish what you cannot achieve on your own. No one can hate his sins unless God grants it, unless He gives him a heart of flesh instead of stone. He must cleanse our polluted hearts and take away our perverse spirit.

Why do I bother to recite these examples of the Lord's mercy taken from the Old Testament? The entire scripture of the old covenant extols the mercy of God. Some men try to make two Gods out of one: one of the Old Testament, who was only just and not good, and one of the New Testament, who was only good and not just. These men are insane rather than heretical. For in the psalms it is often repeated, "O give thanks unto the Lord, for He is gracious; and His mercy endureth forever."

Manichaeus taught that He who spoke to us through the prophets and enacted the laws of Moses was not the true God, but one of the guilty demons. The same God is God of either law, the same truth, the same mercy through Jesus Christ our Lord, except that in the law of Moses there are only shadows; in the Gospel, truth. In the former there are promises, in the latter is their fulfillment. One shows great mercy toward the Jews, the other shows this mercy to all the world, destroying the sins of all mortals. This was the flood of mercy. The flood of old wiped out all sinners, saving only a few people; this flood saves all who believe in the Son of God and wipes out their sin. The Hebrews are promised pardon if they repent; the Gospel says, "Come unto me all ye that labor and are heavy laden, and I will give you rest. Take my yoke upon you and ye shall find rest for your souls, for my yoke is easy and my burden is light."

If you read over the life of Christ, you will see nothing but His perpetual mercy toward all men. He freely healed the sick, fed the hungry, supported those in jeopardy, cleansed the lepers, made the blind see, raised the dead, and absolved the penitent. All His teaching shows God's immense mercy. He impresses this upon us in His many parables. The shepherd carrying the lost sheep home upon his shoulder, the piece of silver that is lost and found, the Pharisee and the publican, the wounded traveler and the Samaritan, the steward who was kind to those entrusted to him, the steward who wasted his lord's goods, and the prodigal son who was received back again are all references to His mercy. The very word Gospel promises mercy. The name of Jesus, that is, Saviour, promises salvation and mercy. If He had come calling Himself a judge, every man would have had reason to be afraid; but He calls Himself Saviour, so why then should you despair of salvation?

Goats' and calves' blood may have seemed insufficient to expiate so many sins. Therefore, in order that we would have more faith in salvation, the Son of God Himself was given on the altar of the cross as a sacrifice for all men's sins. Hanging on the cross, He prayed for those who had crucified Him. And yet you think that He will not pardon you if you recognize your sin and implore His mercy? Have trust in God and you will find mercy, for faith can obtain anything from Christ. For if a man distrusts his physician, he hinders his own recovery.

God will bestow mercy on someone even if another person prays for that mercy. The Canaanite woman wept, and her daughter was healed; the centurion had faith, and his servant was cured; the ruler of the synagogue begged, and his daughter was brought back to life; the father prayed earnestly, and his son was set free from the evil spirits.

The Apostles cry, "Lord save us, we perish," and they are all saved. Often He did not wait until He was called upon. Seeing the faith the palsied one had, He said to him, "Son, be of good cheer, thy sins are forgiven." The dead youth was raised when his mother wept; Lazarus was brought back when Martha and Mary wept; Mary, the sinner, lamented, anointed, and kissed Him, and He said, "Thy sins are forgiven." The woman with a blood disease touched Jesus' clothes and immediately felt the virtue of His mercy. Many others were healed by touching Jesus' clothing.

If you dare not accost Jesus, if you cannot touch Him, at least stealthily touch the hem of His garment. Go to some godly man who can pray for you and commend you to the Lord. He often reveals His virtue in this way, for He is always ready to forgive. He went this far in order to bring sinners to repent. In Genesis the sinners had brought His wrath upon them, but when Abraham prayed, the Lord was ready to pardon any of those cities that were devoted to destruction, if there were only ten righteous men in them. The children of Israel deserved to be destroyed, but Moses' prayers alone were enough to save them.

Those men who despise the Lord's mercy, when it is always so close at hand, are ungrateful and blind. Those who despair at what is there for the asking are even worse off, for He is loath to punish and is easily appeased. What else could this mean, "Why must you choose death, men of Israel?" He laments that He has offered such people His mercy. Again in Micah: "Tell me, my people, what have I done, that you shouldst be a-weary of me?" Likewise in Isaias: "What more could have been done to my vineyard, that I have not done to it?" There is nothing the Lord does not do to save us. Why, then, do we willfully throw away all hope of salvation? In the Gospel He even weeps over Jerusalem, which was bringing destruction upon itself by persisting in its sin. "How often," He says, "would I have gathered thy children together, as a hen would gather her brood under her wings, and you would not." The Lord laments that some men will not let Him save them, thinking He is not capable of saving them, and distrusting Him. In the Gospel the whole house rejoices, because the dead son is alive again and the lost is found. The Lord thinks one repentant sinner is reason for the angels and saints to share His happiness.

Why, then, do you despair, keeping yourself from salvation and the Lord from happiness? For He who grieves over the death of a sinner, and is happy at one's conversion, will not refuse to pardon those who repent. Then why do you tarry and fight against God's mercy? Christ is the wisdom of God. According to Solomon, "And all the while Wisdom is publishing her message, crying aloud in the open streets; never a meeting of the roads, never a gateway, but her voice is raised, echoing above the din of it. What, she says, are you still gaping there, simpletons? Do the reckless still court their own ruin? Rash fools, will you never learn? Pay heed, then, to my protest; listen while I speak out my mind to you, give you open warning."

Why forfeit eternal blessings for the sake of transitory things? It is wiser to win immortality with a little suffering. All who persist in sin are foolish; those who amend their lives are wise. We examine the cheapest metal diligently, yet we despise that great treasure offered to us free. Worse yet, we despair of it. God is rich in mercy. Human wealth can be exhausted by largesse; mercy cannot be exhausted. God has pledged His word to man and, as Paul says, cannot be false to Himself. He does not refuse to be reasoned with, if He does not fulfill what He has promised. For in Isaiah He says to a people deep in sin, "Wash yourself clean, spare me the sight of your wrongdoing and take farewell. Learn, rather, how to do good, setting your hearts on justice, righting the wrong, protecting the orphan, giving the widow redress; then come back, says the Lord, and make trial of me."

You can see that all the Lord asks you to do is change your way of life. The magnitude of your sins will not be held against you in any way, for the Lord says, "Though your sins be scarlet, they shall be as white as snow; though they be red like crimson, they shall be as wool. If ye be willing and obedient, ye shall eat the good of the land." Who is so mad as to refuse to be saved?

God would have us do nothing except that which pertains to our happiness. If you are willing and obedient, He says. No one can save a man against his will. Salvation comes through faith. If a king forgave a group of traitors and only warned them to mend their ways in the future, he would be claimed merciful, since he did not punish or fine them. God actually offers us a reward for mending our ways. "Ye shall eat the good of the land," He says. Even those who continually offend God are not unworthy to eat the good of this world. The Gospel promises, "I will give you a new heart, I will give you a new spirit, through which you shall become the Sons of God instead of servants of the devil, through which you shall be made members of my only begotten Son, through whom you shall succeed to the inheritance of the kingdom of heaven." "This," He says, "is my beloved Son, hear Him."

Why do the Jews follow the Talmudists or rabbis? Why do people follow the teachings of Plato and Aristotle? Do not, as Eve did, listen to the serpent and bring on your own destruction, but listen to the Son of God, who invites you to eternal happiness. "Repent," He says, "the kingdom of heaven is at hand." The Son promises, the Father is surety, and the Spirit is given to us meanwhile, as a pledge. Why hesitate to accept this happiness that is offered to you?

The Apostle's words are the Lord's, "Repent, and be baptized every one of you in the name of Jesus Christ for the remission of sins, and ye shall receive the gift of the Holy Ghost." Forsake a foul life and receive eternal life. Therefore, all sinners, no matter what their sin, should hasten, for the gates of mercy are open to all alike. For if a man repents, his former life shall be forgotten. Although Montanus shut the church doors on those who had fallen away from their baptismal vows, the Lord never shuts the portals of the kingdom of heaven.

There is but one entrance into the Church, baptism, prefigured by the ark, but God's mercy has left us the plank of confession should we fall overboard. Baptism is not repeated, just as the death of Christ is not. Those who have been forgiven, and having been buried with Christ, have risen with Him, should persevere in what they have received. But knowing human weakness, the Lord has made penance available to all, forever. However, God's goodness should not be despised, for no one can tell when he will die. Therefore, if you are in sin, hasten to receive absolution. People who used to put off baptism until their last days were called "deathbed" or "sprinkled" Christians. Even if a baptist is not available, you can confess and swear to amend your life when you are ill. Your tears are enough to cleanse your soul.

It has been doubted whether baptism is efficacious or not in the case of those who resort to it only on their deathbed. For some of them admit that they would sin forever if they could live forever. It has also been doubted, and with better reason, whether repentance that is deferred until one's last day, and that would still be withheld if they did not know it was their last day, is of any use. For just as when the farmer's land that has received ample rain does not produce anything but weeds, the farmer is condemned to be burned, so God sometimes gives men over to a reprobate mind when His mercy has been scorned.

Therefore, my brethren, amend your lives now, when the Lord calls you to give up an unholy life. For if you do not hear the Lord, He may not hear you when you want Him. For He threatens those who refuse to hear Him, "Since my call is unheard, since my hand beckons in vain, since my counsel is despised and all my reproof goes for nothing, it will be mine to laugh, to mock at your discomfiture, when perils close about you. Close about you they will, affliction and sore distress, disaster that sweeps down suddenly, gathering storms of ruin. It will be their turn to call aloud; my turn, then, to refuse an answer. They will be early abroad looking for me, but find me never; fools, who grew weary of instruction and would not fear the Lord. Well for them, if they had followed my counsel, if they had not spurned all the warnings I gave!" The Lord rebukes us so that He may amend us, and when we are beyond all hope, He abandons us and leaves us to our own fate. In the same way a doctor cannot cure a sick man who refuses to be cured, so he leaves him.

"Of mercy and of justice my song shall be," says the psalmist. All men are judged when they have lived out this life. As long as life lasts there is hope of mercy, therefore, repent and seek it. When you give up hope, or are grown old in nonrepentance, you are already dead. The wise Hebrew counsels, "Whoever thou art that drawest the cord of iniquity from day to day, and makest not an end of sinning, return unto the Lord, and forsake thy sins, make thy prayer before his face, and sin less. Turn again to the Most High, and turn away from iniquity, and hate thou abomination vehemently, and recognize the justice and judgments of God. Abide not in the error of the wicked. Confession perisheth from the dead, as from one that is not. Living, thou wilt confess, and praise God and his glory in compassion." You can see how merciful the Lord is, if you only earnestly confess. Yet what about those who continue to think of sin even though their bodies are no longer capable? How shall they confess to the Lord when, throughout their lives, they have sinned? So why do the healthy put off repentance? If you were suddenly struck with dropsy and the cure was readily available, you would not postpone taking it for a year. Therefore, with the diseases of the soul do not wait until your last day for salvation, for who can be sure that you will live until tomorrow?

This is not meant to make anyone give up hope of forgiveness, but only to assure them that they cannot sin continually. There is no sin that is not forgiven, in this world or the next. But it is safest to shun sin altogether. Repentance for sins committed is a second best thing.

In Holy Scripture the Lord sternly remonstrates again and again against wallowing in sin and then expecting ready forgiveness. For the medicine of penance is provided, not that you continue to sin until your dying day and then seek forgiveness, but that, if you should slip, you may still be saved.

In Amos the Lord frequently denounces three or four transgressions: "Shall I not turn away from them?" It is a sin to think of evil, but it is even worse to try to accomplish what you have thought. It is worst of all actually to accomplish what was evilly devised by you. Some add a fourth evil—namely, habitual sin. The Lord will have good cause if he turns away from you now; and He would do so if His mercy did not surpass His justice. In the same prophet there follows directly, "Thus says the Lord God to the house of Israel, 'Seek ye me, and ye shall find, seek the Lord and come.' Listen to the Lord when he threatens, and do not sin; listen to him when he calls you back, and do not despair." For what if He did to us what He threatens to do after the third or fourth transgression, showing us no mercy, leaving us to our own devices? For many it would not do to have the Lord turn away from them after the thousandth transgression. But as soon as justice ceases to prevail, mercy intervenes: "O Lord God, forgive, I beseech thee: by whom shall Jacob arise, for he is small?" And again: "O Lord God, cease, I beseech thee: by whom shall Jacob arise, for he is small?" So that excellent advocate Mercy pleads for the cause of our weakness.

Listen, and you shall hear how ready the Lord is to forgive.

The Lord repented for this: " 'This also shall not be,' said the Lord God." He repents of the vengeance He has threatened. All you need to do is earnestly repent of your transgressions. Surely a mother was never appeased by her son this easily. When there is such a powerful intervener like the Lord, no man should despair and persist in his errors, or revert to the rope like Judas.

The Lord assists us in our hope of salvation by having very great and very good men fall into sin. He hopes that their pardon will inspire hope in us. Who was more admirable in Holy Writ than David? He was a king, a prophet, a man after Christ's own heart, and it was promised that Christ would spring from his seed. Yet what a sinner he was. He heard the threats of the Lord from Nathan, and turned all of the Lord's wrath into mercy with a few simple words. "I have sinned against the Lord," he said. And then Nathan said, "The Lord also hath put away thy sin: thou shalt not die." Abundant are the threats that he may amend, but how prompt are the words of mercy, "Thou shalt not die"? Hezekiah heard this from Isaiah: "Thou shalt die and not live." The prophet who had announced his death had only gone a few steps when the Lord's mercy called him back. "Turn again," He said, "and tell Hezekiah, the captain of my people, 'Thus says the Lord, the God of David thy father, I have heard your prayer, I have seen your tears; behold I will heal you; on the third day you shall go up into the house of the Lord.' " The first Book of Kings has this to say of Ahab: "But there was none like unto Ahab, who did sell himself to work wickedness in the sight of the Lord." These words were spoken to him, "Thou hast killed and also taken possession," for he had killed Naboth and taken his vineyard. When the king became terrified at the Lord's threats, he dressed in sackcloth, and fasted, and hung his head. But Ahab was a hardened sinner, and had often despised the Lord's rebuke, adding sin upon sin. He finally became terrified of the imminent evils rather than repenting. Yet the merciful Lord said to Elijah, "Seest thou how Ahab humbleth himself before me? Because he humbleth himself before me I will not bring the evil in his days."

You see the power that a false repentance has upon God, turning him from vengeance. What, then, will be the effect of one who feels a sincere change of heart, not from fear of punishment, but from love of God?

To illustrate His point He chose Peter, whom He had chosen prince of the Church, to fall into sin. Peter wept and he then obtained mercy. When He entrusted Peter with the care of

His sheep, for whom He had died, He did not reproach him for denying his Lord three times. The Lord did not remember a thing of Peter's past sin.

Paul, the persecutor of the Lord's Church, was cast to the ground and made the teacher of the Gentiles. There are great examples of sinners and great examples of penitents. Do not let these examples of sin provoke you to sin, but if you should fall into sin, you have these examples of penitence so that you will not despair.

It is absurd to follow some person in sin and then refuse to follow him when he repents. Many princes must have glossed over their murders and adulteries with David's example. David, however, had so many other excellent virtues that, considering these, his sin could be forgiven. He gave up the luxuries of his court. He wore sackcloth, and ate ashes, and wept so much every night that his bedding was soaked. He was not ashamed of his penitence in front of the rest of the sinners and used to sing the song of penitence, "Have mercy upon me, O Lord, after thy great goodness, according to the multitude of thy mercies, do away with my offenses." He condemned himself with his own words, "As the Lord liveth, the man that has done this thing shall surely die." God let this guilty man judge himself, and the judge was convicted. But God mercifully overcame him by showing him that he had forgotten his sin. Before he had been drunk with his luckless prosperity, delighting in the woman he loved and his child. But when he turned to the Lord, he at last saw where he was, and the difference between justice and injustice.

When a sinner is sincerely repentant and confesses that he deserves to be punished, then the Lord allows the man to judge himself. Those who set up their own judges make God unjust and a liar, Him who would gladly have his mercy recognized in us all and who would replace sin with his loving kindness.

When Adam was asked to confess, he blamed his wife. Likewise, when she was asked to confess, she blamed the serpent. If they could have repeated David's song, "Have mercy upon me, O God," they would not have been exiled from paradise.

Cain, the true son of his parents, said when called to confess, "Am I my brother's keeper?" If he would have said sincerely, "I have sinned, have mercy," he would have had God's mercy.

There are two kinds of sorrow. There is a sorrow according to the flesh, which causes death, such as that Judas had. There is also a divine sorrow, which brings salvation and true joy.

Paul, who loved all his converts dearly, nevertheless was happy that he could inspire the Corinthians with this kind of sorrow by condemning the man who had intercourse with his father's wife. This kind of sorrow is like a bitter medicine that is followed by genuine happiness. Meanwhile, the hope of salvation, mingled with repentance, tempers the bitterness of the sorrow. David received hope from the Lord's mercy when he frankly confessed his sin. "Thou shalt purge me with hyssop, O Lord," he says, "and I shall be clean; thou shalt wash me and I shall be whiter than snow." It was from sprinkling the blood of the immaculate Lamb that he promised himself cleanness. Though he knew he was polluted with sin from the day of his birth, he hoped for the whiteness of innocence from this washing, a whiteness whiter than snow. He not only hoped that innocence would return, but also that the sorrow of penitence would be made into a spiritual joy. "Thou shalt make me hear of joy and gladness," he says, "that the bones thou hast broken may rejoice. O give me the comfort of thy help again, and establish me with thy free spirit." The confidence of this sinner has promised himself something extra. "And my tongue shall sing of thy righteousness," he says. "Thou shalt open my lips, O Lord, and my mouth shall show thy praise." Having experienced this mercy, he will exhort others to repent. The Lord said to Peter, "When you are converted, strengthen your brethren." David would have perished if he had committed himself to judgment; but being unworthy in this respect, he appealed to mercy, and therefore he sings about the Lord's mercy forever. If a man's court case is in danger, he usually, if he can, goes to another court, although he does not know whether he will find a more propitious judge there. Often, if a man appeals, he ruins his own case.

For us, dearly beloved, the best plan is not to struggle with God's justice, that is, not to kick against the goad but to appeal to His mercy. In temporal affairs the safest course is to rebut the charge against us with some other argument. Lawyers tell us that the poorest defense is to throw oneself on the mercy of the court, saying, I have sinned, forgive me. In these spiritual matters, however, a spontaneous confession of sins and an appeal to God's mercy is the best course.

When both the Scriptures call us and the examples of so many notable men encourage us, why does any man, despairing of himself, prefer to grow old in evil? In God, whose nature is absolute, there is no property that conflicts with another, and yet, if we carefully consider His justice and mercy, there seems to be a conflict. Justice calls for punishment, but mercy, as James has it, κατακαυχᾶνται τῆς κείσεως—

that is, exalts over judgment like a victor. Who has ever exclaimed, "Jesus, have mercy!" without receiving mercy immediately? The Canaanite woman cries, "Lord, have mercy!" and her daughter is healed. If every sinner also cried, "Lord, have mercy!" his soul would be healed. The blind beggar cried, "Thou Son of David, have mercy." He took off his garment and received sight. Therefore let us cry, "Jesus, Son of God, have mercy!" Let us cry long and loud during our evil thoughts, and He will make heirs of the kingdom of heaven out of beggars.

Whoever covets the good things of this life is blind. He is a beggar and asks alms from the people in a filthy garment. Those who covet a kingdom, although they seem to be coveting something great, are doing no more than begging alms from the mob. Those who seek honors and high offices are crying aloud to the people, "Have mercy, give alms." But if any man cries out, "Lord Jesus, have mercy!" He is ready to give us Himself.

The Lord is always with us, calling us to Himself. Why do you unhappy men not go to Him? Why continue in the garments of your misfortune? The altar of mercy is ready to receive you, and you turn to the chains of madness. The asylum of the divine compassion is open, and you fly to the pit of miserable despair. The Saviour holds His hand out to you, and you turn away. Heaven is reserved for you, and you plunge into the abyss. The bosom of the divine goodness is open to you, and you flee to the noose. The thief on the cross hears the words, "Today thou shalt be with me in paradise," and yet you condemn yourself to hell.

I shall now do what I had promised to do at the conclusion, that is, to show how God's mercy can be best obtained. Throughout my discourse, mention has been made of prayers, tears, fasting, sackcloth, and ashes. These things do indeed obtain His mercy for us: but kindness to our neighbor actually, if I may use the expression, wrests it from Him. Each man should show his neighbor what he expects God to show him. The Greek proverb says that favor breeds favor, but with us mercy breeds mercy. Give, and it shall be given unto you; forgive, and you shall be forgiven. God will show you the same mercy that you show your neighbor.

Now I call it mercy, or charity, not only when vengeance is foregone, or a neighbor's poverty is relieved, but also when help is given to a brother with pious intent. He who teaches the erring rebukes the wrongdoer; at times even he who chastises the sinner, if he does it with Christian compassion, bestows mercy on his neighbor. He who admonishes the idle, comforts the ill, or encourages the despairing to hope is merciful toward his neighbor, and is either calling forth or repaying God's mercy.

Christian mercy should not be of the ordinary kind. For even a heathen will give alms to a beggar, almost everyone would cheer up a friend in his illness, and even the Gentiles forgive certain offenses. The Gospel shows the type of mercy we should have. "Be ye merciful, that ye may be the children of your Father, who is in heaven." If God shows us ordinary mercy, then common mercy toward our neighbor will suffice also. But if He bids His sun rise on the good as well as the evil, and allows the godly and the ungodly to share the benefits of this world, then if we want to be His real sons, let us be kind, not only to our friends, but to our enemies as well. For if God gave His only Son for us, idolators that we are, then it is not asking too much to be kind to our enemies, for they are our brothers. And if the Lord sacrificed Himself on the altar of the cross for our sins, then to forgive a neighbor is not too much.

How can a man ask the Lord for mercy when he is unwilling to show mercy to his neighbor and brother? The Gospel says of this, "O you wicked servant, I forgave you all that debt: should not you have had compassion on your fellow servant?"

Whatever kindness we show our neighbor the Lord takes note of. Although He has shown us all the kindnesses that we can show our neighbor, He promises He will repay them with interest. For is it not a fair trade if He allows you into the kingdom of heaven if you give a poor man lodging for the night? To grow poor by bounty of this kind is the best way to become rich. Wise men do not let their money lie idle but deposit it in banks, where it can draw interest. If you wish to become rich in heavenly goods, you should do business with this great Lender.

We call the rich blessed, but in the Gospel the merciful are blessed, for they shall obtain mercy. The wise Hebrew says, "He that hath pity unto the poor, lendeth unto the Lord; and that which he hath given will he pay him again." And the prophet says: "Redeem thy sins with charity, for, as the chief of the Apostles says: 'Charity covereth a multitude of sins.'" You hear what sort of a trade it is. What a great gain is made! Likewise, the mystic psalmist says, "Blessed is the man that is merciful and lendeth." You hear what the loan is, you hear who the Lender is, and also what the recompense is.

He who injures his neighbor is responsible to the injured one: he who does a favor for his neighbor puts his neightbor under an obligation to him. Do not seek vengeance from someone who has, in some way, hurt you. Make this exchange with God: pardon your neighbor's small offense, and God, according to His promise, will forgive all of yours. Do not seek recompense from your neighbor if you have done him a favor, but ask God for whatever you have expended, and He will give you back eternal things for temporal.

God is appeased by several forms of sacrifice, spiritual hymns, songs, prayers, watchings, fastings, poor clothing; but no sacrifice is more effective than mercy toward your brother. "A tender heart," says God, "wins favor with me, not sacrifice." He does not condemn sacrifices, but prefers mercy to sheep. Through the Gospel the Lord Jesus taught us what He had promised to teach us by word of mouth. For Micah says:

> For when the Lord had reproached his people for their invincible obstinacy in evil, the people, anxious to know in what way they can appease God, justly provoked to anger by so many transgressions, say: "What worthy thing shall I offer to the Lord? Shall I bow myself before the high God? Shall I come before Him with burnt offerings, with calves of a year old? Will the Lord be appeased with thousands of rams, or many thousands of fat goats? Shall I give my firstborn for my transgression, the fruit of my body for the sin of my soul?"
>
> "How can I best humble myself before the Lord, that is, God most high? What offering shall I bring? Calf, think you, of a year old, for my burnt sacrifice? Fall rams by the thousands, fattened buck-goats by the ten thousand, will the Lord be better pleased? Shall gift of firstborn for wrongdoing atone, body's fruit for soul's assoiling?"

So say the people, knowing that man cannot offer a sacrifice great enough to atone for their sin, even if they sacrifice their firstborn son, the dearest possession they have.

The prophet shows us a better sacrifice to appease God's wrath: "I will show you, O man, what is good, and what the Lord doth require of you: 'Above all else to act justly, to love mercy, and to walk humbly with thy God.'" What is acting justly? To hurt no man. What is loving mercy? To show kindness even to those who do not deserve it. In his eulogy Paul adds something else. "If I give my body to be burned," he says, "and have not charity, it profits me nothing." Abraham did a magnificent thing when he was ready to sacrifice the only son whom he loved. But he who gives his body to be burned for the love of God will do a greater thing. Charity is more pleasing to God than even this sacrifice. For what is charity to one's neighbor but mercy?

Since we continually need God's mercy in all things, we should always try to relieve each other with mutual mercy and to bear one another's burdens. This would fulfill Christ's law, which requires mercy rather than sacrifice, and which has us purchase its mercy by showing mercy to our neighbor. But as my heart beats with joy, when I think of the Lord's great mercy toward us, and how He would have us attain it, I am overcome with grief when I see how few Christians strive after this mercy.

If we were truly merciful, we would show kindness even to the Turks, in the hope that they would be overcome by our goodness and want to share our religion. As it is, we Christians assail our fellow Christians with war and robbery more cruelly than the wild beast attacks its enemy. What else do we do but live by tearing each other to pieces, after the manner of the fishes. "Who is not ready for the sake of some pretty advantage to defraud his brother, whose need he ought to have succored even without hope of reward?"

Nowadays we make a profit of our brother's needs. My brother is starving to death. As his need for food increases, so does our price. How harsh we are to those we command, how often they rebel against those above them, and how rare is real charity! The whole world is full of brawling, disparagement, and deceit. Not only do we try to avenge these things, but we go out of our way to harm those who do not deserve it.

With all this we fail to see the mercy of the Lord, which has been given to us but which will surely be taken back if we do not show the mercy to our neighbor that we have received. "If you will seek, then seek," says the prophet. If we seek the Lord's mercy, then let us seek it sincerely with our whole heart. "Turn you, come." It will turn to us if we turn to it. God's mercy came to us when the Son of God descended to the earth. Let us in turn come to it.

The Lord compassionately stoops to absolve the adulterous woman. Let us in turn lift up our hearts to Him when He stoops to us. The first step is to put away evil. The physician first bleeds the body so that wholesome fluids can be let in. Then the sinner should discharge the evil desires that God despises: lust, arrogance, avarice, excess, and anger. When a man persists in sin and asks the Lord's forgiveness, he is like a warrior who asks for peace with a sword and shield in his hand. He that asks, receives; he that seeks, finds; to him who knocks, the door is opened. If you ask for God's mercy, ask sincerely; if you knock on the door of mercy, knock sincerely. The prodigal son asked sincerely, but only after he had left the swine and returned to his father; "Father, I have sinned against heaven, and in thy sight: make me as one of thy hired servants."

Listen to the publican, who is afraid, because of his sins, to look up to heaven. He stands far off and beats upon his chest, saying, "God, be merciful to me, a sinner." He has a complete change of heart and becomes: sober rather than drunken, continent rather than unchaste, moderate rather than prodigal, liberal rather than grasping, truthful rather than lying, kindly rather than slanderous, upright instead of deceptive, gentle rather than revengeful, merciful rather than cruel. The Lord knows who does violence, so to speak, to the divine mercy. Cry to the Lord, "Have mercy!"

If you wish to be heard, see that you in your turn listen to Him. He cries in the person of the sick and needy. If you do not hear Him here, He will not hear your cries. He also appears in the person of children; for in them too He is hungry and sick, and in them He is slighted and offended. If a person does not have compassion toward his brother and, besides this, oppresses the weak, maligns the innocent, spoils the needy, and defrauds the unwary, and still asks the Lord to have mercy upon him, then he is worse off than the one who does not hear the Lord's cries. If he perseveres in these deeds, he will call for God's mercy in vain.

Those who do not care for Christ in the person of His children will hear it said to them, "Depart, you cursed of my Father, into everlasting fire." What then will be said to those who assail Christ when He is in the person of His people, who spit upon Him, mock, beat, accuse, and slay Him? There is a famous maxim from Publius, if I am not mistaken, that is worthy of a Christian: "He who does a kindness to a worthy person himself receives one." Why do you hesitate, carefully weighing the results of others? He who does a kindness to a worthy person does it to Christ. He who does a kindness to a worthy person does it to a brother. He who does a kindness to a worthy person does it to a man from love of Jesus. If you seek profit, lend to Him; if you fear evil, you can redeem it here.

After His stern denunciation the Lord says in the Gospel, "But give alms, and behold, all things are clean unto you." When you encounter a storm at sea, you do not hesitate to lose your merchandise, however precious, to save your life. When the vengeance of God threatens you, does it irk you to spend money on your neighbor? What do you do when a fire breaks out? But what fire should you fear more than that of the divine wrath? And when His wrath is kindled, you quench it by the means that was pointed out to you. You may wonder who will point this out to you. Sirach will: "Water will quench a flaming fire, and alms will make an atonement for sins."

There should be no display in almsgiving, otherwise it loses its name. Those who make a great show of giving alms are not giving alms but making a bid for glory. Almsgiving, in the sight of God, is only when the left hand knoweth not what the right hand doeth. Give according to the commandments of the Lord and it will bring you more profit than gold. Give alms to a poor man and it will deliver you from all evil, for a treasure cannot be buried more safely than in the heart of a poor man. It is better to shut it up here than in strong safes. If it be possible, forget that you have given alms and do not let the poor know whence their aid comes.

Your almsgiving will not remain silent in your hour of need but will cry out in your behalf, saying, "Come you blessed of my Father, for I was hungry and you gave me food, thirsty, and you gave me drink; I was naked and you clothed me; when I lacked a roof, you took me in; when I was sick, you visited me; when I was in prison, you came to see me. When it is asked, "When, O Lord, did we see you lacking in these things and supply them?" those who did these things will find an intercessor in their almsgiving. Those on the left, who mention their good works, will hear the words, "Depart into everlasting flames."

Thus there remains nothing, my dearest brethren, but to seek the mercy of the Lord, so that He in turn will give us the strength to aid our neighbor. If we fail in mercy to our neighbor here below, it will be in vain that we expect mercy from our Judge in heaven. Let mercy therefore prevail in our dealing with one another so that the mercy of the Lord will prevail in His treatment of us. In this way it will come to pass that with one heart and one mind we shall sing eternally the mercy of the Lord, proclaiming that his loving mercies surpass all His works. To Him be honor and praise in all places and for all time.

CONCERNING THE EATING
OF FISH

In choosing to entitle what is for many one of the most amusing and at the same time penetrating of his Colloquies, *The Eating of Fish*, Erasmus was influenced neither by the ancient acronym of the catacombs nor what was later to become an unwarranted symbol of Roman Catholicism. Although the religious significance of dietary laws was a common heritage of early Christianity, the laws relating to abstinence from meat did not have in the primitive Church the same vigor as in Erasmus' day. That they were purely voluntary directives was a fact well known to Erasmus from his reading of the Fathers, especially Tertullian and Origen. The gradual introduction of monastic ideals into the entire Church as a result of the Gregorian reform had imposed upon the West dietary regulations that were so much a part of the discipline of the monks. Not only did they give an undue worth to abstinence and fast but they gave the entire matter a widening influence by filling up the Church calendar with a plethora of religious feasts commemorating the heroism of those whose asceticism was judged by their abstemiousness. Canon law after Pope Gregory VII had regulated the eating habits of Latin Christendom to an almost ridiculous point. As in so much else that Erasmus criticizes in his effort to distinguish the essential from the nonessential, he places fasting and the superstitious veneration of relics in the same category of confusing ends and means. The veneration of saints to the exclusion of the Christological mysteries was also in his eyes a part of the evil heritage resulting from the capture of the papacy by fanatical monks during the Hildebrandian reform of the eleventh century.

The multitude of "fish days" had come to exert a great influence on the economic and social life of the late Middle Ages. Control of the North Sea fisheries had been no small factor in the Hundred Years' War, and the repercussions of the Reformation on the fish trade in northern Europe are well known. What was even more disconcerting to many liberal-minded citizens of the time was the fact that in most areas municipal ordinances regulated the eating habits of the citizenry under pain of civil punishment. Many German cities continued to forbid the sale of fish on Fridays long after the territories had been Protestantized. The Church had capitalized on the situation, and not an insignificant source of its revenue was the money paid for dispensations and compositions granting permission to eat meat, eggs, and butter during the many and prolonged periods of fast. The "Butterbrief" letters permitting the eating of certain foods were one aspect of the problem frequently attacked by the reformers of the sixteenth century. Luther in his *Appeal to the Ruling Class* voices an opinion that was widespread:

> In this connection, it should be said that the question of fasting ought to be a matter of free choice, and the foods which may be eaten left unrestricted, as the gospel has ordained. For the people at Rome themselves scoff at fasts, and leave us in the provinces to use as food that with which they would not grease their shoes. But they sell us permission to eat butter and other things, in spite of the holy apostle who says that the gospel gives us complete freedom to do everything.[1]

There was still another and more personal reason why Erasmus may have chosen the eating of fish for the subject of his diatribe. The delicate and squeamish nature of the man revolted at anything that would further impair his poor health. He recounts frequently in his letters his revulsion at the thought of eating fish. Actually he had obtained a dispensation from fast from Cardinal Compegio in 1525.[2]

The ridicule of fasting, however, is eclipsed by a variety of other subjects that revolve about the question of the relationship between divine and ecclesiastical laws. It is only in recent years that Erasmus has been appreciated as a leading figure in the study of jurisprudence in the Renaissance.[3] The conflict between the advocates of positivistic Roman legal science and humanistic equity was very much in the forefront of those forces that were reshaping the political thought of Europe during the Renaissance. Erasmus' influence in the moral and juridical syntheses drawn up by lawyers like Zasius, Vives, and Amerbach was considerable. The references to *aequitas naturalis* in the dialogue are worthy of

[1] *Reformation Writings of Martin Luther,* ed. B. L. Woolf (London: Lutterworth Press, 1952) Vol. I, p. 168.
[2] *E. E.,* VI, 15.
[3] G. Kisch, *Erasmus und die Jurisprudenz seiner Zeit* (Basel: 1960).

deeper study. They demonstrate a certain dependence on the writings of Gerson, champion of ecclesiastical liberties during the great schism. There is for example one open reference to the distinguished chancellor of the University of Paris, but the whole treatise poses problems in morality familiar to the French reformer. Like Gerson, Erasmus is deeply concerned over the moral chaos resulting from the patchwork of conflicting rules and regulations that the canonists had devised to cover almost every aspect of public and private life. Like Gerson he feels that they have made "of the light yoke of Christ and the law of liberty an iron yoke and a heavy burden pressing upon the necks of Christians." [4] Much of the treatise seems to echo the gentle irony of Gerson, who wrote of ecclesiastical laws, "If such a superman as Adam, who had to obey one single command, failed to fulfill it, how shall we escape who are placed among innumerable such commands?" [5] The several references to ecclesiastical laws concerning marriage are, of course, of interest since they bear on the great problem of the time, Henry VIII's celebrated divorce from Catherine of Aragon. Erasmus had dedicated his *Matrimonii Christiani Institutio* to Catherine but generally avoided taking a position in the affair, since his patronage depended to a great extent on the sympathy of the Queen's partisans on the continent.

Historians will find the reference to the New World interesting. His awareness of the exploitation of the Spanish colonies in America and his suggestion that Christianity be made more adaptable to non-European peoples has a timely ring. Las Casas had already perceived the dangers of identifying Christianity with Latin Catholicism, and the great Spanish moralists of the next century, Bellarmine and Suarez, gave a systematic presentation of the natural law more in keeping with the problems of non-Christian peoples. Erasmus had been in contact with Spanish courtiers during a time when enthusiasm for the New World was at its peak. He had met the son and biographer of Columbus, Ferdinand, in Antwerp in the fall of 1520 and presented him with an autographed copy of his *Antibarbari*. The little book is still to be seen in the Biblioteca Capitular Colombina in Seville.

As in all his Colloquies there are thinly veiled references to contemporary acquaintances. Glaucoplitus refers to Ulrich Zazius and Eleutheropolis is the city of Freiburg. Eros is, of course, Erasmus himself. "Vinegar College" is Montaigu College, where Erasmus himself lived during his first stay in Paris in 1495. It was at that time directed by John Standonck (Standoneus), who was, like Erasmus, a product of the Brethren of the Common Life. He is considered as one of the foremost religious reformers in France

[4] *Gersonii Opera Omnia*, ed. Du Pin (Antwerp: 1706), III, 16 D.
[5] *Ibid.*, 17 A.

on the eve of the Reformation, but his strict measures of discipline and enforced frugality hardly endeared him to the Humanist. The school was later to house Loyola and Calvin—it is interesting to speculate on the course of history had they been there thirty years earlier. Neither of them had any time for the tolerance and moderation of the great Humanist, and a great deal of the poor press Erasmus has enjoyed during the centuries is due in no small way to their animosity toward him. Rabelais, who found in Erasmus a kindred spirit, also studied here and the "lousy college" he mentions in the *Gargantua* shows they shared similar sentiments on the institution. Lemantius, or "Bleary-eyed," refers to Egmond, a theologian at the University of Louvain, and Erasmus explains the name as referring to his drinking habits. Amphicholus, or "The Lame One," is James Latomus, his most severe critic at the same university, and Erasmus explains the nomenclature in his case as a reference to the fact that he sprained his ankles making a hasty exodus from apprehension in adultery, *flagrante delicto*.

The *Ichtuophagia* was first published in the Forben edition of the Colloquies in 1526 and met with the usual storm of protest. Martin Lypsius lists it along with *The Praise of Folly* and *On the Eating of Meats* (*De Esu Carnium*) as one of the three most detested of Erasmus' works.[6] Cuthbert Tunstall, then Bishop of London and long-time friend of Erasmus, felt that it would be offensive to many readers, as surely it was, and recommended that Erasmus revise it.[7] Yet the same Tunstall was later to side with Henry and to attack papal primacy, declaring it was a comparatively recent innovation—a position that Erasmus even in his most vituperous mood would never countenance.[8] Erasmus' attitude on this as with his earlier Colloquies was that they were not intended to teach dogma or faith but rather formulae for speaking Latin and thus were conducive to good manners. "Who," he asks, "should be forced to defend himself for having taught how to turn a sentence, though of bad meaning, into good Latin words?" He goes on to say in his letter to the theologians of Louvain, "One must consider the sort of person to whom I attribute these remarks. I do not represent them as a theologian delivering a sermon but rather as a friendly group enjoying a little repartee."[9] Certainly no one enjoyed repartee more than Erasmus, and he knew full well that his gift of ridicule had become the most feared weapon in all of Europe in attacking abuses ecclesiastical as well as secular. The recent Ecumenical Council

[6] *E. E.,* IX, 373.

[7] *Ibid.,* VIII, 291.

[8] P. Hughes, *The Reformation in England* (London: Hoddis & Carter, 1948), p. 274.

[9] *E. E.,* V, 91.

in Rome has revived many of the questions he poses in his rambling discourse on the eating of fish.

Concerning the Eating of Fish

(ΙΧΘΤΟΦΑΓΙΑ)
1526

Si omnis constitutio episcoporum obligat ad poenam gehennae, dura est conditio Christianorum. Si quaedam obligant, quaedam non obligant, nemo melius declarabit mentem suam quam ipse pontifex.

If every episcopal regulation binds under penalty of hell fire, then certainly the condition of Christians is a severe one. If regulations are binding and some are not, no one will better declare his position on the matter than the Pope himself.

> Letter to the Theologians of Louvain
> July, 1522, E. E. V. 93

A BUTCHER AND A SALT-FISHMONGER

Butcher. Tell me silly seller of salt-fish, haven't you bought a halter yet?

Fishmonger. A halter, Butcher?

Butcher. Yes, I said a halter.

Fishmonger. For what?

Butcher. In order to hang yourself.

Fishmonger. Let those who desire it buy halters; I'm not yet weary of my life.

Butcher. But you may become so quickly.

Fishmonger. God willing, it be your case rather than mine. What's the matter?

Butcher. I'll tell you, if you don't know. Soon you and your fellow tradesmen will all be starved to death, and quite ready to end it all.

Fishmonger. Easy, easy, Butcher. God willing, this may be our enemies' case and not ours. But Butcher, how did you become a fortuneteller all of a sudden, to prophesy such a calamity?

Butcher. It's not guesswork, I assure you; it is a matter of fact.

Fishmonger. You frighten me out of my wits; if you have anything to say, say it.

Butcher. I'll tell you to your own detriment. There is to be a dispensation from the College of Cardinals allowing everyone to eat what he wishes. Then what will you and your fellow merchants do, but starve to death in the midst of heaps of your stinking salt-fish?

Fishmonger. Those who wish to may eat snails or nettles for all I care. But is there a prohibition against eating fish?

Butcher. No. But everyone who cares to is at liberty to eat flesh.

Fishmonger. If your prediction is true, you rather than I deserve hanging; and if it is false, you have more need of a halter than I, for I hope for a better trade in the future.

Butcher. You may think you have enough, but your belly is full of fasting. But if you'll listen to the rest of the story, you may live a little more cleanly than before, and no longer wipe your snotty, scabby nose on your elbow.

Fishmonger. Ha, ha, it comes out at last: "The kettle calls the pot black." Is any part of a butcher cleaner and sweeter than his backside? I wish what you say were true, but I fear you feed me nothing but fantasia.

Butcher. What I tell you is too true for jesting. But please tell me how you are assured of a better trade in the light of this.

Fishmonger. Because people by nature are more desirous of that which is forbidden to them.

Butcher. Explain yourself.

Fishmonger. When they are free to eat flesh, they will eat less of it. Then there will be no entertainment greater than the eating of fish, as it used to be in the past. So I shall be glad if there is a license to eat flesh. I also wish the eating of fish was prohibited; then people would desire it more intensely.

Butcher. Well wished, indeed.

Fishmonger. I too would wish it, if I were like you and desired nothing but money, because of which you will send that lumpish, flesh-fed soul of yours to the devil.

Butcher. You make fun of me, but what you say is very silly.

Fishmonger. What makes the See of Rome relax the law prohibiting the eating of flesh, which has been observed for so long?

Butcher. They had thought about doing it a long time ago, and do it now because they think, as is the case, that the city is defiled by salt-fishmongers. Lands, waters, rivers, air, fire, and all the other elements are infected. Men's bodies are corrupted and filled with putrid humors from eating fish, which causes fever, consumption, gout, epilepsy, leprosy, and many other diseases.

Fishmonger. I beseech you to tell me, Hippocrates, why in well-governed cities it is forbidden to kill oxen and hogs within the city walls. It would aid the healthfulness of the city if the killing of sheep were likewise prohibited. Why are butchers appointed to a certain section? Is it not because, if given liberty to move about and settle anywhere, they would infect the entire city? Is there any stench worse than that of the corrupted blood and gore of beasts?

Butcher. They are perfumes compared to stinking fish.

Fishmonger. You, perhaps, may think them perfumes, but your expulsion from the city is a sign the magistrates thought otherwise. The fragrant smell of your slaughterhouses is plainly seen by the way people hold their noses when they pass them. They would rather have ten madams for their neighbors than one butcher.

Butcher. Whole ponds and rivers are not enough to wash your stinking fish. As the old saying goes, "You do but attempt to wash the blackamoor white." A fish will always smell like a fish, though you perfume it. It is no wonder they smell so strong dead, when many stink alive, as soon as they are caught. Pickled flesh far from stinks, but rather smells as sweet as violet even when preserved for many years. No, flesh salted with common salt will never stink, and after being hung up to dry in smoke or wind will have no ill scent. Do what you will to a fish and it will still smell like one. Obviously there is no stench to be compared to that of fish. Fish corrupt even the salt itself, which is basic for preserving things from putrefaction by shutting out, binding up, and forcing out that which produces nauseous things and dries up the humors within from which putrefaction might come.

Fish is the only thing on which salt is not effective. Some nice dandy or other may hold his nose as he passes a butcher's shop, but nobody can bear to be in a boat loaded with your salt-fish. If a traveler chances to meet on the road a cart laden with salt-fish, does he not run away, hold his nose, hawk and spit, and curse the stinking cargo? And if it were possible that salt-fish could be carried sweet into the city, as we do our beef, when killed and dressed, the law would be repealed. Besides, what can be said of something that stinks while being eaten?

Also, how often do we see your condemned ware thrown into the rivers by the market inspectors and a fine imposed upon selling the fish? And we should see it more often, but the inspectors, corrupted by you, regard their own profit more than the city's good. Nor is that the only thing you are notorious for; there is a wicked conspiracy among fishmongers to hinder fresh fish from coming into the town.

Fishmonger. Pray tell me, has no one ever heard of a butcher being fined for killing a measled pig or selling mutton drowned in a ditch or maggoty shoulders of mutton sprinkled with fresh blood to make them look as if newly killed?

Butcher. But there has been no previous incident like the one that was lately perpetrated by you; nine persons were poisoned by one eel baked in a pie. This is what you furnish for the tables of the citizens.

Fishmonger. What you speak of was an accident that no

one can help when it pleases God that it should be so. But it is a daily practice with you to sell young cats for rabbits and puppies for hares, if people don't know them by their ears and rough feet; not to mention your meat pies made of dead men's flesh.

Butcher. What you charge me with is a common failing, and those individuals who are guilty of it should defend themselves. In the same way you can condemn gardeners who mistakenly sell henbane for colworts or apothecaries who administer poison instead of antidotes. No trade or calling is free from these mistakes. But even when you are most faithful to your trade, you sell that which is poison. If you sold an electric ray, a water snake, or a sea hare caught among the other fish, it would be an accident rather than a wrong. Nor do I think guilt any more to be imputed to you than to a physician who sometimes kills the patient he undertakes to cure.

It might be excusable if you sold your stinking wares only in the winter season; then the cold might mitigate the contagion of the infection. But you add putrid matter to the fire of summer and render autumn, which is itself a sickly season, more sickly. In the spring of the year the humors, which have been locked up, begin to flow, endangering the body. Then for two whole months you exercise your tyranny, corrupting the infancy of the springing year by bringing old age upon it. When nature is busy purging the body of unwholesome juices and making it fresh to bloom anew, you throw into it stench and corruption.

If there are any vicious humors in the body, you increase them, making things all the worse and also corrupting the good juices of the body. If you only injured the body, this could be endured; but since different foods spoil the mind, you corrupt the very mind itself. Just gaze upon your fish-eaters; do they not look like fish, pale, stinking, stupid, and mute?

Fishmonger. I beseech you, do not those people who live on beets look themselves like beets? What sort of people are those who eat beef, mutton, and goat flesh? Certainly they look like oxen, sheep, and goats themselves. You sell kids as a great delicacy, and yet this creature is very bad for epilepsy and brings distemper upon flesh-eaters. Would it not be better to satisfy a craving appetite with salt-fish?

Butcher. Do you think what your naturalists write is true? If what they say were true, it is certain that those people who are inclined toward sickness would find good things harmful. We sell kids to those who are troubled with the fever or consumption but not to hypochondriacs.

Fishmonger. If the eating of fish is so dangerous, as you insinuate, why do our superiors allow us to sell our wares all year, but make you keep holy days for a great part of it?

Butcher. That I cannot answer. But it may have been the contrivance of wicked doctors trying to get more money.

Fishmonger. I don't know the doctors you speak of, but I am sure there are no greater enemies to fish than they.

Butcher. Listen, friend, I'd like to get you right on this matter, but not for your sake or for the love of fish. None are more averse than they to eating it; the doctors play their own game. The more people are troubled with cough, consumption, and chronic distemper, the more they profit by it.

Fishmonger. I won't support the doctors in this matter; let them avenge their own quarrel when they get you into their clutches. The ancient respect for life, the authority of the most approved, the majesty of bishops, and the public usage of Christian nations are enough for my purposes. Even if it is madness, I had rather be mad with them than sane with butchers.

Butcher. As you decline to be an advocate for doctors, I decline to be an accuser or censurer of the ancients or common custom. Those it is my custom to revere, not revile.

Fishmonger. If I'm not mistaken, Butcher, you're more cautious than pious on this point.

Butcher. In my opinion they are wisest who have the least to do with those who carry thunderbolts in their hands. However, I won't conceal that which I understand from my Bible, translated into my mother tongue, which I sometimes read.

Fishmonger. What now, the butcher's turned preacher, too.

Butcher. I am of the opinion that early mankind, newly formed from primitive clay, had a more healthy constitution. Their vivacity attests to it. Furthermore, I believe that Paradise was a place commodiously situated with a very healthy climate. People in such a situation might even be sustained without food. Just by breathing the very air and the fragrances of herbs, trees, and flowers, which abounded everywhere, and especially the earth spontaneously producing all things in abundance, man was free of sweating and toiling and was neither infected with distemper nor old age. This Garden was dressed in pleasure rather than toil.

Fishmonger. Until now you seem to be right.

Butcher. In such a fertile Garden nothing was prohibited, save the use of a single tree.

Fishmonger. That's true, too.

Butcher. The sole reason for the prohibition was that they might pay their acknowledgment to their Lord and Creator by an act of obedience.

Fishmonger. All this is quite correct.

Butcher. Moreover, I believe that the new earth produced better and more nutritive things than it does now, since it has grown old and almost past bearing.

Fishmonger. Well, I agree with that.

Butcher. Even concerning Paradise.

Fishmonger. What you say is very probable.

Butcher. If so, then eating was rather for the sake of pleasure than necessity.

Fishmonger. I have heard this.

Butcher. At that time to abstain from eating flesh was human rather than saintly.

Fishmonger. I don't know. I read that the eating of flesh was permitted after the Flood, but I didn't read that it was forbidden before. What purpose would there be in permitting it, if it were not permitted before?

Butcher. Why don't we eat frogs? Not because they are forbidden, but because we have an aversion to them. How can you tell whether God might not have instructed man as to what food human nature required and not what He permitted?

Fishmonger. I don't know.

Butcher. Immediately after man's creation we read, "Rule ye over the fish of the sea, the fowls of the air, and every living creature which moves upon the face of the earth." What use was there in ruling over them, if it were not lawful to eat them?

Fishmonger. O cruel master! Do you eat your men and maidservants, your wife and children? Why don't you at the same time eat your chamberpot, since you are also master of it?

Butcher. I beseech you to listen to me again, you silly Salt-Fishmonger. Every living thing has its use, and many of them have great utility. A horse carries me upon his back, and a camel carries my baggage. But of what use are fish but to be eaten?

Fishmonger. There is an abundance of fish that are good for health. And a great many fish were created merely for the sake of contemplation and for promoting an admiration of their Creator. It may be that you don't believe that dolphins carry men on their backs. But some fish, like the sea urchin, are useful in foretelling calamity. Would you not wish to have such a servant in your own house?

Butcher. Suppose it is granted that before the Flood it was not lawful to eat any food, except the fruits of the earth; it was no great matter to abstain from those things the body did not require and the killing of which was cruelty. Yet in the beginning the eating of living creatures was permitted because of the weakness of humanity. The Deluge brought on a cold climate, and even today we see that those who live in cold climes are greater eaters than those of the hotter climates. The Flood destroyed or at least spoiled the products of the earth.

Fishmonger. That is granted.

Butcher. And yet after the Deluge people lived over two hundred years.

Fishmonger. I believe they did.

Butcher. Why did God after the Deluge, according to the command of Moses, oblige persons of a weaker constitution and of shorter life to eat particular kinds of creatures, when he restricted nothing to the stronger before the Deluge?

Fishmonger. As if it were within my power to give a reason for what God did? But I believe that God did then what masters do now, when they see their servants taking advantage of their leniency. We feed a horse oats and beans, but when he grows pampered and too mettlesome, we give him hay more sparingly and ride him with a curb bridle and a sharper spur. Mankind had thrown off all reverence for the Deity, and lived as licentiously as if there was no God. Because of this, the lattices of the law, the bars of ceremony, and the bridles of threatenings and precepts were used to bring them to know themselves.

Butcher. To what extent do these bars of the law hold us today?

Fishmonger. Inasmuch as the severity of carnal servitude is removed and by the Gospel we have become adopted sons of God, there is an augmentation of grace and a diminution in the number of precepts.

Butcher. Why, when God calls His Covenant everlasting, and Christ denies that He dissolved the law, but fulfilled it, do men dare to abrogate a good part of it?

Fishmonger. The law was not given to the Gentiles; and it seemed to the Apostles that they should not be burdened with circumcision as the Jews have done even to this day, but rather to place their hope for salvation in faith and love for God than in outward observances.

Butcher. I avoid speaking of the Gentiles; where does the Scripture say that if the Jews embraced the Gospel, they would be freed from the servitude of the Mosaic Law?

Fishmonger. It was prophesied by the Prophets, who promised a new Covenant and a new heart. They portrayed God as abhorring their fasts, rejecting their gifts, and desiring a people of circumcised hearts. The Lord Himself confirmed the prophecies by holding forth to the Disciples His Body and Blood, as is stated in the New Testament. If nothing was abolished of the old, why then is this one called the new? The Lord not only abrogated the Jewish choice of meats by His example but by His doctrine, when He denies that man is defiled by meats that go into his stomach and become waste.
He teaches Peter this by a vision. And Peter, with Paul and others, by their example of eating the common meats from which the law commanded them to abstain, carried out the command of the Lord. Paul discusses the matter everywhere in his Epistles; nor can there be any doubt that present Christian practice was handed down to us by tradition from the Apostles themselves.
So the Jews were not set free, but were weaned from superstition, as from the milk to which they had become accustomed and made familiar, but has now grown out of season. The law is not abrogated, but that part of it which was not

essential was modified. Leaves and flowers herald the coming of fruit, but when the tree is laden, no one covets the flowers. Nor is anyone sorry when his son's childishness is replaced by maturity. Nor does anyone light candles and torches when the sun is high in the heavens. Nor does the schoolmaster complain when his son, upon reaching manhood, lays claim to his freedom and himself becomes a master.

A pledge ceases to be one when the thing promised is produced. The spouse comforts herself with her bridegroom's letters, kisses his presents, and embraces his picture until she is married, but when she comes to enjoy his company, she disregards the things she previously admired. The Jews, at first, held tenaciously to that to which they were accustomed, much like a child used to sucking at the breast, even when it has grown robust, will cry for the breast and slight more solid food. But they were forced, as it were, from those symbols, shadows and temporary comforts in order that they might turn themselves entirely to the Lord, whom the law had promised and prefigured.

Butcher. Who would have expected so much theology from a seller of salt fish?

Fishmonger. I used to supply fish to the Dominican College in our city. They often dined with me and I with them; I gathered these things from their discourses.

Butcher. In truth, instead of a seller of salt fish, you deserve to be a seller of fresh fish. But tell me, if you were a Jew (for I cannot very well tell whether you are one or not) and starving to death, would you eat pork or choose death?

Fishmonger. I don't know what I would do; for I do not yet understand what I ought to do.

Butcher. God has forbidden both: "Thou shalt not kill" and "Thou shalt not eat pork." In this case which precept takes precedence?

Fishmonger. It does not appear that God has forbidden the eating of pork, when it comes to a matter of life and death. The Lord allowed David to eat holy bread contrary to the letter of the law. During the Babylonian Captivity the Jews disregarded many of the requirements of the law. I am of the opinion that the law of nature is more obligatory and has never been or never will be abrogated.

Butcher. Why then were the Maccabees, who chose death to eating pork, so much commended?

Fishmonger. I suppose it was because the eating of pork was required by the king and in itself comprised a denial of the general law of the country—as circumcision, which the Jews endeavored to thrust upon the Gentiles, carried with it a profession of the whole law. Just as money given in good faith obliges the performance of the whole contract.

Butcher. If this more unpleasant aspect of the law is abrogated by the Gospel, by what authority are similar things imposed upon us, especially when Lord calls His yoke an easy one, and Peter, in the Acts of the Apostles, calls the law of the Jews a hard one, which neither they nor their fathers were able to bear?

Circumcision was taken away, but baptism took its place, and its features are even more severe. Circumcision was performed eight days after birth, but if during that time anything happened to the child, the vow of the rite sufficed. But now we douse children, scarcely out of the dark cavern of the mother's womb, with cold water, which has stood a long time in a stony font. If the baby chances to die on the first day or at birth, through no fault of the parent or friends, the poor babe is doomed to eternal damnation.

Fishmonger. That is true.

Butcher. The Sabbath is abrogated; no, not abrogated, but transferred to Sunday. What does this signify? The Mosaic Law enjoined a few fast days; but what a multitude have we added to them! They were free to eat sheep, capons, partridges, and kids all year around. The only garments forbidden to them were those that mixed linen and wool. Now besides the prohibition against certain forms and colors of a great many garments, the head must be shaven in some way or another. Many other things render our circumstances much more difficult than that of the Jews. Among these are: the heavy burden of confession, tithes, the strengthened laws relating to matrimony, and the new laws of affinity.

Fishmonger. Indeed, Butcher, you are way off the mark; the yoke of Christ is not to be viewed in this way. A Christian is tied to many more difficult rules and is liable to greater punishment, yet he has greater strength in faith and love, which makes what is by nature more burdensome actually pleasant.

Butcher. Tell me why, when the Holy-Spirit descended from heaven of old, in the shape of fiery tongues to enkindle the hearts of the believers with a greater gift of faith and charity, was the burden of the law taken away from them? Why did Peter, under the inspiration of the Spirit, call this "an intolerable burden"?

Fishmonger. It was taken away so that Judaism could not overwhelm the glory of the Gospel and so that the Gentiles would not find the law a stumbling block with which to alienate Christ. Among the believers there were many weak people, who were in double danger if the law were not removed. On the one hand there was the danger that they would believe there was no salvation without the observation of the law; on the other hand that they would rather remain pagan than accept the yoke of the Mosaic Law. It was necessary to allure these weak minds, as it were, with the bait of liberty.

In addition, to reconcile those who denied any hope of salvation by the profession of the Gospel without the observation of the law, circumcision, Sabbaths, the choice of meats and other things, the change was required. It must be understood that when Peter states he is unable to bear the law, he is not speaking for the stupid and weak Jews, who, though they were satiated with it, fed upon the husk, not having any desire for the spirit.

Butcher. You argue very well, but in my opinion, there is no reason for keeping carnal obligations that are arbitrary and not obligatory.

Fishmonger. Why so?

Butcher. Recently, I saw a map of the whole world and was struck by how small a part of the world truly and sincerely professed the Christian religion, a small part of eastern, northern, and southern Europe, extending no farther than Poland. All the rest of the world is filled with barbarians and brute beasts, schismatics or heretics, or both.

Fishmonger. You did not include the southern seacoast and the islands that lay scattered around it.

Butcher. I saw them, and learned that great spoils were carried from them, but Christianity was not carried to them. When there is such a splendid potential harvest, it seems most advisable for the propagation of the Christian religion to do as the Apostles did when they took away the burden of the Mosaic Law, so that the Gentiles would not fall over it. We should attract the weak by removing the obligation to perform a number of ceremonies, without which the world was saved in the beginning and may now be, if we have faith and Gospel charity.

Again, I both hear and see many for whom religion consists of places, garments, meats, fasts, gestures, and songs, and in the light of these things judge their neighbor contrary to the precept of the Gospel. Thus it happens that the faith and charity that constitute the Christian religion are being extinguished by those superstitions. Anyone who depends upon this activity is far from the faith of the Gospel, and anyone who, for the sake of meat or drink, which a person may lawfully use, exasperates his fellow man, for whose liberty Christ died, is far from Christian charity. What bitter contentions do we see among Christians! What spiteful slander because a garment is differently tied or is of a color different from that which is customary, and contentions concerning food taken from land and sea.

If this evil touched only a few, there would have been no great furor. But the whole world is now aflame because of these deadly altercations. If these things were removed, we would live in greater happiness, unmindful of ceremonies, but attempting to effect those things Christ has taught us. The nations of the world would more readily embrace religion, if it were accompanied by liberty.

Fishmonger. But there is no salvation outside the pale of the Church.

Butcher. That is true.

Fishmonger. Those who do not acknowledge the authority of the Pope are outside the Church.

Butcher. I don't deny that either.

Fishmonger. But those who neglect his injunctions don't recognize his authority.

Butcher. I hope the time will come when the Pope, Clement by name, will mitigate all these things, which have alienated some people from the Roman Church. It is my hope that he may bring all nations into communion with the Church and that he will pursue those things that are good for the Church instead of his own private interest. I hear daily of complaints against yearly offerings, pardons, dispensations, other exactions and Church grievances; but I believe he will so moderate all these things that in the future it will be imprudent to complain.

Fishmonger. I wish all monarchs would do the same, then Christianity, now confined to such a small part of the world, would extend itself. Then barbarous nations would perceive that they were not called to human servitude, but to the liberty of the Gospel; and that they were not sought after to be exploited, but were called to a fellowship of happiness and holiness. If they came to be united with us and found in us true Christian behavior, they would freely offer us more than the greatest violence can now extort from them.

Butcher. I hope this will soon be accomplished; so that the malicious Ate, who engaged the two most powerful monarchs of the world in a bloody war, is cast to the dogs.

Fishmonger. This is soon to take place. No one is more humane than Francis I, nor is anyone more schooled in principles than Charles V, who, as fortune enlarges his Empire, increases his clemency and bounty. Good humor and leniency are peculiar to his age.

Butcher. You'll not find them lacking in anything.

Fishmonger. What, then, hinders the accomplishment of that which everyone wishes?

Butcher. The lawyers have not yet come to any agreement about bounds and limits, and you know that the storm of a comedy always ends in the calm of a matrimony; and the tragedies of princes commonly end in the same way. In comedies matches are made quickly, but among great men matters move slowly. It is better to have a wound heal slowly than to have one that breaks open again in an ulcer.

Fishmonger. Do you think marriages cement bonds of amity?

Butcher. They should; but sometimes the sharpest disputes arise from them. Once war comes between near kin, it is not only more extensive but more difficult to terminate.

Fishmonger. That is quite true.

Butcher. Do you think it proper that everyone should be kept in turmoil because of the disputes and delays of lawyers? As matters are now there is no safety anywhere; unscrupulous men take advantage of every opportunity, while there is neither peace nor war.

Fishmonger. The counsels of princes are no concern of mine. But if I were the Emperor, I know what I would do.

Butcher. Come now, imagine yourself both the Emperor and the Pope, if it pleases you. What would you do?

Fishmonger. I'd rather be the Emperor and the King of France.

Butcher. You can be both of them.

Fishmonger. I would immediately take a vow of peace, publish a truce throughout my dominions, disband my forces, and make it a capital offense to steal so much as a hen. Having settled affairs to my satisfaction, or rather that of the public, I would concern myself with the limits of my dominion or the conditions of a marriage.

Butcher. Have you thought of any former ties than those of a marriage?

Fishmonger. I think I have.

Butcher. Let's hear them.

Fishmonger. If I were the Emperor, I would without delay address the King of France: "My Brother, an evil spirit has set us at war. We don't fight for our lives, but our dominions. You for your part have accounted yourself as a stout and valiant warrior. But fortune has been on my side, having made you captive. What happened to you could have happened to me. Your misfortune admonishes all of our human condition. Both of us have seen that war has not settled our dispute, so let us take another path to settlement. I give you your life, restore your liberty, and make you my friend instead of my enemy. Let past animosities be forgotten; you are free to return to your own country; enjoy what is yours and be a good neighbor.

"In the future let us only rival each other in offices of fidelity and friendship. Let us not vie with each other over who shall govern the largest dominions, but who shall govern his own with the greatest justice and goodness. In the former conflict I gained the prize of fortune, but in this the one who wins will gain far more glory. As for me, the fame derived from my clemency will bring more true glory than if I added all France to my domains.

"You would be more praised for a grateful mind than if you had driven me completely out of Italy. Don't you envy the praise to which I aspire? On the other hand I'll move closer to you, so that you will gladly owe an obligation to such a good friend."

Butcher. Not only France, but all the world might be gained by this method. For if this wound is not properly healed, I fear that at the first opportunity the skin will be broken and all sorts of corrupt matter will issue forth, creating more dangerous consequences.

Fishmonger. How great and glorious would this act of humanity render Charles all over the world! What nation would not readily submit to so generous and kind a prince?

Butcher. You have portrayed the Emperor very well; now do the same with the Pope.

Fishmonger. It would take too long to go through everything. I will sketch it briefly. I would conduct myself so that the whole world could see that, as a Prince of the Church, I would wish nothing but the glory of Christ and the salvation of mankind. It would remove from the name of the Pope all envy and gain him solid and lasting glory. So much for that; we have digressed from our first proposition.

Butcher. I'll bring you back eventually. But is it your position that the Pope's laws are binding on the whole Church?

Fishmonger. Yes, it is my position.

Butcher. What about the punishment of hell?

Fishmonger. I agree with the Pope on this.

Butcher. And are the laws of the bishops obligatory in a like manner?

Fishmonger. They are to everyone in his own diocese.

Butcher. And those of the abbots, too?

Fishmonger. I am in doubt about that. They receive their administration upon certain conditions; nor have they the power to bind inferiors with rules without the agreement of the whole order.

Butcher. But what if a bishop receives his office under the same conditions?

Fishmonger. I doubt that any do.

Butcher. Can a pope annul what a bishop has decreed?

Fishmonger. I believe he can.

Butcher. Can anyone annul papal decrees?

Fishmonger. No, no one.

Butcher. How can it be, then, that the papal constitutions of former popes have been set aside by those succeeding them, because it was claimed they deviated in piety?

Fishmonger. Those were surreptitious and temporary things. The Pope considered as a man may be ignorant of persons and facts. But when he proceeds from the authority of a universal council, he is a heavenly oracle and is of equal authority with the Gospel itself, or at least very near it.

Butcher. Is it lawful to doubt concerning the Gospels?

Fishmonger. Most certainly not; nor the councils, those that were properly assembled by the Holy Spirit, executed, published, and received.

Butcher. What if anyone should doubt that there is any council so constituted? I hear some have rejected the Council of Basle and all do not approve of Constance, not to mention the late Lateran Council.

Fishmonger. Let those who doubt do so at their own peril. I have no doubts.

Butcher. Did Peter have the authority to make new laws?

Fishmonger. He had.

Butcher. Did Paul and the rest of the Apostles also have this right?

Fishmonger. Yes, they had everyone in their own churches committed to them by Christ or Peter.

Butcher. Do the successors of Peter have the same authority he had?

Fishmonger. Why not?

Butcher. Do papal letters have the same weight as the Epistles of St. Peter, and do the constitutions of bishops deserve the same respect as the Epistles of Paul?

Fishmonger. More so if they make a law by authority.

Butcher. Is it lawful to doubt whether Peter and Paul wrote by the inspiration of the Holy Spirit?

Fishmonger. Anyone doubting that must be counted as a heretic.

Butcher. Do you think the same about the ordinances and constitutions of the popes and bishops?

Fishmonger. I accept this concerning the popes, but I have some question about the bishops—although it is most prudent not to be suspicious of any person unless there are very good grounds for it.

Butcher. Why would the Holy Spirit allow a bishop to err but not a pope?

Fishmonger. Because that error which proceeds from the head of the Church is the most dangerous.

Butcher. If the constitutions of the prelates have so much force, then what does the Lord mean in Deuteronomy when it is severely commanded that there shall be no addition or diminution of the law?

Fishmonger. One who explains what is implied in the law and who suggests those things that have a relation to the observation of the law does not add to it. Nor does one diminish it, when he preaches the law, according to the capacity of his audience, declaring some things and concealing others according to the circumstances of the time.

Butcher. Were the constitutions of the Pharisees and the Scribes obligatory?

Fishmonger. I don't think they were.

Butcher. Why is that?

Fishmonger. Because though they had authority to teach, they could not make law.

Butcher. Which is the greater power, that of making human laws or that of interpreting divine laws?

Fishmonger. That of making human laws.

Butcher. I disagree; the one who has the right to interpret His opinion has the force of a divine law.

Fishmonger. I don't understand you.

Butcher. I'll explain it to you. The divine law commands us to assist our parents. The Pharisee interprets it this way: That which we give to the Church we give to the Father, because God is the Father of all. Does not divine law in this way give place to interpretation?

Fishmonger. But that is a false interpretation.

Butcher. But once any interpretation has been received as authoritative, how can I tell which one is true, especially if they differ among themselves?

Fishmonger. If you are not satisfied that all interpretations have a common meaning, accept the authority of the safest prelates.

Butcher. Is the authority of the Scribes and Pharisees passed on to theologians and preachers?

Fishmonger. It is.

Butcher. It seems that there are none more ready to expostulate than those who have hardly studied theology.

Fishmonger. You must hear all candidly and use your judgment, except with those who are quite mad. Concerning them, people should rise and hiss them out of the pulpit to bring them back to their senses. But you ought to believe those who have taken a doctorate in theology.

Butcher. But among them I find a great many who are much more ignorant and foolish than the totally illiterate. I see much controversy among these learned men.

Fishmonger. Single out the best things, leaving those difficult matters to others. Always accept those things approved by the rulers and the great majority of people.

Butcher. I know that is the safest course. But there are false constitutions as well as false interpretations.

Fishmonger. Let others concern themselves whether there are or not. I believe there may be.

Butcher. Did Annas and Caiaphas have the authority to make laws?

Fishmonger. Yes, they did.

Butcher. Did the decrees of these men oblige one to the punishments of hell, if transgressed?

Fishmonger. Give me a specific instance.

Butcher. Suppose that Annas ordered that no one coming from the market could touch a bit of meat before washing his body. Would anyone ignoring this order incur the pain of damnation?

Fishmonger. I think not, unless it were considered a horrendous crime by public authority.

Butcher. Did all the laws of God carry with them the punishment of eternal damnation, if transgressed?

Fishmonger. I don't believe so. According to the theologians God forbids all sin, no matter how venial.

Butcher. Perhaps even a venial sin could send one to hell, if God in His mercy did not assist us in our infirmity.

Fishmonger. The statement is not absurd, but I'd dare not affirm it.

Butcher. When the Israelites were in captivity at Babylon, among the many requirements of the law they did not practice was circumcision. Did they all perish in the hellfires?

Fishmonger. God only knows that.

Butcher. If a starving Jew ate pork, would he be guilty of a crime?

Fishmonger. In my opinion the necessity would excuse the action. David was excused, directly by the word of God, for eating the holy bread, contrary to the precept of the law. Not only did he eat it himself, but he also fed it to his companions.

Butcher. If anyone were faced with either stealing or starving to death, which should he choose?

Fishmonger. Perhaps in this case theft would not be theft.

Butcher. What's that? Is not an egg an egg?

Fishmonger. This would be especially true if he stole with the intention of making restitution and placating the owner, as soon as he was able.

Butcher. Suppose a man were faced with either losing his life or swearing falsely against his neighbor, which should he choose?

Fishmonger. Death.

Butcher. What if he could save his life by committing adultery?

Fishmonger. He should again choose death.

Butcher. What if he could save his life by committing fornication?

Fishmonger. They say he should choose death.

Butcher. Does not an egg cease to be one here, especially if no force was used or injury done?

Fishmonger. There's wrong done to the girl's body.

Butcher. What about perjury?

Fishmonger. He should choose death.

Butcher. What about a simple, harmless lie?

Fishmonger. They say a man must choose death. But it is my opinion that in a situation of urgent necessity or of great advantage, this sort of lie carries no fault or at the most a very small one, unless it opens the way to a dangerous habit of lying injuriously. What if a man by telling a harmless lie could save the bodies and souls of his own country, which should he choose to do? Should he refuse to tell the lie?

Butcher. I can't speak for others, but I'd have no scruples about telling fifteen lies as notorious as those told by Homer, and then washing away my guilt in Holy Water.

Fishmonger. I'd do the same.

Butcher. Then it is not what God has commanded or forbidden that obliges us under pain of damnation.

Fishmonger. It seems to be just the opposite.

Butcher. Then the "modus" of the obligation is not so much from the Author of the law as from the matter of it. Some things give way to necessity, others do not.

Fishmonger. It seems so.

Butcher. If a priest in danger of losing his life could save it by marrying, what should he choose?

Fishmonger. Death.

Butcher. If divine law can give way to necessity, why doesn't human law also do the same?

Fishmonger. It is not the law that hinders, but the vow.

Butcher. If a man vowed to go to Jerusalem but could not do so without losing his life, should he go or should he die?

Fishmonger. He ought to die, unless he can get the Pope to dispense his vow.

Butcher. Why can one vow be dispensed and not another?

Fishmonger. Because one is a solemn vow and the other a private one.

Butcher. What do you mean by a solemn one?

Fishmonger. The usual kind.

Butcher. Why? Is not one that is made daily the same vow?

Fishmonger. Yes, but then it would be a private one.

Butcher. Well, then, if a monk made profession privately before an abbot, would it be a solemn vow?

Fishmonger. You trifle. A private vow is more easily discharged because it can be dispensed with the least offense. Those who take private vows do so with the intention that they may be dispensed, if it be convenient and should they change their mind.

Butcher. Can one vow perpetual chastity in the same manner?

Fishmonger. It should be done this way.

Butcher. Then it would be perpetual and not perpetual. What if a Carthusian monk must either eat meat or die; what should he choose to do?

Fishmonger. Physicians tell us there is no flesh as efficacious but that "gold-water" and jewels would not serve the same purpose.

Butcher. Which is more useful, to help a person in danger of losing his life with the gold and jewels, or to use them to aid many people whose lives are in danger and let the sick man have a chicken?

Fishmonger. I can't say.

Butcher. But the eating of flesh or fish is not one of the essentials.

Fishmonger. Let's leave the Carthusians to their own devices.

Butcher. Let's talk in a more general way. Sabbath-keeping has been diligently, frequently, and largely inculcated in the law of Moses.

Fishmonger. True.

Butcher. Should I relieve a city in danger, neglecting the rule of the Sabbath, or not?

Fishmonger. Do you think I'm a Jew?

Butcher. I wish you were, and I myself wish I were circumcised.

Fishmonger. The Lord Himself has solved that problem, saying, "The Sabbath was made for man, and not man for the Sabbath."

Butcher. Is not the law of force in all human constitutions?

Fishmonger. Yes.

Butcher. What if a lawmaker makes a law that is obligatory under the pain of eternal damnation?

Fishmonger. Friend, it's not within the lawmaker's power to decide to what extent a law shall be binding. He uses his authority to make the law, but what it obliges and what it does not is left to the hand of God.

Butcher. Why, then, do we hear our parish priests from the pulpit crying, "Tomorrow you must fast, under pain of eternal damnation," if it is not apparent to us how far a human law is binding?

Fishmonger. They do so in order to strike terror into the disobedient; such words apply only to them. Whether these words have an effect, I do not know, but they do give weak people qualms and pain. It is a difficult matter to affect both types.

Butcher. The power of law and custom are quite similar.

Fishmonger. Sometimes custom is more powerful.

Butcher. Those who introduce a custom, whether they intend to snare anyone or not, oftentimes bring people under obligation to obey the custom.

Fishmonger. I agree.

Butcher. Well, then, I hope you now see how dangerous a thing it is to impose new laws upon men, which are unnecessary or of no great utility.

Fishmonger. I do see.

Butcher. When the Lord says, "Swear not at all," does He consign everyone who swears to the fires of hell?

Fishmonger. I think not; I take it to be a counsel, not a command.

Butcher. How can you make clear to me that what you say is so, when there is nothing the Lord has forbidden with greater strictness and severity than swearing?

Fishmonger. You must learn from your teachers.

Butcher. When Paul gives advice, are you obliged to follow it under the pain of damnation?

Fishmonger. By no means.

Butcher. Why?

Fishmonger. Because he would not place an impediment before the weak.

Butcher. So it is the maker of the law who decides upon damnation. Thus it is a most sacred thing to insure that we lay no stumbling blocks in the way of the weak with human constitutions.

Fishmonger. It is.

Butcher. If Paul was cautious in this respect, the priests should be much more so because it is uncertain which of them truly have the Spirit and which do not.

Fishmonger. That's true.

Butcher. But a short while ago you denied that it was within the lawgiver's pleasure as to how far the law should oblige a person.

Fishmonger. Here we are dealing with a counsel, not a law.

Butcher. Nothing is easier than to switch these words. "Swear not"—isn't that a command?

Fishmonger. It is.

Butcher. How about, "Resist not evil"?

Fishmonger. It is a counsel.

Butcher. But on the face of it the last implies more a command than the former; we find this in the constitutions, commands, and counsels of the bishops.

Fishmonger. True.

Butcher. But you just denied this strenuously. One who does not have his constitution render anyone guilty of a crime gives advice, not a command.

Fishmonger. True; but it is not expedient that the vulgar mass of men should know this. If they did, they would cry out that they had no intention of following a counsel.

Butcher. Then what would you do about weak consciences, completely perplexed by your silence? I beseech you to tell me whether even learned men can know whether a constitution has the force of a counsel or a command.

Fishmonger. I have heard they can.

Butcher. Can anyone be let in on this secret?

Fishmonger. You may, if you won't blab it out.

Butcher. I'll be as silent as a fish.

Fishmonger. When you hear nothing but, "We exhort, we ordain, we command," it is a counsel; when you hear, "We command, we require," especially when threats of excommunication are added, it is a command.

Butcher. Suppose I owe money to my baker, but can't pay him, and decide to run away rather than be cast into prison. Am I guilty of a capital offense?

Fishmonger. I think not, unless you are trying to escape punishment.

Butcher. Why, then, am I excommunicated?

Fishmonger. That thunderbolt frightens the wicked but does not hurt the innocent. In ancient Rome there were certain dreadful laws in the Twelve Tablets whereby the body of a debtor could be torn apart, which were used for this same purpose. They were never carried out but used as a threat. In the same way that lightning has no effect upon wax or flax, but upon brass, so excommunication does not operate against the penitent, but against the contumacious. On many occasions Christ's thunderbolt is used quite frivolously, in a manner that the ancients would call a "fly in the ointment."

Butcher. Has the master of a house the same power in his household as a bishop has in his diocese?

Fishmonger. In my opinion he has.

Butcher. And do his commands equally oblige?

Fishmonger. Why not?

Butcher. I command that no one eat onions. Are those who fail to obey sinners before God?

Fishmonger. God decides that.

Butcher. In the future I will admonish, not command.

Fishmonger. That will be the wise thing to do.

Butcher. Suppose I see my neighbor in danger and proceed to admonish him privately to withdraw from the society of drunkards and gamblers, but he ignores my admonition and lives more profligately than before. Does my admonition put him under any obligation?

Fishmonger. In my opinion it does.

Butcher. Then neither by counsel nor exhortation do we avoid the snare.

Fishmonger. No, it is not the admonition itself, but the argument of admonition that brings us into the snare. For if I admonish my brother to make use of slippers and he doesn't do it, he is not guilty of a crime.

Butcher. I won't ask you at this time how far the prescriptions of physicians are obligatory. Does a vow make one liable to the pain of eternal damnation?

Fishmonger. Yes.

Butcher. All kinds of vows?

Fishmonger. Yes, all of them, providing they are possible, lawful, and voluntary.

Butcher. What do you mean by voluntary?

Fishmonger. That which is extorted by no necessity.

Butcher. What is necessity?

Fishmonger. Fear falling upon a man of constancy.

Butcher. What of the Stoic of whom Horace says, "if the world fall to pieces about his ears, he would not be afraid"?

Fishmonger. Show me such a Stoic, then I'll give you my answer.

Butcher. Seriously, can the fear of infamy fall upon a man of constancy?

Fishmonger. Why not?

Butcher. Suppose a daughter, for whom it was forbidden to marry privately, should nonetheless marry without the consent of her parents, who would not have given their consent had they known—would the vow be lawful?

Fishmonger. It would.

Butcher. I myself don't know whether it would be or not. But this much I do know: although they may be valid, a great many of these marriages are kept secret, to avoid scandal to the weak. Further, suppose a virgin who, with parental consent, engaged herself in marriage to her lover, then entered the Cloister of St. Clare—is this vow licit and permissible?

Fishmonger. Yes, if it is a solemn one.

Butcher. Can one be solemn that is made in a field or a dark monastery?

Fishmonger. So it is said.

Butcher. Suppose this same person before a few witnesses were to take a vow of perpetual virginity—would it not be a lawful vow?

Fishmonger. No.

Butcher. Why?

Fishmonger. Because a more holy vow stands in the way.

Butcher. If this same girl sold a field, would the contract be valid?

Fishmonger. I don't think so.

Butcher. Would it be valid if she delivered herself into the power of another?

Fishmonger. If she devoted herself to God, she could do so.

Butcher. Does not a private vow devote a person to God? Does not one who receives the holy sacrament of matrimony devote oneself to God? Can those whom God has joined together devote themselves to the Devil? God spoke of married persons when He said, "Whom God has joined, let no man put asunder." When a young man not having reached his majority or a simple maid are forced into a monastery or a convent by the threats of parents, the severity of tutors, the wicked instigation of monks, or by promises and threats, is this vow a free one?

Fishmonger. Yes, if they have reached the age of reason.

Butcher. A virgin that old is certainly of reasonable age and quite easily imposed upon. What if I should decide in my own mind not to drink wine on Friday; would my decision bind me as strongly as a vow?

Fishmonger. I don't think it would.

Butcher. What's the difference between a determined purpose and a vow conceived in the mind?

Fishmonger. The intention to bind oneself.

Butcher. You denied just now that the intention signified anything in this matter. Do I resolve if I am able, and vow whether I am able or not?

Fishmonger. You have it.

Butcher. Have it? What I have are clouds painted upon the wall, which is nothing at all. What, then, is the rationale of the matter to be disregarded in the case of an intention?

Fishmonger. I think so.

Butcher. Must we take care of one because of the law and the other because of the vow?

Fishmonger. Yes.

Butcher. Suppose the Pope were to make it unlawful for anyone to marry within the seventh degree of affinity, would a person marrying a cousin of the sixth degree be guilty of sin?

Fishmonger. In my opinion he would.

Butcher. What if a bishop set forth an edict forbidding a husband to have relations with his wife except on Monday, Thursday and Saturday; would a husband doing so on other than the appointed days be guilty of a sin?

Fishmonger. I think he would.

Butcher. What if he should prohibit anyone from eating bulbous roots?

Fishmonger. What relationship does that have to piety?

Butcher. Because they are aphrodisiacs, but what I say of bulbs I could say of coleworts.

Fishmonger. I don't know.

Butcher. Can't you tell wherein the force of obligation in human laws lies?

Fishmonger. In the words of St. Paul, "Be obedient to those that are set over you."

Butcher. On this basis the constitution of a bishop or a magistrate binds all people.

Fishmonger. Yes, if they are just and lawfully made.

Butcher. But who shall be the judge of that?

Fishmonger. The constitution maker; for only the one who makes the law ought to interpret it.

Butcher. Must we then be obedient to all constitutions without distinction?

Fishmonger. I think we should.

Butcher. What if a fool or a wicked person gains power over us and makes a foolish and wicked law—must we abide by his judgment and must the people obey, as if having no right to judge?

Fishmonger. Such a situation does not exist.

Butcher. Does a man who gives aid to his father only because he is obligated by the law to do so fulfill the law or not?

Fishmonger. No, I don't think he does.

Butcher. Why not?

Fishmonger. First, he does not fulfill the will of the law-maker, and in addition he adds to this hypocrisy.

Butcher. If one fasts, but would not if the Church did not require it, does this satisfy the law?

Fishmonger. You change both the author of the law and the matter of it.

Butcher. Well, then, compare a Jew, who fasts upon the appointed days but would not unless the law required it, with a Christian, who, keeping a fast appointed by men, would not do so if there were no law requiring it. If you'd rather, compare a Jew abstaining from pork with a Christian abstaining from all meat on Friday.

Fishmonger. I believe that there should be some mitigation of the law for infirmity, though the law makes no allowance for it, but none for those who purposely act and murmur against the law.

Butcher. You do allow that divine laws do not always oblige under pain of eternal damnation?

Fishmonger. Why shouldn't I?

Butcher. Would you not dare to agree that there is any human law that does not carry the same penalty, but leaves a person in suspense? You seem to attribute more to the laws of men than to those of God. Lying and backbiting are evil in and of themselves, and are forbidden by God himself, yet you state that some kinds of lies and backbiting do not bind a person to the punishment of hell. Would you dare to exempt a person from the same punishment for eating meat on Friday under certain conditions?

Fishmonger. Acquitting or condemning anyone is none of my business.

Butcher. If divine and human laws bind equally, what is the difference between them?

Fishmonger. This is the difference: he who transgresses a human law sins immediately against man, if you will allow me to use scholastic terms, but mediately against God; a transgression of divine law proceeds conversely.

Butcher. When mixing vinegar and wormwood, what does it matter which goes first, if I must drink both of them? Or of what importance is it whether a stone, having wounded me, rebounds from me, hitting a friend directly or sideways?

Fishmonger. It's not important.

Butcher. If the "modus" of the binding force of the law is measured by matter and circumstances, what is the difference between the authority of God and that of man?

Fishmonger. That indeed is a wicked question!

Butcher. There are a great many who don't think there is any difference. God gave a law through Moses that it is unlawful to violate. He also gives laws through the popes and the councils. What's the difference between these? Moses' law was given through a man, and our laws were given through men. So it would seem that those laws given by God through Moses are of less moment than those the Holy Spirit gives through a council of bishops and learned men.

Fishmonger. It is unlawful to doubt the spirit of Moses.

Butcher. Paul stands in the place of a bishop; what is the difference between the precepts of Paul and those of any other bishop?

Fishmonger. Without doubt Paul wrote through the inspiration of the Spirit.

Butcher. How far does the authority of the writers extend?

Fishmonger. I think no further than the Apostles themselves, unless the authority of the councils has indicated that others be looked upon as inviolable.

Butcher. Why may we not doubt Paul's inspiration?

Fishmonger. Because the Church has adopted this position.

Butcher. May we doubt the pronouncements of the bishops?

Fishmonger. We should not be rashly suspicious of them and only should do so if they show a marked proclivity toward gain and impiety.

Butcher. What do you think of the councils?

Fishmonger. We should not doubt them, if they are rightly constituted and inspired by the Holy Spirit.

Butcher. Is there any council that has not fulfilled these requirements?

Fishmonger. It is possible there may have been, otherwise the theologians would not have made this exception.

Butcher. Then it seems to be lawful to doubt concerning councils themselves.

Fishmonger. I don't think we can, provided they are received and approved by the judgment and consent of Christian nations.

Butcher. But since we have exceeded the boundary set by God, and within which He would have the sacred and inviolable authority of the Scripture circumscribed, it seems to me that there is some other difference between divine and human laws.

Fishmonger. What is it, then?

Butcher. Divine laws are immutable, except those that were given only for a short time, that were used as prefigures or for coercion, that the prophets foretold should terminate, or that the Apostles taught should be omitted. In reference to human laws, sometimes unjust, foolish, and injurious ones are made, and therefore they are either abrogated by the authority of superiors or by the universal neglect of the people. But no such redress exists for divine law. Again, a human law ceases when the causes for its existence cease to exist. For instance, suppose a constitution required all persons yearly to contribute something toward the building

of a Church; when the church is built, the requirement of the
law ceases. In addition a human law is no law at all, unless
it is approved by those who use it.

A divine law cannot be dispensed with or abrogated, although Moses, about to make a law, required the consent of
the people. This was not done because it was necessary, however, but rather that it might render the violation of the law
more criminal. It is indeed an imprudent thing to break a law
to which you gave your approbation during its making.
Finally, inasmuch as human laws commonly concern corporal
matters and are the schoolmasters of piety, they seem to ex-
pire when people arrive at that strength of grace which allows
them to stand with no need of any such restraints. They should
merely endeavor to avoid giving offense to weak persons, who
are conscientiously scrupulous.

For instance, suppose a father enjoins his daughter, who
is under age, not to drink wine, so she may be better able to
preserve her virginity until she is married. When she comes
of age and is delivered to her husband, she is not bound by
her father's injunction. There are many laws that are like a
medicine, that are altered and give way according to the circumstances, and with the approval of the physicians themselves, who, if they should at all times use the remedies of
the ancients, would kill more than they cure.

Fishmonger. You indeed group a great many things together, some of which I like, others I dislike, and some of
which I don't understand.

Butcher. If a bishop's law aims manifestly at gain—that
is, if he ordered every parish priest each year to purchase, at
a gold ducat apiece, the right of absolution in episcopal cases,
so that he might extort more money from those in his juris-
diction—do you think it ought to be obeyed?

Fishmonger. Yes, I think it should; but at the same time
it should be exclaimed against as an unjust law, always avoiding sedition. How come you turn catechizer now, Butcher?
Everyone should stick to his own trade.

Butcher. We are often perplexed by these questions in
discussion at the table and sometimes the contest proceeds
to blows and bloodshed.

Fishmonger. Let those who love fighting fight; I think
we should accept with reverence the laws of our superiors
and religiously observe them, as if they came from God. It is
neither safe nor religious to conceive in the mind or sow

among others any sinister suspicion concerning them. And if there is tyranny in any of the laws, as long as they do not compel impiety, it would be better to bear it than seditiously resist it.

Butcher. I admit this is a very good way to maintain the authority of persons in power. I pretty much agree with you, and as for those in authority, I do not envy them. I'd be quite happy to hear anything that aims at the liberty and advantage of the people.

Fishmonger. God will not forget His people.

Butcher. But where, all this while, is the liberty of the spirit that the Apostles promise in the Gospel, and that Paul so often inculcates, saying, "The Kingdom of God consists not in meat and drink"; and that "we are not children under a schoolmaster"; and that "we do no longer serve the elements of this world"; and an abundance of other expressions? Are Christians tied to the observance of so many more ceremonies than the Jews were; and are not the laws of man more binding than a great many commands of God?

Fishmonger. Well, Butcher, this much I tell you, the liberty of Christians does not consist of it being lawful for them to do what they will, being set free of human ordinances. But rather their liberty consists of doing those things they are enjoined to do with a fervor of spirit and readiness of mind, willingly and cheerfully, as if they were sons rather than servants.

Butcher. Very cleverly answered indeed! But there were sons under the Mosaic Law, and there are now servants under the Gospel. I am afraid the greatest part of mankind are servants who do their duty by compulsion. What difference is there then between the new dispensation and the old?

Fishmonger. In my opinion a great deal. Because the old taught under a veil and the new is laid open to the people. That which the old foretold by parables and riddles the new explains clearly; what the old promised obscurely the new exhibits for the most part manifestly. That which was given to one nation singly now equally teaches all the way to salvation. The old imparted that notable and spiritual grace to a few prophets and famous men, but the new sheds abroad every kind of gift, such as languages, the healing of diseases, prophecies, and miracles, to persons of every age, sex, and nation.

Butcher. Where are those gifts now?

Fishmonger. They have stopped, but are not lost, either because there is no longer any need of them now that the doctrine of Christ has spread abroad, or because many are Christians in name only and desire faith because it is a worker of miracles.

Butcher. If miracles are necessary because of unbelievers, I'm sure the world is full of them now.

Fishmonger. This is a disbelief of simple error, such as that of the Jews murmuring against Peter because he received Cornelius's family into the grace of the Gospel. The same situation prevailed among the Gentiles, who thought the religion they had received from their ancestors sufficient for salvation, and the doctrine of the Apostles a strange superstition. They were converted by seeing miracles. But now those who do not believe the Gospel when it shines so gloriously through the whole world do not just simply err, but being blinded by their evil affections, refuse to see that they should be good. These no miracle can improve.

Butcher. Indeed you have said many things that are probable; however, I am resolved not to depend upon the judgment of a salt-fishmonger. I will go to some theologian, eminent in learning, and what he says concerning all these things, I'll believe.

Fishmonger. Who? Pharetrius?

Butcher. He is feeble before he is old and is fit to preach to nobody but doting old women.

Fishmonger. Well, then, who? Bliteus?

Butcher. Do you think I'd believe anything that prating sophist has to say?

Fishmonger. Well, then, Amphicholus?

Butcher. I'd never trust him to answer questions; he never paid his meat bill, when I trusted him. Can anyone who was always insolvent concerning his debts answer difficult questions?

Fishmonger. Who, then? Lemantius?

Butcher. I wouldn't choose a blind man to show me the way.

Fishmonger. Who, then?

Butcher. If you care to know, it is Cephalus, a man very

well versed in three languages, and accomplished in good literature, familiarly acquainted with the sacred Scripture and the ancient Fathers.

Fishmonger. I'll give you better advice. Go to the Elysian Fields and there you'll find Rabin Druin—he'll cut all your knotty questions in two with a pair of shears.

Butcher. Will you go ahead of me and clear the way?

Fishmonger. All jesting aside, it is true that you told me of a dispensation for flesh-eating?

Butcher. No, I was just teasing you. And if the Pope ever had so much as a thought of doing it, you fishmongers would raise a stink about it. Besides, the world is full of this sort of Pharisee, who has no other way of appearing religious except by such superstitions, and who would neither be deprived of his ostentatious sanctity nor allow his successors to have more liberty than he had himself. Nor would it be in the interest of the butchers to allow people to eat everything, for then our trade would be very uncertain. Now our profit is more certain and we run less risks, as well as have less trouble.

Fishmonger. What you say is true, and we should be in the same condition.

Butcher. I am glad to find at last something upon which a fishmonger and a butcher can agree. But seriously, it would be better if Christians were not tied up in so many ceremonies, especially those that have little to do with true religion. In saying this I'm not against true religion and don't vindicate those people who reject and make light of all human ordinances, just because they are forbidden to do certain things. Yet I can't very well admire some of the absurd notions of mankind in many things.

Fishmonger. Nor can I help wondering about them.

Butcher. We would mix up heaven and earth if we suspected that there is grave danger unless priests abandon some of the weight they attach to their pronouncements. We are all asleep, under imminent danger of attributing so much to the authority of man that the authority of God will suffer. On the horns of a dilemma, we avoid one evil and fall into another even more pernicious. That honor is due bishops no one denies, especially if they act the way they talk. But it is a wicked thing to transfer the honor due to God alone to men;

and in giving too much honor to men, to give too little to God. We should honor and revere God through our neighbor, but we should make sure at the same time that God is not robbed of His honor by this means.

Fishmonger. We see many men who put so much stress upon corporal ceremonies that, relying upon them, they neglect matters of real religion, arrogating to their own merits that which rightly should be attributed to the Divine, and there they rest, when they should begin to ascend to greater perfection, reviling their neighbors for those things that are neither good nor bad in themselves.

Butcher. And when it comes to a choice between two things, one being better than the other, we commonly choose the worse one. The body, and those things that belong to the body, are everywhere preferred to those of the mind. It is rightly considered a great crime to kill a man, but to corrupt the minds of men with poisonous doctrine and pernicious principles is a joke. If a priest lets his hair grow or wears lay clothes, he is thrown into prison and severely punished; but if he sits drinking in a brothel with whores, gambles or debauches the wives of other men and never opens a Bible, he is still a pillar of the Church. Not that I excuse the wearing of lay clothes, but I criticize the absurdity of men's ideas.

Fishmonger. No, if he neglects to say his prayers on the appointed hours, he must be excommunicated; but if he is a usurer, or guilty of simony, he goes scot-free.

Butcher. If anyone sees a Carthusian in other than his prescribed dress or eating flesh, how does he not curse him, tremble before the sight, and take flight, for fear the earth would open and swallow up the Carthusian for his apparel and him for witnessing it. But let the same person see him blind drunk, castigating his neighbor with lies, and openly defrauding him, and he is not at all shocked.

Fishmonger. If a Franciscan is seen in a girdle without knots, or an Augustinian gird in a woolen instead of a leather cord, or a Carmelite without one, or a Rhodian with one, or a Franciscan with shoes on his feet, or a Cruciferian with sandals on, would he not send the whole town into an uproar?

Butcher. Recently in our neighborhood there were two women, both of them considered level-headed; one of them miscarried and the other one fell into a fit upon seeing a canon, who was president of the nuns in a nearby cloister, appear in public without any underwear under his black cloak. But these same women have frequently seen the same kind of cattle out on the town, singing and dancing, not to say more; and their stomachs never so much as heaved at it.

Fishmonger. Perhaps some allowance ought to be made for their sex. But I suppose you know Polythrescus. He was dangerous ill with consumption. The physicians for a long time ordered him to eat eggs and meat, but to no avail. The bishop exhorted him likewise to do so. But being a man of learning and a bachelor in theology, he resolved to die rather than take the advice of either of these physicians. Finally the doctors, in league with his friends, contrived to deceive him, giving him a potion of eggs and goat's milk and telling him it was the juice of almonds. He took it freely. For several days it improved his health, until a certain maid told him of the trick, whereupon he commenced to vomit it up again. But this very same man who was so superstitious in relation to milk had so little religion in him that he refused to pay a sum of money that he owed me. Having gotten an opportunity to destroy the note he had given me, he forswore his obligation and I had to take the loss. He took oaths with so little difficulty, that he seemed to wish he had such complaints made against him every day. Who can be more perverse than that? He sinned against the mind of the Church by not obeying the priest and doctors. But this man whose stomach was so weak in relation to milk had a conscience strong enough to commit perjury.

Butcher. This story brings to mind what I heard a Dominican say, while portraying the death of Christ on Easter Eve in an attempt to temper the sadness of the subject with the pleasantness of a story. A certain young man had gotten a nun pregnant, and the great size of her belly gave it away. A jury of nuns was impaneled, with the abbess sitting as judge of the court. Evidence was given against the nun; the facts were too plain for any denial; she was obliged to plead the unavoidableness of the crime and defended herself this way. She transferred the blame to another, having recourse to the "Status Qualitatis" or rather the "Status Translationis." "I was overcome by one who was too strong for me," she said. The abbess replied, "Then you should have cried out." "I would have," said the prisoner, "had it not been a crime to break silence in the dormitory." Whether this is fact or fiction I do not know, but there are a great many more foolish things than this done.

But now I will tell you what I have seen with my own eyes.

The man's name and his place of residence I shall conceal. There was a cousin of mine, a prior next in degree to the abbot of the Benedictine order. He was the type who doesn't eat flesh, unless out of the place they call the great refectory. He was considered a learned man, and desired to be considered so. He was about fifty years of age. It was his daily practice to drink and live merrily, and once every twelve days he'd go to the public baths to sweat out the diseases of his kidneys.

Fishmonger. Had he the money to live like that?

Butcher. About six hundred florins a year.

Fishmonger. Such poverty I myself would wish for.

Butcher. In short, by drinking and whoring he came down with consumption. The doctors had given him up; the abbot ordered him to eat flesh, adding that terrible sentence, "Under pain of disobedience." But he, though at the point of death, could not be brought to taste flesh, even though for many years he had had no aversion to the flesh.

Fishmonger. A prior and an abbot well matched! I've guessed who they are; I remember having heard the same story from their own mouths.

Butcher. Guess.

Fishmonger. Is not the abbot a lusty, fat man who has a stammer in his speech, and the prior a little man with a straight body and a long face?

Butcher. You've guessed correctly.

Fishmonger. Well, now I'll make amends to you. I'll tell you what I saw the other day with my own eyes; not only was I present, but was in a way the chief actor. Two nuns went to pay a visit to some of their relatives. When they arrived, they found that their manservant had left behind their prayer books, which were special ones according to the custom of the order and place in which they lived. Good God! What a horrible thing that was! They did not dare eat supper before they said their vespers, nor could they read from any book but their own. At the same time all the company was eager to go to supper. The servant ran back and brought back the book; and by the time they had said their prayers and gotten to supper, it was ten o'clock at night.

Butcher. There's nothing greatly wrong with that.

Fishmonger. You have heard only one part of the story. At the supper the nuns began to grow merry with wine; they laughed, joked, and kissed—not too modestly, either—until you could hardly hear what was said for the noise they made. Nobody acted with more freedom than those two virgins who would not go to supper before they had said their prayers. After supper there was dancing, singing of lewd songs, and activity that I dare not describe. I am afraid that night was not a very respectable one; if it was, the wanton plays, nods, and kisses deceived me.

Butcher. I don't blame the nuns for this as much as the priests who look after them. Come on, I'll match you story for story, or rather give you a history of that which I myself was an eyewitness. A little while ago a group of people were sent to prison for baking bread on Sunday, though they were fresh out of it. Indeed, I don't blame the deed, but I do blame the punishment. A little later, on Palm Sunday, I went over to the next street and, at about four o'clock in the afternoon, I saw a sight I don't know whether to call ridiculous or wretched. I don't believe any Bacchanal was ever so lewd. Some were so drunk they reeled to and fro, like a ship tossed on the waves without a rudder. Others, hardly able to stand themselves, were supporting one so drunk he couldn't move. Others fell down and could hardly get up. Some were crowned with leaves of oak.

Fishmonger. Vines and wands would have suited them better.

Butcher. The oldest of the group, acting the part of Silenus, was carried upon men's shoulders like a dead corpse, with his feet forward but his face downward, so that he would not be choked by his own vomiting, which ran down to the heels of those who carried him. There was not a sober man among the bearers; they went along laughing, as if they had all lost their senses. In short, they were all insane. In their pickled condition they made a procession into the city in the daytime.

Fishmonger. How did they all become insane?

Butcher. You know that in the next town wine was sold more cheaply than here. So a group of boon companions went there to obtain a greater amount of insanity for less money. Indeed, they did spend less money and got more insanity. If these men had but tasted an egg, they would have been hauled off to prison as if they had committed parricide. Besides their neglecting divine service and evening prayers on so sacred a day, they committed intemperance with impunity. Yet nobody seemed very displeased about it.

Fishmonger. Don't be too puzzled about it. In the center of the cities and in alehouses next to the churches on the most solemn holidays there was drinking, singing, dancing, fighting, and such noise and tumult that divine services could not be performed, nor could one word the priest said be heard. But if the same men had sown a stitch in a shoe or eaten pork on Friday, they would have been handled severely. Though the Lord's day was instituted chiefly to give people the leisure to concern themselves with the doctrine of the Gospel, it was therefore forbidden to mend shoes, so that there would be leisure to trim souls. But is not this a strange perversion of judgment?

Butcher. An amazing one. There are two elements in the precept of fasting, one abstinence from flesh, the other relating to the type of food. Almost everyone would agree that the first is either a divine command or very close to it. The latter is not only human in origin, but is in opposition to the doctrine really intended by the Apostles. However, we explain it by the preposterous idea that, although it is no crime to eat a meal, yet to taste a bit of meat that is prescribed by man, though permitted by God and the Apostles, is a capital crime. Fasts, although they may not have been commanded by the Apostles, are recommended in their examples and epistles. But as to the prohibition against consuming meat, which God has created to be eaten with acts of thanksgiving, must we now defend this practice before the judgment seat of Paul? Yet almost the world over, men eat plentifully and nobody is offended by it. But if a sick man eats a piece of chicken, the whole of Christianity is in danger. In England the common people have a supper every other day during Lent, and no one is disturbed by it. But if a man at death's door with a fever should take a little chicken broth, it is considered a crime worse than sacrilege. There is nothing of greater antiquity nor more religiously observed among Christians than Lent. The same people who eat supper without penalty during Lent will not allow this to be done outside of Lent on a Friday. If you ask the reason, they say it is the custom of the country, and curse a man for not observing the customs of the land. Yet they forgive themselves for neglecting an ancient custom of the universal Church.

Fishmonger. One who without reason neglects the custom of the country in which he lives should not be praised.

Butcher. In the same way I blame those who divide Lent between God and their bellies, yet there is no reason for preposterous censuring in these matters.

Fishmonger. Although the Lord's day was instituted in order to have people meet together and hear the Gospel preached, one who does not hear the mass is looked upon as an abominable sinner, while one who neglects to hear the sermon and plays ball during that time is not considered a sinner.

Butcher. What a serious crime it is to receive the sacrament into an unwashed mouth! But at the same time many take it with an unpurified mind, defiled with perverse desires.

Fishmonger. How many priests would rather die than celebrate mass with a chalice and paten that have not been consecrated by a bishop, or do so in their everyday clothes? But among all of them, how many do we see not at all afraid to come to the Lord's table drunk after last night's debauchery? How fearful are they of touching the Host with that part of the hand which had not been dipped in consecrated oil? Why are they not as religious in making sure that a filthy mind does not offend the Lord himself?

Butcher. If we happen to so much as touch a consecrated vessel, we'd think ourselves guilty of a heinous offense; and yet how unconcerned are we when we violate the living temples of the Holy Spirit?

Fishmonger. Human constitutions require that no one illegitimate, lame, or one-eyed may be admitted to the priesthood; how strictly do we enforce this? But in the meantime the ignorant, gamblers, drunkards, soldiers, and murderers are admitted everywhere. We are told that the diseases of the mind cannot be seen. I don't speak of those things that are hidden, but of those that are more easily seen than the deformities of the body.

Butcher. There are bishops who have nothing to say for themselves but their sordid accomplishments. The gift of preaching, which is the chief dignity of a bishop, has given way to every sordid thing. This they would never do unless some set of false values hold them.

Fishmonger. Anyone profaning a holy day instituted by a bishop is quickly punished. But there are some great men who, disregarding the constitutions of popes and councils and all their thunderbolts, hinder canonical elections, ravage Church lands, not even sparing almshouses and hospitals, erected through the charity of pious persons for the care of the old, sick, and needy. These think themselves good enough Christians if they indulge their bad temper upon persons who have offended them in trivial matters.

Butcher. We'd better leave great men alone and talk about salt-fish and flesh.

Fishmonger. I agree with you. Let's get back to fasts and fish. I have heard that these papal laws explicitly excuse children, old men, sick and weak persons, those who work hard, pregnant women, breast-fed children, and the very poor.

Butcher. I have often heard this.

Fishmonger. I have also heard that a very excellent theologian, I think his name is Gerson, has said that if there are any other cases of equal weight with those excepted from the papal laws, the precept is mitigated for them also. There are some peculiarities of the body that are a greater excuse for not fasting than disease; and we find that some disorders that do not appear outwardly are more dangerous than those that do. Therefore, one knowing well his own constitution need not consult a priest, just as infants do not, because in both cases their circumstances exempt them from the law.

It follows that those who oblige children, very old men, or physically weak people to fast or to eat fish commit a double sin: the first against brotherly charity, and the second against the Pope himself, who would not require those to observe the law when it would be injurious to them. Whatever Christ ordered he ordained for the health of both body and mind; and furthermore no pope claims for himself the power to endanger a person's life. For example, suppose a person by not eating in the evening is unable to rest well at night and as a result becomes delirious; whoever orders such a person to fast goes against the mind of the Church and the will of God.

Princes, often to suit their own convenience, publish edicts of this sort, threatening transgressors with capital punishment. How far their power extends I do not know, but this much I will say: they would be safer if they inflicted the death penalty for no other reasons than those expressed in the Holy Scriptures. Our Lord urges a pattern of conduct which avoids extremes in this matter. Instead of legislating against perjury he recommends that we avoid swearing of all kinds. If we follow His advice in never becoming angry we will avoid the extreme result of this, homicide. As often as we can we should reasonably follow the dictates of charity and exhort our neighbor, keeping in mind the weakness of human nature. If there is no other apparent reason, it is the role of Christian charity to assume that one's eating habits are done in good faith unless one eats with a manifest contempt of the ecclesiastical law. A civil magistrate justly punishes those who violate dietary laws in public; but what a person eats in his own house is the business of a physician rather than a magistrate. Those who are so wicked that they cause disorder of any kind are guilty of sedition, but hardly the person who consults his own health and breaks no law, neither of God nor man.

In cases like this the authority of the Pope is misapplied. It is absurd to pretend the authority of the Pope in such cases. They are themselves persons of great humanity, and would, if given good reasons on their own accord, protect the health of those who need it with dispensations against slanderous attacks. Besides, throughout Italy flesh is sold in certain markets, for the sake of people who need it for their health. In addition, I have heard theologians, differing little from the Pharisees, say not to be afraid to eat a piece of bread or drink a pint of wine or ale at suppertime to support the weakness of the body. If they take it upon themselves to allow a small supper to those who are in health, contrary to the ordinance of the Church, which requires fasting, may they not permit a much more hardy one for those people whose weakness require it—may not the Pope even approve it? If one treats his body with severity, it can be called zeal, for each person knows his own constitution best; but is there any piety and charity displayed by people who reduce a weak brother, wherein the spirit is willing but the flesh is weak, even to death's door, or cause him to contract a disease worse than death itself, against the law of nature, the law of God, and the sense of papal law?

Butcher. What you mention brings to mind what I myself saw about two years ago. I believe you know the old man, Eros, about sixty years of age, and a man of very weak constitution, who by a lingering illness, acute diseases, and study exhausting enough to fell even the great athlete Milo was brought to death's door. This man had, by a mystery of nature, from early childhood a great aversion to eating fish and an inability to endure fasting. Whenever he did fast, his life was endangered. He finally obtained a dispensation from the Pope to defend him against the tongues of some Pharisaical spirits.

Not long ago he accepted an invitation from friends to go to the city of Eleutheropolis, a city not at all like its name. It was during the Lenten season that he spent a few days devoted to the enjoyment of his friends. All during this time fish was the common diet; he, so as not to give offense to his friends, and even though he had the papal dispensation, ate fish. He felt the old disorder coming upon him, which was worse than death itself. So he prepared to leave his friends and go home, finding this necessary to avoid sickness. Some suspected that he was making a hasty departure because he could not eat fish and persuaded Glaucoplutus, a very learned man and a chief magistrate in that province, to invite Eros to breakfast. Eros, quite tired of company that he could not avoid in a public inn, consented to go, but only on the condition that no preparation would be made for him, save a couple of eggs, which he would eat standing up and immediately take to his horse and be gone. He was promised that his desires would be carried out, but when he arrived, there was fowl provided for him. Eros, taking it poorly, tasted only the eggs, rose from the table, and took to his horse with some learned men accompanying him part of the way.

But in some way or another the smell of the fowl was picked up by a number of parasites. Noise began to issue from the city, sounding as if ten men were being murdered; nor was the tumult only confined to that city, but was carried to places two days' journey from there, and as usual growing in volume as it extended. It was rumored that Eros had not gotten away but had been brought to justice. This was not true, but Glaucoplutus was obliged to give the magistrate satisfaction.

Now considering the circumstances of Eros, had he eaten flesh in public, who would have been justly offended by it? Yet in the same city all during Lent, but especially on holidays, many of these parasites drank until they were insane, howling, dancing, and shooting dice at the church door, so that the priest could not be heard when he was preaching. Yet this was not an offense against the law.

Fishmonger. What a perversion of judgment!

Butcher. I'll tell you another story not unlike the one I just told. It was almost two years ago that the same Eros went to Ferventia for his health, and out of civility I accompanied him. He went to an old friend's home, who had given him frequent invitations by letter. He was a great man and one of the pillars of the Church. When the eating of fish started, so did his old condition. A whole troop of disorders came upon him, fever, severe headache, vomiting, and the stone. His landlord, although he saw his friend in this danger, did not dare give him a bit of fresh meat. But why didn't he? He saw a great many reasons why he might do it and likewise saw the papal dispensation; but he was afraid of public censure. The man excused his inaction by indication that the disease had progressed so far that giving flesh to eat would be of no avail.

Fishmonger. What did Eros do? I know that man; he'd rather die than injure a friend.

Butcher. He shut himself into a room and lived in his accustomed manner. His dinner was one egg and his drink, boiled sugar water. As soon as his fever subsided, he left on his horse, carrying provisions along with him.

Fishmonger. What were they?

Butcher. Almond milk in a bottle and dried grapes in his travel bag. When he returned home, he was seized by the stone and was laid up for a whole month. After he had gone, a torrid but false report of eating flesh followed him, which reached as far as Paris. A great many notorious lies were told about him. What remedy do you think proper for such an offense?

Fishmonger. I would command everyone to empty their chamberpots upon their heads, and if they are encountered in the street, people should hold their noses while they go by, so that they might be brought to a sense of their madness.

Butcher. I think the theologians should write against such Pharisaical impiety. But what is your opinion of this landlord?

Fishmonger. He seems to me a very prudent man who understands the frivolous reasons why the people are excited to such dismal tragedies.

Butcher. This may indeed stem from prudence, and we may interpret the good man's timidity favorably. But how many in a similar case would allow their brother to die, pretending a reticence to act against the usage of the Church and fear of offending the people? The same persons do not fear offending the people by living a publicly scandalous life, by rioting, whoring, and idleness, and by showing the highest contempt for religion by rapine, simony, and cheating.

Fishmonger. There are too many who would act this way. That which they call piety is nothing but a barbarous and impious cruelty. But I think that those who not only leave a man in danger, but also invent dangers for him and force him into a trap, which is dangerous to both body and soul, seem to be more cruel, especially since they have no authority.

Butcher. I'm waiting to hear what else you have to say.

Fishmonger. About thirty years ago I lived in Vinegar College at Paris.

Butcher. That's an appropriate name. But tell me, Salt-Fishmonger, did you really live at that sour college? No wonder you are such an acute disputant in questions of theology; I hear the very walls there teach theology.

Fishmonger. You are correct. But as for me I brought nothing out of there except my body filled with many maladies and my clothes with lice. But to continue, at that time one John Standonck was president. He was a man of attractive personality and desirable qualifications. As I remember it, in his youth, when he was very poor, he was quite charitable, and that is to be commended. He did not at that time have a great deal of money, but what he did have he used to supply the necessities of the young as well as materials for their studies. But this man pushed his students severely, giving them a poor diet and requiring that they study long and hard. Within a year's time, of the many intelligent and hopeful young men in his charge, some he had caused to die, others he blinded, others he drove away insane, still others he caused to contract leprosy, some of whom I knew very well. In short, everyone under him was in danger. Was not this cruelty against his neighbor?

As if this wasn't enough, he required that everyone wear a monastic garb and proscribed the eating of flesh altogether. He then sent his striplings into distant lands. If anyone else gave expression to their desires as he did, their disciples would cover the earth. If monasteries had their origin in this way, what kind of danger did they not present to the popes and kings? It is a pious thing to glory in the conversion of a neighbor to piety, but to seek glory in dress or diet is hypocritical. To supply the need of a neighbor is part of piety; to insure that the liberality of men is not converted to luxury is discipline. But to drive one's fellow man into disorders, insanity, and death is cruelty that amounts to murder. The intention to cause death may indeed be lacking, but murder it is.

Perhaps it can be said that no one is forced into this kind of life and enters it voluntarily; it is contended that they beg to be admitted, and they are free to leave when they become weary of it; but this is a cruel answer. Are we to assume that an inexperienced young man can tell what is good for him better than a man of learning, experience, and age? A man might excuse himself to a wolf, whom he has drawn into a trap when he was almost famished with hunger. But can a man who has set unwholesome and poisonous food before another man who is dying from hunger excuse himself to the dying man by saying, "Nobody forces you to eat it; you ate that which was set before you willingly and eagerly"? Can not the dying man justly answer, "You have not given me food, but poison"? Necessity is widespread and hunger compelling, so those remarks about liberty are untenable. Anyone using these methods really uses force. This cruelty not only destroys the common people, but afflicts the upper classes and ruins many people of intelligence. It is indeed the duty of a father to restrain his son from lewdness.

But what about all of this in face of starvation rations and polluted water? Add to this complete lack of heat in the building. I know many who were reduced to such poor health that they haven't gotten over it to this day. There were rooms on the ground floor filled with rotten plaster and the stench of the nearby latrine. These rooms were so bad that if one were lucky enough to escape death, he would still fall victim to disease. I shall say nothing of the unmerciful whippings, even of innocent people.

This they say is to break their intransigence, for that's what they call youthful industry; thus they lord it over the spirit in order to make those in the monastery more humble. I won't even estimate how many rotten eggs were eaten, or how much sour wine was drunk. Perhaps things have changed now; but it is too late for those already dead or those still suffering from disorders contracted there. I don't mention these things because I bear any ill will toward the college, but I thought it would be worthwhile to give this example of human severity under the pretense of religion to warn the young and inexperienced. How much courtesy or true piety is taught there now I do not know. If it were true that those who donned a cowl put off evil living, I would encourage everyone to wear one. A person of vigorous age should not be frightened into this sort of life, but his mind should be formed for piety. I can scarcely enter a Carthusian monastery without seeing some fools and madmen among the residents. But let's return to our original subject.

Butcher. We lose nothing by digression as long as what we have said has a purpose. Perhaps you have something to add concerning human constitutions.

Fishmonger. In my opinion the person who neglects to do what the author of the human constitution has aimed at does not observe it. The person who on a holy day forbears work, but does not perform his religious duty, profanes the day by neglecting to perform those things for which the day was set aside; therefore one good work is forbidden so that another can be performed. But those who leave their secular employment in order to go out on the town, whoring, fighting, and gambling, are guilty of a double profanation of the day.

Butcher. It is my opinion that the task of saying prayers was imposed upon priests and monks to accustom them to lift their hearts to God. Yet those who neglect saying their prayers are in danger of being punished, but those who only mumble the words with their mouth and do not pay any attention to the meaning of them, nor take pains to so much as learn the language in which they are written, without which they can't tell what the sound means, are considered good men by others, and they think themselves such.

Fishmonger. I know a great many priests who consider it a heinous sin to omit any part of their prayers, or mistakingly have said something of the Virgin Mary, when they should have done so concerning St. Paul. But the same persons consider it no crime to gamble, whore, and drink, though these things are forbidden by the law of both God and man.

Butcher. I myself have known a great many people who would rather die than be persuaded to take the Sacrament after they had chanced to take a bit of food, or let a drop of water go down their throats while they were washing their mouths. Yet these same people will say that they have so much malice against some that, if they had an opportunity, they would kill them; nor are they afraid with such a disposition of mind to approach the Lord's table.

Fishmonger. That they take the sacrament fasting is a human ordinance, but that they lay aside anger before coming to the Lord's table is a command of the Lord himself.

Butcher. How preposterously do we judge perjury! One who swears he has paid a debt, when it is proved he has not, is considered an infamous person. But perjury has not yet been leveled upon the priest who openly lives unchastely, while publicly professing a life of chastity.

Fishmonger. Why don't you tell this to the vicars of the bishop, who swear before the altar that they are all properly entered in holy orders, of the proper age, learning, and manners, when in reality for the most part there are only two or three who are even tolerable, and most of them are scarcely fit to follow the plow?

Butcher. A person who is provoked and swears in passion is punished, but those who swear falsely every three words they speak escape scot-free.

Fishmonger. But they don't swear from their hearts.

Butcher. By the same pretense a man who kills another may be vindicated by saying he had no intention of doing it. Perjury is not lawful in jest or earnest; thus it would be a greater crime to kill a man in jest.

Fishmonger. How can we weigh the oaths taken by princes at their coronation?

Butcher. These royal oaths, though serious in themselves, in this instance are matters of custom and not considered perjuries. There is the same complaint concerning vows. The vow of matrimony is undoubtedly of divine origin, yet it can be dissolved by entering the monastic life, which is an invention of man. And though there is no vow more religious than baptism, yet he who changes his habit or his residence is sought after, apprehended, confined, and sometimes put to death for the honor of the order, as though he had murdered his father. But those who live contrary to their baptismal vows, in that they serve Mammon, their bellies, and the joys of this world, are highly esteemed and are never charged with breaking their vows, nor upbraided, nor called apostates, and are considered good Christians.

Fishmonger. The same situation prevails among the common people in distinguishing good from evil. What a scandal it is for a girl to have been seduced! Yet a lying, scandalous tongue and a malicious, envious mind are greater crimes. Where is a petty theft not punished more severely than adultery? Nobody willingly is the companion of someone accused of theft, but it is considered an honor to be an acquaintance of someone drenched in adultery. No one would condescend to marry a daughter to a hangman, who executes the law for his livelihood, but a judge performs the same function. There is no aversion to a soldier, who has run away from his parents and become a mercenary, even though he has taken part in rape, theft, sacrileges, in camps and retreats. He may be taken as a son-in-law, and though he is worse than any hangman, a girl may love him dearly and consider him a fine person.

Butcher. He who steals a little money must be hanged, but those who swindle the public of their money and impoverish thousands, by monopolies, extortion, tricking, and cheating, are held in great esteem.

Fishmonger. Those who poison one person are hanged for it, but those who poison a whole nation with infectious provisions go unpunished.

Butcher. I know some monks so superstitious that they think themselves in the clutches of the devil if by chance they are without their sacred vestments, but they are not afraid of his claws while they are lying, slandering, drinking, and acting maliciously.

Fishmonger. There are certain citizens who think their house is in danger from evil spirits unless they have holy water, holy leaves, and wax tapers; but they are not afraid of the evil spirits because God is often offended by them, or because the devil is served by them.

Butcher. How many people put more trust in the protection of the Virgin Mary or St. Christopher than in Christ himself? They worship His mother with images, candles, and songs and offend Christ heinously with their impious living. A mariner in a storm is more ready to invoke the Mother of Christ or St. Christopher or some of the other saints than Christ himself. They think they have made the Virgin their friend by singing to her in the evening, the little song, "Salve Regina," though they don't understand what it is they sing. They have more reason to fear that the Virgin should think they jeer her by their singing, when all day and most of the night is spent in obscene talk, drunkenness, and things I will not mention.

Fishmonger. Yes, the same is true of a soldier who embarks on a dangerous mission; he is more ready to remember George or Barbara than Christ. Although nothing is more acceptable to the saints than the imitation of their deeds by which they were approved in the eyes of Christ, most people despise such things. Instead, for example, they think St. Anthony their protector if they consecrate some hogs to him and have him painted on doors and walls with his hog, fire, and bell; but they never fear that which should be more dreaded, namely that he might look with great displeasure upon those houses wherein wickedness reigns, which this holy man always abhorred.

Do we say rosaries and salutations to the Holy Virgin?

Rather we should recount to her the humiliation of our pride, the suppression of our lust, and our forgiveness of injuries. The Mother of Christ takes more delight in songs like these, and they are ways to her and to her Son.

Butcher. A man who is sick is more apt to remember St. Roach or Dionysius than Christ, the only health of mankind. Further, those who from the pulpit interpret the Holy Scriptures, which cannot be done without the assistance of the Holy Spirit, choose rather to invoke the aid of the Virgin Mary than of Christ or his Spirit. Anyone who mutters against this custom, which they call laudable, is suspected of being a heretic. The custom of the ancient Fathers was much more laudable. Such authorities as Origen, Basil, Chrysostom, Cyprian, Ambrose, Jerome, and Augustine invoked the Spirit of Christ but never implored the aid of the Virgin. But there is no hew and cry against those who have presumed to alter so holy a custom, taken from the doctrine of Christ, the Apostles, and the examples of the Holy Fathers.

Fishmonger. A great many monks fall into the same sort of errors when they are convinced that St. Benedict strongly approves if they wear his cowl and cloak, though I don't believe he would have ever worn one so full of folds and costing so much money. But they don't fear his anger, even though they do not imitate his life at all.

Butcher. A monk wearing an ash-colored habit and a canvas girdle is considered a very good son of St. Francis. But compare the lives of some of these with that great saint, and we find nothing more dissimilar. I am speaking of a great many but not all. This is true of all the orders and professions. A preposterous confidence springs from an erroneous judgment, and from both of them, preposterous scandals. Let a Franciscan venture out of doors with a leather girdle because he has lost his cord, or an Augustine with a woolen one, or a monk who ordinarily uses one without it; what an abomination this would be considered! There is a danger that some women seeing this will have a miscarriage! And because of such trifles, how is fraternal charity affected! What bitter envying and virulent slandering! The Lord exclaims against these things in the Gospel, and so does Paul with vehemence, and so should the theologians and preachers of today.

Fishmonger. Indeed they should; and there are a great many among the religious who wish to make the people, princes, and the bishops like themselves. But there are others who have no more understanding about these things than the people themselves; or if they do know better, they conceal it, considering their own bellies before the interest of Jesus Christ. And, hence, as a result, the people everywhere are being corrupted by erroneous judgments, which make them feel secure where there is danger and fearful where there is none; and they sit down satisfied when they should proceed and proceed when they should return. If a man attempts to get people to abandon these erroneous principles, he is accused of sedition; as if it were seditious for anyone with better remedies to try to cure a vicious habit of the body, which an ignorant charlatan had for a long time nourished and almost made natural. But it is time to stop our complaining, but certainly not because we have exhausted the subject. If the people hear our discourse, we will have a new proverb raised against us, to wit, that a salt-fishmonger and a butcher trouble their heads about such things.

Butcher. If they did, I'd retort with this proverb. "A truck gardener often speaks with a purpose." A little while ago I was talking of these things at the table, and as luck would have it, there sat a ragged, lousy, stern, old, withered, white-clothed fellow; he scarcely had three hairs on his head, and when he opened his mouth, his eyes shut. They said he was a theologian, and he called me a disciple of Antichrist and a great many other things.

Fishmonger. What did you do? Did you say anything?

Butcher. I wished him an ounce of sound judgment in his stinking brain, if he had one.

Fishmonger. I'd like to hear the whole story.

Butcher. You shall, if you dine with me next Thursday; you'll have veal pie for dinner, baked so tender that you can suck it through a straw.

Fishmonger. I promise I'll come, if you'll dine with me on Friday. I'll convince you that we fishmongers don't live merely on stinking salt-fish.

ON MENDING THE PEACE
OF THE CHURCH

Liber de Sarcienda Ecclesiae Concordia,* or *On Mending the Peace of the Church,* is in a certain sense the last will and testament of Erasmus. For more than thirty years he had dedicated his life to the cause of sacred learning, Church reform, and peace among men. He was, by the standards of the time, an old man when he wrote it. Yet advanced age and a lingering ailment were the least of the ills that were sapping his vigor and dampening his enthusiasm. The peace for which he had striven so tirelessly and the concord that was the aim of so much of his literary efforts were becoming more and more an illusion. By 1533, when Erasmus compiled the little work on ecclesiastical concord, all of Europe seemed in travail. "The King's Proceedings," the royal act of supremacy, had torn his beloved England from the universal Church, and More's fate had been sealed. In the Estates of the Empire the Schmalkaldic League had stiffened its resistance to compromise, and the Roman Curia was bogged down in a fruitless effort to negotiate peace with the Protestants. France, Italy, and Spain were the scenes of religious riots. The peasants' revolt and the division among the Lutherans themselves had shaken men's belief in the benefits of Christian liberties. Mistrusted by both Catholic and Protestant alike, Erasmus feared above all that any official endeavor on his part to reconcile them would lead to a failure if an Erasmian third party were to consolidate. He had written to his friend Coelius Calcagnius some years earlier: "It is my fate to be pelted by both parties while I endeavor to satisfy them both. In your country [Italy] and in Brabant I am considered to be a Lutheran, and the whole of Germany, where I live so

* The Leclerc edition uses the title, *De Amabili Ecclesiae Concordia*

much, an anti-Lutheran, that his ardent followers rave against no one as against me and they mainly blame me that they do not triumph over the Pope." [1] The religious turbulence in Basle in 1529 had forced him to leave what had been his home for so many years and take refuge in Freiburg. He expresses his weariness in a letter to his friend John Vlatten of Cleve's court, telling him of his new book. [2]

Yet strangely enough Erasmus was then and was to remain for many years after his death in July, 1536, the guiding spirit of a group of Christian humanists who still hoped to restore peace and reform the Church on an Erasmian program that fostered tolerance and evangelical enlightenment. Like the disciples of the Aufklärung two centuries later they were represented at almost every court in Europe and their aims transcended religious and political partisanship. Granvella and Valdes of the Imperial Court as well as Mary of Hungary were strong supporters of Erasmus. Christopher Stadion, Bishop of Augsburg, the Polish bishop, John Dantiscus, Tunstall, now of Durham, Cardinal Cles of Trent were but a small cross-section of Church dignitaries who embraced his ideals. Yet it was especially among the compromise theologians of the day, Cardinal Sadoleto, Cardinal Contarini, John Gropper, later Chancellor of Cologne, Julius Pflug, and the great publicist George Witzel, that the hope that Erasmus would take up the cudgels for Church union was strongest. All of them shared the common conviction that reunion could be achieved only through a cleansing of the Church of its nonessential trappings and a return to that pristine purity reflected in the Gospels and the Fathers. It was largely due to Pflug that the tiring Erasmus condescended to write his work on church concord.

The book itself is a commentary on the eighty-third (eightyfourth) psalm that weaves a beautiful allegory on the Church as the *Domus Domini,* the House of the Lord.

Here we see, as in all his works, the great central themes of Erasmus' theology, spiritualism and interiorization. Silently bypassed are the strident questions on the juridic elements of the Church. In Erasmus' estimation this spiritualism is the expression of an inner, intellectual renewal based on the hope that it will bear fruit in a personalization of religion. As Etienne remarks, Erasmus leaves in the shadow the aspects of sacramental efficacy. "The rite is reduced to the role of a pure symbol, thus constituting an inferior level which must be hastily by-passed to other reality. The rite is not the means by which I encounter God actually and continually, it is but the figuration of this encounter, which I must

---

[1] *E. E.,* VI, 76.
[2] "Totam hanc aestatem langui, nec adhuc rediit vigor" *E. E.,* X, 269.

realize by other means." [3] Although he treats of the sacraments in the work on ecclesiastical concord, he does not attempt to formulate a speculative system to confine their operation. He denies neither the Real Presence in the Eucharist nor the reality of baptismal purification. In an age of extreme formalism his apparent insensibility to sacramental values cannot be taken as heresy. If true charity is free and spontaneous, not constrained by laws and ceremonies, it will lead to true concord by its very nature. His enthusiasm is directed more to the universal assembly of faith and charity than to the hierarchical structured visible organization. Yet this individualistic piety is counterbalanced by the most universal expression of charity itself, the Body of Christ. It is perhaps one of the great merits of Erasmus that he sees clearly the difference between analysis and living religion, between the superstructure and the inner edifice. The great value of his critique of the external Church is his perception of the unsuitability of temporal or physical means to spiritual ends, especially when these means involve dishonesty or deceit.

In advocating tolerance he reiterates his deep conviction that since Christ conquered by truth, the suppression of truth, much less conceit, cannot be used in His name. The strength of Christianity does not consist in ignorance. If in his day the invisible Church was in danger of being absorbed into the visible, then it is the peace of Christ that is the sole principle that can once again make the visible Church the authentic expression of the invisible.

After reading *On Mending the Peace of the Church* it is difficult to agree with certain of Erasmus' critics who feel that he laid out a program for a third church. Renaudet gives in detail what he considers the Erasmian plan for what he terms *le troisième Église;* the third church could be born only at Rome, with the approval of the Pope.[4] It would be characterized by Gospel discipline and respect for Christian liberty. But in Renaudet's estimation this church would be a betrayal of the fundamental principles of Catholicism, since Erasmus is quite insensitive to the Church's mystical foundations and his taste for reason and clear ideas had turned him away from the sacred books of Israel.[5] Renaudet seems to imply that Erasmus' reason for rejecting heresy is more moral than doctrinal, but the view that the chief evil or heresy is its disruption of the peace and unity of the Church is an authentic and traditional element in Catholic thinking, at least as

[3] J. Etienne, *Spiritualisme Érasmien et Théologiens Louvainistes* (Louvain: 1956), p. 42.

[4] A. Renaudet, *Érasme et l'Italie* (Geneva: 1954), pp. 170–177.

[5] A. Renaudet, *Érasme, Sa Pensée Religeuse et Son Action, d'apres Son Correspondence* (Paris: 1926) p. 4.

ancient as the treatise of St. Cyprian, *On Church Unity*. It is a beautiful expression of a messianic hope that just as God kept his promise of mercy to the Chosen People so he will restore and mend the Church if it will but expurgate its sins.

Reflected in the *Liber de Sarcienda* is Erasmus' steady determination to remain above religious partisanship. The extreme radicalism of the reformers, which had led them to do away with ancient ecclesiastical institutions, he impartially laments. The Mass is defended as well as the intercession of the saints and the veneration of images. Of special interest is his treatment of the necessity of good works. Here, as in his commentary on the twenty-second psalm,[6] he formulates what came to be termed the notion of a twofold justice (*iustitia duplex*), immanent and imputed. He speaks of the innocence imparted by baptism as well as the righteousness that faith works in charity. In this bisectioning he saw the possibility of a reconciliatory formula that would do justice to the aims of both religious parties. This concept received its classical formulation at the Diet of Regensburg in 1541 and was incorporated into the famous "Book of Ratisbon" accepted by both Catholics and Protestants. We encounter it also in the writings of John Fisher, John Gropper, and the Louvain theologian Albert Pigge.[7] Later, Cardinal Seripando was to propose it at the Council of Trent. It was an important factor in removing the terrible misconception that the Catholic faith prejudiced Christ's mediatorship and the universal efficaciousness of His grace.

As was the case with most of Erasmus' writings, *On Mending the Peace of the Church* was met with anything but universal acceptance. The papal nuncio Vergerio forwarded a German translation of the book to the Pope, remarking that its reception in Germany created the impression that Erasmus had defected.[8] Luther himself described the work as an Arian intrusion, and the University of Louvain condemned it a few years later.[9]

Yet the book continued to exert for many centuries an influence upon those sincerely interested in terminating the internecine conflict between Christians. Hugo Grotius, a pioneer in international law, found in it an ideal basis for his world court of arbitration.

---

[6] "Duplex est iustitia, prior est innocentia cui per fidem ac baptisma restituimur, altera est fidei per dilectionem operantis." Op. V, 325. For a discussion of this see J. P. Dolan, *The Erasmian Influences in the Cleve Church Ordinances* (Münster: 1957), pp. 19–23.

[7] See H. Jedin, *Studien über die Schriftstellertätigkeit Albert Pigge* (Munster: 1931), pp. 123–127.

[8] W. Friedensburg, *Nuntiaturberichte aus Deutschland* (Gotha: 1892), I., p. 139.

[9] E. Gossart, "Un Livre d'Érasme reprouve par l'Université de Louvain," *Bulletin de l'Academie Royale de Belgique*, Classe des Lettres (1902), p. 438.

Herman Conring relied upon it in his efforts toward ecumenism. The message it contains—tolerance, avoidance of extreme dogmatism, respect for the religious convictions of others—is as needed today as it was then.

On Mending the Peace of the Church

(DE SARCIENDA ECCLESIAE CONCORDIA) 1533

Dogmatum definitio synodo reservetur. Nec arbitror necesse ut de quibuslibet opinionibus pronunciet synodus, sed tantum de praecipuis in quibus Christianae doctrinae cardo versatur.

The definition of dogmas should be reserved to a synod. Nor do I think it necessary that the synod pronounce on each and every opinion but rather upon those matters that form the essentials of Christian doctrine.

Letter to Pope Paul III
February, 1535, E. E. XI, 62

We have selected the eighty-third psalm for commentary because in this psalm the Holy Spirit with many arguments both from evidence and vehemence urges to our attention this beautiful and holy unity within the Church. This message of the Holy Spirit is true and profitable at all times, but especially does it appear of importance in this vicious age of sects, as it has in no other age. Those, then, who love that peace which, in the words of St. Paul, "surpasses all senses," and which alone has kept and will protect our hearts from all evils in the peacemaker Our Lord Jesus Christ, must devote their whole attention to this discussion.

The title of the psalm has a few variations, but we will treat these with all possible brevity and quickly proceed to the examination of the beautiful and pleasing message of the psalm.

The title, then, is given variously in different codices, a variety due either to the zeal of the scribes, or simply to the ambiguity of the Hebrew itself. The Septuagint has it thus: "Unto the end; the winepresses; the sons of Core." St. Jerome gives it as, "To the conqueror for the winepresses of the sons of Core." The words "unto the end" are to be understood as referring to Christ, i.e., the end and perfection of the law to every believer. For there is no perfect and true justice, except through a sincere faith in Him who alone purifies through faith the hearts of men.

By "to the conqueror" or "for victory" the words of St. Paul should be recalled to mind: that no one attains that blessed crown of glory that is never effaced, except him who lawfully struggles for it. There are some skilled in Hebrew who mention that "Vincenti" can be translated as "To one who sheds his blood," i.e., not as in an easy and bloodless war, but as in a bloody battle, what the Greeks call "war without quarter" (ἄσπονδον πόλεμον). Indeed, since soldiers in the life so often expose their bodies to the weapons of the enemy, entrust their lives to the uncertain luck of Mars to achieve supplication, applause, or even a triumph—and this so much more inane and ludicrous than marvelous that no serious man can restrain his laughter at the sight—whose pomp is over in a day; to what lengths should not the Christian soldier go to attain an eternal triumph in heaven? How great now is the glory of the martyrs who in pouring out their blood through their faith have conquered kingdoms, accomplished justice, and attained to the blessed promises? Their praise indeed does resound through the whole world, and to the praise of the angels they enjoy with Christ their Leader an eternal triumph in the heavenly Jerusalem. There are those also who heed the advice of St. Paul and mortify their members. They rise above the things of this life—namely, lust and greed, which battle the spirit—and conquer Satan in a bloody warfare. Furthermore, there is in this psalm a mention of tents or encampments, "tabernacles," a word certainly of military connotation.

The words *pro tocularibus*, "for the winepresses," which are added to the title, caused some distress to St. Augustine since there is no mention of winepresses in the psalm itself. So he turned to allegory for explanation. It can, of course, be observed that the titles of the psalms do indicate at times an historical event, e.g., Psalm 33, "A psalm of David when he changed his face before Abimelech, and he sent him away and he departed," sometimes a feast day on which the psalm should be recited, e.g., Psalm 91 carries the title, "A psalm for the Sabbath," Psalm 92, "A song of praise of David for the day before the Sabbath," and Psalm 93, "A psalm of David for the fourth Sabbath." Nor should the historical sense be rejected to make room for allegory, since the former is the foundation and basis of the latter in that it provided the understanding wherewith the hidden and mystical meaning may be treated.

So when the title of the psalm has added to it, "for the winepresses," the seventh month is meant—September. For the ancients determined the beginning of the year from the month of March, the time when the sun enters the sign of Aries. Reckoning from this month, then, the fifth month (July) was called "Quintilis," the sixth month (August) "Sextilis," and so in order until December. Since the month of September is the time of harvest, it was more significant and more appropriate to the mystery to say "for the winepresses" than to say "September." So Horace, in marking the beginning of spring, uses a not unpleasant figure, "gentle breezes and first storms." In like manner are indicated feast days on which contests of songs were celebrated among the prophets. Thus some titles of the psalms have the words "roses" and "lilies" to indicate spring and its feasts.

The Jews celebrated three special feasts, the Passover in memory of the Red Sea crossing, Pentecost in memory of the law given on Mt. Sinai, and the Feast of Tabernacles, about which we shall speak later. The Pasch was celebrated in early spring, Pentecost in late spring, Tabernacles in autumn. The fifteenth day of the seventh month was the feast of scenopagia, so called from the fixing of tents or tabernacles. The people were ordered to stay in their homes in memory of their ancient history, that driven from Egypt they wandered through a vast and terrible desert for forty years and lived in their tents, God showing them the way at night in a column of fire, by day through a pillar of cloud; by His kindness they lacked neither food nor drink, nor did their shoes or clothing wear out. At this time the Ark of the Covenant was the temple and remained so until Solomon built the renowned temple at Jerusalem, an object of veneration even to the pagans.

Lest the people ever be able to forget the providence of God, or the knowledge of such a great miracle be not handed on to later generations, the people were commanded each year at harvest time to celebrate the Feast of Tabernacles for eight days in the month of September. This month is in a way the sabbath among months, just as among days the seventh day and among years the seventh year is the sabbath, which provides rest for the farmlands, and in the calculation of years the jubilee of seven years.

Of these eight days in September the first was a sabbath, the beginning of the third week, and the eighth as well, the beginning of the fourth week. On both were observed rest and fast. The days that fell between these two sabbaths were given over to sacrifices, hymns, thanksgiving, and solemn joy. The eighth day was, as it were, the actual beginning of a new feast, that of "collections," on which, because of the expense of sacrifices and offerings, collections were taken from all for the use of the temple. Further treatment of these matters can be found in Leviticus 23 and Numbers 29.

Though in the title, therefore, there is no express mention of tabernacles, it is tacitly implied, since mention is made of the month in which the Scenopagia feast is celebrated after all the fruits of the land have been collected. This month was almost entirely devoted to feasts and sacrifices, a month in which provision was made for the Levites and the people acknowledged they owed to divine providence whatever their lands produced. Thus they were not to squander in senseless luxury the bountiful harvest, nor suffer despondency at unproductive years, reminded as they were by the tabernacles that when journeying through barren and arid regions, God had not permitted them to lack anything, but had provided them with manna from the heavens and water from a rock. How indeed can it be possible that He who clothes the lilies of the field and provides bread for the sparrows would allow His own people to lack the necessities, especially since the temperance of the pious is content with so little?

All the more disgraceful, then, are those Christians in our time, when divine providence provides such abundant goods, who turn His bounty not to thanksgiving and alms to the priests and poor, but to luxury, ostentation, and lusts of all kinds. But if on the other hand the year is a poor one, then, forgetful of the past abundance and unconcerned about the future, they are intent on prices, stingy with the poor; they consume for themselves what is owed to the priests and put off their creditors. How much more worthy would it be of those who boast of the title of Christian that, the more difficult a year has been, the more generous is the charity of the rich to the poor. God has not given a wondrous harvest that the grain might rot in your barns, but that the surplus might be dispensed for the use of the poor. Only in this fashion will you appear worthy of the past bounty of God and, in bad years, deserving of the Lord's greater liberality.

That the Feast of Tabernacles designates the sobriety of the Catholic Church is made clear in Zachariah, Chapter 14: "A ruin will come by which the Lord will strike all the nations who have not come up to celebrate the Feast of Tabernacles." In this same chapter mention is made of winepresses, so that the argument of this psalm seems to have been taken from this reference in the prophet.

St. Jerome carefully notes that there are three psalms whose titles mention winepresses: the eighth psalm, which is entitled "David," the eightieth, entitled "Asaph," and this eighty-third psalm, which is entitled "to the sons of Core." All three have in common the word "victory."

The number "eight" has been dedicated to the glory of the resurrection, for this is the day the Lord had made in rising from the dead, and on which we are ordered to rejoice and be happy with spiritual festivities. For where there is the resurrection there also is the life. But where there is life there also is innocence, just as where there is sin there is death.

The first day was in honor of man made to the likeness of God; this the eighth psalm treats, showing man to be so created as to be nearest the angels. The second day was for man recalled to justification, which the number "eight" multiplied by "ten" shows, a figure of the decalogue. The third day shows man drawn through the grace of the gospel to such a state of perfection that even though his body stays on earth, through faith and hope his "conversation is in heaven"; to eight times ten is added three, because through the light of the gospel the whole world knows clearly the mystery of the Holy Trinity. The Jews knew the Father, but afterward the Son, having taken on human nature, appeared and dealt with men on earth, and was taken into heaven; from heaven the Holy Spirit was sent, renewing the minds and tongues of all. The world knew clearly that there is in Three persons one God, and in the divine nature three Persons, Father, Son, and Holy Spirit.

The pagans were wont to celebrate the harvest with profane and impious rites in honor of their ridiculous god Bacchus, rioting with unrestrained games, indecent dances, and obscene remarks (we grieve to realize that some traces of this foolishness can be seen even today). For this reason Moses transformed the public rejoicing into a religious thanksgiving, the obscene jigs into dances of the prophets (for David himself is said to have danced before the Ark of the Covenant), and the

impious songs and impure verses into the mystical psalms—
thus he made over this impious cult shown by the pagans to
demons into the worship of the true God.

The pagans had in their festal celebrations contests in which
drunkards, their faces covered with filth, would sing from a
platform stupid songs to the crowds: the prize for the winner
was a goat—certainly an appropriate prize. Among the
prophets, too, there was a contest, but one filled with devotion
and reverence. This is why so many psalms have in their titles
"for victory."

Such contests were held even in Apostolic times and in
gatherings of Christians. One spoke with tongues, many more
participated in the gift of prophecy. Nor among these were
unseemly contentions rife, but if something had been revealed
to a certain person, others kept silent; nor did the defeated
feel displeased, but rather gave thanks to the Spirit who
through another person wished to teach what had escaped
them. Nor was the winner uplifted in spirit, realizing that all
this was the work of the Spirit who gives His gifts to each as
He wishes. This was the nature of the contests among these
prophets.

This example teaches us that whether we labor in afflictions
or find ourselves in prosperous circumstances, we should do all
for the glory of God. Many Christians of our day invoke
God only in sickness, times of war, or other such dangers.
They carefully distinguish circumstances: sorrowful circumstances are given to God, fortunate ones to Satan. At funerals
of dear ones you can see a sort of appearance of piety, but
at weddings, victorious celebrations, banquets—at all these you
find no trace of a Christian mentality.

So long as we are in this life there are different times for
things. There is a time of being born and a time for dying; a
time for marrying, and a time for abstaining from marriage; a
time for rejoicing that children are born, a time for grief that
they are dead: but for the Christian there must be no time
separated from piety. In preparation for a feast day there
should be fasting, but a religious fast; the feast day requires
joy, but a religious joy. In the former we mortify ourselves,
but according to God; in the latter we rejoice, but rejoice in
the presence of God.

Speaking of these evangelical joys, Isaias says in Chapter 9:
"They shall rejoice in your presence, as do those who rejoice
at the harvest." Well do we rejoice in the presence of God
when with a pure conscience we give Him thanks equally for
our sorrows and joys. But those who in times of joy devote

themselves to gambling, drunkenness, filthy speech, and prostitutes, these rejoice in the presence of the world but are insane in the presence of God. Perhaps we are dwelling longer on these points than we should, but if only this were done without sufficient reason!

So much for the mystery of the title. The eighth psalm is inscribed to David, which in Hebrew means "hand-picked"; the eightieth psalm to Asaph, "the one who gathers"; and this eighty-third psalm to "the sons of Core," that is, "Calvary." In a figurative sense these three terms all signify Christ. For He created mankind justified: "The Father established the earth and all that is in it through the Son." This only the Omnipotent can accomplish. Thus Paul, writing to the Hebrews, terms the Son the Word of the paternal power. God likewise through the law has recalled man so wounded through sin and cast down that he could be compared to beasts and become like them, if not worse than them: He enclosed man in a cage, as it were, until the fullness of time had come. Hence the expression synagogue. The psalmist Asaph reprovingly called for the observance of the law. "Israel," he says, "if you will harken to me, there will be no new God among you." Finally, the Lord professed His role as the one who gathers when in the Gospel He exclaimed: "Jerusalem, Jerusalem, thou that killest the prophets, and stonest them that are sent unto thee, how often would I have gathered together thy children, as the hen doth gather her chickens under her wings, and thou wouldst not."

But when the fullness of time had come, this same son of Core, raised on Calvary's cross, gathered the whole world to himself and, in the same moment, conquered Satan in his triumph.

Perhaps at this point a small problem will occur to the reader as to how Christ the Son of God is called the son of Core: this man was first among the Levites and attained the rank of High Priest, yet joined with Dathan and Abiron and led nearly the whole multitude against Moses and Aaron, as is mentioned in Numbers, Chapter 16. Those who followed him were destroyed either in an earthquake or from fire sent from heaven.

But comparison is not ridiculous. According to the flesh Christ took his origin from the Jewish race, a people in rebellion against God. Isaias the prophet says, "I have held out my hands each day to a people who do not believe or obey me." Again, in the psalms we read, "Forty years I was close to this people in the desert and I said: these people sin in their hearts." St. Stephen blames them for this pertinacious rebellion in the Acts of the Apostles: "You have always resisted the Holy Spirit."

Many psalms have in their title "sons of Core," nor is any other name indicated, as though it were sufficient to praise them to call them sons of Core, since in common estimation there is ignominy to be called by the name of a father so evil and one condemned by such a terrible example. Who, for instance, could endure being known as the son or descendant of the traitor Judas? And yet Scripture notes in praise that the sons of Core, sons of a father whose impiety but enlightened their own piety, tied as they were by the bonds of nature to that author of sedition, still permitted the love of religion to overcome the effects of nature. We may probably conjecture that either, heeding Moses, they separated themselves from their father, or remained with him without consenting to his evil proposition; they were saved when he was destroyed with his followers (Numbers 26) and were not removed from their office in the service of the Ark, as is said in I Paralipomenon, Chapter 26. They are, further, shown to be outstanding in the spirit of prophecy.

Since God does not impute the sins of parents to the sons unless they imitate them, mankind acts foolishly when it does not disavow for children the sins and punishment of their ancestors, but treats them as though the children themselves had done them. "Your father," they say, "was convicted of embezzlement and was put to death for it; do you dare to speak to us, even to appear in men's sight?" But it seems more wonderful that children renowned for their virtue should spring from evil parents than that a good person come from good parents.

In like manner are they unjust who attribute to children not the sins of their parents, but rather the parent's misfortunes or calamities, in order to demonstrate their own probity. "I knew his father," they say; "he was a servant." Or, "I saw his father acting as a beggar." Those who speak thus are excusing themselves because, dedicated to their vices, they are but servants of Satan, enriching themselves by stealing from the poor. But to be born from a father who is a servant is not base, while to be a slave to lust, avarice, and other vices is most base; to beg one's bread when necessity requires is not shameful, but to refuse the necessities to the poor or to live on what has been stolen from them is a contemptible crime. Those who excuse their own sins always blame their neighbors for another's misfortune.

But how much more condescending is God to us! He does

not impute our sins to us once we have repented of them. What crime was more detestable than that of Core, what punishment more dreadful? This, not from man's judgment, which is often fallible, but from God's judgment. Yet the prophet preferred to show honor to his sons by calling them after him, rather than by their own proper names.

Of similar inhumanity is it to call "Marani" those who have turned from the impiety of their parents to the true faith: more honor, rather, is due them for this reason. Furthermore, if the imputing to descendants of ancestors' faults were just, what precisely is our own origin? Is it not from those who in contempt of the true God worshipped trees and rocks and shed the blood of the martyrs?

But to return to our subject. Core, Dathan, Abiron, and Hon attempted to divide the tabernacle, as heretics and schismatics have always tried to rend the Church. Just as the wrath of God destroyed them, so for those who will not be warned to return to reason and abandon their impious sects and seditious attempts there remains the fire of hell. By the same token, then, all should be sons of Core so that none in opposition to true religion should stand by anyone else—not son by father, brother by brother, wife by husband, son-in-law by father-in-law. All should, rather, disassociate themselves from the dwellings of the impious, if not in body, then at least in spirit. If any error has crept in through thoughtlessness, let us heed Moses and be warned to follow a wiser path. After the exhausting labors of this life we shall drink the wine of everlasting joy, and living in union in the tabernacle of God that is the Church, we shall be received into the celestial tabernacle of the Church triumphant.

I observe that in explaining the title I have taken more time than I intended. We shall now move on to the psalm itself.

"How wonderful are your tabernacles, Lord God of hosts."

The rather abrupt beginning of this psalm demonstrates the unfulfilled desire of the spirit. Of this type is also Psalm 72: "How wonderful, Israel, is God to those who are of right heart." To the point is St. Augustine's comment: "How lovable—in Greek ἀγαπητά. Nothing is more beautiful, more wonderful, safer, or more steadfast than the assent of the good among the good: nothing, on the other hand, is uglier, more disgusting, or weaker than the conspiracy of the evil among the evil.

Impious men have their own tabernacles, which the psalmist calls to mind here and in the preceeding psalm: "Since they have taken counsel together, they have planned against you: the tabernacles of the Idumaeans and Ishmaelites, Moab and Agareni, Gebal and Ammon, Amalech, foreigners with those who inhabit Tyre." And the second psalm: "The rulers have held common council against the Lord and against his Christ."

Just as there is one Church and St. Paul still speaks "as I teach in all the Churches," perceiving that there are many churches by distinction of persons and place, only one by profession of faith and communion of sacraments, so too there are said to be many tabernacles of God, although actually there is but one which embraces all the others, for all in Christ are one. But the impious, on the other hand, differing in religion and dogmas of the faith, have no such common tabernacle, but so disagree among themselves that they dissent from the tabernacle of God in various modes and names, but all with the same impiety.

Formerly the Greeks and Romans ridiculed the Egyptians for worshipping the Bull, Serapis, Cercopitheca, and even Caepe, instead of the true God, while all the while they themselves were worshipping rocks and trees, or the spirits in them, instead of the true God. Gaul had its Druids, priests of a special religion who fought against the true religion. Of this type were Dathan, Abiron, and Hon. Each in his own tabernacle stood ready for battle. Divided among themselves, but in agreement to battle Moses, they are like the different religions of various peoples, all fighting among themselves, yet united in harmony and agreement to persecute the Jews and, afterward, with an even greater assent, to fight the Christians.

Core prefigured the dissent of the heretics in that he did not bodily separate himself from the tabernacle of God, though in spirit he was far removed from it. Sometimes heretics insist they are the champions of the true religion; just as Core attempted to remove Aaron from his sacred ministry, so these heretics attempt to show that adherents to the Catholic faith are but tyrants and enemies of the Church. Just as each heresiarch cries out that Christ is here, not there, so Core spoke of the flock, the whole people, asserting that in them was the Lord.

Before the coming of the Redeemer the Sadducees and Herodians had their own tabernacles, but they were neither attractive nor beautiful. But now that the light of the Gospel has been diffused throughout the world, how many abominable tabernacles have not been raised against the tabernacle of God? Who does not shudder to read of the disgraceful scenes in the tabernacles of the Ophitae, who worship a serpent instead of Christ, or of the Cainists, who esteem Cain the murderer and Judas the traitor as the special saints? Or of the Nicolaitae, who consider their wives common property? Or of the Adamites, among whom both sexes worshipped naked, on the representation that they were thus a figure of Adam and Eve still innocent in paradise, and, of course, opposed to marriage? What portents of dogmas, what monstrosities of lust were not carried out in the tabernacles of Basilis, Colorbasus, Priscillus, or Marcion? Who can read or tell of the disgraceful mysteries of the Manichees without revulsion? Who would not have contempt for the Sebellians, Arians, Eunominians, and the blasphemies against Christ, or their assemblies of blasphemy against the whole Trinity?

It would be worthwhile, I feel, to relate some of their stratagems, that by them may be illustrated the malice with which their tabernacles are imbued.

These people had decided to oppress with false criminal charges Athanasius, that renowned champion of Catholic truth, since they were unable to conquer him with Scripture and argumentation. They so stirred up the Emperor Constantinus against this saintly man with their lying reports that he ordered a commission convoked at Tyre to investigate Athanasius, and to this commission as its prefect he sent a legate *a latere*.

Two principal crimes were stated: a woman who had been raped, and an arm cut from a dead man for the practice of the black arts. It was not difficult to discover a woman who would play her part in this tragedy; to prove the crime of black magic they had summoned a certain Arsenius, formerly Athanasius' lector, who in fear of correction by his bishop, whom he had offended, had fled from him. The Arians concealed this man for a period of time that they might claim that he was dead. But when Arsenius saw the plot against Athanasius, either fearing the atrocity of the crime, or desiring on this occasion to return to the good graces of his bishop, he fled in the dark of night and came to Tyre by boat and exposed the whole plot to Athanasius.

Athanasius, a man at once of outstanding virtue coupled with a clever genius, as those who follow the Lord's warning to mix the dove's simplicity with the serpent's astuteness, ordered Arsenius to conceal himself until he would be needed.

When the commission was opened, the woman was presented and, in a grisly spectacle, a coffin was brought in, containing the amputated arm of a man. Horror gripped the hearts of all. Who would have dreamed that such things were perpetrated by priests?

First the woman, carefully instructed, told how she had accepted hospitality from Athanasius, and since she had no fear of him, was forcibly assaulted during the night by him. Athanasius then was called in to answer this accusation. But in keeping with his cleverness, Athanasius asked Timothy, his priest, to answer for him; he knew that the woman did not even know his face. When she had finished her accusation, Timothy asked, "Do you say, woman, that you were forcibly assaulted by me?" The woman answered, "Yes, by you. At that time, at that place, you forcibly violated my purity." They were embarrassed, of course, that the calumny had been so easily detected. But Athanasius was not set free, nor was the woman punished for perjury: at this trial both judges and accusers were the same.

They then proceeded to the second charge. "Here," they said, "the matter speaks for itself—this is the arm of Arsenius. For what use you amputated it, Athanasius, you shall now explain to us." Athanasius with similar cleverness asked whether they knew Arsenius well, to whom this arm was supposed to belong. A few said they knew him quite well. Athanasius then asked if he might call in someone whose help he needed in this case. Permission was granted. Arsenius was then brought in and his face exposed. "See," said Athanasius, "here is Arsenius alive—here is his right arm and left arm. Suppose you tell us where you got that arm over there."

But you would scarcely expect that Athanasius would be freed from the charge. Indeed, he would have been torn apart by the hands of his enemies had not Archelaus, imperial legate and president of the commission, secretly freed and dismissed the holy man. What other traps could they lay, since they had been so clearly found out? They screamed that he was a Magus, that he deceived the eyes of men with his tricks, that such a magician should not continue to live.

The commission was reassembled, and with a specious legality Athanasius was finally condemned. Throughout the whole world was spread the ugly word that this saintly man was being sought, at the imperial edicts, in every corner both on land and sea; a reward was promised if he were brought in alive, or if this proved impossible, if his head were brought in.

Did not the Jews plot similarly against Christ? Who has ever heard of a worse crime even among pagans? I have given examples: these are the tabernacles of the heretics and schismatics. Should I even go into the cruelty of the Circumcellionists?—the subtle tricks and violence of the Donatists? Those who have read Augustine's commentaries on their acts are certainly aware of these things.

But these examples are all in the past. Surely much more to be deplored is that within recent memory there have been discovered nightly gatherings at which, after praise has been given to God, the lights are extinguished and the men and women consort in promiscuous love. Or the ceremonies in which mothers freely hand over their infants to be butchered, and even watch serenely the horrid crime, so persuaded are they that their children will thus find a high place in heaven.

This madness seems to have taken its origin from the heresy καταφρύγας, which would make the Eucharist from flour mixed with the blood of an infant. This blood they would draw from small pinpricks, and if in the process the child died, it was venerated as a martyr.

You can see into what excesses men fall when, having abandoned the tabernacle of God, they purchase for themselves the tabernacles of the impious. If you put a beautiful girl next to a deformed old hag, the one will seem even more beautiful, the other more repulsive. So the prophetic and spiritual eye compares the tabernacles of Satan with those of God in which the heavenly truth reigns, in which peace surpassing all peace is present, where there is charity unaware of deceit, where faith is unconquered, where all with one voice and soul chant the praises of God: such a comparison makes the spirit cry out even more: "How lovable are your tabernacles, Lord of hosts."

This union of the pious is for us a figure of that heavenly church in which there is no difference of opinions—there the glory of God is contemplated, not enshrouded in mystery, but face to face. With great unanimity of heart and the greatest charity, all in perfect unison praise God with hymns. The eye of the spirit, made all-seeing through the light of faith, discovers more than does the eye of the body. What more does it see? It sees Christ sitting in the midst of his own and blessing the gathering, as he told us in the Gospel: "Where two or three are gathered in my name, there am I in the midst of them." It sees the protecting and ministering angels of the holy congregation, worshiping in deepest reverence.

But in the tabernacles of the impious everything is divided; as ruler over them Satan, never more dangerous than when he assumes the role of angel of light, assisted by the evil spirits suggesting each evil action.

Now to turn to their different destructions. All are aware of what happened to Core and his associates in conspiracy. It was a horrible thing to see the earth yawn and swallow living bodies; to see fire dropped down from heaven, or thunderbolts consuming so many thousands. For on the next day, when sedition flared up again, 14,000 perished from the heavenly destruction. But it is even more horrible for body and soul to be sent into hell.

Nor is what certain ones say false: the Church is invisible. Only God knows the hearts of men and truly knows who belongs to Him. By many arguments it is often disputed where the Church of God is and where the synagogue of Satan. But this visible Church, which contains the good mixed with the evil, brings to the cult of piety all its ardor and majesty.

When someone is given the gift of prophecy, the people listen with religious attention and devotion, hearing not the word of man, but the word of God. The preacher himself is so affected that one can perceive that the spirit of Christ is speaking through the mouth of man. The evidence of the work of the Spirit can be seen as well in the listeners: some sigh, others burst into tears, while others have a happy countenance—in a word, all are transfigured.

Again, when in solemn worship, each one is busy with his own duty—one reading the holy lessons, another singing the praise of God, another, praying in the name of the whole multitude, performs the mysteries while others assist him— the whole people in religious silence venerate all these mysteries. Who on seeing this spectacle would not admit that the tabernacles of God are wonderful? Or when there occurs a great supplication on the part of the Church in proper and decorous order, are not even those who look on simply to see such a spectacle themselves touched with emotion?

Every legitimate gathering of men for some good cause has a certain dignity and, therefore, a certain joy. These are the feelings of students at examinations, of nearly all men at a public debate. When Alcibiades was about to give his first address to the Athenians, he felt a certain fear in his heart. Socrates cured him of this as follows. He asked of Alcibiades, "Can you fear any leatherworker?" "No." "Can you fear any bricklayer, builder, or mason?" When Alcibiades answered that he could speak without fear to any of these, Socrates answered, "And yet this crowd you fear is composed of just such men."

But if the very gathering of the lowest ranks stirs up a certain dignity and reverence, how much more venerable is the gathering of pious men assembled for the worship of God? Such power has the chorus of those who worship God as one that it brings pagans to reverence, as Paul testifies; when the stranger or unbeliever enters the Church of the saints, he falls on his face, adores God, and testifies that God truly is in the midst of His own.

Balaam was a prophet, indeed, but an impious one. But when he saw from a mountaintop the tabernacles of the Israelites, he was compelled to cry out, "How wondrous are your tabernacles, Jacob, and your tents, O Israel." He saw as well the happy death of those who remain the camp of the Church.

"May my soul," he said, "die the death of the just, and let my last end be like theirs." The holy prophet saw the beauty of these tabernacles when he said in the gradual psalm, "See how good and wonderful it is for brothers to dwell in unity." Peter saw this as well, but as in a dream, when on the mount he had contemplated the glory of the Lord and had heard Moses and Elias speaking of the glory of the Lord's death: "Lord," he said, "it is good for us to be here—let us build here three tabernacles."

There is indeed true concord where the law and the prophets preach in agreement that Christ is the mediator of the New Testament, not by the letter but by the spirit. This is not done in the synagogues of the Jews, who twist the law to refer not to Christ but to some other Messiah, for whom they have so unfruitfully waited so many centuries. Nor is it done in the tabernacles of the Manichees, who reject the entire Old Testament as the work not of God, but of the prince of darkness: the New Testament, falsified in many places, they accept or reject according to their whims. Nor, finally, is it done in the tabernacles of the heretics, where the Scriptures are turned not to Christ the Truth, but to some human interpretation—a practice always proper to heretics. So the Priscillians rejected the authority of none of the books either of the Old or New Testament; but when their absurd teachings were in conflict with something from Scripture, they would twist Scripture to fit their own peculiar interpretation.

But to return again to the psalm. If by the "tabernacles of God" one understands the Church militant in this life, consider this verse as spoken by a catechumen, a pagan, a Jew, a sinner, or even a heretic or schismatic returning to his senses. But if you understand it to be of the Church triumphant with Christ, consider it spoken by a pious man, wishing with St. Paul to be freed and to be with Christ.

The rather abrupt beginning of this verse indicates the intensity of the desire arising from the profound contemplation on the part of the wayfarer. Nor is it without significance that the word "your" is used as referring to the Lord. Whatever power, strength, or happiness is in the Church, it comes from God, not man. God has freely redeemed for Himself the Church, He governs it, He protects it against all storms. He who attacks the Church attacks not man, but God. This is clearly stated to us in the words of Zachariah, Chapter 2: "He who touches you touches the apple of my eye." St. Paul heard these words: "Saul, Saul, why do you persecute me?" In the Gospel, also, Christ recognizes as offered to Him whatever kindness is given to the least and lowest in the name of

Christ: He considers, then, any harm done to the Church as harm done to Himself.

Since the Catholic Church has such a ruler and defender, in vain are all the conspiracies of the impious against her. For this reason the psalm adds: "Lord of hosts." By "hosts" or "virtus" here is meant not "virtue" (ἀρετάς), which is opposed to vice, but rather "power" (δυνάμεις). Scripture often calls God by this name, as in Psalm 23: "The Lord of power, He is the King of Kings in glory"—(δυνάμεων). Just before this are the words: "The Lord is strong and powerful in battle."

In the books of the Old Testament God is frequently called the "Lord of Sabaoth," which in Hebrew means "power" or "armies"; this is the meaning in this psalm. δυνάμεις, "power," in mystical writings can mean several things; especially it refers to the angels whose ministry God uses for the protection of His own. Elizaeus saw this army and said to a servant disheartened at the sight of the Syrians: "Do not fear—there are more with us than with them." At the prayers of the prophet the servant's eyes were opened, and he saw the mountain covered with horsemen and fiery chariots. "No one," said Christ, "can take from my hands those whom my Father has given me." In similar vein is the gradual psalm: "Unless the Lord be the builder, in vain do the laborers build the house."

In the time of St. Paul the Church was fortified by no wealth, numbers, or other protections of this world, yet he said with great confidence, "If God is for us, who is against us?" And soon he came to such a degree of confidence that when the Church was oppressed on all sides, he did not hesitate to say, "I am certain that neither death, nor life, nor angels, nor principalities, nor present, nor future, neither height nor depth, nor any creature will be able to separate us from the love of God which is in Christ Jesus our Lord."

Whence comes such confidence, Paul, amidst so many deaths, dangers, and difficulties both internal and external? Whence this spirit to men so few, unlearned, of little influence, weak, and oppressed? "Of ourselves," he says, "we can do nothing, but our Lord is the Lord of hosts."

Whether, then, you take "virtus" as referring to angels, the protectors of the Church, or as miracles, both meanings declare the Lord of the Church to be unconquered since He is omnipotent; at His will the legions of angels are prepared; He alone it is who does great wonders, and He alone, whether in heaven or on earth, does whatever He wills.

The beginnings of the Church drew their strength from miracles, not from human protection. Since those who wish to live in Christ Jesus suffer the persecution of the impious, since they are lowly according to the world and few in proportion to those who oppose them, for the consolation of the flock was it said, "Lord of hosts." This is the meaning of the verse in the Gospel, "Do not fear, little flock, for yours is the kingdom of heaven." Again, "Have confidence, for I have conquered the world." Only Christ could bind the strong one and take away his possessions.

"We are considered," He said, "as sheep for slaughter." What animal is more peaceful and unwarlike than a sheep? And what does Paul, once a wolf but now a sheep, say? "Our weapons are not those of the world, but the power of God, used to destroy those against us, upsetting their plans and bringing low all pride that raises itself up against the wisdom of God." In the same place he criticizes the Corinthians on the grounds that since they were carnal they saw only according to appearances and judged the Apostles only from the exterior. He finds fault with them that they are not weak in the eyes of the world, humble, even persecuted, wealthy in the spiritual goods, armed with spiritual weapons.

So those whose eyes are occupied with the powers of this world measure the Church according to external appearances; not only do they have contempt for the Church, but they repudiate it and turn away from it. Of such a kind are those who formerly deferred baptism until their last day, and would not come to the temple of God except in tears of regret. But those whose spiritual sight perceives the glory of the daughter of the King from within say with the prophet, "My heart has desired and grown weak in the temple of the Lord."

Lesser goods are sought with equally lesser desires, but those things no eye has seen, no ear has heard, nor has it entered into the hearts of any man to know what God has prepared for those who love Him, must be sought with a mighty affection. The magnitude of this desire is expressed by the prophet: "and has grown weak in the temple of the Lord." ἐπιθυμεῖν (desire) is common enough, but ἐκλείπεν (grow weak) belongs only to those who desire above human measure. The Greeks use λειποθυμίαν when they refer to a man who, due to some violent and sudden movement of the spirit, loses his senses for a time. Overpowering fear or admiration sometimes produces this in men: so we speak of them as "stupefied," "thunderstruck." Sometimes, too, a great sorrow or joy beyond all hope, or even an impotent love, can have this same effect.

In profane tragedies we read how Phaedra fell as though dead at the sight of Hippolytus. We are told in history how a woman dropped dead on the entrance of her son whom she had heard had died in battle. Psalm 108 uses the word in the same sense: "My soul grows weak in the presence of your salvation." Pertinent to this are the words of the spouse in the canticle of Solomon: "Cover me with flowers and with fruits, because I am languishing from love." She asks for support, for she is in danger of falling.

This same thing occurs in spiritual as well as external matters. There is required a proportionate relation between a potency and its object. Otherwise, if that which is offered to a sense lacks this proportion, the sense itself is destroyed: if, for example, one looks at the sun on a cloudless day, his sight is ruined, and too loud a noise induces deafness. So in the works of learned men we read that at Stadisis, a town where the Nile roars over a fall with a tremendous racket, the natives are born deaf. We have, further, very often seen how those who apply their minds to matters of great difficulty beyond their ability often fall into madness. About Aristotle, for example, we are told (whether true or false is not now pertinent) that after he had applied his whole genius in attempting to discover why the sea of Euboia, unlike other bodies of water, had seven tides, cast himself into the sea saying, "Because I cannot understand you, you shall have me." So, too, it is no great cause for wonder that those who are not content with what Scripture tells us, but scrutinize beyond human power the Holy Trinity, fall into a madness: thus they who wish to learn beyond human capability end up lacking even common sense. Solomon spoke of these: "He who investigates God's majesty will be overwhelmed by His glory." In like manner Isaias: "Those who investigate the secret shall be as if they did not exist."

For some time now you have been wishing to hear the nature of these marvelous goods, surpassing human senses, which he saw who had such a desire to enter into the temple of the Lord that he grew weak in spirit. Or can anyone really estimate the dignity and the happiness of a man who is a sinner, captured in the snares of Satan, and who through faith and baptism has been freely loosed from bondage to the Devil and made one of the number of the sons of God, a member of the body of Christ, and become one with Him; from an inheritor of hell to become a son of heaven, to be taken into that glorious assembly of all the saints, from the beginning of the world and to the end of the world, whether in heaven or earth?

Such honor is rendered by the catechumens in the forecourt of the temple of the Lord. So he who with the vision of faith sees the majesty of the house of God—small wonder that he faints in spirit before divine matters, matters higher than human nature, and seized with an impotent desire no longer is in possession of his faculties in the face of such a desire? Horace, hardly an unlearned man, when summoned to Maecenas, spoke little and that, as he admits, haltingly. Nor does it rarely happen that great and erudite men, about to speak in the august presence of pontiffs or princes, suffer from a form of dizziness and so lose control of themselves that they are not able to speak what they had so carefully worked out. How can we compare the majesty of such an assembly as this with the glory of the Church? More surely can we see with the eyes of faith than with the eyes of the body.

Those who come to baptism in coldness and unwillingness, as it were, do not yet see to what happiness they are being received, and are to that extent unworthy of attaining that to which they are called. If a messenger should come to a commoner starving in a filthy jail and announce, "Be of good cheer, today you shall enter the royal palace, be among the assistants of the Court, a favorite of the King Himself," would there not be some danger lest he pass out from sudden joy, or, when admitted to the light of the palace after the darkness of the prison, lest he lose his senses? But what prison, what cell could be more terrible than that in which those are retained whom Satan has bound with the chains of sin? Or what palace is there anywhere, even if you lump all their splendors together, that can be compared with the majesty of the Church? And if they are to be censured who receive such a favor calmly and disinterestedly, how much more are to be censured those who live in the palace filthily and ungraciously? I feel that the very words of the prophet throw some light on the mystery. He does not say that he himself grows weak but "my soul grows weak." Nor does he say, "I exult," but rather, "my heart and flesh exult."

The word "soul" in Holy Scripture sometimes is used for something human and lowly, as when Paul speaks to the Corinthians of the animal soul (ψυχικός) saying that the animal man does not receive what is God's. So, too, James calls "animal" the wisdom of this world, which rejects faith and investigates the things of God with human reasoning (so, too, "flesh of man" signifies something rather crass, which wars perpetually with the Spirit of God). By the word "heart" is indicated the spirit of man or his mind, for, according to the physicians, the source of vital spirits is the heart. It is, therefore, the flesh that, according to Paul, cannot possess the kingdom of God, and it is the flesh that the spirit of God

does not consort with. Realize that this is the lowest part of
man. And so it is the soul that repels the Spirit of God, as
St. Jude says, indicating as it were with his hand those who,
following the things of this world, secede from union with the
Church by sects and schisms. These, he says, are those who
separate themselves, animalistic, without souls. There is also
the heart of man, to which do not arise the things that God
has prepared for those who love Him.

Since, therefore, the entire man, in concentrating all his
powers on one object, is not capable of receiving heavenly
gifts, what is left except that he becomes entirely deficient in
himself and falls (to the point) whence, renewed and raised
up by the Spirit of God, he sees by faith the greatness of the
gifts bestowed upon us by the goodness of God through His
Son and worthily draws nigh to His tabernacles. Thus, to fail
is to advance; thus, to lose one's life is to be vivified; to fail
oneself is to be returned to oneself; to fall is to be raised up;
to lose one's strength is to become strong in Christ; to die is
to be transformed into God. For unless that which is animal
dies, that which is spiritual does not begin to live. In the same
fashion, in the things of nature, the dry and unformed seed
is corrupted that the green tree may spring up; the ugly cater-
pillar dies that the gleaming and varicolored butterfly may fly
out; the aged cicada withers up that from its dried skin may
come forth a new and succulent songstress. Therefore, after
the whole man fails—fails for the tabernacles of God—then
his flesh and the soul and heart exult together in the living
God, for the Spirit of God by faith renews all things, and the
whole man becomes a new creature in Christ Jesus. For then
it is the flesh that sees the salvation of God and, according to
Paul, there is a spiritual body and a clean heart that God
creates in us, as well as a right spirit that He renews within
us. That spiritual exultation is thus born, not in riches or
honors or pleasures of this world, not in beauty and strength
of body, not in human wisdom, but in the living God, who
gives life to the dead. He, in short, safely glories who, as
blessed Paul tells us, glories in the Lord.

Scripture often gives this attribute "living" to God, not
only to distinguish Him from lifeless images, but also to set
forth His omnipotence. For that which works is called living.
It is not great to believe that God is living, since brute animals, too, live, but He alone is living in such a way that He
is life itself, whence, as from a fountain, emanates all life. "I,"
said the Lord, "am the way, the truth, and the life." Therefore, once the old man has died and been buried in baptism,
the new man, dead in himself but having the living Christ

within himself, exults in his entirety, thanking Him by whose gratuitous munificence he was thus transformed. Sarah did not give birth to Isaias, that is, to joy in the spirit, until after her female organs had failed her. From whom did she conceive him? From Abraham, dead as to the flesh but living and lively with the vigor of faith. The prophet preferred to express the cause of her exultation in allegory: the sparrow has found for itself a home and the turtledove a nest wherein to place her young. With what a lowly figure the spirit of the prophet expressed such a wondrous thing! Why is it that you exult and thus rejoice, you who just before had been failing yourself? Because, he says, the sparrow has found a home and the turtledove a nest wherein to put her young. By a natural instinct all kinds of living beings prepare homes for themselves, wherein to rest in safety after their labor, and in this they display a marvelous variety of means. Many retire into pathless and inaccessible places, scarcely capable of being investigated by hunters, like deer. Bears hide in brambles, lions and dragons in the depths of caves. The hare deceives the hunter by backward leaps, lest its bed be discovered. The snake is safe in its hole. Rabbits protect themselves by underground labyrinths. Ants pass the winter in burrows they have dug. Bees build their cells in holes in trees and seal them with a sticky and bitter coating, which protects them against harm. Fish, too, have their recesses and hiding places. Many birds live in accessible ravines and swamps. The eagle builds its nest on precipices, the partridge on the ground. Kingfishers place upon the water a nest so artfully constructed that it cannot be broken by a sword, and no one has yet found out how it is made. Many birds nest in twigs and branches artfully put together in chimneys or hung in trees. Sparrows and swallows have taught us how to make walls of wet clay and chaff. Not to drag this out by mentioning every one, all animals have gotten happiness when they have found where they can rest securely and bring up their young, and they desire nothing more. For they have the principles of nature, which are self-defense and propagation of the species.

Someone may wonder why I mention, of all kinds of living beings, only birds, and among them, only the sparrow and the turtledove. Of all kinds of living beings the birds are the smallest. The earth has elephants, the sea has whales—huge creatures. Among the birds the smallest is the sparrow, whose worthlessness and life, free from care, are spoken of to us by the Lord. The Holy Spirit does not love souls that are swollen with pride, burdened with love for corporeal goods and therefore walking on the ground; He loves souls that are birds and rejoices in dealing with the heavens; He loves those who are little in their own eyes and disregarded by the world; He loves all who depend upon the providence of God. If God so clothes, so feeds the sparrows, which are sold two for a cent, why do you torture yourself into extreme old age, to which perchance you will not come, and pile up riches, by right or wrong, for your children, grandchildren, and great-grandchildren, which perchance will go to persons you do not wish? And if a sparrow does not fall to the ground—this sometimes happens, from immoderate sexual congress, as some say—why do you, who were brought into the number of those of whom the Saviour said that not even a hair of their head would fall without the knowledge of the Father, run to soothsayers and astrologers, in fear lest you die before your day? The turtledove has in common with doves that it sighs instead of singing, knows neither adultery nor bigamy: for it is said that when one's partner dies, it does not consort with another. For this reason its voice is pleasing to the spouse, for it is said in the mystical Canticle of Solomon, "The voice of the turtledove is heard in our land." To some, larks and nightingales sing more sweetly in the springtime, but to the spouse the sight of the turtledove is ever pleasing.

For all those who condemn this world out of hope for a life in heaven mourn as long as they live in the tabernacle of this body, burdened, as the Apostle says, because they wish not to be unclothed but to be clothed over, so that what is mortal may be absorbed by life. Add the fact that in the Old Testament the turtledove was the offering given by the poor, so that in cheapness this bird is put on a par with the sparrow. He must be cheap in his own eyes who truthfully recognizes that in himself there is nothing good. Who is more sublime than Paul? Nevertheless, he speaks like a sparrow when he calls himself born out of due time, and the least of the Apostles, and unworthy of the name "Apostle," and the refuse and dregs of this world. This cheapness is the one thing that makes us valuable in the eyes of God. This littleness makes us great and high in the presence of the just Judge. Do you want to hear how great is this sparrow? "I can," he says, "do all things in Him who strengthens me." Will you not say that he, from a sparrow or turtledove, has become a lion? Directly opposed are the judgments of God and the judgments of this world, and so, just as the world loves and makes much of those who are of the world, it hates and condemns those who are not of the world. They go about, says Paul, in the skins of sheep and goats, needy, distressed, afflicted, wandering in solitudes and in the mountains. But listen to their worth: of whom, says Paul, the world was not worthy. To the world, what is more abject than Paul, who calls himself refuse, that is, excrement, which is cast aside? But how precious to Christ is he who is so despised by the world, he whom Christ testified was a vase of election to Him! What do I say about the other saints, since the Lord of glory Himself says through David, I am a worm and not a man. But He, most condemned by the world, is the one in whose name every knee bends, in heaven, on earth, and in hell, and who is equal in glory to God the Father.

Therefore, let no one who lives holily be displeasing to himself, as he is condemned and hated by those who have drunk the spirit of this world. We must strive mightily not to offer provocation to God if we are without our fault hated by the world. When I say "world," I do not mean possessions, clothing, food, or titles, but a spirit that does not have the spirit of Christ. Ordinary people abuse this word, as they do other words, by calling "worldly" those who are not in Holy Orders or are not monks. Those who have the monastic vows they call out-of-this-world and dead-to-the-world. But, as under any vesture, even though it is cheap or holy, a worldly spirit can lurk, so under lay or military vesture can lie a spirit that is unworldy, even though the plume of an ostrich adorns his helmet.

But perhaps someone will wonder how suddenly from the exultation of the whole man we slip to the mention of sighs, like a spur (as people say) into the charcoal burner. For although exultation and sighs seem opposed to each other, nevertheless they cannot be separated from each other as long as we live in this mortal tabernacle and carry our heavenly treasure in vessels of class—nay, more, each one in turn arises from the other. All the exultation of us who walk in faith rests in the hope of future goods. The more clearly we see those goods with the eyes of faith, and the more certainly we hope for them, the greater sighs we make, just as every deferment is troublesome to strong desires. And the more we sigh for that life, the more do our heart and flesh exult in the living God, while we have sadness in this life and solace only in Christ. Nothing here is perfect, and hardly anything is safe. We know in part and in part we prophesy. And he who stands must see to it that he does not fall. We walk amid traps; to avoid all is most difficult if not impossible. But even if the trials of this life cannot withdraw us from the charity which is in Christ Jesus, nevertheless they often call us away from the spiritual exultation of mind and compel us to groan with longing for that day when perfection will be accomplished. Who, in such an exile, does not yearn for such a homeland? Do you wish to hear the sigh of the turtledove? Read Psalm 119: "Woe is me! My sojourn is prolonged; I have dwelt with those who live in Cedar; long was my soul a dweller there. Lord, deliver my soul from the lips of the wicked and from the deceitful tongue." For good men it is a great affliction to endure the ways of life and tongues of the wicked. Here is relevant what Ecclesiastes says: "He who brings wisdom brings pain, and in much knowledge there is much indignation. The light of the sun belongs to all, not to all belongs the light of faith." In Hebrew "cedar" means "darkness." Whatever is done by those who have the spirit of this world is mere darkness; they hate the light of truth and love rather than darkness. And although there is almost more difference between the spiritual man illuminated by faith and the carnal man without faith, nevertheless in this pilgrimage (on earth) the good are forced to live in the same city and the same home with diverse souls. Thus, Lot, living in Sodom, was tortured in his soul, desiring to be freed from association with the wicked. But now listen to the turtledove which you just heard sigh deeply: "Woe is me! My sojourn is prolonged"; now it exults with the hope in the happiness that has been promised: "I have rejoiced at what was said to me: we shall go into the house of the Lord." Listen to another famous turtledove, groaning deeply with longing for its heavenly homeland: "Unhappy me! Who will deliver me from the body of this death?" Now hear him exulting: "I am filled with consolation; I abound exceedingly with joy in my every affliction."

We see that these groans were always deepest in those who longed for heaven's beatitude. For this reason the prophets withdrew into the deserts. For this reason after the passion of Christ so many crowds of men, who would not serve the savageness and wickedness of idolatry, took possession of the solitudes of Thebaid. For this reason monasticism was instituted. They thought it better to live with lions and panthers than with wicked men. Some withdrew into the wastes of Syria, one of whom was blessed Jerome; others hid on deserted islands; others occupied the almost inaccessible summits of mountains, like Benedict; some looked for rough swamps, hardly habitable even by animals, like Patrick and Bernard; others chose mountains and places that were horrible to look at, like Bruno or whoever was the founder of the Carthusians. These refuges were urged upon holy men by their disgust with the world. They sought to leave those who dwelt in Cedar. But here you are in exile wherever you hide. Seek and look for whatever hidden places you want, you still go to men as a man, and fleeing all consort with men, you take man with you, you carry with you the mortal body with which, lamented the Apostle, man is burdened. We read that Basil called back to life in the city the monks who dwelt in solitudes far from association with men, because he in his wisdom realized that many of them did not become truly holy but were rather supercilious, proud with a false conviction of their holiness, irritable, vengeful, morose, lacking in human kindness, and incapable of doing anything. Chrysostom says that the same thing is proved by experience, whenever monks are called to the episcopate from their fasting, watches, and sleeping on the ground. They sought outside themselves what they should have looked for within themselves. They made nests, but not in the halls of the Lord, although the kingdom of God is within us. The very current of language urges us to return to our nests. A nest is that in which man's desire is satisfied, in which he tranquilly nourishes his chicks, that is, his desires and wants. For he is said to be fortunate who wants nothing else when he is filled. This cannot befall any man in this life. Nature sets the limits of blessedness for other animals, and they attain their beatitude when they come to that for which they were made. But the soul of man, because it is divine and immortal, finds nothing in this life in which it can truly rest unless it attains that for which it was made. For what, then, was man made? To know, love, and glorify with soul and body as a unit its God—creator and redeemer—and its Lord. "This," said the Lord, "is eternal life, that they knew you, the one true God, and Him whom you have sent, Jesus Christ." To know is to see, to see is to enjoy; enjoyment is the last terminus of beatitude. This blessedness will be had only in the resurrection of the dead. There is, however, a nest in the halls of the Church, but it is suspended in the hope of the future. For outside the Church there is no real hope of blessedness. So immense and so capacious a thing is the human soul that only God can fill it, even if you add to it, besides God, six hundred worlds.

What about the fact that even in animate things you see each one brought to its proper end? As soon as a stone thrown from above hits the ground, it rests; how mightily is a flame borne to its place? What is it that so strikes the earth as to shatter even mountains of rock except the north wind, struggling to break forth to its own place? A bag filled with wind and forcibly sunk into water springs out. The soul of man is a fiery thing, and although it is weighed down by this earthly body, it does not rest until it rises to the place for which it is born. By nature all men hunt leisure, they seek something in which the soul can find rest; but because they build their nests in empty and perishable things, they become involved in larger crowds the more they seek rest. What else is the goal of so many books of the ancients—*De summo bono, De bonorum finibus,* and *De animi tranquillitate,* which the Greeks call contentment? One puts his nest in knowledge, another in freedom from pain, another in pleasure; some in that habit of virtue which is called wisdom, some in the acts and practice of a particular virtue. But all of them, as Paul says, "vanished in their thoughts," and although with their tongues they promised in glowing words contentment to others, they themselves had unquiet hearts. Why? Because they did not rejoice in the living God. If princes among the wise were so insane, what can be said of the unlearned, who estimate happiness by riches? After they acquire what they set out to get, they realize the complete truthfulness of what the Venusian wrote: "Worry accompanies wealth as it grows," and "Love for money increases to the extent that the money increases." Others care not for wealth but seek kingdoms and rule. What else sought Alexander the Great to the disturbance of the world? And how small a part of the world was he able to subjugate? Even if he had subjugated all of it, after he heard from Democritus that there were many worlds, he lamented because he had struggled so long in one part of the world. What did not Julius Caesar do and endure to obtain the principate of the Roman world? He obtained it, but his soul found no rest there; he yielded before the worries and the consciousness of his crimes, because of the pressure of his mind, and sought death because of his dissatisfaction with life, a death he did not expect.

There can be no real rest when the soul is conscious of its evildoing. Men's desires are endless. One promises himself contentment if he gets as a wife a very beautiful and well-dowried girl, but instead of peace he acquires a host of troubles. Another promises himself happiness if he gets such and such a benefice, but when he gets it, his hunger-thirst becomes more intense. Benefice is added to benefice, he strives for the dignity of abbot, seeks a bishop's miter, and changes the miter for a more wealth-producing one; then he pants after the cardinalate; when he gets this, he seeks the tiara. Does his soul finally find rest here? Let Julius II answer, whose extreme old age was tossed about on the unbearable waves of secular affairs. Let others judge of the others. It is not absurd that Augustine takes chicks to mean our good works, which are useless unless done in the nest of the Catholic

Church. Phocian and Aristides, Trajan and Antony, and many others did deeds of justice, devotion, and bravery for their countries. Zeno is praised for his continence, Xenocrates for his integrity, Socrates for his patience, but what they did did not give them true happiness, for it was not done with Christ. Emperor Julian spent much money in helping the poor, but he did this against Christ. Similarly, of many heretics some extraordinary and almost incredible acts of virtue are mentioned—great contempt of wealth among the Ebionites, mighty assiduity in prayer among the Euchites, extreme abstinence and severity of life among the Manichaeans—but all they did was fruitless because they did not put their chicks in the nest of the Church but built nests in their own tabernacles; to them applies the ancient proverbs, "From a bad crow is born a bad egg," and, "You will expect turtledove chicks but get asps." Therefore if we seek true peace of soul, let us persevere in the tabernacle of the Lord of Hosts, let us remain in union with the Catholic Church, which is Jerusalem and is built as a city, whose participation is in itself. This is that blessed rest, of which another psalm says, "As soon as I sleep I shall rest, for Thou, O Lord, hast established me in peace in a singular way."

Sion is a mountain in Jerusalem, where were the tabernacle and the palace. *Sion* is the Hebrew word for "mirror." So let us climb up this mountain. How shall we climb it? By contempt of earthly things and a longing for the heavenly life. There, after long and treacherous wanderings, exhausted by fruitless concern with human affairs, we shall find a nest in which to renew our wings, we shall find rest, as says Psalm 14: "Lord, who will dwell in Your tabernacle? Who will rest in Your holy mountain?" Let us enter without the stain of heresy and, advancing in faith, which works by love, practice justice, not of the law but of the Gospel, attributing to God all that we seem to do rightly. To fly up to this mountain, let us be sparrows in lowliness of soul, cheap and valueless in our own eyes, not solicitous for the morrow but casting all our concern upon Him who takes care of us. Let us be turtledoves in innocence and chastity, and realizing that we have not here a lasting city, sigh constantly for the heavenly Jerusalem. Let us harken to the voice of the Lord, inviting us to true peace of soul: "Come to Me, all you who labor and are burdened, and I shall refresh you. Take My yoke upon you and learn of Me because I am meek and humble of heart, and you will find rest for your souls." To human ways of thinking this is an absurd statement. What rest is had by the meek and humble, who are trod upon and driven from their homes? What repose is there for those who carry a yoke? The yoke is a synonym for slavery; according to the Greek proverb, "There is no leisure among the slaves." But they who in imitation of Christ are meek shall possess the land; they who according to the world are lowly are lofty in Christ and reach up even to heaven; they who subject their necks to the placid yoke of Christ are truly free. They submit to it who trust in His promises without any hesitation. Let us follow the mystic-teaching prophet, who by his example shows us how lovable and beautiful are the halls of the Lord and how peaceful the rest possessed by souls becomes in them.

Now from the atrium he shows us the altars of the Lord, which make up the holier and more beautiful part of the temple: "Your altar, O Lord of Hosts, my King and my God." Among the Jews there was a great reverence for the temple and its equipment, and the altars were magnificently ornamented. Hence those words: "Temple of the Lord, temple of the Lord"; and to swear most inviolably was to swear by the temple and the altar. Not with impunity did the Lord say "Destroy this temple." But the temple and the altar were only a type of spiritual thing. When the prophet uttered those words, he was contemplating another tabernacle not made by hands, he was looking at other altars, admiration for which so astounded him that words failed him. Some refer these words, "Your altars, O Lord," to the ones above: "How beloved are your tabernacles, how beloved your altars." Augustine connects them with the ones that immediately precede: "The sparrow finds herself a home, the turtledove a nest," so that "Your altars" follows and is in apposition, with the result that we understand that the altars are nests, in which we rest. It seems to me more correct to take the words absolutely, as a better expression of admiration. For when we see the magnificently constructed home of a prince, we say in wonder, "The royal palace." As here the emphasis is on "royal," so in what the prophet said the strongest emphasis is on the pronoun "your." You alone are the Lord of Hosts, and these are Your altars, worthy of You, pleasing to You. Again, the Greek word for "hosts" is power, of which we said before that the Hebrew is "sabaoth," that is, "armies." It is repeated here so that we may understand that the Church, although it is according to the world condemned and unarmed, is nonetheless unconquerable because it is protected by the Lord of hosts and unconquered by the very gates of hell. These are not altars that are bloodied by the blood of oxen, goats, and rams. The Lord had formerly, in the mouth of Isaias, expressed His disfavor with this kind of victim. What do we conclude? God is a spirit and takes delight in spiritual victims. He cares not for the flesh of sheep but wants the mortification of desires that fight against the spirit.

If for the love of Christ you have killed within yourself the craving for money, and have given to the members of Christ what you formerly cared for, you have offered to God a most pleasing victim. If you have strangled luxury and lust, and from being a drunkard and incontinent have become sober and chaste, you have offered a sacrifice acceptable to God. If, when injured by a neighbor, you restrain your anger for the sake of Christ and forgo revenge, you have offered a most pleasing sacrifice to God. If, firm in faith and fervent in charity, you give yourself and all you have to the will of God, ready to suffer death and hell if He so wishes, you have offered a most pleasing holocaust to the Lord of Hosts. This is the rational or spiritual worship and the living victim, holy and pleasing to God, to which the Apostle pleadingly exhorts us, Romans 12. God is not pleased by the fumes of incense or of myrrh or balsam but likes spiritual perfume, the vows and prayers of devoted minds, gratitude and the sacrifice of praises, with which He wishes to be honored. It is by these victims that we walk to see the salvation of God, who is the goal also of this psalm: "He shall see the God of Gods in Sion." Prayers are received by God only when they are made in faith; and thanksgiving in the name of Christ is to be offered not only in prosperity but also in adversity. The sacrifice of praise will be acceptable if, according to Paul's teaching, whatever we do, in word and in action, we do, not for our own glory, but for God's glory. This offering, which is truly because it is spiritual, is offered continually throughout the world on the altars of the Church. In this nest we repose safely for a time, because altars are not of men but of the Lord of Hosts, whose will no one can resist, who wishes to be worshipped by the simple and humble, who wishes to give to little ones the gifts of the heavenly kingdom. In this name He (Himself gives thanks to the Father in the gospel (Matthew 11): "You have hidden these things from the wise and learned but revealed them to little ones; yes, Father, because it was pleasing to You." There is no reason to fear the world or Satan if the Lord of Hosts has received you in His tabernacles. He protects what He has created; He rules, walking in the midst of His own; He finishes what He has made.

The Lord of Hosts protects, the King rules, God raises up to the kingdoms of heavens: "My King and my God." So, too, says Psalm 43: "You are my King and my God." This can in a proper sense be accommodated to the Christ, King of the

Church, who says in the second psalm, "I have been made king by Him, over Sion His holy mountain." Under the rule of God are all things. The demons, too, recognize His omnipotence, and tremble; but only the voice of faith can say "My King and my God." No one can say "Lord Jesus" except in the Holy Spirit. Everywhere, however, we hear voices of persons calling the Lord Jesus. So, too, no one can say "My King and my God" except him who entrusts himself, full of confidence, to the will of God and awaits from Him alone the reward of eternal happiness. Another psalm says that blessed is the people to which the Lord is God. Likewise, when in some other passages in Scripture and in Leviticus 26, the Lord says, "I will build My tabernacle among you, and My soul will not cast you aside. I shall walk among you and I shall be your God and you will be My people." Whom he here calls King he later calls Legislator. Therefore, if we recognize Him as our King, let us obey His laws. If we recognize Him as our God, let us love nothing more than Him; nay, let us love nothing except for Him. By the word "King" we are reminded of something else: that we have been redeemed by the blood of Christ from the rule of the devil and that from being under a most foul and cruel lord we have come into the rule of the most merciful King.

Up to this point our mystic-leader or hierophant has shown us the lovable tabernacle of the Lord, has brought us into its atrium, has shown us its altars and spiritual victims. Now he shows us those extraordinary and God-worthy priests who deal with sacred things in the temple of the Lord. "Blessed," he says, "are those who dwell in Your house, Lord; for all ages they will praise You." They who are strong in faith and rooted in charity dwell already not in the atrium but in the house of the Lord, for "dwell" is a word that connotes stability. Why are they blessed? Because they have many possessions or gleam with honors or abound in good things? Not at all. Why, then? "Because," he says, "they will praise You for all ages." Here is the tranquil home that the sparrow has found, here is the restful nest that the turtledove has found. For here is the ultimate end for which man was made: to know, love, and celebrate in hymns his Creator, Redeemer, Ruler, and Remunerator. In human opinion they who are praised are blessed rather than they who praise. But in the things of God it is otherwise. For God does not become more blessed by being praised, for He is the eternal font of all glory. But all who praise Him become blessed simply because they praise. But not all persons praise Him who sing, "Glory to You, Lord," but they in whose hearts dwell charity, "which is the bond of perfection," and who rejoice in the peace of Christ, to which they are called who have joined in one body, and who exhort one another in psalms and hymns and spiritual canticles in grace, singing in their hearts to God. But if God is to be praised with corporeal voice, "Let us sing psalms in spirit and in mind."

Praise in the mouth of the sinner is not beautiful, nor is singing pleasing when voices are out of harmony. Outside the house of God, which is the Church, hymns are not accepted by God. If we wish to be blessed, let us with one voice praise God as the angels praise Him; in them there is no dissension. All creatures praise the Lord in their own fashion, for not only do the heavens announce the glory of God but every kind of living being, the elements and what comes from them, shout out the praises of God when their very sight declares to us the omnipotence, the wisdom, and the goodness of the Creator. For this reason, in the psalms and the Canticle of the Three Children, not only the sun and the moon, but beasts and fish and mountains and hills and seas and rivers call upon us to praise the name of the Lord. Only the evil spirits and wicked men are not invited to join this chorus, because by them, to the extent they are able, the name of the Lord is rather blasphemed. What is meant by what the prophet adds, "They will praise You for all ages," where the word *sela* is subjoined? This Jerome translated by "always," even though some deny that the word means "eternity," because it is not found in Scripture except in the psalms—and then sometimes in passages where it does not mean "eternity." Hence they think that *sela* means the same as *diapsalma,* which word was a directive to change the melody (psalms were sung to organs). Musicians today have signs to indicate a change in the melody. Not every melody befits every sentiment. Thus, in dialogue in comedy flutes gave out certain modes by which the people might know that the type of sentiment was serious or otherwise. In this psalm, at least, this clause seems to indicate the beginning of another part. But, however this may be, the words "for all ages" mean "eternity," which is not applicable to the temple that was in Jerusalem; it lasted not much more than two hundred years, although the Jews had convinced themselves that the law and their temple would last until the end of the world, just as the Romans were sure that the Capitolium would be eternal—but today at Rome not even a vestige of the Capitolium can be seen or at Jerusalem of the temple. Therefore, the eye of the prophet saw a different temple in which the name of the Lord would be praised forever, that is, the Catholic Church.

But what can this perpetual praise be since they who praise are mortal? This Church, which praises the Lord, awaits its perfection and knows not an end. And as in the good charity never fails, so praise of God is made now and is perfected in heaven. As soon as the soul flies from this terrestrial domicile, with the angels and the souls of the blessed it clearly sings the praises of God. When the body, no longer animal but spiritual, is united with it, the whole man without end and without interruption will sing forth the praises of its Creator. For the Church militant upon earth and the Church triumphant in heaven is one and the same house, except that the latter is more pure, just as the air on the moon, according to some, is purer than the atmosphere of the earth. But there is nothing to prevent each one of us, burdened by this mortal body, from praising his God without interruption. How can he, you ask, if whatever we think, say, or do we do for the glory of God, even when we eat or drink or sleep or refresh our body with games, we praise God. "Glorify," says the Apostle, "and carry the Lord in your bodies." Not all members speak, but all members of our bodies glorify God when they serve justice even though the tongue is silent. After the prophet, as though rapt in ecstasy, came to the heavenly Jerusalem, where no trouble interrupts the melody, no dissension vitiates it, nothing urgent interrupts hymns to God—or, as Blessed Paul says, "whether we exceed, to God, whether we are sober, to ourselves"—returning, as it were, to himself, he remembers that he is a man and to those living in this exile he shows the road by which one arrives at that blessed tranquillity. He said, "Blessed are they who dwell in Your house, Lord," including even the angels and holy souls dwelling with the angels. Then, changing the kind of harmony, he says, "Blessed is the man," or, as Jerome translates from the Hebrew, "the human being." The word "man" does not exclude women: "In Christ there is neither man or woman, slave or free, but the new creature." The word "human being" warns us of our weakness, for unless God extends the hand of His mercy, we cannot approach the atrium even of the Church, not to speak of flying to the lofty home of the blessed.

Entrance to the Church is faith, without which baptism is of no avail. But no one gives himself faith; it is a gift from God, by which God gives preliminary help to whom He wills and draws him to Christ. For man as man is carnal and smacks of nothing but of the world. Aware of this, the prophet now sings in lower modes, "Blessed is the man whose help is in You," or, as Augustine read the text, "whose assumption" —the Greek is succor, which word refers to one who extends his hand to one who is trying to climb. For the Church is a city located on an elevation, as the temple of Jerusalem was located on Mt. Sion. Jerome translated *auxilio* by *fortitudine* (which means "strength"). The words are different, the meaning is the same. Those who struggle in difficulties need strength. But man can do nothing of himself. Faith really adds strength to a man so that he no longer fears the world or Satan. And so they who place all their faith in God are strengthened by the Spirit and are able to climb the mountain of the Lord. Fifteen steps led up to the Jewish temple built by Solomon. On the first step the prophet complains of the wickedness of tongues and of exhaustion with life. On the second he is strengthened by the gift of faith and says, "I raised my eyes to the mountains, whence comes help; my help is from the Lord, who made heaven and earth." Faith it is that makes stable our walk so that it wavers not; Paul wrote to the Corinthians, "Stand in faith"; to the Romans, "But you stand in faith." And Blessed Peter urges us to "resist the devil, strong in faith." He is verily strong who, weak in himself, has fortitude from God; Isaias, indicating this, says that it will come to pass that "this song be sung in the land of Juda." The song is of profession of the gospel, for "*Juda*" is the Hebrew word for "confess." What song, then? "A mighty city is our Sion." *Sion* is the Church, but whence comes strength to the weak person? "As a saviour let there be placed in it a wall and a fore-wall."

Hear of the impregnable fortification: The same one says, "In silence and hope will be your strength." He waits in silence who has complete confidence in what has been promised and in his hope for such great happiness that does not cause embarrassment because it does not fail us and exhilarates the soul even in the midst of affliction and death. In this there is no perfect beatitude; yet there is much blessedness so long as we consider in our souls the brevity of this entire life and "the unworthiness of our affliction in comparison with the glory that will be revealed in us."

In addition we should consider the reliability of Him who made the promises. By His faithfulness He even allows us to deny Him, yet He cannot deny Himself to us so long as we persevere in faith and charity, keeping ourselves within the walls of the house of God and growing in it to the measure of the fullness of Christ. We climb the fifteen mystical steps into the eternal tabernacle and pass joyfully through the forty-two mansions to the third mansion of rest that the Lord promised in the gospel to the meek. What we seek is difficult; extraordinary, too, is that toward which we tend. No one passes from the depths to the heights. We need someone to show us the way, as God was a guide through the pathless desert to the Israelites, who prefigured us. We need someone who will stretch out a hand to us from above and draw us heavenward in our struggles. "It is the Lord who works in us the will as well as operation." He opens our eyes by faith to see where we are, to shudder at what we are, to hope for what we as yet are not. The first help given us by God, that is, the first step to beatitude, is that when we raise our eyes to the mountains. From heaven comes our desire for heavenly things and our contempt of earthly things. They who look at their own wisdom, their own strength, their own merits, who look only to ceremonies, privileges, and papal documents, never arrive at that blessedness. What does that candidate for blessedness do to whom the Lord by faith granted a distaste for the low cares of the world and a predilection to raise his eyes to the mountains of eternity. He disposes in his heart the steps that he must climb. What he here terms "steps" he refers to in the gradual psalms as the scale or ladder that individuals are actually climbing, although the Latin expressions connote descent as well as ascent.

In the business of piety we must never go back but must forget those whom we have left behind and tend ever to the more perfect. Eurydice looked back and fell back into hell; Lot's wife looked back and turned into a pillar of salt. Piety has its steps, too, as does man's life span. Catechumens are born; once baptized they are fed, as infants, milk; as adults they receive for solid food the more obtuse mysteries. Paul "speaks wisdom among the perfect"; among the weak he says nothing "except Jesus Christ and him crucified." So he who raises his eyes to the mountains arranges the steps that climb. Where does he do this? "In his heart." This is not surprising because one climbs that mountain, not on foot, but by his internal movements. There are external steps, which are not to be belittled but are not useful unless they are disposed in our hearts. From a layman one becomes a cleric, from a cleric a subdeacon, from a subdeacon a deacon, from a deacon an archdeacon, from this a priest, from a priest a bishop; again, from a layman a monk, from a Canon Regular a Dominican, from a Dominican a Franciscan, from a Franciscan a Benedictine, from a Benedictine a Carthusian. Nevertheless there is much controversy about these grades among those who arrange them and evaluate them according to externals. Some think the Franciscans are higher because they walk half barefoot and do not touch money. Others prefer the Dominicans to them because they do not eat meat at home. Some prefer the Benedictines to both because they chant the various hours in churches and never leave their houses. Among them all they possess the highest rank who rub their skin with metal breastplates instead of shirts. All these ranks or grades are beneficial if they, with the help of the Lord, are true and are distributed in heart. Not to live by rapine is a step toward devotion. Not only to restore ill-gotten goods but to give your possessions to the poor for the love of Christ is a step higher. If from being violent and fierce you become harmless, you have climbed a step in your heart. You seek to do good to everyone: you have lifted yourself up a step. You not only refrain from revenge on those by whom you have been injured but take joy in wishing and doing them well for the sake of Christ: you have gotten up to a truly lofty step.

These things I have set forth as examples; let each consider the rest for himself. These steps are arranged in the heart of a man, in the inmost recesses of his soul. These steps by which we tend to perfection are arranged by the blessed man in his heart, by the man who does not boast among men but submits himself for the approval of the inspector of hearts and looks for help to no one but the Lord. And he considers all this in the valley of tears. What else is this entire world but a dark valley, full of opportunities for being born, giving birth, dying, being sick and needy, sailing, waging war, and a thousand other tears? From these things neither the powerful nor the rich nor kings are free. This is the valley of *Achor*, that is, tumult and perturbations, into which was hurled Acham, as is said in Joshua (7:24). God put us in this valley after we lost Paradise through disobedience, so that living for a while in exile we might by the obedience of faith and keeping of God's commandments contrive a return to our homeland. There is no reason for us to dislike this valley: the Son of God Himself deigned to come down to it to be our "way, life, and truth." Therefore, as long as we live in this mortal body we live in the valley of tears. Someone may object: in vain does a man arrange in his heart the steps that climb, if he must remain in the valley of tears. But this valley of Achor is changed into rest for warriors, according to Isaias 65. And Jerusalem is given in declaration of hope (Hosea 2). Besides, we must remember that we climb to the citadel of Sion by our emotions, not our feet; in our heart, not by stairs. The body clings to the valley, the soul struggles for the mountain. Therefore it seemed good to our King to have us attain to the crown of immortality by the temporary afflictions of this world. And the regulations of this warfare do not appear harsh. Our King, who gave us these regulations, observed them Himself. There is no reason for us to disengage our soul: He who calls us to combat will give His blessing, helping us in dangers, consoling us in afflictions, so that we may endure them. Our Gamemaster calls His followers to the contest; He offers rich rewards to those who contest according to rules; He presides, not as spectator and judge, but also as helper. He furnishes the strength, He urges eagerness. For here "blessing" is not the word that means "praise" but the word that means "generosity"—as the Apostle says, "He who sows sparingly reaps sparingly; he who sows in blessings receives eternal life from blessings." Rigorous are the regulations: "He who does not take up his cross daily and follow Me cannot be My disciple. He who does not hate his father and even his own life is not worthy of Me." Rigorous, I say, and fearful unless there is present a generous outpouring of grace; to show that the grace is abundant and not at all sparse, He preferred to call it by the word bounty than by any other. In the time of the Mosaic Law the giving of grace was less, but as soon as there shone forth the humanness and goodness of our God, who not in accordance with the works of justice that we do but according to His mercy saved us by the water of rebirth and regeneration and poured out His Spirit generously upon all flesh.

Among men there is sometimes a difference between saying well and doing well; frequently, as a matter of fact, a man's saying well is a curse, not a doing well, but to God saying well is the same as doing well. They act religiously who fall down and receive a bishop's blessing; how much more correct is it to fall down before God to receive His blessing? Listen to the effectiveness of God's blessing: "They will go," He says, "from virtue to virtue and will see the God of Gods in Sion." Some may wonder at the sudden change of number in the verb. He just said, "Blessed is he whose help is from You, and who arranged in his heart." Here He says, "They will go from virtue to virtue." Why the sudden change to the plural? In the sacred writings God's blessing brings fecundity as His curse brings barrenness: "Cursed is the earth in its activity; when you work it, it will bring forth thorns and briars." On the other hand, when God created man from wet clay and his wife from a rib on his left side, He blessed them, saying, "Grow and multiply and fill the earth." So, too, Psalm 106: "He blessed them, and they increased exceedingly." And all this is a type of spiritual thing.

So after we were freed from the curse of the law by the grace of the Gospel and a blessing was given the Apostles by the Holy Spirit, the cult of the true God, which among the Jews was restricted to a small corner of the world, spread with amazing speed throughout the world. Swarms of virgins, martyrs, and confessors broke forth! Whence this prodigious fecundity? Whence, if not from the blessing of God? "Your sons," He says, "will come from afar, and your sons will arise from the side." And so that deserted widow marvels at her unexpected fecundity and says, "And where have your sons come from?" They came from every nation under the sun: from India, Gades, Thrace, the Goths, the Scots, and the Irish. They multiplied because of the blessing of God, and animated by faith and eager in hope, "they will go from virtue to virtue." Not even here does he use the word "goodness" but "from power to power," which Jerome translated from the Hebrew into *de fortitudine in fortitudinem*. It is real bravery to care not for pleasures, wealth, and the honors of this world for the sake of Christ; but more bravery is needed to triumph over the bonds of affection for parents, wife, and children; bravest of all is to disregard death and the tortures that are mightier than death out of love for life in heaven.

The higher they who strive to mount the steps to the heights climb, the more tired they become, but the farther they go who climb these steps, the more strong and eager they become. How is this except that it is a matter, not of human strength, but of God's blessing? How else could there be the ready strength and eagerness of the Apostles, young men, and virgins in the filth of prisons, in whips and scourges, in death itself, at even the mention of which the spirit of man shudders? From no other source except our Gamemaster and Lawgiver, who increases His blessing in proportion to our trials. Men wonder, for they see the external affliction but do not see the inner blessing. Not without elegance was it said of monks living an austere life by one who is well known for his piety: "Many see our crosses but not our anointings. They see the body weakened by watching, fasting, and labor; they see the loneliness and the abstention from all pleasure, but they do not see in these weak bodies the delights by which the soul is strengthened in its desire for heaven." But what is the reward they seek for their great labors? "They will see," he says, "the God of Gods in Sion," or, as Jerome translates it, "they will appear before the God of Gods in Sion." This is the reward for all the struggles, this is the rest for which all yearn, this is the height of felicity. "Lord," he says, "show us Your face, and we shall be saved"; and Phillip says, "Show us the Father, and we are content." But "no one sees God":

He is invisible to the eyes of the body, but visible to the clean of heart.

Accordingly, the Lord in the gospel calls blessed "those who are clean of heart, for they shall see God." By "heart" here understand not the bodily organ, the font of life and blood, but the mind of man illuminated by light. He is seen sometimes in this life, too, by those who have been cleansed in mind, but only as by a mirror and enigmatically, and only in Sion. For outside the Church no one sees God because no one has a pure mind. And they who think they see Him are hallucinated; they see a specter, not God. Not a blessing shared by everyone is "appearing before the God of Gods." What does "appearing before Him" mean? It means to come with complete confidence into the sight of Him who knows the secret places of the human heart. Only one with a pure and completely sincere conscience dares do this. God will also be seen by the wicked, but the sight of Him will be horrible to them while it is lovable to the good. God is not different here; it is the eyes that are different. It is like light that is hurtful to weak eyes but healthful to sound eyes. "For we all shall stand before the tribunal of the highest Judge," and there will be no appeal from Him. The soldier who gave faithful and hearty service in war, the servant who wisely invested his master's talents, go joyfully into the sight of their general and master, and will hear the words: "Receive the crown of eternal life, and enter into the joy of your Lord." Blessed is he who is not afraid to open up his conscience to the Lord, and says to King Ezechia: "I pray, Lord; remember, I ask, how I walked before You in truth and with a perfect heart and that I did what is good in Your eyes."

With similar confidence that brave soldier of Christ proclaims, in the sight of the Emperor, "Behold, we speak before God in Christ." And addressing the same Corinthians he speaks of himself, saying, "We do not walk in deception, adulterating the word of God, but in the manifestation of truth, commending ourselves to the conscience of men before God." Elsewhere he says, "I have fought the good fight, I have completed the course, I have preserved the faith, as for all else, a crown of justice awaits me." Is this not a great happiness, to be able to appear before the God of Gods in Sion, in the tower of evangelical perfection? "The God of Gods," he says, thus indicating the Judge of all. Whether you take this to mean the judges of the people, or the holy men to whom this was addressed, or the angels whom they called gods, or the demons and their human ministers who allowed themselves to be worshiped as gods, He alone is the one God of Gods, the Judge of all, as the eighty-first psalm indicates: "God stood in the Synagogue of the gods and in their midst he judged them"—He was judged by no one.

The power of neither the angels nor the prophets nor the saints confers true beatitude on man; this is only accomplished by the God of Gods. If we may explain this a little better, the Lord demands a blessing, but only for those who are praying. He does this, not that He might admonish us, but rather that we may be made worthy to ask for a more generous blessing. We thus make an agreement with God to often call upon Him with pure prayer, or give thanks for His benefits. "O Lord of powers, hear my prayer, give ear O God of Jacob." He is the God of angels and thus is called the God of powers. He is the God of men who must imitate the patriarch Jacob, who, when wrestling with the angel, merited a benediction and said, "I have seen the Lord face to face and my soul is saved."

There follows the verse, "Behold, O God our Protector; and look upon the face of thy Christ." Whoever requires protection has not really obtained security. He still fears the fiery darts of the evil spirits that threaten him. Against this he implores the God of armies that He might be his shield. Jerome uses the term shield, whereas the Septuagint has over-shield. The power of the demons is great, but that of the Lord of powers is greater than all others. If He deigns to be our shield, we will have no fears of weapons. He will be quite safe under Thy shield who says, "The Lord is the Protector of my life, whom shall I fear?" and again, "O Lord, you have girded us with the shield of your good will." There is really no shield that can protect a person from every injury, but whom the shield of the Lord covers can in no way be wounded. To be seen by the Lord is to be protected. He looks upon whom He favors and makes him well. Hence in the psalm I've just cited, the word "shield" means "benevolence." Jerome translated this as placability. Those who protect themselves with their own merits and trust in these as in a shield shall see whether or not they are really safe. Whoever places his confidence in ceremonies, in the cult of saints, or particular garb, as if these make him safe from Satan, does not use a dependable shield. True confidence can be placed only in the grace of God and His promises.

To look upon God is true beatitude, but we are unable to behold Him until He has first looked upon us. Since we were blind and living in darkness rather than mist, He has deigned to look upon us and has opened our eyes. And since we became His enemies by loving ourselves, He has enabled us to love Him once again. "Look upon the face of your Christ."

I don't feel that it should be a matter of concern whether this text referred to David or to certain others. Christ in Greek means the "anointed one"; in Hebrew it signifies the "Messiah." Yet all of us are Christ's since we have been reborn in Him. We are those from whose face the Lord does not remove His gaze, but guards us like the pupil of His eye, provided we do not turn our face from Him. It is a practice to anoint kings and priests. Both of these, in a way, correspond to their nomenclature. Peter indicates this, saying, "You are a chosen people, a royal priesthood." But He is the Prince of all Christians who is the Prince of Peace, a priest in eternity according to the order of Melchisedech whom God has singularly anointed with the oil of joy beyond His participants.

Upon His face, since it is without blemish, the Lord is pleased to look. Him He has proclaimed as His only beloved Son, in whom He is well pleased.

What did the prophet wish for you when he said, "Behold the face of your Christ"? Whatever God has given to you He has given through His Son and because of His Son, not because of the works of justice that we perform. "For all of us have offended in many things." He alone is the lamb without spot. Therefore O God our Protector, if our face or our conscience offend You, then look upon the face of Christ Thy Son, whom You love without exception and through whose merits you have granted us what we do not deserve.

The Jews, since they were unaware of the mystery of the Incarnation besought God through the memory of the patriarchs Abraham, Isaac and Jacob, whose piety was accepted by God. Christians, on the other hand, ask nothing of the Father except through Christ, whom we have in heaven as an efficacious advocate who binds us with His faith. If we would receive anything, we must request the Father in His Name.

He who wrote this psalm did not see Christ in the flesh but with the eyes of faith that, looking into the future, saw his coming in the same way that Abraham and all those who lived before Christ saw His coming and were glad.

Therefore, as often as we ask for something from God, we must do so with faith, but we must find this faith, not in our own works, but in the gratuitous promises of Christ. Let us not say, "Behold my fastings, or my offerings or my privations, but behold the face of thy Christ." Paul in his letter to the Ephesians says the same thing: "In Christ Jesus Our Lord let us have boldness and access with confidence by faith in Him." "Why by His faith?" Because we must trust with our entire heart in Him who never fails in His promises even when they appear impossible. Who could conceivably believe it possible that divine and human nature would so unite as to go together into one person? Yet He promised and fulfilled this. Who could believe that man could sit at the right hand of God? Yet this He also promised and accomplished. What is there that we cannot hope for from God provided we look upon the face of His Christ?

So that you will not think that I have dreamed up this interpretation but rather that the prophet recognizes his dignity in having recourse to the face of Christ, listen to what follows: "One day in Your courts are more than a thousand elsewhere."

Nothing would stand in the way of taking a more down to earth interpretation of this as referring to the Israelites' captivity in Babylonia. They were obsessed with a great desire for their homeland, the superstition of the pagans disturbed them, and they longed once again for the earlier rites and the magnificent temple constructed by Solomon. Already long association with the pagans made them appear as paganized.

We do not wish to give this retrospective interpretation. The psalmist does not give the number "thousand" but "beyond a thousand," that you may understand an infinite designation. Nor does he say "in your home," or "in your temple," but "in your courts." That is to say, in the vestibule or outer area where even the ordinary crowd could enter. Hence Paul in writing to the Hebrews refers to it as the holy world ($\kappa o\sigma\mu\iota\kappa\acute{o}\nu$) open to all. Nor is the expression "one day" found in the Hebrew, but rather "day." Where the sun of justice and purified truth fail to shine, there is no day. There can never be day unless in the Church. Those who are outside it live in the night as Zachariah prophesied, when speaking of the unbelieving: "In that day there will be no light, but cold and freezing." Later on this could be said of the Church, "And there will be one day that is known to the Lord, being neither day nor night." The rising of the sun makes the day, its setting the night. What is this—being neither day nor night? Isaias explains it in his sixtieth chapter: "You will have no sun in the light of the day, nor will the rising of the moon illuminate you through the night, but the Lord will be for you an eternal light." He who wrote the Apocalypse imitated both of the prophets when he stated: "And the city will not have the benefit of sunlight, since the Almighty will be its light." Furthermore, there can be no light except in the Church. Isaias testifies to this in the text cited above and it applies to those who have not accepted the faith of the Gospel: "Behold darkness has covered the earth, and a mist the people. Yet the

Lord will rise above you and his glory will be seen in you."
He speaks also of those who, rejecting their superstitious past,
have embraced the Gospel: "And the gentiles will walk in
thy light, and kings in the splendor of your rising." When he
adds the expression "over a thousand," he implies a universal
group which is unthinkable outside of the Church.

No happiness is possible for one who walks in darkness.
As long as we fight in this temple, we behold the sun through
our faith. In Thy heavenly temple there is continued daylight,
since neither change, nor the shadow of necessitude, nor the
cloud of ignorance and error can blot out the light. For there
is nothing in the riches and glories of this world that offers
the happiness of those who walk in the light of faith and follow in simplicity Him who says, "Who follows me will not
walk in darkness."

This may appear a foolishness to those whom Christ has not
enlightened. Yet if you question those whose hearts Christ has
illuminated as to whether they would not want to gain the
entire world by rejecting their religion, they would detest and
abominate your suggestion. They know full well the inestimable value of what they have acquired, and they cling to it
as to a most precious reward. Their tenacity is summed up in
these words: "I have chosen to be abject in the house of the
Lord rather than to dwell in the tabernacles of sinners."
What does the expression "abject" mean other than to lie at
the threshold and in the antechambers of the temple? In
short, to be a beggar. Yet the majesty and happiness of the
Church are such that even what is most contemptible in it, far
surpasses the greatest splendors in the world. Just as in the
heavenly Jerusalem there are many mansions, the lowliest of
which surpasses the regal dwellings of the earth, so in the
Church there is a diversity of appointments, the poorest of
which is superior to the finest the world can offer.

In the human body there is a diversity of functions and
parts. Yet all are nourished by the same soul. It is the same in
the mystical body of Christ which is the Church. There are
different orders of men, different gifts of the Holy Spirit, yet
all expect the same reward as members of Christ. Whatever
here is lowly still ranks higher than the great things of the
world. The foot of a human is superior to the eye of a pig, or
a dog. The alimentary tract in the human is superior to the
head of a monkey.

The prophet has explained why so many mortals either
refuse to join the Church, leave it, or are expelled from it.
Those who are puffed up with mundane honors are quite
reluctant to relinquish their camel humps and enter humbly

through the lowly door. We have historical instances of certain heresiarchs who refused to relinquish their episcopal dignity. They preferred to hold first place among dogs and swine rather than a lower position among the sheep of Christ. This life of stupidity has provided us with such names as Basilides, Marcion, and others less auspicious. What did these unhappy wretches gain other than the everlasting ignominy of men and eternal hellfire from God? Provided one has his name written in the book of life, it is much preferable to suffer even the greatest humiliation among the sheep of the Church. We can say the same regarding the insanity of those who, having been excluded from the Church through great and manifest crimes, refuse to confess their guilt and be reconciled. They feel that a return to the Church would involve only standing in the churchyard barefoot and bareheaded, imploring on their knees the prayers of the congregation, exchanging purple for sackcloth and ointment for ashes. Why is this? It is because they fail to perceive the dignity, the joy, and the security enjoyed by those living in the courts of the Lord. The danger of being for even one hour outside the house of God points to this.

The Emperor Theodosius, a person dear to God, preferred to set aside the business of the empire and seek a place of abject penance rather than be outside the house of the Lord. Even those penitents who are filthy and emaciated from fasting and tears, who stand as beggars at the threshold of the Church, are happier than those who reign in the tents of Satan. For they, provided they are penitent, are spiritually within the Church, although corporally they may still remain outside it. This is what the prophet desires so eagerly when he petitions God through the face of His Christ—that he might be allowed in the threshold or at least be considered the most lowly of Christ's members. For outside the Church there is no hope of salvation.

Whether we are approaching for the first time or returning to the threshold of God's house, we will find that the mercy of God is there, ready to lift us up in our infirmity and aid us in the path to perfection. His truth stands ready to increase our spiritual knowledge, His grace to enrich our charismatic gifts, and finally His glory is prepared to transform us into the image of God.

Christ is truth; He is also our justice. Isaias says, "Your justice will go before my face and the glory of the Lord will collect you." Mercy condones error; truth enlightens the mind lest we return to error; grace brings the gifts of the Holy Spirit that, being converted, we may confirm our brethren. Many have been thus recalled from their erring ways, as, for

example, David tested the mercy of God and was recalled to
truth by Nathan. "I will teach the wicked Thy ways, and they
will be converted to Thee." These sentiments are expressed by
the prophet showing how God loves mercy and truth and the
Lord gives grace and glory. Paul says the same thing in telling
how, through God's mercy, he was recalled from the fury of
persecuting and, through the truth of the Gospel, led to the
way of the Lord. Finally, through grace he was filled with the
special gifts of the Holy Spirit and became a chosen vessel to
the point that in the midst of his sufferings he could be glorified in the Lord. The verse is also open to other interpretations. It is divine mercy that attracts us to recognition of truth.
Jeremiah writes, "Therefore in my mercy I have attracted
thee." David, so long as he concealed his sin, was a liar and
attempted to deceive not only men but God as well. Truly it
was God's mercy operating through Nathan that recalled him
to confess the folly of trying to deceive men, since no one is
able to hide from the eyes of God. Glory and grace follow
once mercy has recalled and truth brought about the confession of the sinner. Once penitential sorrow has taken place
and we have punished our crimes, we will serve justice with
justice as we once did evil with evil in the temple of the Holy
Spirit. The Church will be glorified since where once sin
abounded, grace will more abound, and there is greater joy
among the angels over one sinner recalled than over ninety-
nine just. What Augustine adds to this makes sense. He refers
this truth to faith in the promises of God. God alone is truthful, for all men are liars. They are so not because they deliberately deceive one another but because they lack the ability
to fulfill what they promise, being uncertain as to whether
they will be alive from one day to the next.

As long as we live in this mortal body, liable to so many
dangers and evils, mercy will safely protect us, lest we fall
again into our erring ways. The truth of God will support and
lift up our minds so that with a total disregard for the things
of this life we will be borne to celestial things. The thirty-fifth
psalm expresses this with the words, "Extend Thy mercy to
them that know Thee, and Thy justice to them that are right
in heart." Justice renders to each his own. What does God
give to us, since He is no man's debtor? There is nothing we
have that we have not received from His benignity. Yet liberality is one thing, justice another. This kind of justice is that
which fulfills what was promised gratuitously. For this reason
God places Himself, as it were, as a debtor in our regard so
that, granted we cannot speak of our own merits, yet we can
refer to them as promises.

If we would recall our duties, we would not resent being called unjust when we fail to fulfill what was promised. "Come and accuse Me, says the Lord." David refers to this justice of the Lord when he says, "In order that you be justified in your words, you will conquer whom you judge." Meanwhile the Lord demands that we await our judgment which will not fail. Those who are unaware of this truth may murmur and doubt, as was the case with the two Apostles who claimed they awaited the redemption of Israel. I am always amazed at the thinking of the Apostles who, because they did not believe in the resurrection, thought that they would be given a verbal confirmation of its veracity. There is a certain amount of discrepancy among translators of the Septuagint as to the meaning of this expression "truth." The Hebrew itself contains the key to its interpretation, often misread by the scribes.

If we look at the Hebrew, we will see the meaning: "Because the Lord is the Sun and the Shield, He will give glory and grace." The word "Sun" refers to Christ, who illuminates every man who comes into the world. "Shield" signifies His mercy which protects the faithful against all attacks of Satan. The thirty-first psalm tells us, "Those who hope in the Lord abound with His mercy." Paul tells us to take up the shield of faith, and elsewhere the psalmist says, "His truth will surround you with a shield and you will not fear the night."

Do you wish to be safe from every evil? Then do not be blown about by the wind of doctrinal change, but hold fast to what the Catholic Church has handed down to us from Holy Scripture. What it commands, carry out with simple obedience; what it promises, let us expect with a ready hope. To those who walk in simple faith, neither mercy, nor truth, nor grace, nor whatever else is necessary for beatitude will ever be lacking. Add to this "the Lord does not take away, He does not defraud those who walk in innocence of their goods." The Septuagint uses the word "guilelessness" (ἐν ἀκακίᾳ), and this is rendered better by the simplicity that is lacking in all fraud and malice. The Holy Spirit loves the souls of little doves. He gives them the glory of a sincere conscience and promises them an unspeakable glory in the future. Meanwhile, content with such a precious reward, look forward to the goods of the age to come, rejoicing in hope so that you may say with the prophet, "Lord of virtues, happy the man who hopes in Thee."

We find that the psalms contain many expressions of this nature, so that they may be ever fixed in our minds. The second says, "Blessed are those who trust"; the thirty-third, "They will not be abandoned who hope in Thee"; the fourth,

"For thou, O Lord, singularly hast settled me in Hope"; "Expect the Lord, act manfully, and let thy heart take courage, and expect the Lord"; "In His holy name we have hoped."

Nor is this hope expressed in the Scriptures that which common usage implies. The farmer hopes for a bountiful crop, the sailor for a prosperous voyage, the pregnant woman for a safe delivery, the sick for health. But the pious individual puts his entire hope in the Lord and joins his every confidence to God. He is persuaded that everything—sadness, death, and life—will come to a reward through the mercy of God who inscrutably tempers all human affairs.

Therefore, O Lord, since man is made blessed by placing his entire confidence in Thee, grant, I implore Thee, that we may open our eyes and see how lovable, how beautiful, safe, and happy are Thy tabernacles. Let us see how unlike them are the tabernacles of the impious, who follow their own opinions and preferences. Grant us that same concord that pervades the assembly of the blessed, so that it may truthfully be said of us—Behold, how good and how joyous it is for brethren to live in union.

We will, however, never attain to this union unless we place our hope equally in Christ Jesus the King of Sion and our Lord. He alone should be our goal. Wherever ambition, avarice, or a blindness that tries to defend what is indefensible in writing, speech, or wherever self-justification carries the cord of contention, there concord will not be achieved.

We should realize how stupid it is to despise the immorality of certain pontiffs, priests, and monks to the extent that we ourselves become just as detestable. It is more detestable to withdraw from the Church and take up heresy or schism than to live impurely and remain orthodox in our belief. It is even worse for us excessively to inquire into the vices of others while we take a molelike attitude toward our own. Seeing a straw in our own eyes and making it a beam in the eyes of others is a human fault.

If they who defect from the institutes of St. Benedict or St. Francis are branded with the terrible name "apostate," how much more do they deserve the term who, once having professed contempt for the world in baptism, now serve the world entirely and transfer their allegiance from Christ the Emperor to Satan. The crime of adultery, which the pagans punished with the sword and the Jews with stoning, is now considered nothing more than an object for humorous anecdotes. If you look a little more closely, you will find that everything is filled with fraud, rapine, and perjury. Lest I forget to mention it, how much evil does not the Lernaean shadow of war cover over?

It is of no use to speak of this either to petty officials or to those whose title seems to give them license or even to higher magistrates. Wherever you look there is no end of complaints. But this is the nature of human affairs, in the manner of the sea, to carry away much that does not belong. Vices may change, they do not desist. What is left other than that we break down and flee to the mercy of God? Certain slight vices are of such a nature that a strong medicine ought to be applied as a remedy. Certain others could be concealed with little inconvenience to religion rather than being forcefully extricated. Those that are of such a nature as to require concealment ought to be treated with a trained hand to avoid the fate of those who sometimes fall victim to an ignorant doctor who in curing either kills the patient or through wrong dosage makes further treatment useless.

Most evils creep in little by little and on different occasions. They ought to be eliminated in the same way, provided this does not cause a disturbance. Otherwise they should be concealed until an opportunity presents itself for removing them.

This same dexterity ought to be used in dogmatic problems. There are those who outrageously shout, "Heresy! To the flames!" and misconstrue harmless assertions interpreting what even is pious in a malign fashion. Many of those whom they deem worthy of destruction they could reconcile with good will. On the other hand, others under cover of the Gospel treat too gently things that are in direct opposition to the evangelical spirit, actually aiding those whom they suppress. One faction is unwilling to accept changes, while the other wishes nothing of the old to remain. Thus an interminable storm arises and a tug of war ensues, with both parties falling to the ground when the rope breaks.

The Church itself, founded on the rock of Christ, is not going to fall since it can outride any storm. But rather, they will fall who, though without evil intent but rather misguided zeal, look upon the Church in this manner.

This fire will be extinguished only if we remove the fuel. The chief source of the disturbance is a breakdown of morals. And certainly accusing another will not bring a solution. We have an example of this in the unhappy explanation of our first parent: "The woman has deceived me, the serpent has deceived me." All of us are guilty of calling down God's wrath, and it is essential that all of us turn with a contrite heart to our Saviour. He will, on his part, unquestionably turn to us and transform those confused with this disturbance once

again into a state of tranquillity, awarding each of us a jus
portion of what we strive for.

How, you ask, will this be accomplished? In the first plac
each individual must fulfill his proper duties. If you are a pope
then act as the Vicar of Christ and care for the flock of th
Lord with a sincere heart. As far as princes are concerned, le
them act as ministers of divine justice, as those who are t
render an account to God, whom it behooves them to fear, free
from the fetters of public opinion. Let magistrates fulfill thei
civil duties with good faith. Monks ought to demonstrate with
improved morals the perfection to which they have devote
themselves. Priests should meditate day and night on the law
of the Lord and thus become the salt of the people. Let th
laity keep their proper place and reverently give ear to th
instructions of the clergy, as well as faithful obedience to thei
civil leaders. Let each one perform his duties conscientiously
before the great Knower of hearts. Let us freely use th
works of St. Luke. Whoever is a tradesman, let him carry o
his business in good faith. The producer, the miller, the artisan
the clothier, ought to act in the same manner, having faith in
Him who does not abandon the sincere of heart. Let no on
be deceived by the saying, "This is a condoned practice," o
that "everyone is doing it." Don't let your excuse be that
others are doing the same things, but rather bear in mind that
regardless of whether you are a king or a pauper you will one
day stand before the tribunal of that supreme Judge to whom
all is known. And here the reluctance expressed in the fact
that it was a condoned practice or "everyone does it" will be
of no avail.

Meanwhile put aside ambition and the obstinate endeavor to
overcome opposition; give in to your private hates and tone
down the filthy bawling of your insane quarrels. In this way
peaceful truth will finally come to light. Thus a spirit of accommodation will prevail so that each party will be willing to
make concessions to the other, concessions without which no
accord will be achieved. But care must be taken that the funda-
mentals be not removed and that human weakness be considered. In this way we will gradually arrive at the things that
are more perfect. However, this should be borne in mind, that
it is neither safe nor conducive to concord rashly to do away
with those things that have been handed down with the authority of the past and that long usage and general agreement
have confirmed. Nor should anything be changed except under
pressure of necessity or for evident benefit.

Concerning *The Freedom of the Will*, this is a thorny question rather than something that can be profitably debated. If

it must be ironed out, however, let us leave it to competent theologians. Meanwhile we can at least agree that, of his own power, man can do nothing and is wholly dependent on the grace of God, in virtue of which we are what we are, so that in all things we recognize our weakness and glorify the mercy of God. We must all agree in acknowledging the importance of faith, providing we admit that it is a special gift of the Holy Spirit and that it is open to more meanings than the ordinary individual can comprehend. It cannot be adequately explained by merely saying, "I believe Christ has suffered for me." Let us agree that we are justified by faith, i.e., the hearts of the faithful are thereby purified, provided we admit that the works of charity are necessary for salvation. Nor is true faith inoperative, since it is the font and garden of all good works. Rather, let us distinguish that justice that cleanses the dwelling place of our mind, which is rightly termed innocence, and that embellished faith that is enriched with good works. God is, properly speaking, no man's debtor, unless perhaps because of a gratuitous promise. And even here, since we must fulfill certain conditions, it is from His own munificence. The expressions reward or merit ought not to be rejected because God accepts and weighs that grace that is in us or operates through us. Let's not have any argument, then, concerning words, provided they agree on the essentials. If not, the false doctrines will fall within hearing distance of the ignorant crowds. Although true in a sense, the expressions that the quality of our works, provided we have faith, have no special meaning, or that all our actions are really sinful, will be misunderstood by the ordinary person.

Take the expression, "Christ died for our sins." Does it mean that He died so that we might live in sin, or rather that washed by His blood we might abstain from all contamination? He died and rose again that in imitation of Him we might die to sin and rise in a newness of life. He tasted of the cross for us but at the same time He tells us, "Whoever does not take up his cross and follow Me is not worthy of Me." Whoever crucify Christ who dwells within them by their daily crimes will profit nothing more from His death other than that it delays the impending approach of punishment. It is characteristic of certain pious individuals to believe that the prayers and good works of the living may profit the dead, particularly if they take care that this be done during their lifetime. To this practice I would give this warning: whoever provides for pompous funerals and masses for his own glory loses his reward. It would be much more profitable if their legacies were used for pious purposes in aiding those who are still alive and healthy. But if we are not of this persuasion we should not disturb the simplicity of those who are; rather, we should be more generous to the needs of the poor. It is better to apply oneself to good works than to believe that the devil can be helped by the good deeds of the living.

It is also a religious practice to believe that certain saints who while living were able to expel demons and recall the dead to life are still able to do this. Those who do not share this opinion should pray with sincere belief to the Father, Son, and Holy Spirit, and should not disturb those who, out of superstition, implore the intercession of the saints. Superstition, which I must admit is quite widespread in the invocation of the saints, should be corrected. Yet we must tolerate the pious simplicity of some, even when there is a certain amount of error involved. If our prayers are not heard by the saints, Christ, who loves simple souls, will give us what we request through the saints.

Those who rage against the image of saints have perhaps done so with reason, but to my way of thinking they have been a bit immoderate. Idolatry is certainly a terrible sin, and although the worship of images was removed in times past, there is the danger that diabolical devices might facilitate its return for the unwary. Statuary and painting have a place among the liberal arts as a kind of silent poetry. They occasionally catch the emotional state of man far better than the eloquence of words. Plato, recognizing that poetry had much to offer the well-being of the state, did not exclude all poets from the ideal city, but only Homer and those similar to him. This he did because he attributed to the gods and their offspring adultery, pederasty, theft, lying, uncontained anger, and other terrible vices that no decent ruler would allow in his city, or family head tolerate in his wife, children, or domestics. Certain corrections are in order here. The superstitious element should be eliminated; whatever is useful should be retained. Would that every dwelling had the life of Christ depicted on its walls. In churches the decree of the African Council ought to be followed, which states that here nothing should be recited other than Holy Scripture and no paintings allowed other than those that have a scriptural theme. In courts and parks it would be all right to depict scenes from human events, provided they lead to good morals. Whatever depicts what is foolish or obscene or seditious should be removed not only from churches but also from public places. And just as it is a crime of blasphemy to reduce sacred words to stupid and profane jokes, so reducing biblical themes to the ridiculous should also be punished. If you want to be foolish, take your arguments from

Philostratus, since the pagan writers have many arguments that to the uncultured eye may appear useful. If you feel that the images of the saints are devoid of any sense and are not to be honored, keep your thoughts to yourself. But do not disturb those who without superstition lovingly cherish images, as for example a newlywed kisses the ring or the bracelet her absent husband has left behind or sent to her. This affection is certainly pleasing to God when it is done, not out of superstition, but rather proceeds from an abundance of love. We might say the same of those who from the same motive kiss the bones and other relics of saints. St. Paul would allow each person to follow his own opinion in this matter. I know a certain theologian who, seeing a man walking through a cemetery on a public road, noticed that he did not lift his hat to a crucifix. He failed to do so because he was engaged in conversation with his companion. The theologian immediately said, "I'll swear that he is a Lutheran." Obviously he was mistaken, and I think the same applies to those who loudly attack the importance of images. I think we can say without vexing anyone that the saints are best venerated by imitating their lives.

Certain individuals cannot bring themselves to be persuaded that what in these times is termed sacramental confession was instituted by Christ. They ought at least to agree to retain it as something that is salutary and useful to many and has the approval of many centuries of practice. It is safer in this matter to recognize that its usefulness depends upon ourselves. We should choose an upright, educated priest who can hold his tongue to whom we should confess as to Almighty God our certain and serious sins. This we should do without forcing him to extract our sins because of our vague and ambiguous manner of stating them. The serious sins I would list are adultery, murder, theft, voluntary drunkenness, detraction, which is a type of murder, perjury, deception, raping, and sins of that nature. They are serious whether they have actually been perpetrated or whether they have been merely intended, lacking the occasion to perform them.

There should be no superstition, repetition of confession, no minute enumeration of circumstances, no flying to another priest if we have forgotten something in a previous confession. Our chief concern ought to be to detest the sin we have committed and to return to our original innocence. Most important of all we should determine to lead such a life as to avoid serious sin entirely. If we do this, there is no need for confession.

It is hardly possible in this life to avoid little failings, yet with God's help we can avoid serious sin, provided we have a

deep love of God and our neighbor. This should be the basi
on which we should center our actions. If by accident w
should fall into sin, we should immediately make our peac
with God and await a favorable opportunity to confess th
sin to a priest, rather than rushing off to a confessor. Certainly
a priest can be consulted in dubious matters relating to th
legality of actions. There are many cases of this type; fo
example, questions concerning usury, marriage, restitution
and vows. In general, let those who believe that Chris
founded confession in its present form observe it with the ut
most care; but on the other hand, they should allow others to
retain their own ideas on the matter until a council of the
Church has given a definite judgment. In this way Christian
concord will be preserved and the weak will not fall into ope
licentiousness. As far as the Mass is concerned, wherever there
is superstition or corruption it should be reasonably corrected
I see no reason why the Mass itself should be suppressed. I
consists of psalmody; the introit; the doxology; prayer and
canticles; lessons from the prophets and from the Apostles
and from the Gospels; the creed; thanksgiving or, as it is
called, the Eucharist, the commemoration of Christ's death
then prayer again, including the Lord's Prayer; after this the
symbol of Christian peace; then the communion; the sacred
canticle, and prayer. Finally the priest blesses the people and
as a group commended to his protection, bids them depart in
piety and mutual charity.

What is there in this that is not pious or does not arouse
reverence? Those who dislike the dirty crowd of hired priests
should dismiss the unworthy and retain the good. Those who
do not approve of the prose, especially the unlettered, should
permit this feature to be bypassed. The Church of Rome does
not have this practice. The same holds for the various songs
that are sung in some churches after the consecration—for
peace, against pestilence, or for a good crop. They can be
omitted without any bad effect on religion. The same holds
for other novelties. In ancient times the people did not run
about to see what the priest did, but rather in a prostrate position gave thanks to Christ the Redeemer who cleansed us
with His blood and redeemed us by His death. This practice
is not known in Rome. In the chapel of the Pope there is bu
one altar and one divine service. There are many churches
today where, in imitation of the practice in Rome, it is no
permitted to celebrate private Masses, especially when Mass is
being offered at the main altar. We must reprove the insolence
of those who walk about the Church when Mass is being
celebrated, talking of their own private affairs, and when it is

finished go find a priest of their own to say a special Mass for them. The same holds for those who at vespers seize upon any priest they meet and compel him, even with violent threats, to say separate vespers for them, though he may have already finished his own. This practice, whether done publicly or privately, ought to be condemned.

Some may not approve of modern harmonized music and the use of organs. These can be omitted without any loss of piety. If they are retained, then care should be taken that the music is suitable for divine service. However, whatever is in the service by prescription should not be omitted or curtailed because of preference for music, as happens in some churches. Sometimes the readings take up almost an hour, whereas the creed is abbreviated and the Lord's Prayer is omitted. There are large concentrated passages, a single verse often taking up a considerable time span, which lengthens the usual form of the service and makes it tedious.

There is a great deal of superstition also in increased numbers of special Masses; the Mass of the crown of thorns, the Mass of the three nails, the Mass of the foreskin of Christ, Masses for those who travel by land and sea, for barren women, for persons sick of quartan and tertian fevers. In this matter a great deal could be either tolerated or corrected. There is no need that the Mass, accepted for so many centuries, should be stamped out like some impiety or pestilence. Those problems relating to the quality of the Mass, the *ex opere operato* and the *ex opere operantis* elements, ought to be laid aside until a general council has made a pronouncement concerning them, or left it to the judgment of some arbiter. The expressions "sacrifice" and "immolation" were accepted by the ancient Fathers.

I must admit, the Christ having once died, will die no more, but this one sacrifice is renewed daily in symbolic rites, whereby we receive new grace as from an inexhaustible font. We offer up the victim for the living and the dead, in the sense that we implore God the Father through His Son. Finally, since every prayerful action that consists of praise and thanksgiving is a sacrifice, this would seem an appropriate term for the Mass, as it contains all these holy actions.

There are those who demand that all participate in Holy Communion at Mass. And surely this is the way Christ instituted it and the manner in which it was so long observed. The fact that this is no longer so is not due to the priests but rather the laxity of the laity in whom charity has grown cold. The celestial food should not be forced upon those who do not wish it, or upon the sick, but given, rather, to those who request it. How can there be general communion when in many cases the churches are almost empty at the time for receiving it? Some people leave after the "Asperges," even before the "Introit." Others leave the moment the Gospel has been read, which, of course, they don't understand. At the time of the "Preface," after the priest has said, "Lift up your hearts," and "Let us give thanks," then especially there should be a participation with the priest in silent communion with God. Instead they stand gossiping in the marketplace or carousing in wineshops, which practice, bad as it is, is not so disgraceful a thing as the irreverence of those who stay in Church chatting during the entire service.

And finally, even today, there is not, just as there was not in antiquity, a complete sharing of the symbols of the sacrament on the part of those assisting at Mass. Nevertheless there is a participation in the same divine doctrine, the pious prayers and exhortations as well as the acts of praise and thanksgiving. This is the communion that vivifies, and it does so without this sharing of the elements. Some may have objections to the adoration given to the Eucharist. If Christ is totally present in the sacrament, why should it not be adored? Although He is only there in the form of bread and wine to be received in a pure devotion, not to be made a display of at public games or processions nor to be carried about on horseback through the fields. This may be an ancient practice but it is at the same time a concession to ignorant fancy that never should have been made.

Certain individuals think themselves quite pious if, whenever they see a priest exposing the Host, they rush up and gaze fixedly upon it. It would be much more religious if, like the publican, they stayed at a distance or prostrated themselves in adoration of the Crucified.

There is nothing so stupid as to adore what is human as divine in the person of Christ or to worship the bread and wine instead of Him. Since no one is really certain, however, except the priest himself, as to whether he actually consecrates the elements, all adore with this tacit condition. Furthermore, what we adore in Christ is always present with us. Besides, if there is no sacrament so lowly that we do not uncover our heads when it is administered, as for example with baptism and confirmation, who would want to call this idolatrous that we bare our head to this sacrament even if Christ be there only symbolically?

How many different forms there are of the sacramentals! How often do not authorities change their minds about them! How often do they not quarrel with others about them. Only recently someone has conceived of the impious idea that there can be a sacrament without an external sign, an idea that would eliminate the sacraments altogether and make them a mere state of mind. People who make these conjectures have lost all sense of the seriousness of the subject. If they are not clear on the matter, they ought to acquiesce in what the Church has handed down, namely, that the living body and blood of the Lord are here present. If we believe that in the sepulcher the divine nature of Christ was not separated from His lifeless body, then how much more credible to hold that His living body is not separated in the sacrament? If we can reach agreement in this matter, then other questions that are causing dissension—how the body and blood are present under the substance of bread or under the species of bread and wine, and the like—can be taken up at the synod and defined. As it is, the diversity of private opinions turns what could be a comfort and joy to pious souls into something that they have come almost to dislike.

The plethora of feast days, which either bishops in deference to popular wish have introduced, or popes have instituted for no real reason, they themselves ought to discreetly reduce in number. I would list among these the feast of the Immaculate Conception, the Nativity of the Blessed Virgin, and the Presentation. I really feel that no feasts should be celebrated that have no basis in Scripture—with the exception, of course, of Sunday. There would be no objection to fewer feasts provided we keep those we have with greater devotion. We need not consider that a day is profaned when a man by honest labor earns enough to support his wife and children or helps his neighbor in need. Those feasts that sodalities have set up on their own authority ought to be suppressed by the civil magistrates. They are nothing more than the ancient revelries of Comae and Bacchus.

Fasting and special regulations about food are only enjoined by the Church for health of body and mind and are not binding on those who cannot stomach fish or who find their strength diminished by fasting. But when people are all the better for these abstinences, it is mere contumacy to reject useful practices just because they are ordained by the Church. Let no one sit in judgment, then. If you eat meat, don't condemn those who do not, and vice versa. Let God be our judge. I feel the same way with regard to the other constitutions of bishops. If they are good and useful, let them be observed as laws. If the idea of enforcement is repulsive, then consider them as merely counsels. If a servant whom you have employed for little or nothing offers you advice that is useful, then listen to him, not because he is your servant, but because what he says is for your best interests. Should we reject the advice of those who are in public office and those who take the place of the Fathers and the Doctors of the Church? I take this stand, not because what I say should be taken as absolutely certain or because I wish to dictate what the Church should do. It is rather that while awaiting a council we must cut off, so far as in us lies, the causes of dissension. Let us not do anything by force, and certainly do unto others what we would wish them to do unto us. Let us beseech heaven and earth but in no way force anyone into a religion that repels him. It is equally important that those who do not want to be forced in the matter of religion refrain from attacking the religion of others, especially when that religion is sheltered behind ancient practices.

Let this warning be listened to by both factions: if moderate accommodation lessens the intensity of the disagreements, the medicine of the council will more easily work toward concord, just as the physician, before he administers a strong medicine, prepares the patient with bland potions, which we call syrups. Would that we could all imitate this practice. Yet I fear that there are some who, through lack of judgment or because they wish to secure their own position, only hasten to inflame the situation, so that a council will come to naught. For I fear that they have fallen into error, and it is this rather than malice that hastens them to their doom. Is not that baptism that was good enough for over fourteen hundred years for the Church satisfactory to them? Even at the time of Augustine it was an immemorial practice, and it is easy to conjecture that it was practiced by the Apostles even though not expressly stated in the Bible. Paul tells us that he baptized three families, those of Crispin, Cajus, and Stephen. And among the Philippians he baptized his jailer and his entire family at night. Peter, as we read in the Acts, baptized Cornelius and at the same time not only his family but also his entire household, whom he summoned on the occasion of Peter's visit. It is safe to assume that among these there were a number of children.

Christ commands, "Render to Caesar the things that are Caesar's." And the princes of the Apostles, Peter and Paul, diligently recommended that Christians obey civil authorities even though they were pagans. They wish the baptized servant to be more servile to his master than before he was baptized, and they make difficulties for those who were washed in the same rite and profess the same religion. They are said to demand a sharing of all their possessions. This practice of communism was found only in the primitive Church, and there it was not universally practiced. As the gospel spread it became impossible and led only to sedition. Concord will be achieved if we agree that property should remain in the hands of its legal owners and its common use be directed, when occasion arises, out of charity.

We hear also that among the Bohemians a new type of Judaism has arisen. They call themselves Sabbatarians and observe the sabbath so scrupulously that they will not even remove a foreign object from their eye on this day. As though Christ had not taught us how to observe the sabbath! Or as if Sunday which was sacred to the Apostles is not sufficient. Blessed Paul treats with anathema even an angel who would introduce from heaven anything contrary to his own message. At these times men's minds are so unsteady that regardless of the stature of the person who introduces it or the ridiculousness of the new doctrine, he will find new disciples. What has caused this vacillation among the Germans who have always been distinguished above other nations for courage and constancy?

How happy would we not be if we could lay aside dissensions and dwell with one head and one mind in the House of the Lord. The Emperor Charles V is doing all he can in this regard, as is the king of the Romans, or Hungary and Bohemia, Ferdinand I. Nor is the most Christian king of France acting in a way that would compromise his title. The king of England is not forgetful of the fact that he merited the special title, Defender of the Catholic Faith. Those who are close to Pope Clement promise that he is prepared to condescend to whatever equitable conditions will preserve the peace of the Church. The good will of the educated cardinals can also be counted upon. The affair will have a happy ending under the guidance of Christ if other rulers and cities will come around to this way of thinking. We have put up for too long a time with strife; perhaps mere exhaustion may enable us to find peace.

If the leniency of the Lord leads us to license whereas it should lead us to penance, then it is to be feared lest anger be more frequent than injured patience or, as Paul wrote concerning the Jews, "The anger of the Lord will reach out to you in the end." We should not abuse the forbearance of the rulers who have been consulted in this affair. They are quite aware of the use of force, but they prefer to use mild means rather than the knife. Perhaps we think that the Emperor is sleeping; he is, however, vigilant in the matter. He proceeds deliberately, as behooves a man of his power, and prefers a final settlement rather than a hasty generalization. King

Ferdinand, a man endowed with those qualities of character that Plato depicts in his ideal prince, also demands our respect and religious obedience. A rash temerity never succeeded in escaping the Cyclops. Or as the bard so adroitly expresses it, "Power that is lacking in discretion falls to the ground with its own weight." The gods carry tempered power to greater heights. Therefore if we apply ourselves to the task of establishing peace in the Church with moderate advice and calm minds, that which Isaias prophesies will take place. "And my people will sit down in the beauty of peace, in the tabernacles of confidence and in opulent rest. Let us all say as we rejoice with one another—How lovable, O Lord of power, are Thy tabernacles."

Suggestions for Further Reading

Allen, P. S., *Erasmus, Lectures and Wayfaring Sketches*. Oxford: Clarendon Press; New York: Oxford University Press, 1934.

A series of lectures delivered by the editor of Erasmus' letters, with a penetrating appraisal of Erasmus' service to learning and a good description of his relationship with his printers.

Bouyer, L., *Erasmus and His Times*. Westminster, Md.: Newman Press; London: G. Chapman Ltd., 1959.

Translated from the French by F. X. Murphy. The author, in opposition to Renaudet, attempts to so refurbish Erasmus as to make him acceptable in all respects to contemporary Catholicism. For this author Erasmus symbolizes the renewal of the world of ideas, he was the Christian conscience of his age.

Gilmore, M. P., *The World of Humanism*. New York: Harper & Brothers; London: Hamish Hamilton, 1952.

This author singles out Erasmus and Savonarola as extremes in contrast between intellectual and mystical reformers. Erasmus is a precursor of the Council of Trent because he accepted a disappointment of his hopes rather than a division of the Church.

Harbison, E. H., *The Christian Scholar in the Age of the Reformation*. New York: Charles Scribner's Sons, 1956.

The essay on Erasmus forms part of a book on scholarship as a Christian vocation and quite naturally focuses on Erasmus as a Christian scholar. In the main Harbison's observations are quite sound, especially when he discusses the reformatory significance of Erasmian scholarship.

Huizinga, J., *Erasmus and the Age of the Reformation*. New York: Harper & Brothers, 1957.

In this illuminating character study the author maintains that Erasmus' classicism radically alienated him from traditional Catholicism and that his sensitive nature was unable to come to a final determination on the great doctrinal issues of the day.

Phillips, M. M., *Erasmus and the Northern Renaissance*. New York: The Macmillan Co.; London: Hodder & Stoughton, 1949.

A very readable and sympathetic biography of Erasmus; dispels much of the popular misunderstanding surrounding his character while at the same time avoiding the entanglements of abstruse scholarship.

Smith, P. S., *Erasmus, A Study of His Life, Ideals, and Place in History*. New York: Harper & Brothers, 1923; New York: Frederick Ungar, 1962.

First published in 1923, so it does not include the findings of more recent research; nevertheless, this remains one of the finest biographies on Erasmus. The author depicts Erasmus as the hero of liberal Christianity and often interprets his departure from traditional opinions as evidence of a rationalistic rejection of dogma.

————, *A Key to the Colloquies of Erasmus*. Cambridge: Harvard University Press; London: Oxford University Press, 1927.

A study of the various editions of the Colloquies with interesting historical data on the contemporary situations and personalities involved.

INDEX

Index of Names Cited by Erasmus

SIGNET and MENTOR Books of Related Interest

☐ **THE STORY BIBLE: VOLUME I by Pearl S. Buck.** The winner of the Nobel and Pulitzer Prizes retells the Greatest Story Ever Told in the living language of our times. In VOLUME I the immortal stories of the Old Testament are brought to life with a power and immediacy for the modern reader.   (#Y5080—$1.25)

☐ **THE STORY BIBLE: VOLUME II by Pearl S. Buck.** This superlative rendering of the New Testament brings the crowning achievement of Pearl Buck's career, THE STORY BIBLE, to a triumphant conclusion. Here, adding relevance to its wisdom and freshness to its beauty, is the story of the birth, life, death and resurrection of Jesus. "Compelling, moving . . ."—**Library Journal**
(#Y5079—$1.25)

☐ **THE MENTOR BIBLE: A Literary Abridgement edited and with Commentary by Michael Fixler.** A splendid modern interpretation of the Old and New Testaments in the King James version.   (#MJ1251—$1.95)

☐ **THE SERMON ON THE MOUNT According To Vedanta by Swami Prabhavananda.** A fascinating and superbly enlightening Hindu reading of the central gospel of Christianity by the renowned author of books on Indian religious philosophy.   (#MW1518—$1.50)

THE NEW AMERICAN LIBRARY, INC.,
P.O. Box 999, Bergenfield, New Jersey 07621

Please send me the SIGNET and MENTOR BOOKS I have checked above. I am enclosing $_____(check or money order—no currency or C.O.D.'s). Please include the list price plus 35¢ a copy to cover handling and mailing costs. (Prices and numbers are subject to change without notice.)

Name_____

Address_____

City_____State_____Zip Code_____
Allow at least 4 weeks for delivery

MENTOR Religious Classics

☐ **THE MEANING OF THE GLORIOUS KORAN: An Explanatory Translation by Mohammed Marmaduke Pickthall.** The complete sacred book of Mohammedanism, translated with reverence and scholarship.
(#ME1652—$2.50)

☐ **THE SONG OF GOD: BHAGAVAD-GITA—The Hindu epic** translated by Swami Prabhavananda and Christopher Isherwood. (#MW1590—$1.50)

☐ **THE SAYINGS OF CONFUCIUS translated by James R. Ware.** The sayings of the greatest wise man of ancient China, teaching the ageless virtues of civilized men.
(#MY1557—$1.25)

☐ **THE TEACHINGS OF THE COMPASSIONATE BUDDHA edited by E. A. Burtt.** The basic texts, early discourses, the Dhammapada, and later writings of Buddhism.
(#MW1632—$1.50)

☐ **THE UPANISHADS: Breath of the Eternal.** The wisdom of the Hindu mystics, translated by Swami Prabhavananda and Frederick Manchester. (#MW1589—$1.50)

☐ **THE WAY OF LIFE: TAO TÊ CHING.** Eighty-one brief poems embodying the beliefs of Taoism, in a fresh translation by R. B. Blakney. (#MW1459—$1.50)

THE NEW AMERICAN LIBRARY, INC.,
P.O. Box 999, Bergenfield, New Jersey 07621

Please send me the MENTOR BOOKS I have checked above. I am enclosing $_____(check or money order—no currency or C.O.D.'s). Please include the list price plus 35¢ a copy to cover handling and mailing costs. (Prices and numbers are subject to change without notice.)

Name_____

Address_____

City_____State_____Zip Code_____
Allow at least 4 weeks for delivery

The MENTOR Philosophers

A distinguished series of six volumes presenting in historical order the basic writings of the outstanding philosophers of the Western world—from the Middle Ages to the present time.

☐ **THE AGE OF BELIEF: THE MEDIEVAL PHILOSOPHERS edited by Anne Fremantle.** Basic writings of St. Augustine, Boethius, Abelard, St. Bernard, St. Thomas Aquinas, Duns Scotus, William of Ockham and others.
(#ME1536—$1.75)

☐ **THE AGE OF REASON: THE 17TH CENTURY PHILOSOPHERS edited by Stuart Hampshire.** Bacon, Pascal, Hobbes, Galileo, Descartes, Spinoza, Leibniz.
(#MY1186—$1.25)

☐ **THE AGE OF ENLIGHTENMENT: THE 18TH CENTURY PHILOSOPHERS edited by Isaiah Berlin.** Locke, Berkeley, Voltaire, Hume, Reid, Condillac, Hamann.
(#ME1591—$1.75)

☐ **THE AGE OF IDEOLOGY: THE 19TH CENTURY PHILOSOPHERS edited by Henry D. Aiken.** Kant, Fichte, Hegel, Schopenhauer, Comte, Mill, Spencer, Marx, Nietzsche, Kierkegaard.
(#MW1494—$1.50)

☐ **THE AGE OF ANALYSIS: 20TH CENTURY PHILOSOPHERS edited by Morton White.** Peirce, Whitehead, James, Dewey, Bertrand Russell, Wittgenstein, Croce, Bergson, Sartre, Santayana and others.
(#MW1452—$1.50)